Consider Leviathan

Consider Leviathan

Narratives of Nature and the Self in Job

Brian R. Doak

Fortress Press
Minneapolis

CONSIDER LEVIATHAN

Narratives of Nature and the Self in Job

Cover design: Ivy Palmer Skrade

Cover image: The Pierpont Morgan Library / Art Resource, NY

Library of Congress Cataloging-in-Publication Data is available

Print ISBN: 978-1-4514-6993-6

eBook ISBN: 978-1-4514-8951-4

The paper used in this publication meets the minimum requirements of American National Standard for Information Sciences — Permanence of Paper for Printed Library Materials, ANSI Z329.48-1984.

Manufactured in the U.S.A.

This book was produced using PressBooks.com, and PDF rendering was done by PrinceXML.

For Junia

"Shinn had stood at the curb drinking his first Coke of his first day at the Post and felt his clothes unwrinkle and sag slightly in the humidity, smelling the same honeysuckle and cut grass as suburban Chicago, listening to the songs of dawn-stirred birds in the locust trees along Self-Storage, and his thoughts had drifted all over the place, and suddenly it occurred that the birds, whose twitters and repeated songs sounded so pretty and affirming of nature and the coming day, might actually, in a code known only to other birds, be the birds each saying 'Get away' or 'This branch is mine!' or 'This tree is mine! I'll kill you! Kill, kill!' Or any other manner of dark, brutal, or self-protective stuff—they might be listening to war cries. The thought came from nowhere and made his spirits dip for some reason."

—David Foster Wallace, The Pale King (New York: Little, Brown, 2011), 372.

Contents

Illustrations

All drawings by Christian Reed (with the exception of Figure 1), modeled after the images in the following sources:

Figure 1. How Activation of Expectation Sets Compromise Intuitive Ontologies; Justin L. Barrett, *Cognitive Science, Religion, and Theology: From Human Minds to Divine Minds* (Templeton Science and Religion Series; West Conshohocken, PA: Templeton Press, 2011), 67, Fig. 1.

Figure 2. Palace relief from Mari, with investiture of Zimri-Lim (18th c. BCE); André Parrot, *Mission archéologique de Mari, II: Le palais. Peintures murals* (Paris: Geuthner, 1958), pls. IX, XI, A.

Figure 3. Glazed brick panel of Shalmanesar III (9th c. BCE); Irene J. Winter, "Ornament and the 'Rhetoric of Abundance' in Assyria," in *eadem, On Art in the Ancient Near East*, Vol. I (Culture and History of the Ancient Near East 34.1; Leiden: Brill, 2010), 163–83, at 179.

Figure 4. Painting on stucco, Deir el Medinah, Tomb of Amenakht (no. 218), ca. 14th–11th centuries BCE; Othmar Keel, *The Symbolism of the Biblical World: Ancient Near Eastern Iconography and* the Book of Psalms, trans. Timothy J. Hallett (New York: Seabury Press, 1978; first published in German in 1972), 354, ill. 479.

Figure 5. Assyrian palace relief; irrigated royal garden (mid-7th c. BCE); Richard David Barnett and the British Museum, *Sculptures from the North Palace of Ashurbanipal at Nineveh (668–627 B.C.)* (London: British Museum Publications, 1976), pl. XXIII.

Figure 6. Assyrian palace relief of Sargon II at Khorsabad (8th c. BCE); Lawrence Stager, "Jerusalem and the Garden of Eden," *Eretz-Israel* 26 (Frank Moore Cross Volume, ed. Baruch A. Levine) (1999): 186, fig. 3.

Figure 7. Master of animals seals, Iron IIB; Othmar Keel and Christoph Uehlinger, *Gods, Goddesses, and Images of God in Ancient Israel*, trans. Thomas H. Trapp (Minneapolis: Fortress Press, 1998), 183: 196a–b, 197a.

Figure 8. Assyrian lion hunt relief, palace of Assurbanipal; 7th c. BCE; British Museum; Richard David Barnett and the British Museum, *Sculptures from the North Palace of Ashurbanipal at Nineveh (668–627 B.C.)* (London: British Museum Publications, 1976), pl. VII.

Figure 9. "Master of ostriches" motif on various seals; Othmar Keel, *Jawhes Entgegnung an Ijob. Eine Deutung von Ijob 38–41 vor dem Hintergrund der zeitgenössischen Bildkunst* (Göttingen: Vandenhoeck & Ruprecht, 1978), 104:40–42; 106:43.

Abbreviations

AB   Anchor Bible

ANET   James B. Pritchard, ed., *Ancient Near Eastern Texts Relating to the Old Testament*, with Supplement, 3d ed. (Princeton: Princeton University Press, 1969)

BETL   Bibliotheca Ephemeridum Theologicarum Lovaniensium

BTB   *Biblical Theology Bulletin*

BZAW   *Beihefte zur Zeitschrift für die alttestamentliche Wissenschaft*

CAD   Erica Reiner, et al., eds., *The Assyrian Dictionary of the Oriental Institute of the University of Chicago*, 21 vols. (Chicago: University of Chicago Press, 1964–2010)

CBQ   *Catholic Biblical Quarterly*

COS   William W. Hallo, ed., *The Context of Scripture*. Vol. I, *Canonical Compositions from the Biblical World*; Vol. II, *Monumental Inscriptions from the Biblical World*; Vol. III, *Archival Documents from the Biblical World* (Leiden: Brill, 2003)

DDD   Karel van der Toorn, Bob Becking, and Pieter W. van der Horst, eds., *Dictionary of Deities and Demons in the Bible*, 2d ed. (Leiden: Brill, 1999)

FOTL   Forms of the Old Testament Literature

HSCP   Harvard Studies in Classical Philology

HTR   *Harvard Theological Review*

HTS   Harvard Theological Studies

JBL   *Journal of Biblical Literature*

JSJSS   Journal for the Study of Judaism Supplement Series

JSOT	*Journal for the Study of the Old Testament*
JSOTSS	Journal for the Study of the Old Testament Supplement Series
OTL	Old Testament Library
TDOT	G. Johannes Botterweck and Helmer Ringgren, et al., eds., *Theological Dictionary of the Old Testament*, trans. David E. Green, J. T. Willis, et al., 15 vols. (Grand Rapids: Eerdmans, 1974–2004).
ESWT	Norman C. Habel and Shirley Wurst, eds., *The Earth Story in Wisdom Traditions* (The Earth Bible 3; Sheffield: Sheffield Academic Press, 2001).
VT	*Vetus Testamentum*
ZAW	*Zeitschrift für die Alttestamentliche Wissenschaft*
ZTK	*Zeitschrift für Theologie und Kirche*

Prologue

The question of nature's meaning or non-meaning is a loaded one, capable of eliciting ferocious responses, even tearing apart the moral and intellectual fabric of a society. Consider, for example, the 1755 Lisbon earthquake, an event powerfully analyzed by Susan Neiman in her book *Evil: An Alternative History of Philosophy* (Princeton University Press, 2004). Now-famous thinkers of the period, such as Kant, Voltaire, Rousseau, and even Goethe as a six-year-old boy could all be counted among those agitated by the disaster, which in ten minutes of intense shaking killed some 15,000 people and threw Europe into panic about the goodness of God. Though wealthy and notable, mid-eighteenth-century Lisbon was by no means so notorious as to have "deserved" such a fate in the eyes of many, but its position in a period of "massive intellectual ferment," as Neiman puts it, meant that the history of ideas in the West was bound to be affected. Philosophers and natural scientists made a decisive split in the quake's aftermath, as the very physical earth itself acted out a drama whose results had come to fruition. The sentiment behind Job's sardonic cry, "What is man, that thou shouldest magnify him . . ." (Job 7:17, KJV) could easily have been uttered there, as many wondered in new ways how God could possibly care enough about people to ruin their lives in such a way. The irony of Job's cry comes from the fact that, as most agree, Job cites an earlier use of a nearly-identical phrase in Psalm 8, where the poet utters these words to praise the goodness of God in light of nature's perfection.

Two hundred fifty years later such questions of nature and meaning have scarcely faded. A recent book by the philosopher Thomas Nagel (*Mind and Cosmos*, Oxford University Press, 2012) claims that the universe operates with a kind of "natural teleology," a logic driving it from within. Even though Nagel does not identify this logic with God or any other being, and even though, as Michael Chorost has pointed out in a recent article in *The Chronicle of Higher Education* ("Where Thomas Nagel Went Wrong," May 2013), Nobel-Prize-winning scientists have made similar claims for decades, leading public intellectuals used the immediacy of social media to condemn Nagel out of hand, denouncing his book on Twitter and lamenting his work as a heresy of science.

Should humans pillage the natural world for philosophical analogies, statements of purpose, or cues about the meaning of existence? In what sense? Which kinds of analogies? It hardly seems adventurous to propose that nature will play an inevitable, ongoing role for questions of human meaning. There is no avoiding nature's effect on the structure of our thinking and our stories about ourselves; indeed, whatever meaning nature implicitly has or does not have, there is no avoiding the *narrativizing* of nature. Though the *sapiens* aspect of *Homo sapiens* comes under frequent scrutiny, no one can doubt our identity as *Homo narrans*, the human storyteller. To the extent that the Bible serves as "The Great Code," in Northrop Frye's memorable phrase, for the history of the West, the Bible's nature narratives have become canonical for us, whether as a normative and benevolent guiding spirit or an ignorant ghost raving in the background. Plants and animals are everywhere in the Hebrew Bible, and for obvious reasons: in non-industrial societies of all kinds the connection to rain, land, plant, and animal had to be constant and obvious. Survival depended on it, as it does today, and widespread participation at the ground level of agriculture guaranteed a certain kind of familiarity. Even though the notion that "primitive man" lived in earthy and beautiful symbiosis with the natural world is a romantic myth, it is easy for those of us who love the study of the past to treasure earthy narratives of hunters and gatherers and village-folk inhabiting austere landscapes while tending their animals, eventually returning home to close-knit tribes and reveries of mythical thinking, fire dances, and frequent sex.

In fact, ancient humans most often perceived nature as a fierce threat, capable not only of killing them through droughts or animal attacks but also of implicating them in moral and religious schemes lost to secular audiences in the modern period. The very word "nature," as a reified concept in contemporary speech, indicates forces somehow *detached* from the divine realm or from any purpose—we may speak of an "act of God" as an insurance term, but for the most part winds blow where they blow, and crop failure or success is the result of hard work and wise planning. Moreover, the category of "nature" is potentially all-encompassing; what would a "non-natural" object truly be, if "nature" is defined as the totality of objects and things and interactions among these things in the universe? Of course, what we usually mean when we call something "natural" is that the thing is pure, organic (living or once living), wholesome, and so on. "Unnatural" is then a pejorative term, denoting what is impure, fake, immoral.

In this book I examine the famous story of an ancient sufferer in the Bible, Job, and the relationships that are forged and denied between the human self and nature in Job's story. Perhaps more than any other book in the Bible, Job evokes a world of flourishing and dying plants and animals to speak of the human moral situation. In every distinct movement of Job we see that the narrator, human characters in dialogue, and the Deity set the key terms of their discussion in the theater of ecology, a fact usually lost in debates about Job's meaning that focus on legal metaphors or the problem of theodicy generally. Job has plenty to say about the meaning of nature, perhaps more than we can handle, and the Joban natural world offers us a panoply of actors rivaling any human voice in this most complicated of biblical books.

To put it simply, I make two central arguments. First, I contend that the plant and animal metaphors constitute the primary terms of debate within the Dialogues (Job chapters 4–37), and the nature metaphors within these Dialogues need to be considered along with the evocation of nature in the Prologue (Job 1–2) as well as the towering Divine Speech (Job 38–41). In this way we discover not only that plant and animal images occur with far greater frequency than most readers assume, but also that nature is drawn into a complex web of images within the Bible as it attempts to narrate nature in terms of covenant. These attempts at narrating nature have implications for the formation of the discrete human being and the human community within Job and the Bible more broadly—wresting the distinct Joban "self" out of the control of the Deuteronomic and Proverbial nature traditions and into a wild and uncertain new world. The center of my work in this project is the heightened consideration of plant and animal images in the book of Job by way of close readings of key texts; in one sense, for me, this stands on its own as the beginning of what I hope are renewed efforts to see Job as a central voice in considerations of what constitutes a "biblical view of nature," either as a chapter in the intellectual history of the ancient world or as a theological project.

On the other hand, I seek something more than this set of close readings. I go on to argue that in Job's prevalent but under-studied nature images we find symbols of a divine economy and a social world—ancient Israel/Palestine in the late sixth and early fifth centuries BCE—in a period of ecological flux and great political confusion. Thus I want to make a historical argument—no matter how tentative and open to criticism as such arguments are bound to be—about the circumstances of Job's composition and earliest reception in this particular context. Though it is not especially controversial to place the book of Job in this era, very few attempts have been made to understand how Job's nature imagery participates in or constructs a symbolic universe that would have been precisely meaningful in this early post-exilic setting. To this end I argue that the Joban conversation about nature mirrors geographical and political concerns about land and covenant in the early years of Persian domination over the province of Judah/Yehud, and that the Joban Divine Speech points its audience directly into the savage paradoxes of their new efforts to cultivate and control their space.

As a specific point of entry into these Joban nature narratives I take up the theoretical lens of the "self," a rubric that is at once vague and penetrating for considering Job's fate amid his fluctuating worlds of plants and animals. Israelite wisdom literature engages in a multifaceted project of self-making in the face of nature, and Job needs to be considered as a major contributor to this project, not merely relegated to the sidelines as too complicated for historical analysis or too risky for theological consideration. As I will demonstrate in Chapter One, when I use the term "self" in this book I am invoking an awareness of recent studies that speak of the "self" very self-consciously. Moreover, as indicated above, I am invoking a version of the self that is explicitly forged by narrative—in this case, Israel's narratives about the human position within nature. The ancient Israelite self exists not only within "nature" but also within a community of narration, and Job offers us a flashpoint for reading these communities in the midst of fierce debate about the meaning of the individual within nature and the human community. At the very least my theoretical gestures involving self and narrative—though preliminary and incomplete—help remind me as an author (and I hope readers as well) that inquiry is not launched from a vacuum, and that the historical-critical method (a method I also cherish) is not an inevitable starting or ending point for every academic study of the Bible.

In this book I do not make a systematic or scientifically-oriented attempt to understand the exact species of plant or animal that correlates to a particular Hebrew word in every case, except where such knowledge is helpful for understanding a precise nuance in the text. Moreover, this book does not participate in the genre of "ecological hermeneutics" as it is sometimes understood—that is, as *advocating* for a particular course of spiritual or political action with regard to the environment based on the text. If, however, that rubric of ecological hermeneutics implies any broad attempt to understand a textual or cultural tradition in light of historical or symbolic ecologies, then my work does indeed fall squarely into this rubric. Whatever the case, I hope that readers interested in plants and animals as biological phenomena, or those concerned with the fate of our environment today in light of the Bible, will still find much that is valuable in the way the book of Job invokes these topics.

অঅঅ

In Chapter One ("Consider the Ostrich") I explain my theoretical approach to Job in terms of narrative and the language of the "self" and relate this search for a self, as both an ancient and a modern project, to ecological concerns. Moreover, I give a review of previous scholarly work relating to the book of Job, specifically as previous studies address eco-anthropological questions in Job and as those studies attempt to place Job in a particular (ancient) social and interpretive world. By engaging with and, at points, endorsing and expanding upon biblical-studies scholarship under the "eco-theology" rubric, I do not ignore historical-critical, linguistic, or history of religions concerns—indeed, these latter historical-critical categories form the core of my analysis in this book.

In Chapter Two ("Eco-Anthropologies of Wisdom in the Hebrew Bible"), I explore the context of the juxtaposition of plant, animal, and human selves in the Hebrew Bible. The notion that *nature responds* to human and divine activity is fundamental to the biblical corpus, and for many exegetes the mandate of human control over the natural world in Genesis 1:26 stands as the normative template for this response. However, I contend that there are other striking images of the human relationship to nature that severely complicate a naïve or straightforward understanding of Genesis 1:26 as a programmatic text. Elsewhere we find nature—particularly animals—operating far outside the realm of human mastery, and nature's existence as punisher of or rival to humans suggests that the problem of defining the human place alongside plants and animals was an ongoing concern and even a source of angst and bewilderment in ancient Israel. Specifically, I examine the use of plant and animal metaphors for the human self in wisdom literature, arguing that the wisdom fixation with these metaphors represents a significant Israelite contribution to ancient Near Eastern categories of the human vis-à-vis the natural world.

In Chapter Three ("Eco-Anthropologies in the Joban Dialogues") I turn directly to the book of Job, where key elements of the debate between Job and the Friends (and even among the Friends themselves) hinge on particular understandings of the human place within nature. In differing ways the Friends offer ruminations on

Job's predicament that rely on specific plant and animal analogies. These images prompt the question: Under what concept of the self are the characters in the book of Job working if they see fit to compare human states of suffering and morality to plants? Indeed, the debate between Job and his companions directly addresses the question of self-agency versus a deterministic natural order; within the core of the Joban dialogues (chapters 3–31) characters make numerous appeals to models of creation, animal life, and plant growth as analogies for human order and suffering. For example, the Eliphaz speech in Job 4 makes shrewd references to cycles of precipitation by way of anchoring a conventional appeal to divine justice, and further reference to covenants with the animal kingdom and the prospect of flourishing grass suggests that the trials of the suffering self can be straightforwardly tested against floral and faunal responses. In 8:11-12, Bildad evokes seemingly common-sense agricultural norms as an analogy for human faith. Later in the book Eliphaz compares defiant humans to failing branches, grapes, and olive trees (15:32-33), Bildad equates humans with maggots and worms (25:6), and other speakers in chapters 26 and 28 introduce radical and strange images of monstrous animals and impenetrable earth.

As a counter-model to these eco-anthropologies, Job himself offers a shocking rejoinder in chapter 12 in which animal and cosmological imagery serves as evidence for a world that can only be an inverted parody of the Friends' concept of natural theology (i.e., the notion that God's activity can be accurately perceived through a "rational," conventionally-conceived image of the physical order). Moreover, the ominous references to Leviathan (Job 3:8; 41:1) and other mythological creatures (7:12; 26:12-13) heighten the philosophical problem inherent in the natural drama from Job's (and eventually, God's) perspective, since they introduce further distance between humans and the rest of the created order and thus insert confusion into the anthropology of suffering as it is related to the state of non-human life forms. Moreover, Job points to strong disjunctions between the human self and plant life (14:1-2 and 14:13-19) and argues against identification with trees (cf. 29:18-20). His laments refer to his new animal companions, ostriches and jackals (31:38-40)—the steppeland photographic negatives of the domestic cattle of the prosperous years—and Job's final plea in 31:38-40 significantly invokes plants as witnesses to decide the case.

The three Friends, who are typically viewed as naïve and rigid traditionalists, do in fact offer a range of speculation on plant and animal life that is more complex and provocative than anything the supposed Deuteronomists or Proverbialists had to offer on the topic, and Job's own musings—though obviously defensive and oriented around opposing the claims of the Friends—not only offer a rejection of the other paradigms but oscillate between human identification with the fate and morality of nature generally and the outright rejection of floral and faunal metaphors for the position of human-as-sufferer.

God famously responds to the argument in Job 38–40, and in Chapter Four ("Eco-Anthropologies in the Joban God-Speech") I examine the recitation of animal lore and cosmological lists that define the Divine self in terms of its relationship with nature. Though many analyses of the divine speech are simply content to notice God's obvious mastery over nature, most have stopped short of naming the profound theological indeterminacy created in these chapters, which, through its strange cocktail of beauty and cruelty, asserts a vision of nature that is identical with neither Job's nor the Friends' visions (and yet reflects elements of nearly all the views). Since the Divine Speech—arguably the pinnacle of the book's poetic and thematic expression—is so directly concerned with providing resounding statements on animals, weather, and cosmology generally, I conclude that it is most appropriate to read the speech not as an *avoidance* of the key moral questions at stake but rather as the most *direct engagement* with the book's central metaphors, that is, the plants and animals that stand as transparent ciphers for the suffering or thriving human body—indeed, for Israel itself.

Having analyzed the texts within Job to this extent, in Chapter Five ("Natural Theologies of the Post-Exilic Self in Job") I situate Job within a context of literature addressing the fate of the early post-exilic community in the late-sixth and early-fifth centuries BCE. As best we can tell, archaeological work informs us that the land itself in this historical context had to be beaten back into shape by new, small, and vulnerable communities of settlers, making the question of nature's relationship with human morality an explicit concern. Indeed, on these very questions Job was not a lone voice in this period, and other "ecological competitors" such as Haggai, Isaiah 40–55, Genesis 1, and the finalized book of Deuteronomy also put forth their own narratives of nature and the self, against which Job stands in sharp relief. Having set this context, I provide an exploration of Job's participation within the category "natural theology," distinct from a mere "theology of nature" and yet including the observable nature-world in Job. There is no sustained scholarly work of which I am aware that treats Job in light of natural theology, which is surprising since the book deals so heavily and directly with questions of how the deity and the self may be known through observable natural phenomena. I review some parameters of the natural theology debate in both ancient and modern contexts and show how the book of Job evokes at least a starting point for thinking about nature and human rationality in light of the historical and ecological context of empire in the post-exilic period. Key elements of Job's presentation of suffering and nature fly in the face of doctrinally correct pictures of "natural religion," marking Job as the effort of a powerful "little community" attempting to forge a new physical and psychological landscape for the future. In this way Job takes a place alongside other products of its era such as Ruth, Jonah, and even Esther, all of which, in different ways, use fictive scenarios to raise subversive questions about the meaning of Israel's failed attempt at national independence and the broader question of the meaning of empire in the ancient Near East.

অঅঅ

All translations from the Hebrew Bible in this book are my own, unless otherwise noted, and are drawn first from the Masoretic Text (though I consult other manuscripts). I represent Hebrew words using a transliteration system that I hope is simplified enough to give non-Hebrew readers some sense of the words' sounds, but also technical enough for Hebrew readers to follow the original language. Readers coming from outside the disciplines of Hebrew Bible and ancient Near Eastern studies will need to know that Job presents unique problems for translation, as the book seems to be written in some strange mélange of dialects and with an intentionally arcane vocabulary—perhaps an affected technique employed by the author(s) to give the book an "ancient" or "foreign" feel. Though I have attempted wherever possible to address problems of translation and some technical aspects of philology and textual criticism, readers looking for more detailed commentary on this aspect should consult any number of the studies cited in the notes.

In particular, the following works are excellent resources, and I rely on them as dialogue partners and guides for my own philological approach: Choon-Leong Seow, *Job 1–21* (Illuminations; 2013); Edouard Dhorme, *A Commentary on the Book of Job* (trans. Harold Knight; London: Thomas Nelson & Sons, 1967 [French orig. 1926]);

Marvin Pope, *Job* (AB 15; Garden City, NY: Doubleday, 1965; 3d ed. 1973); Norman Habel, *The Book of Job* (OTL; Philadelphia: Westminster, 1985); and David J. A. Clines's three-volume Word Biblical Commentary (*Job 1–20* [Dallas: Word Books, 1989]; *Job 21–37* [Nashville: Thomas Nelson, 2006]; *Job 38–42* [Nashville: Thomas Nelson, 2011]). Samuel Balentine's *Job* (Macon, GA: Smyth & Helwys, 2006) provides a treasure trove of insight for theologians and those interested in the profound reception history of Job in art and literature, and two excellent recent books on Job and creation give analyses that are analogous to the work I attempt in this study: Abigail Pelham, *Contested Creations in the Book of Job* (Leiden: Brill, 2012), and Kathryn Schifferdecker, *Out of the Whirlwind: Creation Theology in the Book of Job* (HTS 61; Cambridge, MA: Harvard University Press, 2008). Carol Newsom's *The Book of Job: A Contest of Moral Imaginations* (Oxford: Oxford University Press, 2003) anticipates several important points of focus in my own work here, and her outstanding treatment has influenced my argument in every chapter.

ৰৰৰ

I first presented ideas from this book in a session on the Hebrew Bible and theology at the 2012 Society of Biblical Literature meeting in Chicago; sparsely attended though that session was, were it not for the friendly response and positive feedback I received there I would not have continued with the project. My doctoral advisor, Peter Machinist (Harvard University) continues to play his role for me after I have left his direct educational care, offering advice, suggestions for bibliography, and encouragement just when it is needed. Two faculty research grants from the George Fox University Faculty Development Committee (2012, 2013) provided financial support while I was writing the manuscript. Many of the ideas here were first presented in teaching contexts, for courses on Wisdom Literature (Spring 2012, Spring 2013) and the book of Job specifically (Summer 2013), all at George Fox University. I thank the students in these classes for their thoughtful participation, and I also want to single out my teaching and research assistant Brandon Brown, who spent many hours helping with various aspects of the research process. The members of my weekly writing group at George Fox University—Paul Anderson, Joseph Clair, and Roger Nam—read this entire manuscript at the draft level as I wrote it over the past two years, and their insight, patience, and attention should be held up as a model for faculty writing groups everywhere.

Two other colleagues here at George Fox, Abigail Rine and Ed Higgins, saved me from many errors at the level of style and grammar, and both in their own ways strengthened my resolve to finish the project. Samuel Balentine (Union Presbyterian Seminary) was one of the first to read the completed manuscript and gave me encouragement at a time when I needed it. Victor Matthews (Missouri State University) gave me many ideas for bibliography, and Ron Simkins (Creighton University) helped me to think about how I might better integrate the theoretical gestures into the main body of the book. Abigail Pelham offered many thoughtful suggestions on the style of argumentation and pushed me to think about central issues of content in new ways. William Brown (Columbia Theological Seminary) served as a continual guide through his published work on Job, and gave specific feedback that helped make the book better in a number of important ways. I hold these individuals specifically responsible for what the reader finds good and useful in what follows—and nothing else.

A project of this scope requires moral support and psychological interventions of various kinds, and for this I am grateful to Susan

Melendez Doak, Nova Doak, Michael Favale, Abigail Rine, and Patrick Ray. I began writing this manuscript in a fit of vaguely-Joban despair during the Spring of 2012; just over a year later my second daughter, Junia Taylor Doak, was born (17 May 2013), and I dedicate this book to her.

1

Consider the Ostrich

Consider the Ostrich and the Papyrus

In some of the more subtly cruel lines spoken by a deity in world literature, the Joban God, in the midst of an elongated zoological lecture, has the following to say about the "ostrich" (Hebrew *rĕnānîm*, literally "joyous one"):[1]

> The wings of the ostrich flutter jubilantly,
> even though she lacks pinions or the right kind of feathers for flying.
> She leaves her eggs on the ground,
> and upon the dust they grow warm;
> she forgets that a foot might crush them,
> or a beast of the field might trample them.
> She acts harshly against her sons,
> as if they were not her own;
> her labor is for nothing, but not to worry;
> Eloah made her forget wisdom, he gave her no share of understanding.

---

1. Like so many words in Job, *rĕnānîm* is a *hapax legomenon*. I offer commentary on this passage in Chapter Four.

But another time comes, she rises up on the height,
she laughs at horse and its rider. (Job 39:13-18)

The image presented here—if the interpretive choices of this translation are correct—is of a pompous but ultimately impotent animal. Her wings flap wildly, but she does not have the power of flight; she produces eggs but does not (or cannot) care for them. Despite these inabilities, the bird confidently rises up to mock "horse and its rider," a stock image in the Hebrew Bible of military power, thus confirming the bird's stance toward the world: arrogance matched with ignorance, futile displays of power undercut by inability. This *rĕnānîm* is at least a joyous creature, though. The root *rānan* alludes to jubilant shouting (as in Job 3:7; 20:5; 29:13; 38:7), and the verb used to indicate the flapping of the bird's un-flying wings (*ne'ĕlāsāh*), which also describes some kind of joy (even sexual delight in Prov. 7:18), again highlights the bird's attitude.

What lesson is a reader supposed to take from this little allegory of the naïve and negligent bird-parent? One does not need to plumb the depths of one's literary sensitivities to imagine the chilling implications of this obtuse creature's existence for Job's own situation: as the book's opening narrative reveals, Job's children are killed during an infamous heavenly ideological duel, and Job's own body, once strong and monarchic in status, falls into ruin. Thus Job is like the arrogant but ultimately overconfident bird in this analogy, and the unguarded baby ostriches are like Job's dead children. And God is like . . . God—which is precisely the point: the all-important link between the fate of Job and that of the ostrich might be that God sees humanity as inhabiting the same stunted world of morality, causality, life, and death as any other animal. This is *nature*, for all living things. The harsh deity of the ostrich, who erases wisdom and facilitates the trampling of the eggs, is also the harsh deity of Job's own suffering, his own loss of children.

But who could have accused Job of being neglectful of his offspring? The first chapter of the book is entirely devoted to over-selling Job's perfect parenting, to the point that he offers vicarious sacrifices—not having any sins of his own—for imaginary offenses committed secretly in the hearts of his children. Perhaps one detects a sort of troubling paranoia in all this hypothetical atonement, or at least an inflated sense of the self. But had Job *flaunted* his wealth or status? Why should God treat Job like a mere bird—even like *this* bird?

Consider another example of an analogy to nature in Job offered in the aftermath of the protagonist's suffering, this time in the midst of the dense argument between Job and his three Friends in 8:11-13. One of the Friends, a certain Bildad the Shuhite, speaks to Job:

> Will papyrus sprout up where there is no marsh?
> Will reed-grass flourish without water?
> Still in its early stage of growth, will it not be cut down,
> and wither before any other foliage?
> Such are the paths of all who forget El,
> and the hope of the impious (*ḥānēp*) perishes!

Much could be said about Bildad's statement, which in fact continues for several verses after the portion quoted here, and I will return to it later in this study. This fragment of discourse could be read as a type of riddle: the first few lines are the question, after which there is an implied answer, followed by a punch line. The answers to the questions are so obvious as to not require an answer—papyrus will not sprout up outside a marsh, the reed-grass will not grow without water, and such plants would have to be prematurely harvested or simply removed. These actions of cutting and withering draw the riddle into the realm of polemic against Job, as Bildad shrewdly combines a moral category, "impious" or "godless" (adj. *ḥānēp*), with a cycle of natural plant life and the conditions required for that life. Can plants be *ḥānēp*, though? Have they failed in some human sense of the word "fail"? The passive "be cut down" (*yiqqāṭēp*), in the midst of a rhetorical negative question ("will it not be cut down" = "it will be cut down"), leaves one to ponder who it is that does the cutting, or why anyone would be doting over papyrus and reed-grass in the middle of the Uzzian steppeland.[2]

One could always appeal to the logic of riddle metaphors to argue that the grasses here are only a convenient image of something growing and dying. Bildad could have used another example to make the same point about causes and effects: A house does not burn down unless it catches fire. A child does not cry unless she is hungry. The appeal to plant life here, however, is not simply an arbitrary metaphor; rather, it is one of a long line of similar comparisons made by the Friends, rooted in the appeal to what they see as a commonsense pattern of moral agency among humans, plants, animals, and the earth itself (see, e.g., Job 4:8-11; 5:5-13; 5:22-27; 25:6; 15:32-33; cf. Job's similarly themed responses in 12:7-8; 14:1-12; 14:18-19; 27:18-23; 29:21-23; 31:38-40).[3] The implication here in Job 8:11-13, at least, is that God's cosmic justice is equated with a type of natural justice; there is simply "order," and order is order everywhere, for all things. In perhaps the Bible's

2. Tradition has it that the "Land of Uz" (*'ereṣ 'ûṣ*), where Job is said to live in the first verse of the book, is somewhere in the desert region south and east of Israel. "Uz" is a descendant or relative of Aram (northeast of Israel) in Gen. 10:23 and 1 Chr. 1:17 (cf. 1 Chr. 1:42), and directly associated with Edom (southeast of Israel) via the genealogy in Gen. 36:28 and the poetic parallel in Lam. 4:21. Note also a contextless reference to the "kings of Uz" in Jer. 25:20.

3. Here I firmly agree with Carol Newsom, "The Moral Sense of Nature: Ethics in the Light of God's Speech to Job," *Princeton Seminary Bulletin* (1994): 9–27, at 19, where she argues that the anthropomorphic language God uses to refer to nature in Job "should not be dismissed as 'mere poetry.' Metaphorically transferring the language of human moral activity to the natural world is a claim that there is an analogy between the vital purposeness of the natural world and the moral purposiveness of the human world."

most famous statement of the human relationship vis-à-vis nature, in Genesis 1:26, humans are created to rule over the created cosmos and its animals—in water, land, and sky. These images of the ostrich and the papyrus, however, suggest not a discrete, masterly human self but rather a world of human fumbling and of identification with plant and animal failures.

The Narrative and the Self

What are we to make of this relationship among plants, animals, and the human being in the book of Job? Is the ebb and flow of nature, in the Joban vision, a reliable witness to the ebb and flow of the human being? Is non-human, animal violence an appropriate model for thinking about human suffering? Does the human self flourish or fail in the moral universe of plants, or in some other universe? Is plant withering a faithful model for human withering? Are humans a part of nature, or a special part, or somehow apart from it? Does the harmony or violence of plants and animals have anything to say, in Job, about God? If so, what? To address these questions we must explore the specifically ecological context of suffering in the book of Job in order to delineate the competing definitions of the Joban self/selves through the prism of plant and animal life. On the most basic level I contend that the cycles and behavior of floral and faunal worlds present the primary metaphor through which the suffering human self is defined in Job. A close look at the texts I examine in this study indicates that something is very much at stake regarding the relationship among plants, animals, and the meaning of human experience for the Joban authors; the dialogues and the divine speech in Job can be investigated as though they are a kind of workshop in which the meaning and place of the human body vis-à-vis the plant and animal body is hammered out.

Using a more violent (and perhaps more appropriate) image, Job can be viewed as an anthropological ground zero for the traumatic definition of the post-exilic human self in ancient Israel, and the battered shape of the Joban experience provides a reconfigured—though not altogether unique—starting point for thinking about "natural theology" as a category of intellectual history in the ancient world.[4] To be sure, the question of the development of the "self" or "subject" in specific historical or cultural situations has received much attention from a variety of fields (in both the humanities and the sciences), though biblical scholars have yet to systematically engage with the topic so as to allow the Bible to take its rightful place as a witness to the historical evolution of moral agency (is one in control of one's actions?), psychological formation (how are emotions and thought processes shaped?), and anthropology generally (what does it mean to be a "human"?).[5] Though related questions of anthropology and the definition of self have long been part of the modern scholarly investigation of many ancient literatures—including, prominently, the Christian New Testament[6]—the Hebrew Bible has been under-explored in this

4. On the Hebrew Bible and the "natural theology" rubric see, e.g., James Barr, *Biblical Faith and Natural Theology*, The Gifford Lectures for 1991, Delivered at the University of Edinburgh (Oxford: Oxford University Press, 1995). Even though I hope the contents of this study would be helpful for contemporary theological thinking, here, and throughout the book, I attempt to use the word "theology" in some relatively neutral sense of "historical theology" (as opposed to, say, various types of prescriptive Christian or Jewish theologies or systematic theology), i.e., an attempt to explain religious thinking as it occurred in ancient Israelite communities through time. See the discussion in James Barr, *The Concept of Biblical Theology: An Old Testament Perspective* (Minneapolis: Augsburg Fortress, 1999), 209–21. Of course, in Christian formulations "historical" theology (as distinct from "speculative" theology) still maintains an apologetic framework of "revelation" or "salvation history"; see, e.g., Frederick J. Cwiekowski, "Biblical Theology as Historical Theology," *CBQ* 24 (1962): 404–11.

5. Carol Newsom, "Models of the Moral Self: Hebrew Bible and Second Temple Judaism," *JBL* 131 (2012): 5–25; idem, "Flesh, Spirit, and the Indigenous Psychology of the *Hodayot*," 339–54 in Jeremy Penner, Ken M. Penner, and Cecilia Wassen, eds., *Prayer and Poetry in the Dead Sea Scrolls and Related Literature: Essays in Honor of Eileen Schuller on the Occasion of Her 65th Birthday* (Leiden: Brill, 2012).

respect. In a recent and programmatic essay Carol Newsom draws attention to the neglect of the fields of "moral psychology" and "anthropology" in the scholarly discipline of Hebrew Bible studies, though she is able to point to a recent surge of scholarship by German-language academics.[7] Whatever insight biblical scholars can offer regarding these issues should take an important place alongside other similar investigations, such as those conducted within fields such as Greek and Latin classics, the history of philosophy, and modern literary studies of all kinds.

As Jacobus Wentzel van Huyssteen and Erik Wiebe point out in the Introduction to their recent edited volume (*In Search of Self*, 2011), "the search for the self" is "one of the most salient interdisciplinary academic discussions of our time," and religious literature has found its way right to the center of this discussion.[8]

6. E.g., Louise J. Lawrence, *Reading with Anthropology: Exhibiting Aspects of New Testament Religion* (Waynesboro, GA: Paternoster, 2005); Christian Strecker, *Die liminale Theologie des Paulus: Zugänge zur paulinischen Theolgie aus Kulturanthropologischer Perspektive* (Göttingen: Vandenhoeck & Ruprecht, 1999); Robert H. Gundry, Sōma *in Biblical Theology with Emphasis on Pauline Anthropology* (SNTSMS 29; Cambridge: Cambridge University Press, 1976); Ernst Käsemann, "On Paul's Anthropology," 1–31 in idem, *Perspectives on Paul*, trans. Margaret Kohl (London: SCM, 1971).

7. Newsom, "Models of the Moral Self," 5–6. Newsom cites three edited volumes as evidence of the German-speaking interest in the anthropology of the Hebrew Bible: Bernd Janowski and Kathrin Liess, eds., *Der Mensch im Alten Israel: Neue Forschungen zur alttestamentlichen Anthropologie* (Freiburg: Herder, 2009); A. Wagner, *Anthropologische Aufbrüche: Alttestamentliche und interdisziplinäre Zugänge zur historichen Anthropologie* (FRLANT 232; Göttingen: Vandenhoeck & Ruprecht, 2009); Christian Frevel, ed., *Biblische Anthropologie: Neue Einsichten aus dem Alten Testament* (QD 237; Freiburg: Herder, 2010). For Job and anthropology see Leo G. Perdue's *Wisdom in Revolt: Metaphorical Theology in the Book of Job* (Bible and Literature Series 29; Sheffield: Almond Press, 1991), 69, where he speaks of Job in terms of a "clash of anthropological metaphors." See also the recently published volume by Angelika Berlejung, Jan Dietrich, and Joachim F. Quack, eds., *Menschenbilder und Körperkonzepte im Alten Israel, in Ägypten und im Alten Orient* (Tübingen: Mohr Siebeck, 2012), esp. the following essays: Bruce J. Malina, "The Idea of Man and Concepts of the 'Body' in the Ancient Near East," 43–60; Jan Dietrich, "Individualität im Alten Testament, Alten Ägypten und Alten Orient," 77–96. For an earlier attempt to use anthropological categories for reading the Hebrew Bible see Thomas Overholt, *Cultural Anthropology and the Old Testament* (Minneapolis: Fortress Press, 1996). For a recent work engaging Job and psychology see Jeffrey Boss, *Human Consciousness of God in the Book of Job: A Theological and Psychological Commentary* (London: Bloomsbury T & T Clark, 2010), esp. 249–53 on nature and Job.

Even as this rubric of the "self" is salient and timely in contemporary discourse, like religious language generally, the philosophical language of the self comprises a veritable blizzard of terminologies and approaches. For example, Wentzel van Huyssteen and Wiebe refer to the notion of "multiple selves" as an "increasingly popular idea" in the field, and point to "a large, if not bewildering number of notions of self" in current usage: "the premodern self, the modern self, and the postmodern self . . . the plural self, the empty self, the multiple self, the emergent self, the saturated self, the erotic self, and the posthuman self."[9] It would be a mistake, however, to artificially calm this methodological storm and settle on single, strict definitions. As Helene Russel and Marjorie Suchocki remind us, although the ideal "self" of traditional Western theological and philosophical traditions is essentially a monolith, a "hierarchical unity of internal parts," personhood is better understood in terms of "multiple internal and external relations, with changing forms of relating these relations to self and others."[10] On a benign level, appeal to a single or "core" self

8. Jacobus Wentzel van Huyssteen and Erik P. Wiebe, "Introduction," in idem, *In Search of Self: Interdisciplinary Perspectives on Personhood* (Grand Rapids: Eerdmans, 2011), 1. Related to the sociological and anthropological quest for the "self" is a burgeoning body of literature exploring the intersection of religion and biology (i.e., the human body as viewed through the fields of cognitive science and/or neuroscience); see, e.g., Justin L. Barrett, *Cognitive Science, Religion, and Theology: From Human Minds to Divine Minds* (Templeton Science and Religion Series; West Conshohocken, PA: Templeton Press, 2011); Patrick McNamara, *The Neuroscience of Religious Experience* (Cambridge: Cambridge University Press, 2009); David Cave and Rebecca Sachs Norris, eds., *Religion and the Body: Modern Science and the Construction of Religious Meaning* (Leiden: Brill, 2012); Harvey Whitehouse, *Modes of Religiosity: A Cognitive Theory of Religious Transmission* (Walnut Creek, CA: AltaMira Press, 2004); idem, *Inside the Cult: Religious Innovation and Transmission in Papua New Guinea* (Oxford Studies in Social and Cultural Anthropology; Oxford: Oxford University Press, 1995); idem, *Arguments and Icons: Divergent Modes of Religiosity* (Oxford: Oxford University Press, 2000); Harvey Whitehouse and James Laidlaw, eds., *Religion, Anthropology, and Cognitive Science* (Durham, NC: Carolina Academic Press, 2007); Harvey Whitehouse and Robert N. McCauley, eds., *Mind and Religion: Psychological and Cognitive Foundations of Religiosity* (Walnut Creek, CA: AltaMira Press, 2005). I deal specifically in chap. 5 with some of this literature (particularly the works of Whitehouse and Barrett) as it interfaces with the notion of natural theology.
9. Wentzel van Huyssteen and Wiebe, "Introduction," 2–3.

("the real me") may be a convenient but immature and misguided method of ignoring dissonant aspects of one's own behavior or, worse, "a solitary construct of what it means to be human participates in an exaggerated heroic narrative, which cannot be disentangled from the myths of conquest that undergird both imperialism and colonialism."[11]

The question of the self in terms of "moral agency," that is, the extent to which selves are perceived as being in control of their own actions and moral outcomes, could be made a particularly relevant model for discussing Job, since this problem emerges constantly in the dialogues, specifically in the face of plant and animal flourishing. In one well-known attempt to map categories of the indigenous psychology of the self, Andrew Lock locates various "dimensions" of the self.[12] The relationships between culture and object become questions of symbolic relationship and, specifically, the *control* one is thought to have within one's broader environments: *"Man will necessarily conceive of himself in terms of an underlying construct of control."*[13]

Lock then maps out the "dimensions" of this control on two basic axes that reveal the orientation of "mind" and self within the grid. Where are the (inevitable, but not at all culturally uniform) boundaries between what a self considers to be the world "intrinsic" to the self (i.e., a part of the self) and what is "extrinsic" to the self (externalized versus internalized conceptions)? And to what extent is

10. Helene T. Russell and Marjorie H. Suchocki, 182–97 in "The Multiple Self," in Wentzel van Huyssteen and Wiebe, *In Search of Self*, at 182.
11. Pamela Cooper-White, "Reenactors: Theological and Psychological Reflections on 'Core Selves,' Multiplicity, and the Sense of Cohesion," 141–62 in Wentzel van Huyssteen and Wiebe, *In Search of Self*, at 151; on this same concept, and in the same volume, see Hetty Zock, "The Existential Self in a Culture of Multiplicity: Hubert Hermans's Theory of the Dialogical Self," 163–81.
12. Andrew Lock, "Universals in Human Conception," in Paul Heelas and Andrew Lock, eds., *Indigenous Psychologies: The Anthropology of the Self* (London: Academic Press, 1981), 19–36.
13. Lock, "Universals," 28 (emphasis in original).

the self perceived as being in control of the "game" of interactions of which one is a part—is the self "in control" or "under control" of an outside force?[14] The psychological drama represented by these dimensions is openly at the heart of the Joban conflict, as characters within the book take stances and generate opposition to each other based on assumptions regarding locus of control: Job is in control, out of control, vying for control; Job is part of an ecological context in which moral control is the result of decision-making, and yet the divine voice questions the viability of human decision-making and all morality and control; the heavenly banter in the Prologue (Job 1–2) quickly veers into questions of moral choice and rigged quotients of the flourishing self. Notable also in Lock's map is the dimension of *time*, which allows for understanding change and (dis-)continuity in a self. Notions of internal versus external control allow for differing views of change in time: internal controlling agents conceive of time in terms of memory, mood, and goals, while externally controlled agents speak of ghosts, the spirit world, and magic snares into which they may haplessly fall.[15] The floral and faunal dimensions of the Joban struggle make for a particularly important site to observe the categories of psychological belonging and control, and the Joban ecology has been mostly overlooked as one of the book's major contributions to ancient conceptions of the self.

The Bible (as either a Christian or a Jewish document) does not identify or advocate for any single ideal self. Instead, we find a seemingly contemporary focus on multiple selves, always plural, always negotiated through time. As a move toward addressing what we might call the "indigenous psychology" of the Joban actors,[16] my own approach here is to single out one set of relational categories of

---

14. See diagram in ibid., 33, Fig. 2.
15. Ibid., 32, 34.
16. Adopting the terminology of (among others) Paul Heelas, "Introduction: Indigenous Psychologies," in Heelas and Lock, *Indigenous Psychologies*, 3–18.

the self—the self that reflects and/or affects the status of the natural world. The "natural world" to which I refer here could maximally include all living things and material bodies besides humans: plants, various animals, clouds, tectonic plates, astral bodies, and water. More specifically, and as a pointed reflection of the texts I have already mentioned, the "natural world" I deal with in this study most specifically includes the living plants and animals that inhabit the chapters of the book of Job.[17] Indeed, Job's world is heavily populated with deliberate references to plants and animals, perhaps more so than any other book in the Bible as a whole, and the debate that develops in Job most often evokes non-human living things (plants and animals) as analogies for the human moral self. Of course, Job's world is also a fictional, literary one—which is all the more intriguing, since the plants and animals in the book would thus seem to appear as highly intentional, ideologically-driven symbols for the core ideas present in the narrative and dialogues. Indeed, Job, his family, his friends, and his God are part of a carefully constructed cosmic geography, the blueprint for which tells a story about all of its inhabitants. The ecological context of the self—even within imaginary or purely narrative geographies—is an important but often neglected aspect of biblical studies generally, but this context has been emphasized as central in studies of the self within indigenous psychology methodologies.[18]

The question of the human relationship with plants and other animals is not a straightforward one in the Hebrew Bible. Rather,

---

17. These categories will receive further specification in chap. 2; see Barrett, *Cognitive Science*, 58–69.
18. Note the repeated reference to the "ecological context" in Uichol Kim, Kuo-Shu Yang, and Kwang-Kuo Hwang, "Contributions to Indigenous and Cultural Psychology: Understanding People in Context," in idem, eds., *Indigenous and Cultural Psychology: Understanding People in Context* (New York: Springer 2006), 3–24, as well as in James Georgas and Kostas Mylonas, "Cultures Are Like All Other Cultures, Like Some Other Cultures, Like No Other Culture," in ibid., 197–221.

we find disparate images, and the particularly contested and focused character of the plant and animal discussion in Job suggests that the book can be viewed as an experimental textual zone for the development of a distinctly Israelite eco-anthropology. I use this admittedly cumbersome phrase, "eco-anthropology," to address the exact intersection of the human self with plants, animals, and earth generally. The Greek prefix *eco-*, from *oikos* ("house"), frames the question of ecology—and thus eco-anthropology—in terms not only of the four walls of domicile or property boundaries but more broadly in terms of "environment," "habitat," and the growing things resident in the world household. The opening chapters of the book of Genesis have understandably taken center stage in these kinds of discussions in the past although, I will contend, they should not be read as singular, emblematic, or authoritative beyond the many other descriptions of humans in combat with, or as victims under, or as masters over the natural world. There are other plant narratives and other animal voices in the Hebrew Bible, and where these narratives and voices appear we gain valuable insight into the biblical conceptions of the natural world generally, the historical theologies of sin and redemption, covenant, punishment, prophetic metaphor, and the definition of the human. The book of Job stands as a pinnacle of literary and philosophical expression on these topics insofar as they concern floral and faunal worlds, hence my focus here on the precise intersection of the book of Job's local anthropology of human righteousness, local botany, and local zoology.

Thus by invoking the language of the self in this study I attempt to draw attention to the oscillation and contestation among competing attempts within the book of Job to define the human self and its appropriate floral and faunal analogies. In fact, language about the "self" need not be limited to humans; if "self" is taken broadly to refer to living things with "mechanisms that allow them to detect and react to entities and events beyond their own boundaries," then the entire spectrum of plant and animal life participates in self-making.[19] A recent special volume of the journal *Cultural Anthropology* (2010) is dedicated to considering "multispecies ethnography" as "a new genre of writing and mode of research" in the social sciences, and many researchers are now looking toward "an anthropology that is not just confined to the human but is concerned with the effects of our entanglement with other kinds of living selves."[20] To be sure, such research could be focused scientifically on the cause-and-effect relationships among human systems of politics, economy, culture, and other living organisms, and much recent discussion of the environment in the academic field of biblical studies appears as an engagement with the pressing environmental concerns of our time.

But the focus has also turned to reflection on story, and to elements of nature that are somehow constitutive of the narrative expression of religion itself. A significant portion of the contemporary outburst of apocalyptic literature and film contains themes that are specifically eco-apocalyptic;[21] the demise of the modern West, whether an overblown, politicized fever dream conjured by threatened elites or a deep, mystical reaction to imminent change links our visions of human travail with visions of failure, success, or change in the

19. Ian Tattersall, "Origin of the Human Sense of Self," 33–49 in Wentzel van Huyssteen and Wiebe, *In Search of Self*, at 33. Note also, in the same volume, B. J. King, "Are Apes and Elephants Persons?" 70–82.
20. S. Eben Kirksey and Stefan Helmreich, "The Emergence of Multispecies Ethnography," *Cultural Anthropology* 25 (2010): 545–76, at 545. See also Christopher Southgate, *The Groaning of Creation: God, Evolution, and the Problem of Evil* (Louisville: Westminster John Knox, 2008), 60–72 on animal "selving."
21. For example, Cormac McCarthy's *The Road* (New York: Alfred A. Knopf, 2006) in both novel and film versions uses a destroyed ecological landscape as a primary character throughout the story. The eco-apocalypse theme can be found in many other recent novels (mostly involving the effects of climate change), such as Martine McDonagh's *I Have Waited, and You Have Come* (Brighton: Myriad Editions, 2006), films such as *The Happening* (2008) and *Chrysalis* (2008) (both of which received highly negative reviews), and various levels of non-fiction speculation regarding life on earth after humans, e.g., Alan Weisman, *The World Without Us* (New York: Picador, 2006).

natural world. Recent scientific studies on "insect love" or "delectable mushrooms that flourish in the aftermath of ecological destruction" are not simply arcane and culturally dislocated studies of entomology and mycology;[22] rather, they are a meditation on the silliness or impossibility or seriousness or biology of *human* love. They raise implicit questions about the frailty of human life—the flourishing post-apocalyptic mushrooms are a cipher for understanding what it would take for humans to live in a very different world. The plant self and the human self reflect and evoke one another.[23]

In the pre-modern world, and in some of the contemporary world as well, the relationship between humanity and the rest of nature could be conceived in quasi- (or straightforwardly) mystical terms.[24] Famines, earthquakes, or volcanoes can easily take on metaphysical overtones; crimes and immorality of various kinds are cited as harbingers of natural disaster. In such systems, human moral states are yoked to the land itself, and in this sense the observable, natural world of plants and animals provides a ready-made guide for the analysis of the self.

One may compare such a view with the development of an inner self that is distinct from the group or nature or anything else, often cited as a primary feature of modernity. As Charles Taylor has documented in his now famous tome, *Sources of the Self*, the recognizably "modern" self exhibits a specific type of detachment or self-control. In this system "personal commitment," or the ability

---

22. See Kirksey and Helmreich, "The Emergence of Multispecies Ethnography," 545.
23. See, recently, Matthew Hall, *Plants as Persons: A Philosophical Botany* (Albany: SUNY Press, 2011), which I discuss further below, as well as Jakob von Uexküll, *A Foray into the Worlds of Animals and Humans: With a Theory of Meaning*, trans. Joseph D. O'Neil (Posthumanities 12; Minneapolis: University of Minnesota Press, 2010), and, from a more strictly scientific perspective, Marc Bekoff and Jessica Pierce, *Wild Justice: The Moral Lives of Animals* (Chicago: University of Chicago Press, 2009).
24. See Charlotte Hardman, "The Psychology of Conformity and Self-expression Among the Lohorung Rai of East Nepal," 161–180, esp. 163–65, and Signe Howell, "Rules Not Words," 133–44, esp. 138, both in Heelas and Lock, *Indigenous Psychologies*.

to act with one's full force of will toward the good, becomes the very definition of thriving "human moral power" (at least in the Augustinian traditions).[25] This development of an "inner self," this interiority, provides an opportunity for every human self to willfully embrace what is good. "Commitment" is now the decisive moral element, and "no way of life is truly good, no matter how much it may be in line with nature, unless it is endorsed with the whole will."[26] Taylor's overall project—ambitious far beyond the scope of any review I could provide here—is to do nothing less than "to articulate and write a history of the modern identity,"[27] and one elemental part of that identity, against which Taylor's own vision is formulated, is labeled "naturalism," specifically defined as "the belief that we ought to understand human beings in terms continuous with the sciences of extra-human nature." For the "naturalist," in this sense, "human affairs ought to be maximally described in external, non-culture-bound terms."[28] Naturalist philosophy seeks to "reject all qualitative distinctions and to construe all human goals as on the same footing, susceptible therefore of common quantification and calculation according to some common 'currency.'"[29]

To bend Taylor's concepts a bit in anticipation of the discussion regarding the natural world within Job, we might say that the actors in the book (both human and divine) are engaged in an ancient philosophical diatribe on the relationship of the suffering self to the reactions, order, and disorder of extra-human natural experience. The

---

25. Charles Taylor, *Sources of the Self: The Making of the Modern Identity* (Cambridge: Cambridge University Press, 1989). Many others have spoken of this phenomenon of "self-detachment," such as Norbert Elias, "*Homo clausus* and the civilizing process," 286–98 in Paul du Gay, Jessica Evans, and Peter Redman, eds., *Identity: A Reader* (London: Sage, 2000), esp. 291–93, where he comments on the role of human control vis-à-vis nature.
26. Taylor, *Sources of the Self*, 185.
27. Ibid., ix.
28. Ibid., 80–81.
29. Ibid., 22–23.

fate of land (or *The* Land)—its produce, its plants, its people—is held up to the scrutiny of a type of ancient naturalism embodied in a primitive botany or zoology, and the actors contend for competing visions of how best conceive to of the human self in light of plants and animals. As readers have readily noted for generations, a great deal of the discussion as it shapes up in the book of Job concerns the exact question of individual commitment to what is good—namely, Job's commitment to doing what is right before God—and the supposed results of this commitment as they may be observed in nature. By calling this set of relationships into question (indeed, by even exposing such questions to scrutiny in the first place), the book of Job reveals a breaking point in Israel's dominant narrative of the self, one that is important not only for thinking about the relationship between nature and the self in the ancient world but also for considering modernity and secularity as contemporary phenomena.

For the character of Job himself, however, such lofty debates are often overshadowed in the moment by sheer personal pain. Whatever native senses of self may be derived from the book, the authors of this complex ancient poetry were certainly concerned with providing, on their own terms, an anthropology of thriving, suffering, and punishment, all of which is played out in one individual body.[30] Since Job is the quintessential biblical sufferer, we cannot help but read Job's own identity in terms of the suffering self. For one notable explicator of the self, the philosopher Paul Ricoeur, suffering is a central concept of the person, and Ricoeur defined one of his central terms in his exploration of self, *attestation*, as "the *assurance of being*

---

30. The concept of a "body," often linked to theoretical notions of the self, is now beginning to receive attention in biblical studies; see recently, and on Job specifically, Amy Erickson, "'Without My Flesh I Will See God': Job's Rhetoric of the Body," *JBL* 132 (2013): 295–313, and Jürgen van Oorschot, "Beredte Sprachlosigkeit im Ijobbuch. Körpererfahrung an den Grenzen von Weisheit und Wissen," 239–53 in Berlejung, Dietrich, and Quack, *Menschenbilder*.

oneself acting and suffering."[31] Ricoeur distinguishes between "self" as *idem*, "sameness," and *ipse*, "selfhood"; the latter "involves a dialectic complementary to that of selfhood and sameness, namely the dialectic of self and the other than self," with this "otherness" being "of a kind that can be constitutive of selfhood as such"—and he uses this *ipse* concept of otherness within the self as the guiding concept of selfhood in his later work.[32] For Ricoeur the definition of the self is not the self-confidence of the pithy Cartesian motto, *cogito ergo sum*, but rather is bound up in the layers and palimpsests of memory and story: "in many narratives the self seeks its identity on the scale of an entire life." At the risk of simplifying, it can be said that Descartes' model has one looking inward, doubting the senses and the external world, while Ricoeur would have us look outward, at others, at narration, and at the embodied world. For Ricoeur the self depends upon others, and this style of approach affirms the person as an element of nature in a non-naïve manner while requiring vulnerability in the face of other humans and the physical world.

The self as I will analyze it here in this study, following Ricoeur, is about narrative, and others, and one's physical environment—but also it is about believing, and about trust. Ricoeur loads the word *assurance* ("*the assurance of being oneself acting and suffering*") with quite a bit of pressure, perhaps not so unlike the author of Hebrews 11:1 in the famous Christian formulation, "Faith is the assurance (*hypostasis*) of

---

31. Paul Ricoeur, *Oneself as Another*, trans. Kathleen Blamey (Chicago: University of Chicago Press, 1992), 22 (emphasis in original). Ricoeur's views of self and suffering have been the subject of productive analyses; see, e.g., Pamela Sue Anderson, "On Loss of Confidence: Dissymmetry, Doubt, Deprivation in the Power to Act and (the Power) to Suffer," in Joseph Carlisle, James C. Carter, and Daniel Whistler, eds., *Moral Powers, Fragile Beliefs: Essays in Moral and Religious Philosophy* (London: Continuum, 2011), 83–108; Declan Sheerin, *Deleuze and Ricoeur: Disavowed Affinities and the Narrative Self* (London: Continuum, 2009), 48, 57, 61, 106, etc.

32. Ricoeur, *Oneself as Another*, 3.

things hoped for, the conviction of things unseen." For, as Ricoeur puts it:

> The assurance remains the ultimate recourse against all suspicion; even if it is always in some sense received from another, it still remains *self-attestation*. It is self-attestation that, at every level—linguistic, praxic, narrative, and prescriptive—will preserve the question "who?" from being replaced by the questions "what?" or "why?" Conversely, at the center of the aporia, only the persistence of the question "who?"—in a way laid bare for lack of a response—will reveal itself to be the impregnable refuge of attestation. . . . As credence without any guarantee, but also as trust greater than any suspicion, the hermeneutics of the self can claim to hold itself at an equal distance from the *cogito* exalted by Descartes and from the *cogito* that Nietzsche proclaimed forfeit.[33]

Ricoeur's focus on narrative and the definition of the self vis-à-vis the "other" that constitutes the self is a helpful starting point for framing the Joban drama as it strives toward the definition of the human in the face of a plurality of other "selves"—not only among Job, Job's Friends, and God, but also among the writhing and dying plants and the proud, monstrous, or negligent animals that are invoked to inhabit the Joban moral universe. My intention here, then, is to use these categories of nature and the self to re-frame the central debate in Job and to examine the big ideas at the center of this book of ideas through the prism of the Joban natural world.[34] Though obviously I do not claim to uncover "the meaning"—as if such a thing could exist, in the singular—of the book of Job, an investigation of the Joban natural world in relation to the human body reveals an underexplored vista for seeing Job's distinct expression of ancient Israelite human selfhood in a period of religious change.

---

33. Ricoeur, *Oneself as Another*, 22–23.
34. Here I echo William Brown's assertion in *The Seven Pillars of Creation: The Bible, Science, and the Ecology of Wonder* (Oxford: Oxford University Press, 2010), 115–16, that Job is a type of "thought experiment."

Nature and History in Job and the Hebrew Bible

Before moving directly into my engagement with the texts in question I would like briefly to situate my project within the history of academic studies on the book of Job and the Hebrew Bible, specifically as those studies address the issue of the human identity as opposed to plants and animals and the question of Job's early reception in a historical context. Is Israel's deity perceived as "above" or "apart from" nature, or somehow *in* it, a part of it, or even implicated by it? Such questions have received a fair amount of attention from biblical scholars in the second half of the twentieth century, spurred on in part by Gerhard von Rad's often-cited essay, "The Theological Problem of the Old Testament Doctrine of Creation."[35] Von Rad canonized a dichotomy between God and nature by making a distinction between Israel's putatively *historically-* oriented worldview and the *nature* orientation of Mesopotamian myth. In this view "creation" and "redemption" have nothing to do with one another; Israel's religion was to be oriented around strict opposition to "Canaanite" religious forms involving Baal. Such "nature religions" were not to be opposed by the prophets or the Deuteronomistic Historian(s) on the basis of an Israelite view of nature or creation, but rather on the basis of Israel's history of redemption.[36]

---

35. Gerhard von Rad, "The Theological Problem of the Old Testament Doctrine of Creation," 131–43 in Bernhard W. Anderson, ed., *Creation in the Old Testament* (Issues in Religion and Theology 6; Philadelphia: Fortress Press, 1984; first published 1936). Ronald Simkins (*Creator & Creation: Nature in the Worldview of Ancient Israel* [Peabody, MA: Hendrickson, 1994], 8) sees the beginning of this type of dichotomy in Western intellectual traditions in the philosophical framework of Hegel, while others have identified the basic framework of the dichotomy in Plato (see, e.g., Hall, *Plants as Persons*, as discussed below). On the question of Israel's "distinctive" posture vis-à-vis Mesopotamia on this question and others see Peter Machinist, "The Question of Distinctiveness in Ancient Israel," reprinted in Frederick E. Greenspahn, ed., *Essential Papers on Israel and the Ancient Near East* (New York: New York University Press, 1991), 420–442, at 424.

According to von Rad, even materials that discuss both nature and the history of redemption side by side (such as Psalms 136 and 148) in fact somehow manage to create a disjointed situation in which nature and history are "wholly unrelated" to one another.[37] One might simply ask how these themes can be truly and "wholly unrelated" while appearing in the same psalm (when presumably the author could have omitted one of the themes if he did not want them to be related in any way). When in the Psalms creation does play a decisive role in characterizing God's being or activity, as in Psalms 19 and 104, it turns out, in von Rad's conception, that these psalms were "Canaanitish" or Egyptian in origin. Themes of nature and creation are thus always epiphenomena, subordinated to the *Heilsgeschichte* theme.[38] I do not mean to make von Rad's work an isolated or all-too-simplistic target for what has appeared to many later interpreters (including myself) to be an overly rigid system for dismissing the intimately conceived connection Israel's divinity apparently had with the created order.[39] The assertion that Yhwh's domain was history as opposed to the mythico-natural world of Egypt and Mesopotamia had been a common trope in early- and mid-twentieth-century European and American scholarship, and more recent interpreters, such as Yosef Yerushalmi in his justly celebrated book *Zakhor: Jewish History and Jewish Memory*, have argued for Israel's unique status over and against the rest of the

---

36. Von Rad, "Theological Problem," 54. See the thorough review of von Rad and others on this theme in Theodore Hiebert, *The Yahwist's Landscape: Nature and Religion in Early Israel* (Oxford: Oxford University Press, 1996), 4–23, and William P. Brown, *The Ethos of Cosmos: The Genesis of Moral Imagination in the Bible* (Grand Rapids: Eerdmans, 1999), 4–10.

37. Von Rad, "Theological Problem," 55.

38. See the clear statements of von Rad ("Theological Problem," 59, 63) on this; cf. Machinist, "The Question of Distinctiveness," 424, 434.

39. See the review of von Rad's position(s) on this issue in John W. Rogerson, "The Old Testament View of Nature: Some Preliminary Questions," 67–84 in Hendrik Antonie Brongers, et al., eds., *Instruction and Interpretation: Studies in Hebrew Language, Palestinian Archaeology and Biblical Exegesis* (Leiden: Brill, 1977), as well as Perdue, *Wisdom in Revolt*, 17–18.

ancient Near East in rejecting the traditional ancient connection between nature and history.[40]

Others, however, were more willing to tease out the ways in which Israel participated in myth and Mesopotamia constructed history,[41] and the specific question of the role of nature within the Hebrew Bible took on its own momentum. Only a few examples must suffice. Klaus Koch asserts that a proper understanding of ancient Israel's God must admit that God *includes* nature—which represents not quite a Spinozan pantheism (*Deus sive natura*), "but perhaps it is not Theism either in the sense of our western theology."[42] Reading the conflation of human and natural success in texts like Psalm 72 and Ezekiel 17, Koch points to the attribution of moral categories (*sĕdāqāh*) to hills and the analogy of tree growth to kings as evidence of direct connections among morality, the deity, humans, and nature. Such connections, for Koch, are not "purely metaphorical" or subordinated to some other higher theological framework; rather, they are the very substance of the theology in question.[43] Regarding the book of Job specifically, Robert Gordis asserts that the divine speech in Job 38–41 sets up an "analogy" of "beauty and harmony" between the natural world and the human sphere within that world—yet the speech is shot through with images of nature that are "without any reference to man's desires or needs, or even his existence."[44] Hence creation

40. Joseph Hayim Yerushalmi, *Zakhor: Jewish History and Jewish Memory* (paperback, with a new preface and a Foreword by Howard Bloom; Seattle: University of Washington Press, 1996), 8; cf. Ronald Hendel, *Remembering Abraham: Culture, Memory, and History in the Hebrew Bible* (Oxford: Oxford University Press, 2005), 98–99.

41. E.g., Bertil Albrektson, *History and the Gods: An Essay on the Idea of Historical Events as Divine Manifestations in the Ancient Near East and Israel* (Lund: Gleerup, 1967); J. J. M. Roberts, "Myth versus History: Relaying the Comparative Foundations," 59–71 in idem, *The Bible and the Ancient Near East: Collected Essays of J. J. M. Roberts* (Winona Lake, IN: Eisenbrauns, 2002).

42. Klaus Koch, "The Old Testament View of Nature," *Anticipation* 25 (1979): 47–52, at 47.

43. Koch, "The Old Testament View of Nature," 50.

44. Robert Gordis, "Job and Ecology (and the Significance of Job 40:15)," *Hebrew Annual Review* 9 (1985): 189–202, at 195 (this last quoted phrase is italicized in the source).

and nature are not always subordinated to a *Heilsgeschichte* scheme, but rather exist in idiosyncratic or mystical communion with some inscrutable divine purpose.

In his *Creator & Creation* (1994), Ronald Simkins gives us the first systematic attempt to interpret the world of ancient Israel in light of nature. Simkins notes the almost total lack of reference to the natural world in shaping ancient Israel's view of humanity and God in biblical interpretation before 1970; rather, as outlined through von Rad's essay above, nature was merely the "stage for the historical drama of salvation, or nature served as God's instrument in that drama."[45] Simkins takes on the challenge of articulating an Israelite "worldview" regarding nature, in which he attempts to delineate the "cognitive categories" within which nature and the Self were viewed. Simkins locates Israelite culture as "collective," in which people share a common fate, and identity is located primarily within the group. The "Other," then, is "all that is not the Self," which would include non-domesticated plants and animals, as well as humans outside of the "ingroup."[46] When faced with the outgroup, *disharmony* is the ruling idea—whether the outgroup includes humans, plants, or animals—while *harmony* is stressed within the social cosmos of the ingroup.[47] Thus there is no strict division between "nature" and "human" as such, but rather a division between all that is associated with the Self and the Other.

We will find many occasions to revisit this question of the relationship between "God" and "Nature" in Job and the Hebrew Bible, and the past few decades have seen an explosion of

---

45. Simkins, *Creator & Creation*, 1.
46. Ibid., 26–29.
47. Ibid., 30. I have discussed this question of human harmony with nature using Simkins's categories elsewhere; see Brian R. Doak, *The Last of the Rephaim: Conquest and Cataclysm in the Heroic Ages of Ancient Israel* (Ilex Series 7; Boston: Ilex Foundation; Cambridge, MA: Harvard University Press, 2012), 147.

philosophical and religious literature on the meaning of humans within the natural environment, much of it related to the Bible in some way. Indeed, sophisticated ecological readings have been fashionable lately, no doubt spurred on by the "green movement" and the creeping realization that problematic trends in climate change, water availability, and population density are beginning to interact with one another with increasingly disastrous results.[48] Scholars from many disciplines are rethinking the now centuries-old dichotomy that establishes humans and the natural world on separate sides of a massive chasm. In a recent book on the religious and philosophical understanding of plants in various traditions, for example, Matthew Hall takes up the challenge to situate "'humans in ecological terms and non-humans in ethical terms' and apply them in terms of a separately theorized nature of diversity, abundance, and individual (as well as collective) presence."[49] Tracing the history of the contemporary dichotomy between humans and plants, Hall finds early evidence of disregard for plants as "passive creatures" in Platonic philosophy and, in his view, an overly-sharp divide between plants and humans in the biblical book of Genesis.[50]

---

48. See David G. Horrell, Cherryl Hunt, Christopher Southgate, and Francesca Stavrakopoulou, eds., *Ecological Hermeneutics: Biblical, Historical, and Theological Perspectives* (London: T & T Clark, 2010); Celia Deane-Drummond, *Eco-theology* (Toronto: Novalis, 2008); and Norman Habel and Peter Trudinger, eds., *Exploring Ecological Hermeneutics (Atlanta: Society of Biblical Literature, 2008); Richard Bauckham, Living with Other Creatures: Green Exegesis and Theology (Waco, TX: Baylor University Press, 2011); Arthur Walker-Jones, The Green Psalter: Resources for an Ecological Spirituality (Minneapolis: Fortress Press, 2009)*. For a more popular treatment see Matthew J. Sleeth, *The Gospel According to the Earth: Why the Good Book is a Green Book* (New York: HarperOne, 2010).

49. Hall, *Plants as Persons*, 2.

50. Hall, *Plants as Persons*, 16, 60, with many helpful sources cited there. In his influential *The Secular City*, for example, Harvey Cox argues that "man" is the "master and commander" of the animal world. "It is his task to subdue the earth . . . . For the Bible, neither man nor God is defined by his relationship to nature. This not only frees both of them for history, it also makes nature itself available for man's use." Harvey Cox, *The Secular City: Secularization and Urbanization in Theological Perspective* (New York: Macmillian, 1965), 23.

Hall's perception of the way biblical texts in general function for this question, however, is relatively superficial; important though Genesis 1–3 are for Jewish and Christians traditions, they hardly need to represent the "center" or totality of meaningful or normative thought on the topic.[51] The Bible's wisdom literature, though traditionally given no pride of place among ancient Israel's intellectual contributions to theology or moral thinking generally, provides many and provocative models for thinking about the symbiosis or clash among humans, plants, and other animals. Indeed, the close interrelationship among the Hebrew Bible's wisdom literature and the encounter between humanity and nature is obvious, and many studies have already appeared to address these interrelationships. In a very helpful review of the question, Katharine Dell affirms that the "quest for an ecological hermeneutic" of any theological kind will have to reckon with biblical wisdom literature at or near its center.[52] Dell shows how texts like Proverbs 30:15–33,

---

51. Most of Hall's review of the Bible and the Christian traditions that use it for thinking about plants focuses on the opening chapter of Genesis. In this sense Hall follows the lead of the often-cited article by Lynn White, Jr., which focused attention on the (putatively negative) influence of the Genesis creation narrative on the environmental views of generations of Americans; see Lynn White, Jr., "The Historical Roots of our Ecologic Crisis," *Science* 155 (1967): 1203–7. Citing the fact that most of the Bible's references to plants have to do with agriculture, Hall (*Plants as Persons*, 64) claims that Genesis provides "a description of an agricultural setup in which plant life has no other purpose. The only thing of importance is the satisfaction of human needs." Nevertheless, Hall's overall point that the "hyperseparation" of nature and humanity in the Western tradition found warrant in certain parts of the Bible, and particularly the opening chapters of Genesis, is well supported. For biblical scholars and theologians, however, this type of critique would also be focused on those in the history of interpretation (even within the Bible itself) who chose to emphasize certain themes or biblical texts about nature over others. *Pace* Hall and White, the problem is not so much the inherent or inevitable message about nature provided by Genesis or any other text, but rather a particularly productive combination of available themes regarding human dominion in Genesis with modern ideologies of empire. See also the accurate critiques of White in Simkins, *Creator & Creation*, 5–7.

52. Katharine J. Dell, "The Significance of the Wisdom Tradition in the Ecological Debate," 56–69 in Horrell, Hunt, Southgate, and Stavrakopoulou, *Ecological Hermeneutics*, at 56. A sampling of relatively recent forays into the topic of ecology and wisdom literature by biblical scholars (many of which are cited by Dell in her essay) includes Leo G. Perdue, *Wisdom & Creation: The Theology of Wisdom Literature* (Eugene, OR: Wipf & Stock, 2009); Terence E. Fretheim, *God and the World in the Old Testament: A Relational Theology of Creation* (Nashville: Abingdon,

for example, fail to distinguish non-human life from human life, demonstrating a "complete interlinking of worlds," and she further highlights the contributions of Qoheleth and Job to important questions of creation and theology generally.[53]

Job's own engagement with plants and animals as analogies for human moral states is particularly noteworthy for its explicit and extended focus on these very topics, and thus should represent a central contribution to the discussion of "what the Bible says" about humans and nature.[54] In his *The Seven Pillars of Creation*, William Brown has taken up this challenge in an insightful and even stunning manner. Brown describes the Joban natural world as "creation thriving at the margins of human culture," and rightly observes that for too many interpreters the lesson in the Joban God-speech is merely a divine power trip (which is to say, a cover-up of the main moral problems of the book). Rather, Brown rightly contends, this divine speech contains *information*—about nature and the human place within that nature.[55] As God begins his four-chapter response to the human conversation throughout the book (chapters 38–41), we find the constant refrain of the word "where" (*'êpōh, 'ê*), which

2005); Katharine J. Dell, "Plumbing the Depths of Earth: Job 28 and Deep Ecology," *ESWT*, 116–25; and Hans-Jürgen Hermisson, "Observations on the Creation Theology in Wisdom," in Anderson, ed., *Creation in the Old Testament*, 118–34. The reader will find ample reference to older scholarship in these sources, and additional examples are discussed in more detail below.

53. Dell, "The Significance," 61–62. Biblical scholarship generally has witnessed a striking surge of interest in animals, with recent studies not only of the classic focal points in Genesis and wisdom literature but also in prophetic writings and other narrative traditions. E.g., for monographs see recently Tova L. Forti, *Animal Imagery in the Book of Proverbs* (Leiden: Brill, 2008), and Benjamin A. Foreman, *Animal Metaphors and the People of Israel in the Book of Jeremiah* (Göttingen: Vandenhoeck and Ruprecht,2011), as well as Mary R. Windham, "An Examination of the Relationship Between Humans and Animals in the Hebrew Bible," PhD dissertation (Harvard University, 2012).

54. For a popular work on this topic see Bill McKibben, *The Comforting Whirlwind: God, Job, and the Scale of Creation* (Cambridge, MA: Cowley, 2005).

55. Brown, *Seven Pillars*, 116, 124. See also Gordis, "Job and Ecology," 193: ". . . if the functions of the God Speeches were merely to assure Job that God was aware of his presence and responsive to his pain, a few lines to that effect would have sufficed. . . . Not merely *that God speaks*, but *what He says* must surely carry significance in this context."

focuses attention on space and ecology. In this redefined space "Job explores a new world of broadened horizons and alien creatures. Job is taken on a grand tour of creation's fringes, a cosmic field trip of unimaginable proportions."[56] God's animals here are conspicuously not under human control; they are not under Job's command and not for Job to name. Rather, as Brown perceptively notices, the conceptual order of creation in chapters 38–41 moves not from chaos to order (as in traditional ancient Near Eastern creation narratives) but from order into chaos.[57] In this ecological vision, creation is "terrifyingly vast and alien" and represents a world that is pluralistic and polycentric. Job cannot eat from a tree of knowledge in this world—rather, he is force-fed a vision of the entire world of plants, animals, monsters, and meteorological phenomena.[58]

Humans cannot act as masters of creation in the world of Job's God. Even generally speaking, in Simkins's conception of the ancient Israelites, "mastery over nature" was not something to be attained: "nature was beyond their control; they either felt subjugated to nature or linked with it in precarious balance."[59] Of significance for my project is the way Simkins characterizes the book of Job within the Israelite worldview concerning nature. After Job, or at least within the book of Job, nature can no longer be viewed as in "harmony" with humanity: "the character of Job gives preference on the subjugation-to-nature solution of the human-relationship-to-nature problem."[60] Human righteousness and nature are de-synched.[61] Moreover, Job presents a challenge to what is usually viewed as the "standard" biblical idea that "nature is an unambiguous

56. Brown, *Seven Pillars*, 125.
57. Ibid., 126–28.
58. Ibid., 129–31.
59. Simkins, *Creator & Creation*, 39.
60. Ibid., 123.
61. Ibid., 162.

witness to the character of human actions."[62] Of course, if, as Simkins states, ancient Israelites never really felt themselves to be in control of nature to begin with, then God's thundering assertion of the human position as out of control in Job 38–41 would come as less of a disjunction with tradition. The point here, though, concerns the question of the *link* between humans and nature: *is nature a reliable cipher for understanding the cosmos?* My contention is that, within the Joban drama, nature is, or can be, a "reliable" witness. The crux of the problem comes, however, when we begin to characterize the message of this reliable witness. Nature does indeed speak for the Joban characters in many ways, but it is only comprehensible or reliable within one's idiosyncratic experience, from positions of power or positions of loss and pain.

Considered philosophically (in the abstract) or as a question of ethics for our own time, the problem of God's relationship to plants, animals, and environment is a daunting one. But how is the Joban vision with regard to nature to be understood historically—that is to say, as a response to a particular social and historical context? Wisdom literature, most often situated in the period following the destruction of Israel's temple and monarchy in 586 BCE, is widely characterized as the embodiment of cosmopolitan, individual, non-cultic, and ahistorical concerns. Odil Hannes Steck, for example, seems to view wisdom literature as a sort of historical (and ecological) afterthought, not involving the Israelite community as such:

> Matters present themselves in a different light to Jerusalem cultic poetry and to Wisdom in the postexilic period, for their starting point is not a serious counter-experiences [*sic*] on Israel's part which have relevance for theology. The creation statements are not drawn into the problems of the still-unfulfilled and expected realization of salvation for Israel.

62. Ibid., 163. See also the summary comments on the role of nature and creation in the Joban dialogues in Katherine Shifferdecker, *Out of the Whirlwind: Creation Theology in the Book of Job* (Harvard Theological Studies 61; Cambridge, MA: Harvard University Press, 2008), 34–54.

... The questions do not emerge in the field of salvation history, with Israel's political and social existence; they are initiated by the fate of the individual. The problem is individual suffering and premature death, in contrast to Yahweh's activity in the world of creation as a whole, which guarantees life.[63]

Despite the focus in much Israelite wisdom literature on "timeless" single individuals (e.g., Job), or the singular voice of the sage as narrator in wisdom texts (e.g., Proverbs, Qoheleth), I think it would be a mistake to read these products as though they were written in an impossible historical or social vacuum. My assumption is that all authors, including the authors of Job, were situated individuals whose products reflect circumstances of upheaval, intellectual debate, and religious contention within their communities.[64] Even though it is also the case that wisdom compositions in Egypt and Mesopotamia generally feature individuals as speakers or protagonists, one may not automatically assume that those texts must have been produced in times when the nation or empire was in total collapse or disarray—indeed, periods of national strength or great societal concern can prompt wisdom speculation of all kinds, and there is no *a priori* reason to restrict the production of literature invoking the community and its history to periods of national disintegration. Though the narrative action in Job occurs in a kind of historical and geographical No-Man's Land, I do not presume that the book is devoid of historical, ecological, and political concerns.

On the contrary, I assume that Job can and must be made meaningful in light of some particular historical situation or social

---

63. Odil Hannes Steck, *World & Environment*, trans. Margaret Kohl(Biblical Encounter Series; Nashville: Abingdon, 1980), 217.

64. Of course, the very concept of an "author" in the singular is anachronistic, or at least problematic, when applied to ancient scribal contexts; see David M. Carr, *Writing on the Tablet of the Heart: Origins of Scripture and Literature* (Oxford: Oxford University Press, 2005); Susan Niditch, *Oral World and Written Word: Ancient Israelite Literature* (Louisville: Westminster John Knox, 1996).

occasion, difficult as this task may be, and indeed, there have been other attempts to make such correlations. In a recent article James Sanders has attempted to understand Job's role for a community living in the sixth or fifth century BCE.[65] In Sanders's view, in the fifth century BCE the formal Torah would come to canonize various struggles, not least of which is the problem of suffering and retribution in the face of the notion of a generational curse.[66] Among the prophets, Isaiah had offered a model for *communal* punishment and restoration, but, Sanders claims, such a model proved inadequate for dealing with the case of the *individual*.[67] Job then stands in this explanatory gap, as the "Rebel Job" challenges the Friends' reading of corporate tradition. Sanders thus places Job within what he sees as a great transformation in Judaism, initiated with the exile and expressed through prophets of "personal responsibility" (Jeremiah, Ezekiel) who would come to supplant older ideas of corporate identity.[68] No longer could the corporate view be applied, with national covenants of crime and punishment, to individuals; rather, Torah and Prophets had to be adapted as already part of an ongoing canonical process in antiquity.[69] Karel van der Toorn has tackled the question of Job as a transition point between "natural theology" and "revelation," and situates the book specifically in the "Persian era" (but not in any specific part of this period).[70] For van der Toorn, Job's theology

---

65. James Sanders, "The Book of Job and the Origins of Judaism," *BTB* 39 (2009): 60–70.

66. See Exod. 20:5; 34:7; Num. 14:18; cf. Deut. 24:16; Jer. 31:29–30; Ezek. 18:1–4.

67. Sanders, "Book of Job," 63–64. In making this claim Sanders seems to discount the possibility that the "Servant" (*'ebed*) figure of Second Isaiah (e.g., in Isa. 42:1, 15; 49:3-6; 53:11) could be understood in terms of individual suffering. Moreover, the Torah's own generational curse debate seems explicitly addressed to the individual in Deut. 24:16, and indeed it is taken as such when quoted and applied in the narrative of 2 Kgs. 14:5-6.

68. Sanders, "Book of Job," 66.

69. Sanders ("Book of Job," 67) assumes, problematically in my view, that the Torah and Prophets were "discerned by static readings" in the pre-exilic Iron Age." One may want to know which elements of the Torah or the Prophets *actually existed* in the pre-exilic period in order to know what was read statically, not to mention the many problems associated with the assertion that these materials really would have been read statically.

is social and historical in every way, and Job's status as an upper-class individual reflects the changed economic circumstances for "old money" in the face of the *nouveaux riche*: "increased taxation and the rise of an aggressive money economy based on the circulation of coinage" created a reversal of social fortunes as an "upcoming class of merchants outstripped" the traditional ruling class (see references such as Job 9:24; 15:19; 20:18-19).[71]

Perhaps the most important major work on Job written within the past decade is Carol Newsom's *The Book of Job: A Contest of Moral Imaginations* (2003), and my own project here lays claim to several of Newsom's conclusions and takes up some of her most important methodological cues.[72] Newsom embraces the approach of Mikhail Bakhtin to read Job as a "polyphonic" text and insists that a proper understanding of genre must provide a starting point for understanding readers' "horizon of expectation" before a literary work.[73] Especially important in Newsom's argument is the recognition of a variety of voices populating the narrative—and no single voice, not even the divine voice, ultimately claims narrative privilege in the text.[74] Following Bakhtin's work in *Problems of Dostoevsky's Poetics*, Newsom identifies three aspects of the polyphonic text: it exhibits a dialogic sense of truth; the author's position is not the "privileged" one in the text, though it may appear

---

70. Karel van der Toorn, "Sources in Heaven: Revelation as a Scholarly Construct in Second Temple Judaism," 265–77 in Ulrich Hübner and Ernst A. Knauf, eds., *Kein Land für sich allein. Studien zum Kulturkontakt in Kanaan, Israel/Palästina und Ebirnâri für Manfred Weippert zum 65. Geburtstag* (OBO 186; Göttingen: Vandenhoeck & Ruprecht, 2002).

71. Van der Toorn, "Sources," 268–69.

72. Carol Newsom, *The Book of Job: A Contest of Moral Imaginations* (Oxford: Oxford University Press, 2003). Leading up to this book, Newsom had published a series of essays on related topics such as "The Moral Sense of Nature: Cultural Politics in the Reading of Job," *Biblical Interpretation* 2 (1993): 119–34; "Job and His Friends: A Conflict of Moral Imaginations," *Interpretation* 53 (1999): 239–53; "The Book of Job as Polyphonic Text," *JSOT* 97 (2002): 87–108.

73. Newsom, *The Book of Job*, 11.

74. Ibid., 18–31.

in the text; and the polyphonic text resists final closure.[75] I endorse these particular tenets of the Bakhtinian perspective in this study, at least generically, and I provide elaboration on this front specifically in relation to the use of plant and animal imagery to define the struggling human self. Because dialogic truth has—or even requires—"an embodied, personal quality," through which we hear not "no-man's thoughts" but "voice-ideas,"[76] such a perspective is most appropriate for speaking about a plurality of animal and plant voices in a narrative and the emergence of diverging conceptions of the human self in the world of Joban debate.

As a scholarly conceit (or "heuristic fiction"), Newsom takes up the assumption that, with the exception of the Elihu speech (chapters 32–37), Job was written by a single author, and that author was deliberately attempting to compose a wisdom text by conflating several distinct yet overlapping genres (prose tale, dialogues, wisdom poems) into a single presentation for readers.[77] Job is thus a kind of *Bildungsroman*, exploring the question of individual suffering. I consider my own heuristic fiction for the book's composition, however, the details of which will become clear later on, to be something more than a fiction. In juxtaposition to Newsom's position I take up the argument that Job is not only (or not even primarily) a *Bildungsroman* but also something like a *Staatsroman*, a political treatise or national allegory for Israel's position in the early post-exilic period. The weaknesses of such a view may be immediately apparent. The language of the book is notoriously obtuse, frustrating philological analyses of a specific date or social setting for its composition, and since we do not know when or where or for whom

75. Ibid., 21. See Mikhail Bakhtin, *Problems of Dostoevsky's Poetics*, ed. and trans. Caryl Emerson (Theory and History of Literature 8; Minneapolis: University of Minnesota Press, 1984).
76. Newsom, *The Book of Job*, 22–23.
77. Ibid., 16–17.

Job was written, discussing the book's politics or national-allegorical possibilities can only seem imaginative.

But the strengths of such an approach will, I hope, become apparent as well. The *Staatsroman* category allows us to situate the book historically by reading the absence of the land/Israel/history as significant and by claiming that void as historically and symbolically meaningful. As many commentators on Job have noted, there are obvious parallels between the views and language of the Friends and the so-called "Deuteronomistic" conceptions of covenant, punishment, and divine responsibility. If these correlations are historically (and not just thematically) valid, and I think they are, this can only indicate that the author of the book was enmeshed in a thick position of religio-political entanglement with an already-existing corpus of religious thought, with severe implications for the national situation in the sixth and fifth centuries BCE.

2

Eco-Anthropologies of Wisdom in the Hebrew Bible

Wisdom as Floral and Faunal Knowledge

In ancient Israel, Egypt, and Mesopotamia the category of "wisdom" (Hebrew *ḥokmāh*; *ḥākām*) could encompass many different activities and skill sets, exemplified through diverse sub-categories such as upstanding moral behavior, religious observance, expert craftsmanship, scribal prowess, esoteric abilities, political savvy, and storytelling powers.[1] Perhaps the most frequently discussed aspect of wisdom discourse with relation to ecological concerns is the category of creation, strikingly on display through the recitation of a creation narrative or isolated creation motifs.[2] Specifically, and related to the

---

1. For the many different Akkadian terms designating wisdom activities see Ronald F. G. Sweet, "The Sage in Akkadian Literature: A Philological Study," 45–65 in John G. Gammie and Leo G. Perdue, eds., *The Sage in Israel and the Ancient Near East* (Winona Lake, IN: Eisenbrauns, 1990), esp. 47–50.
2. The most compelling introduction to the intersection between creation and wisdom is Leo G. Perdue, *Wisdom & Creation: The Theology of Wisdom Literature* (Eugene, OR: Wipf & Stock, 2009); see also Katherine Shifferdecker, *Out of the Whirlwind: Creation Theology in the Book of*

creation theme, wisdom activity could include compiling lists or delivering learned discourse on plants and animals, and we find evidence of this type of wisdom throughout the ancient Near East. In the Hebrew Bible, for example, consider this summary of the Solomonic golden age of wealth and achievement in 1 Kings 5:9-14 (English 4:29-34):

> (5:9) And God gave wisdom (*ḥokmāh*) to Solomon, and very great insight (*těbûnāh*), and breadth of understanding (*lēb*) like the sand of the seashore, (10) so that the wisdom of Solomon was greater than all of the Easterners and all the wisdom of Egypt. (11) And he was wiser (*ḥākam*) than every human, from Eytan the Ezrachite to Heyman, Kalkol, and Darda, the Sons of Machol. His fame was (known) in all of the surrounding nations. (12) He spoke three thousand proverbs, and his songs (numbered) one thousand and five. (13) He spoke about the trees, from the cedar that is in Lebanon to the hyssop that sprouts forth from the wall; he spoke about beasts (*běhēmāh*) and birds (*'ôp*) and creeping things (*remeś*) and fish (*dāgîm*) (14). People from everywhere came to hear the wisdom of Solomon—all of the kings of the earth heard his wisdom.

Solomon's wise status among the "Easterners" (*běnê qedem*) mirrors the use of this same terminology in Job 1:3 to describe Job's superiority over an identical (albeit broad) geographical category.[3] Curiously enough, the narrator of 1 Kings embeds within this précis only one specific indicator of Solomon's wisdom: his knowledge of

---

Job (HTS 61; Cambridge, MA: Harvard University Press, 2008); several essays (related to Job in particular) in *ESWT*; Roland E. Murphy, "Wisdom and Creation," *JBL* 104 (1985): 3–11; Hans-Jürgen Hermisson, "Observations on the Creation Theology in Wisdom," 118–34 in Bernhard W. Anderson, ed., *Creation in the Old Testament* (Issues in Religion and Theology 6; Philadelphia: Fortress Press, 1984); and reference to many studies on creation themes in Proverbs 8, e.g., Gale A. Yee, "The Theology of Creation in Proverbs 8:22-31," 85–96 in Richard J. Clifford and John J. Collins, eds., *Creation in the Biblical Traditions* (CBQMS 24; Washington, DC: Catholic Biblical Association, 1992).

3. *Běnê qedem* apparently describes inhabitants of northern Mesopotamia (near Haran) in Gen. 29:1, territory in the south (Judg. 6:33 and Isa. 11:4), and the heart of Mesopotamia in Babylonia (Ezek. 25:4, assuming the *běnê qedem* are a cipher for Babylon).

plants and animals.[4] The reference to cedars of Lebanon in tandem with hyssops sprouting out of walls in verse 13 is a merism, inclusive of all plants—from the majestic to the common shrub[5]—and the list of animals in the latter half of the same verse echoes the animals mentioned in the creation account of Genesis 1.[6]

The Solomonic wisdom emphasis, represented both in the passage above and in parts of the putatively-Solomon-authored book of Proverbs,[7] provokes different reactions. For von Rad the Solomonic empire constituted a complete break with the very provisional and charismatic rule of Saul, and even with David, with whom the process of hereditary leadership began and the monarchy took on new power.[8] According to this romantic view, cultural life opened up under Solomon; wealth and peace characterized this late-tenth-century setting and the royal court became "a centre of international wisdom-lore, as the Egyptian courts had been in an earlier age."[9] Von Rad called this achievement an "enlightenment," producing not only a flourishing court of wisdom but also the first genuinely historical writing in Israel.[10] Along these lines, Albrecht Alt seized on the reference in 1 Kings 5:13, in conjunction with animal references in Proverbs, and posited a non-biblical collection of plant and animal literature that circulated in ancient Israel.[11] For Alt this literature

---

4. See the brief comments on this passage in Mordecai Cogan, *1 Kings* (AB 10; New York: Doubleday, 2000), 222–23, and the thorough review of animal and plant control as royal achievement in Baruch Halpern, *David's Secret Demons: Messiah, Murderer, Traitor, King* (Grand Rapids: Eerdmans, 2001), 114–21.

5. Heb. *'ēzôb* could refer to the "hyssop" or any number of shrublike plants.

6. Though in Genesis 1 the animals occur in a different order: see Gen. 1:11, tree/vegetation (*'ēṣ*); 1:20, fish and sea creatures, then birds (*'ôp*); 1:24, *bĕhēmāh, remeś*. The plants-then-animals order may represent a way of listing such things among the learned in ancient Israel.

7. I.e., Solomon appears as an author or sponsor of proverbs in Prov. 1:1; 10:1; 25:1.

8. Gerhard von Rad, "The Beginnings of Historical Writing in Ancient Israel," 166–204 in idem, *The Problem of the Hexateuch and Other Essays*, trans. E. W. Trueman Dicken (Gesammelte Studien zum Alten Testament, Vol. 1; New York: McGraw-Hill, 1966); idem, *Wisdom in Israel*, trans. James D. Martin (Nashville: Abingdon, 1972).

9. Von Rad, "The Beginnings of Historical Writing," 203.

10. Ibid., 203–4.

comprised its own *Gattung*, "nature wisdom," and could be compared with other known products of this type from Egypt and Mesopotamia.[12]

Such speculation about the Solomon wisdom enlightenment has justifiably come under heavy criticism—on purely historical grounds relating to the existence of a grand Solomonic empire in the tenth century[13] and also for methodological questions involving the existence of "wisdom schools" in Israel generally.[14] Still others view Solomon and his wisdom connections as (at least) a social reality and yet criticize the monarch as he is presented in the Bible on moral or theological grounds. Walter Brueggemann, for example, finds the putative Solomonic wisdom obsession a morally sordid

11. Albrecht Alt, "Solomonic Wisdom," 102–12 in James Crenshaw, ed., *Studies in Ancient Israelite Wisdom* (first published 1951; New York: Ktav, 1976), at 103–4; in the same volume see Ernst Würthwein, "Egyptian Wisdom and the Old Testament," 113–33. James Crenshaw finds it odd that we do not have a wisdom-oriented plant or animal list in the Hebrew Bible: "Proverbs, Book of," 513–20 in David Noel Freedman, ed., *The Anchor Bible Dictionary*, Vol. V (New York: Doubleday, 1992), at 514.

12. Alt, "Solomonic Wisdom," 104–10.

13. Recently the battle over the historical Solomon has moved to archaeology, as represented in the "high chronology" versus "low chronology" debate; for a convenient summary see Israel Finkelstein and Amihai Mazar, *The Quest for the Historical Israel: Debating Archaeology and the History of Early Israel*, ed. Brian B. Schmidt (Archaeology and Biblical Studies 17; Atlanta: Society of Biblical Literature, 2007), esp. Part 4, 99–140, as well as Gary N. Knoppers, "The Vanishing Solomon: The Disappearance of the United Monarchy from Recent Histories of Ancient Israel," *JBL* 116 (1997): 19–44. But see Katharine J. Dell, "How Much Wisdom Literature Has its Roots in the Pre-Exilic Period?" 251–71 in John Day, ed., *In Search of Pre-exilic Israel* (Proceedings of the Oxford Old Testament Seminar; JSOTSS 406; London: T & T Clark, 2004), at 267.

14. The most prominent exponent of the "wisdom school" hypothesis is Moshe Weinfeld, *Deuteronomy and the Deuteronomistic School* (Oxford: Oxford University Press, 1972). For the critique of a "Solomonic enlightenment" and other wisdom school concepts see, e.g., Roger N. Whybray, "Wisdom Literature in the Reigns of David and Solomon," 13–26 in Tomoo Ishida, ed., *Studies in the Period of David and Solomon and Other Essays* (Winona Lake, IN: Eisenbrauns, 1982); James Crenshaw, "Method in Determining Wisdom Influence upon 'Historical' Literature," 481–94 in idem, ed., *Studies in Ancient Israelite Wisdom*; idem, *Education in Ancient Israel: Across the Deadening Silence* (New Haven: Yale University Press, 1998), and sources cited there; but cf. Christopher A. Rollston, *Writing and Literacy in the World of Ancient Israel: Epigraphic Evidence from the Iron Age* (Atlanta: Society of Biblical Literature, 2010), who does not engage the question of "wisdom schools" but makes an argument, based on epigraphic evidence, for flourishing scribal circles and elite literacy in Iron Age Israel.

affair, imagining a corrupt king huddled over volumes of botanical lore in a corner of his sumptuous palace while orphans languish in the street.[15] Such thinking ignores the extent to which the proper understanding and management of flora and fauna in this ancient context were viewed as integral to the maintenance of justice and the proper construction of the entire cosmos. In this chapter I argue for the existence of native ancient Israelite "nature wisdom," embodied in a constellation of texts, that demonstrates a significant engagement with the nature-wisdom category across several genres (law, narrative, poetry, and proverbial sayings). In ancient Israel's wisdom traditions one finds a close relationship among plants, animals, wisdom, and human community. Indeed, many wisdom texts from the ancient world take up the human place within the natural world as a topic of explicit concern. In order to situate this category of wisdom in Israel's ancient context, then, I review elements of Mesopotamian and Egyptian texts that exhibit nature-wisdom tropes, such as the Egyptian Onomastica, Mesopotamian lexical texts, wisdom parables, dialogues, narrative traditions, and monumental art, as well as Greek sources.

Having established this context, I discuss the ancient Israelite adaptation of this ancient Near Eastern nature-wisdom genre. A review of all relevant materials is clearly beyond the scope of what I mean to accomplish here; thus I focus on selected moments in which the plant or animal self comes into interpretive unity with the human self in wisdom-oriented texts. For example, we have several sapiential motifs in Deuteronomy involving plants and animals in relationship with the emerging nation (e.g., Deut. 6:11; 7:13; 8:8; 11:14-15; 20:19; 22:6); in storytelling traditions, plants and animals take the

---

15. Walter Brueggemann, *The Prophetic Imagination*, 2d ed. (Minneapolis: Fortress Press, 2001), 24; see also Brueggemann's comments in "The Social Significance of Solomon as a Patron of Wisdom," 117–32 in John G. Gammie and Leo G. Perdue, eds., *The Sage in Israel and the Ancient Near East* (Winona Lake, IN: Eisenbrauns, 1990).

stage as wisdom actors (e.g., Judges 9, 2 Kings 14, Ezekiel 17); the book of Proverbs employs animal observation as wisdom exhortation (e.g., Prov. 3:18; 11:30; 27:18); the wisdom-oriented Psalms (e.g., Psalms 1, 37) evoke thriving and dying plant worlds as metaphors of theodicy and righteous community; and Qoheleth (Eccl. 2:4-8) uses vineyards and royal gardens as markers of the ideal wise king in search of a perfect life. My goal in discussing these passages is of course to provide a context for the Joban engagement with these very themes, and yet the materials I examine here—from the Bible and elsewhere—deserve attention in their own right as important moments in the search for effective metaphors of the self from the ancient Near East.

A Word on Metaphor, Analogy, and Intuitive Ontologies

Before analyzing ancient examples of plant and animal wisdom I must briefly clarify some of the core language used in this study regarding questions of metaphor, representation, and analogy: what do we mean when we say that a plant "represents" a human self or that, in the Joban dialogues, Job's situation is "like" that of a particular animal?[16] On the simplest level all one needs is a recognizable and

16. Many recent studies of metaphor in the Hebrew Bible give explicit attention to clarifying terminology and recounting the history of metaphor studies from Aristotle to the present day. Excellent examples, to which the reader should turn for lengthier reviews of terminology and sources, include Benjamin A. Foreman, *Animal Metaphors and the People of Israel in the Book of Jeremiah* (Göttingen: Vandenhoeck & Ruprecht, 2011), 4–33; Martien Halvorson-Taylor, *Enduring Exile: The Metaphorization of Exile in the Hebrew Bible* (Leiden: Brill, 2010), 16–21; S. Tamar Kamionkowski, *Gender Reversal and Cosmic Chaos: A Study on the Book of Ezekiel* (London: Sheffield Academic Press, 2003), 30–57; Brad E. Kelle, *Hosea 2: Metaphor and Rhetoric in Historical Perspective* (Atlanta: Society of Biblical Literature, 2005), 21–46; several essays in Pierre Van Hecke, ed., *Metaphor in the Hebrew Bible* (Leuven: Leuven University Press, 2005), esp. the introductory essay by Pierre Van Hecke, "Metaphor in the Hebrew Bible: An Introduction," 1–18; and a very helpful review in Claudia D. Bergmann, *Childbirth as a Metaphor for Crisis: Evidence from the Ancient Near East, the Hebrew Bible, and 1QH XI, 1–18* (Berlin: de Gruyter, 2008), 1–8. Most of these studies draw inspiration from (or criticize) the seminal works of Ivor A. Richards, *The Philosophy of Rhetoric* (London: Oxford University

culturally relevant thread running from one concept or item to another in order for a metaphor to function.[17] But metaphors accomplish more than the unidirectional pointing of a simple hand, corralling attention from one sign to another (Greek *metaphora*, "transfer, carry over")—they also *create* new realities, call into question traditional definitions of the primary object and/or its metaphor, and forge plurality out of singularity and singularity out of plurality.[18] In his foundational study, *The Rule of Metaphor*, Paul Ricoeur persuasively argues that metaphors create realities and generate meaning beyond the mere use of metaphor-words as decorations.[19] Ricoeur describes his view as a switch to a "*hermeneutic* point of view" as opposed to a focus on "the form of metaphor as a word-focused figure of speech"; metaphor redescribes reality and "presents itself as a strategy of discourse that, while preserving and developing the creative power of language, preserves and develops the heuristic power wielded by fiction."[20]

To compare a suffering human to a fading flower, then, is not simply to use ornamental language that inherently privileges the human and offers the image of a flower as a side-model, but rather to draw plant and human into interpretive conversation. Metaphors are *arguments* in which identity and difference are what is at stake in the debate.[21] Whatever the case, it should be clear that I follow the

Press, 1936) and George B. Caird, *The Language and Imagery of the Bible* (London: Duckworth, 1980).

17. As recognized by Renita J. Weems, *Battered Love: Marriage, Sex, and Violence in the Hebrew Prophets* (Minneapolis: Fortress Press, 1995), 24.

18. Compare with language used by Adele Berlin, who in her *The Dynamics of Biblical Parallelism* (Bloomington: Indiana University Press, 1985), 16, asserts that Hebrew poetic parallelism "forges oneness out of twoness." On the generative power of nature metaphor see Howard Eilberg-Schwartz, *The Savage in Judaism: An Anthropology of Israelite Religion and Ancient Judaism* (Bloomington: Indiana University Press, 1990), 118.

19. Paul Ricoeur, *The Rule of Metaphor: Multi-Disciplinary Studies of the Creation of Meaning in Language*, trans. Robert Czerny (Toronto: University of Toronto Press, 1977).

20. Ibid., 6 (italics in original).

(now commonly accepted) view of metaphor that sees this type of communication as deeply transformative and evocative. The critical question we need to ask involves the human self and the way that self is contorted and reconfigured through floral and faunal symbols and the narratives those symbols represent—whether we choose to call comparisons "similes" when involving words such as "like" or "as" and so on is not usually relevant.[22] I am content to use the terms "metaphor" and "analogy" to designate the close relationship created by a text between at least two items, with "metaphor" acting as a more specific or direct style of comparison (A is B) and "analogy" referring broadly to comparisons of parallel qualities evoked for any constellation of images (A is to B as C is to D, etc.).

Analogy may operate on what we could call a "kind-of" relationship—for example, *the heart is a (kind of) pump*, which is to say, "a pump is to a hydraulic system as the heart is to the blood circulation system."[23] In this case the analogy gives legitimacy or "license" for thinking of the heart directly as a "pump" (i.e., a mechanical device). Descriptions of grain and grass flourishing, as in

21. "'To metaphorize well,' said Aristotle, 'implies an intuitive perception of the similarity in dissimilars.' Thus, resemblance itself must be understood as a tension between identity and difference in the predicative operation set in motion by semantic innovation" (Ricoeur, *Rule of Metaphor*, 6). See discussion in Victor H. Matthews, *More Than Meets the Ear: Discovering the Hidden Contexts of Old Testament Conversations* (Grand Rapids: Eerdmans, 2008), 12–16.

22. See, e.g., William P. Brown, *Seeing the Psalms: A Theology of Metaphor* (Louisville: Westminster John Knox, 2002), 7. Moreover, I agree with Foreman, *Animal Metaphors*, 16–20, that it is not possible or helpful to distinguish between "dead metaphors" (i.e., a once-living metaphor that has become frozen and thus "literal" for the speaker) and other metaphors in the biblical text. On the failure of the "dead metaphor" theory see also George Lakoff and Mark Turner, *More than Cool Reason: A Field Guide to Poetic Metaphor* (Chicago: University of Chicago Press, 1989), 128–31. This does not mean that metaphors cannot be conventional (i.e., "routine and unconscious"); Lakoff and Turner (107) use the word "withered"—applied to humans as well as plants—as an example of this phenomenon. Indeed, Lakoff and Turner use the "people are plants" metaphor for numerous examples in their study (see 12–14, 25–28, 73–75, etc.).

23. For the following discussion of the "kind-of" relationship and animal metaphor I draw directly from Francisco José Ruiz de Mendoza Ibáñez and Lorena Pérez Hernández, "The Contemporary Theory of Metaphor: Myths, Development, and Challenges," *Metaphor and Symbol* 26 (2011): 161–85, at 166–67.

Job 5:22-27, function as analogy for human thriving or dying in the sense that vegetation can stand erect or grow robustly like a human body; its "skin" may be healthy and clear or mottled and broken, a "kind-of" human skin, which itself may be healthy and clear or mottled and broken. In other cases the "kind-of" relationship may be strictly lacking—the phrase *lawyers are sharks* is a metaphor based on analogy, since we may think of lawyers exhibiting qualities in relation to their clients or opponents in the same manner as sharks behave toward prey, but sharks cannot be "dishonest" or "greedy" in the human sense. Even so, the metaphor *lawyers are sharks* (whether stated bluntly or drawn out as a narrative motif) could very well require audiences to consider difficult questions of how human behavior coheres or does not cohere with notions of wild animal justice in terms of dishonesty and greed.[24] Other metaphorical statements, such as *seeing is knowing* neither require nor make use of any strict system of analogy, even though the definition of analogical reasoning can be (and is sometimes) extended to cover "any form of alignment between structures."[25]

Besides asserting sameness between things, metaphor relies on some element of *incongruity*, and metaphorical identification further requires an understanding of (at least) the immediate literary context of the metaphor and can include historical concerns at the time of authorship or in communities of reception.[26] The nature of this

---

24. Abigail Pelham (personal communication) reminds me that humans often displace negative human characteristics onto animals; on this idea see Mary Midgley, *Beast and Man: The Roots of Human Nature* (Routledge Classics Edition; London: Routledge, 2002; first published 1979).

25. Ibáñez and Hernández, "The Contemporary Theory," 166; these authors go on to suggest that "analogy is a more complex phenomenon than correlation and . . . it may make use of either resemblance or a combination of correlation and resemblance operations to give rise to some kinds of metaphorical thought. Other kinds of metaphor are purely correlational and are therefore not based on analogy" (167).

26. Here I follow the summary in Foreman, *Animal Metaphors*, 12–13, as he discusses the work of Eva Feder Kittay, *Metaphor: Its Cognitive Force and Linguistic Structure* (Oxford: Clarendon Press, 1987) on identifying metaphors.

incongruity (for both metaphor and analogy) is precisely the point of argument in a text and must be left open to examination and debate. Thus we see the problem with a technical term such as "catachresis," the use of inappropriate or mixed images, since the categorization of catachresis easily begs the question. The power of metaphor relies not on some inherent or pre-set cognitive map of what must be incongruous; metaphor is a factor in shaping or reshaping human cognition itself. Thus, for the Joban characters in dialogue we find a rollicking argument concerning just which metaphors for the self are appropriate. Understanding what is at stake politically, historically, and personally within the terms of any metaphor world requires intuition and metaphorical perception on the part of the audience or interpreter that matches the visions of the speaker or text. As William Brown puts it: "What is written with imagination must also be read with imagination."[27]

Comparisons of any kind among humans, animals, and plants require both analogical and metaphorical thinking, and thus thoughtful attention to congruity and incongruity. Since I have already raised the question of whether we can speak of plant or animal "selves" in Chapter One, I ask: How might we begin organizing the differences between plants, animals, and humans in terms of the "self"? What kinds of shared and unshared sense of self might we expect? In an attempt to delineate boundaries of the self, cognitive scientist Justin Barrett identifies the "where" as the first category of "making sense of the world": there are physical boundaries, there are objects within those boundaries, and there are limits within that space.[28] The next order of sense is closely related to the first, the "what." A basic set of what Barrett calls "intuitive

27. Brown, *Seeing the Psalms*, 4–8.
28. Justin L. Barrett, *Cognitive Science, Religion, and Theology: From Human Minds to Divine Minds* (Templeton Science and Religion Series; West Conshohocken, PA: Templeton Press, 2011), 59.

ontologies" places objects into roughly five categories: *Spatial Entities*, *Solid Objects*, *Living Things* (that do not appear to move themselves), *Animates*, and *Persons*.[29] These categories are animated by "expectation sets," which are assumptions about the way these ontologies behave or their relation to one another: *Spatiality*, *Physicality*, *Biology*, *Animacy*, and *Mentality*.[30] Of interest here are the categories of *Living Things* (plants; non-self-propelled or un-forceful animals), *Animates* (animals, or self-propelled objects such as robots), and *Persons* (humans, deities). In Barrett's schema only *Persons* are animated by all five "expectation sets," while *Living Things* lack *Animacy* (goals; self-propulsion or force), and both *Living Things* and *Animates* lack *Mentality* (e.g., desires, awareness, or understanding of communication). The set of cognitively "intuitive" relations between categories and expectation sets, then, could be mapped in the diagram here (see Figure 1).

However, these sets of relations are obviously not the end of the story. *Counterintuitive* ideas—formed by the reconceptualization ("transfer") of the expectation sets attached to the ontological categories or by unmet expectations ("breach")—can break the intuitive arrangements in any number of ways. A straightforward counterintuitive breach may involve a tree flying through a mountain (a breach of our expectation that physical boundaries are solid), whereas a transfer could involve a talking animal (i.e., applying *Mentality* to an *Animate*, which is perhaps less of a conceptual stretch).[31] *Animates* and *Living Things* in Barrett's categorization share similar expectation sets, though they differ with regard to *Animacy*.[32]

---

29. Ibid., 61, and 178 nn. 1-9 for the research base for these categories, including an earlier study by Barrett, "Coding and Quantifying Counterintuitiveness in Religious Concepts: Theoretical and Methodological Reflections," *Method and Theory in the Study of Religion* 20 (2008): 308–38.
30. Barrett, *Cognitive Science*, 61–62.
31. Ibid., 68.

Barrett's "transfers" can overlap or engage with metaphors, and strict modern notions of congruity can of course interfere with our understanding of ancient metaphor.

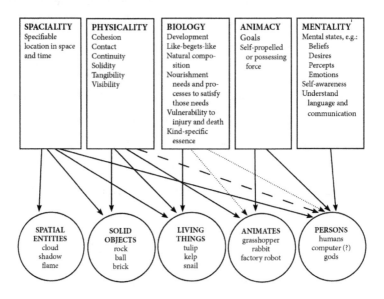

Figure 1: How Activation of Expectation Sets Compromise Intuitive Ontologies

Indeed, the religious world of the ancient Near East allowed for many counterintuitive visions of the non-human natural world that blur the lines between the tidy categories outlined here. Under what conception, for example, is the post-exilic prophet Haggai working when he boldly asserts that his audience is suffering the effects of

32. Cf. Foreman, *Animal Metaphors*, 3: "Animals, as opposed to flora . . . live and move in time and space. They, like humans, breathe, eat, roam to and fro, make noises, have feelings, behave in certain ways, have relationships with other animals, and also die." Opposing animals to flora on these terms is of course not quite correct, since plants live and move in time and space, breathe, eat, behave in certain ways, have relationships of various kinds with other plants and animals, and they also die.

natural failure because of their human failure to rebuild the Temple quickly enough?

> Therefore the heavens above you withhold moisture, and the earth withholds its produce; and I called forth a drought upon the earth, and upon the hills, and upon the grain, and upon the new wine, and upon the oil, and upon all that the earth brings forth, and upon human and upon beast, and upon all the labor of their hands. (Hag. 1:10-11)

Here we find a "transfer," on Barrett's terms, whereby *Solid Objects* (the sky, the earth) take on *Animacy* and *Mentality*—at least as part of a theological schema whereby Israel's deity punishes humans through *Solid Objects*, and at most as part of a cosmos that was thought to have inbuilt physical consequences for human states of righteousness and unrighteousness.[33] The notion that the heavens or the earth could "withhold" (Heb. *kāla'*) their blessing metaphorizes these elements (via personification), with the putative incongruity being the product of an assumed categorization of earth and heavens as *Solid Objects*. On these terms we have obviously left the realm of viewing humans or plants in a detached, instrumental relationship (such that hard work produces a good harvest). For Haggai, frantic human effort cannot compensate for the moral work of cosmos-rebuilding-righteousness that people must do in order to rebuild the Temple. Plant and animal flourishing is thus a special kind of moral category, directly related to a view of human moral anthropology.[34] In this anthropology the

---

33. I allude here to the essay of Klaus Koch, "Gibt es ein Vergeltungsdogma im Alten Testament?" *ZTK* (1955): 1–42.
34. On the correlation between human behavior and natural health in terms of the "indigenous psychology" discussion (raised in the Introduction) see Signe Howell, "Rules Not Words," 133–44, esp. 135–38, and Charlotte Hardmann, "The Psychology of Conformity and Self-Expression Among the Lohorung Rai of East Nepal," 161–80, esp. 164–65, both in Paul Heelas and Andrew Lock, eds., *Indigenous Psychologies: The Anthropology of the Self* (London: Academic Press, 1981). See also Carol Delany, "Seeds of Honor, Fields of Shame," 35–48 in David D. Gilmore, ed., *Honor and Shame and the Unity of the Mediterranean* (American Anthropological Association Special Publication 22; Washington, DC: American Anthropological Association, 1987), who discusses metaphors of sexuality in relation to natural landscapes.

human inner state is an open book, mirrored in nature.[35] One could classify this situation for Haggai as a metaphor, *disobedience is drought,* or an analogy: the human failure to produce is to the Temple as the skies' failure to produce is to vegetation. One could even say that, for Haggai, this is not even a metaphor or analogy at all—the natural world is simply an actor on its own terms (compare Jer. 3:2-3).

Whenever one speaks of metaphor or analogy one runs the risk of tautology: the identity of a thing with anything other than itself—which is to say, any way of talking about the identity of a thing in human language—would seem to require metaphorical and analogical linguistic scaffolding of all kinds, operating on many levels through all speech. Notwithstanding such Wittegensteinian language traps, the appropriate use of metaphor and analogy is always up for debate, often polemical, and usually contested, and in this realm of contestation lies the opportunity for imaginative projection. When animals and plants become wisdom themes, as comparative and symbolic phenomena they participate in what could rightly be considered metaphor, analogy, and the formation (or rejection) of intuitive religious ontologies of human interaction with non-human living things. And we will find that the wisdom evocation of the natural world was a profound manner of searching for appropriate representations of self and human community in the ancient world.

Eco-Anthropologies of Wisdom in the Ancient Near East

Aristotle's mid-fourth-century BCE *Historia animalium* ("History of Animals") is perhaps the most famous ancient attempt to integrate animal and plant knowledge into a philosophical system of understanding the human being within the natural world.[36]

---

35. On this see John B. Geyer, "Desolation and Cosmos," *VT* 49 (1999): 49–64.
36. For a critical edition of the text see Aristotle, *Historia Animalium*, Vol. I, Books I–X: text, ed. David M. Balme, with Allan Gotthelf (Cambridge Classical Texts and Commentaries 38;

Beginning with physical bodily structures and moving into sexual activity and psychological behavior, Aristotle works his way through diverse creatures and animal oddities, arriving eventually at the human. To be sure, the presentation in *Historia animalium* draws humans and other animals into close interpretive relationship, even if, for Aristotle, the characteristics animals exhibit shine forth most extremely or clearly in humans. It would be hard to read Aristotle's catalogue of adversarial animal relationships and animal warfare (e.g., Book VIII.I, II, XI, XVIII) without thinking of the state of seemingly perpetual conflict in the Greek Mediterranean in the sixth to third centuries BCE and the formative effect of those wars on prominent Greek thinkers. Non-human animals cultivate enemies, enact construction projects, take mates, delineate the politics of leadership, exhibit differing work ethics, and so on.[37] As Ann Michelini has shown, for ancient Greek authors the notable language of *hybris* functions not only for humans but also for the living natural world; both Aristotle and his most prominent student, Theophrastus (in *De historia plantarum* and *De causis plantarum*), use verbs like *hybrizō* and *exubrizō* to refer to excessive plant grown and exuberance.[38] By evoking this language Greek authors drew plants, animals, and humans into interpretive conversation—all can suffer from a "superabundance of nature" or "madness" as a mental disease, and on the positive side humans and their communities can sprout like branches (as in the common poetic metaphor).[39] The solution to plant

---

Cambridge: Cambridge University Press, 2002). For translation, Aristotle, *History of Animals*, Books I–III, trans. Arthur L. Peck (LCL 437; Cambridge, MA: Harvard University Press, 1965); idem, Books IV–VI (LCL 438; Cambridge MA: Harvard University Press, 1970); idem, Books VII–X, ed. and trans. David M. Balme (LCL 439; Cambridge MA: Harvard University Press, 1991).

37. See esp. *Historia animalium*, Book IX (*passim*) for these types of characterizations, and Book VII for the turn toward human reproduction.

38. Ann Michelini, "Hybris and Plants," *Harvard Studies in Classical Philology* 82 (1978): 35–44. Michelini notes (pp. 35–36) that *hybris* language for animals is elusive (animal *hybris* may denote unruly animals affected by overeating), while the connection with plants is more obvious.

hybris, pruning (*kolouō*, "cut short, prune") is closely related to the verb *kolazō*, "punish." Cutting down the overgrown is thus an apt image for political domination and for cosmological maintenance—in Herodotus's famous metaphor Thrasybulus offers Pesiander a blunt object-lesson on population control by clipping off the tallest shoots of grain in a field.[40] Animal fables play a prominent role in some archaic Greek texts, ranging from the *Aesopica* all the way back to Archilochos (seventh century BCE) and Hesiod's fable of the hawk and the nightingale in *Works and Days* 203–12 (eighth century BCE).[41]

Though these examples are not strictly "wisdom" texts they demonstrate something of the extent to which plant and animal behaviors act as a correlative to human moral states, and certainly in the case of Aristotle we find attention to the natural world under the purview of a broadly-conceived philosophical program. Even earlier than the Greeks, however, understanding types of plants and animals was a known wisdom trope. Evidence comes through a range of documents from the ancient Near Eastern world, from Egypt to Mesopotamia, from the third millennium BCE onward. A first-millennium Babylonian lexical list entitled "Interest-Bearing Loan" (HAR-ra *ḫubullu*) classifies animals in various ways,[42] as does as a

39. Ibid., 38; 40–41.

40. All discussed in ibid., 43; see also Brian R. Doak, *The Last of the Rephaim: Conquest and Cataclysm in the Heroic Ages of Ancient Israel* (Ilex Series 7; Ilex Foundation; Cambridge, MA: Harvard University Press, 2012), 119–23.

41. The fable in *Works and Days* 203–12 has received extensive treatment for its application to the politics of kingship and justice; see, e.g., Gregory Nagy, *Greek Mythology and Poetics* (Ithaca: Cornell University Press, 1990), 64–75; Deborah Steiner, "Fables and Frames: The Poetics and Politics of Animal Fables in Hesiod, Archilochus, and the *Aesopica*," *Arethusa* 45 (2012): 1–41; Stephanie Nelson, *God and the Land: The Metaphysics of Farming in Hesiod and Vergil*, with a translation of Hesiod's *Works and Days* by David Grene (Oxford: Oxford University Press, 1998), 77–81.

42. See Benjamin R. Foster, "Animals in Mesopotamian Literature," 271–88 in Billie J. Collins, ed., *A History of the Animal World in the Ancient Near East* (Leiden: Brill, 2002), at 272. On animals in the ancient Near East generally see, e.g., the other essays in Collins, *History of the Animal World*; Benno Landsberger, *The Fauna of Ancient Mesopotamia, First Part* and *Second Part*, MSL VIII/1–2 (Rome: Pontifical Biblical Institute, 1960, 1962); Paula Wapnish, "Towards

third-millennium Sumerian bird list.[43] According to Foster these lists are not random; rather, they set out an "implicit typology, but less than a systematic treatise."[44] Certain ancient Egyptian onomastica—"catalogues of things arranged under their kinds," to be differentiated from a glossary or various types of lexical lists—contain entries suggesting that the organization of plants and animals served some kind of instructional purpose in Egypt.[45] Here I refer specifically to the circa-twelfth- to tenth-century BCE "Onomasticon of Amenope," often cited as an example of Egyptian didactic literature with relation to categories of living things, which unsystematically lists agricultural plants and parts of an ox among classifications of human occupations, towns, and cosmological elements. In addition, and even more relevant with its inclusion of plants and animals, the fragmentary "Ramesseum Onomasticon" (allegedly Middle Kingdom, early second millennium) seems to have contained columns of entries devoted to plant names, seeds, birds, fishes, quadrupeds, and animal body parts.[46]

These Egyptian onomastica in particular provoked discussion among biblical scholars with reference to the book of Job, insofar as

Establishing a Conceptual Basis for Animal Categories in Archaeology," 233–73 in David B. Small, ed., *Methods in the Mediterranean: Historical and Archaeological Views on Texts and Archaeology* (Leiden: Brill, 1995); Allan S. Gilbert, "The Flora and Fauna of the Ancient Near East," 153–74 in Jack M. Sasson, ed., *Civilizations of the Ancient Near East*, Vols. I–II (Peabody, MA: Hendrickson, 2000).

43. See Foster, "Animals," 273, and references there, esp. Giovanni Pettinato, "Liste presargoniche di uccelli nella documentazione di Fara ed Ebla," *Oriens antiquus* 17 (1978): 165–78.

44. Foster, "Animals," 273.

45. Alan H. Gardiner, *Ancient Egyptian Onomastica*, Vol. I (Oxford: Oxford University Press, 1947), 5; see also the review of Gardiner's work and topic by Charles F. Nims, "Egyptian Catalogues of Things," *Journal of Near Eastern Studies* 9 (1950): 252–62. See the review of these onomastica as a comparison for biblical wisdom materials by Michael V. Fox, "Egyptian Onomastica and Biblical Wisdom," *VT* 36 (1986): 302–10; John Day, "Foreign Semitic Influence on the Wisdom of Israel and its Appropriation in the Book of Proverbs," 55–70 in John Day, Robert P. Gordon, and H. G. M. Williamson, eds., *Wisdom in Ancient Israel: Essays in Honor of J. A. Emerton* (Cambridge: Cambridge University Press, 1995) esp. 61–62.

46. Gardiner, *Ancient Egyptian Onomastica*, 8–9; Alan H. Gardiner, *The Ramesseum Papyri* (Oxford: Oxford University Press, 1955).

God's nature harangue in Job 38–41 involves a litany of ultra-wild animals and cosmological phenomena. Von Rad attempted just such a comparison, focusing specifically on meteorological elements (hail, snow, etc.) in both Amenope and Job 38:12-38.[47] Though he did not claim direct literary dependence or exactly parallel formulations, von Rad did believe the Joban author drew upon at least the spirit of onomasticon-like lists to compose elements of God's speech, and he claimed that another biblical text, Psalm 148, bears an even closer resemblance to the order of elements in the Amenope list.[48] Turning from the lists, von Rad finally concluded that the questions in the Papyrus Anastasi I inspired the Joban God's "Where were you" rhetorical questions, suggesting that the Papyrus Anastasi I questions were real school-exercise queries, and thus God's questions reflect this educational genre.[49] Michael Fox later demonstrated the unconvincing nature of von Rad's specific comparison of the onomastica to the lists in Job 38, and he further questions the extent to which the Egyptian materials themselves can be read as participating in an encyclopedic project.[50]

The extent to which such lists fall under the "wisdom" rubric is not entirely clear, but several literary works from Mesopotamia make use of the fable or disputation genre to cast plants and animals in the role of wisdom actors.[51] In the Sumerian "Heron and the Turtle" fable a villainous turtle attacks a heron, resulting in a legal

47. Gerhard von Rad, "Job xxxviii and Ancient Egyptian Wisdom," 267–80 in James L. Crenshaw, ed., *Studies in Ancient Israelite Wisdom* (New York: Ktav, 1976). See also John Gray, "The Book of Job in the Context of Near Eastern Literature," *ZAW* 82 (1970): 251–69, at 252, who suggests the style of Job 38 is a "poetic development" from the Egyptian-style lists, and Henry Rowold, "Yahweh's Challenge to Rival: The Form and Function of the Yahweh-Speech in Job 38–39," *CBQ* 47 (1985): 199–211, who speculates (on p. 211) that the Joban Divine Speech "incorporates and adapts possible nature traditions (*Listenwissenschaft?*)," as well as Hans Strauss, "Motiv und Strukturen von Umkehrungssprüchen in Ägypten und im Alten Testament (Buch Hiob)," *ZAW* 115 (2003): 25–37.
48. Von Rad, "Job xxxviii," 285–86.
49. Ibid., 287–90.
50. Fox, "Egyptian Onomastica," 303–4, 308.

dispute and some undetermined conclusion (the ending of the story is fragmentary). A "Disputation Between Ewe and Wheat" notably begins with a cosmology and portrays a generation of humans in the "distant (past) days" who drink ditch-water and are unable to make bread or proper clothing. Ewe and Wheat—apparently ciphers for the benefits of animal husbandry and crops—descend from on high and bring happiness and prosperity to the world. Soon Ewe and Wheat argue for preeminence, with Wheat finally gaining the upper hand. The "Disputation Between Bird and Fish" stands as a particularly noteworthy example of this apparently popular genre. After a brief cosmological introduction and a declaration on the divine nature of kingship ("A king he gave them for a shepherd, and raised him to sovereignty over them; the king rose as daylight over the countries"), Bird and Fish contend with one another for supremacy, offering up insults and arguments of all kinds based on the characteristics of each animal. In the thick of the dispute Fish violently attacks Bird, raising questions about the efficacy of argumentation and the place of violence in the midst of political gridlock.[52] Since the fable is grounded in cosmology and the authority of kingship, the animal dispute provides a point of meditation for the wisdom of human relationships and the politics of power—as with a fish and a fish-

---

51. A fable is "a story that takes place in the world of animals, plants, or inanimate objects, told in the past tense but applied to the present by virtue of the epimythium," as defined in Eli Yassif, *The Hebrew Folktale: History, Genre, Meaning*, trans. Jacqueline S. Teitelbaum (Bloomington: Indiana University Press, 1999), 23. For the examples below see, conveniently in English translation in *COS* I: Gene B. Gregg, "The Heron and the Turtle," 571–73; Herman L. Vanstiphout, "The Disputation Between Ewe and Wheat," 575–78; idem, "The Disputation Between Bird and Fish," 581–84; in *ANET* see Robert H. Pfeiffer, "Dispute Between the Date Palm and the Tamarisk," 410–11, and Robert D. Biggs, "Dispute Between the Tamarisk and the Date Palm," 592–93. The summaries I give below refer to these translations. For critical notes and further bibliography see Wilfred G. Lambert, "Fables or Contest Literature," 150–212 in his *Babylonian Wisdom Literature* (Oxford: Clarendon Press, 1960).

52. The translator/editor of the Bird and Fish text, Herman Vanstiphout ("The Disputation Between Bird and Fish," 581), suggests that "the burden seems to be that stern moral righteousness can never excuse violence away."

eating-bird, enmity is built into nature and the sheer power of attack serves as the only recourse in the face of endless posturing.[53]

The seventh- to sixth-century BCE wisdom text "The Words of Ahiqar," one of the best-known writings of the ancient world in any genre, also uses plant- and animal-fable elements as wisdom teaching.[54] Roughly the second half of this Aramaic document contains a series of over one hundred wisdom sayings, beginning with an apparently incomplete animal riddle (Saying 1), "What is stronger than a braying ass? . . ." and employing animal motifs throughout.[55] For example, Ahiqar cites a Proverbs-like animal observation-saying (7): "The scorpion finds bread and will not eat it; but if he finds something foul, he is more pleased than if he were sumptuously fed"; a direct animal metaphor (15): "For a word is a bird, and he who releases it is a fool" (compare Eccl. 10:20); a sophisticated philological animal wordplay: "There is no lion in the sea; therefore the sea-snake is called *labbu*";[56] a plant fable: "The

53. Also relevant here is an enigmatic Hurro-Hittite bilingual text, part of which compares various animals (deer, dog, rodent) to humans as a wisdom motif. Translation by Gary Beckman, "Excerpt from the Hurro-Hittite Bilingual Wisdom Text," *COS* I, 216–17, and brief comments in Billie Jean Collins, "On the Trail of the Deer: Hittite *kūrala*," 73–82 in Gary Beckman, Richard Beal, and Gregory McMahon, eds., *Hittite Studies in Honor of Harry A. Hoffner, Jr. on the Occasion of His 65th Birthday* (Winona Lake, IN: Eisenbrauns, 2003), at 77–78.

54. See the introduction and translation by James M. Lindenberger, "Ahiqar," 479–507 in James H. Charlesworth, ed., *The Old Testament Pseudepigrapha*, Vol. 2 (Peabody, MA: Hendrickson, 1983), as well as Lindenberger's *Aramaic Proverbs of Ahiqar* (Baltimore: Johns Hopkins University Press, 1983) and the older standard, Arthur E. Cowley, *Aramaic Papyri of the Fifth Century B.C.* (Oxford: Clarendon Press, 1923). A newer edition of the text by Bezalel Porten and Ada Yardeni, eds. and trans., *Textbook of Aramaic Documents from Ancient Egypt*, Vol. 3, *Literature, Accounts, Lists* (Jerusalem: Hebrew University Press, 1993), 23–53, calls into question some famous aspects of Ahiqar, such as its putative contribution to the concept of "personified Wisdom," but this does not affect my treatment here; see Seth A. Bledsoe, "Can Ahiqar Tell Us Anything About Personified Wisdom?" *JBL* 132 (2013): 119–37. In Porten's and Yardeni's edition animal and plant sayings appear in Cols. 6.17, 7.23, 9.79–81, 12.84 ("What is stronger than an ass braying . . ."—here not the beginning of the sayings portion of Ahiqar as for Lindenberger), 12.90-94, 13.109, and 14.115.

55. Translations and saying numbers here from Lindenberger, "Ahiqar." I have removed brackets and parentheses from the translations; these indicate reconstructed text and implied words. Readers should know that the Ahiqar text is fragmentary and readings are tentative. Cf. the translations in Porten and Yardeni, *Textbook*.

bramble sent a message to the pomegranate as follows: 'Dear Pomegranate, what good are all your thorns to him who touches your fruit?' The pomegranate replied to the bramble, 'You are nothing but thorns to him who touches you!'"; an animal-to-human dialogue: "A man said one day to the wild ass, 'Let me ride on you, and I will provide for you!' The wild ass replied, 'Keep your care and fodder; I want nothing to do with your riding!'"; and various animal fables involving lions, asses, leopards, bears, and lambs (see Sayings 28, 35-36). In one case (Saying 36) Ahiqar gives explicit application of the animal interaction to human religious politics: "Once upon a time a bear came to the lambs and said, 'Let me take just one of you and I will be content.' The lambs replied to him, 'Take whichever one of us you will. We are only sheep, but you are a bear! For it is not in men's own power to lift their feet or set them down apart from the gods.'"[57]

In an example that brings us closer to the type of faunal analogy used in Job, the famed "Babylonian Theodicy," a Mesopotamian cuneiform text composed ca. 1000 BCE, has both the human Sufferer and Friend in dialogue attempting to marshal an animal analogy in their favor.[58] First the Sufferer uses what he sees as the non-moral nature of animal satiety to distance his own state of suffering from moral activity:

---

56. Lindenberger ("Ahiqar," 502) explains: "The Akkadian word *labbu* (written *lb'* in Aram.) means 'lion' but is also the name of a mythological sea monster. Evidently a serpentlike sea creature named for the legendary monster (perhaps the vicious moray eel) has been popularly identified with the homonymous word 'lion.' Thus the saying is a rather erudite bilingual play on words."

57. Porten and Yardeni (*Textbook*, 47) are less confident about the translation here and leave significant lacunae in this saying.

58. Translation here from Benjamin R. Foster, "The Babylonian Theodicy," COS I, 492–95; specific quotations below from sections V–VI, 493. See also Lambert, *Babylonian Wisdom Literature*, 73–74, for these passages, with further discussion in Peter Riede, *Im Spiegel der Tier: Studien zum Verhältnis von Mensch und Tier im alten Israel* (OBO 187; Fribourg: Universitätsverlag, 2002), 135.

The onager, the wild ass, that had its fill of [. . .],
Did it pay attention to carry out a god's intentions?
The savage lion that devoured the choicest meat,
Did it bring its offerings to appease a goddess's anger?
The animal examples immediately transition to the human realm:
The parvenu who multiplies his wealth,
Did he weigh out precious gold to the mother goddess for a family?
Have I withheld my offerings?
Not to be so easily outdone, the Friend counters (invoking the same
    animals):
Consider that magnificent wild ass on the plain,
The arrow will gash that headstrong trampler of the leas!
Come, look at that lion you called to mind, the enemy of livestock,
For the atrocity that lion committed, the pit yawns for him.
The well-heeled parvenu who treasured up possessions,
The king will put him to the flames before his time.
Would you wish to go the way these have gone?

When animals enter the debate as analogies or metaphors for the human self we enter the realm of polemic—the proper analogy for the suffering self is contested, but in both cases it is predicated on a proper understanding of the natural world.

Admittedly, the examples cited here are not always close parallels to the way plants and animals are used as wisdom tropes in Job, nor do these examples represent an exhaustive list of *comparanda* from the non-biblical ancient Near East. The point here is to notice the popularity of floral and faunal imagery in a wide range of wisdom-oriented texts from the ancient Near Eastern world. Though fables appear infrequently in the Hebrew Bible, these types of natural analogies lead us directly into the arena of contestation and polemic found in the floral and faunal analogies of the Joban dialogues. Such analogies are inherent in many wisdom-oriented literatures; as Deborah Steiner perceptively notes in her study of archaic Greek animal fables, nature images function as competitive devices deployed by performers within agonistic situations: they are rhetorical strategies that promote their tellers' claims to victory in ongoing contests that involve issues of opposing poetics, modes of discourse, and genres, and that additionally form part of an individual's bid for the political-*cum*-civic authority that can be achieved with a display of verbal artistry and *sophia* over a performative rival. At stake here is not only the fable-tellers' verbal ascendancy, but also . . . the question of which . . . contested modes of poetic production individuals and communities should pursue.[59]

Steiner further concludes that animal motifs signal cultural upheaval:

It has become critical commonplace that archaic and classical Greek sources blur the boundaries between men and animals at moments of crisis, particularly when social and political institutions break down. When beasts speak and act like men (or men like beasts), this signals the failure of human discourse and men's broader inability to regulate their communal affairs.[60]

These conclusions will, we will come to see, hold true for biblical invocations of nature wisdom, especially when the human self or the political community is drawn into close comparison with animals and plants. Nature analogies come out swinging—the language is polemical, the identity is contested, and the narrative is charged.

Plant and Animal Wisdom in the Hebrew Bible

Humans, plants, and animals are related in a universe of mastery, punishment, cause, and effect in the Hebrew Bible. To be sure, the natural world appears so prevalently and prominently in the Bible that it is difficult to categorize "nature" as a whole, or even plants or animals specifically. Scholars involved with this quest to better understand nature's role in the Bible continue to produce volumes of studies, most of which are quite specific—a study of Isaiah's tree

---

59. Steiner, "Fables and Frames," 1–2.
60. Ibid., 36.

metaphors, or animal life in Jeremiah.[61] Indeed, the prophetic corpus alone contains a massive amount of nature imagery. The earth itself becomes a prophetic actor, as these writings often use the image of an earth in mourning (Isa. 24:4; 33:9; Jer. 4:28; 12:4; Joel 1:10; Amos 1:2);[62] wayward animals graphically sniff the wind in sexual heat as metaphors of human spiritual adultery (Jer. 2:24);[63] locusts, like a military force, devour the land (Joel 1:4-12); Israel becomes a vineyard tended by God the vinedresser (Isaiah 5); land is parched because of covenant infidelity, but later restored to abundance by way of righteous actions (Hos. 2:5, 14, 23-25 [English 2:2, 12, 21-23]); dangerous snakes crouch in walls to bite humans already fleeing from lions and bears (Amos 5:19).[64] In the book of Jonah both plants and animals stand as central actors in the drama, with animals curating the prophet's comical journey to the underworld and back (in the stomach of a fish, Jon. 2:1; 2:11 [English 1:17; 2:10]) and repenting along with the Ninevites (3:7-8). Plants grow and fade as ciphers for God's inscrutable will (4:6-7). The book ends on an animal question (4:11), as God asks Jonah to consider the place of cattle and plants within the arena of divine care.

Examples of this kind could obviously be multiplied and expanded to include the role of the natural world as metaphors, analogies, and actors in genres as diverse as parables, historiography, poetry, and

---

61. See, e.g., Foreman, *Animal Metaphors,* and Kirsten Nielsen, *There is Hope for a Tree: The Tree as Metaphor in Isaiah* (JSOTSS 65. Sheffield: JSOT Press, 1989). Two of the most comprehensive studies are Riede, *Im Spiegel der Tier* (with several chapters focusing on Job in particular), and Brent Strawn, *What is Stronger Than a Lion? Leonine Image and Metaphor in the Hebrew Bible and the Ancient Near East* (OBO 212; Fribourg: Academic Press, 2005).

62. Katherine M. Hayes, *The Earth Mourns: Prophetic Metaphor and Oral Aesthetic* (Atlanta: Society of Biblical Literature, 2002); on these types of images in Isaiah 24 and elsewhere see Geyer, "Desolation."

63. See Foreman, *Animal Metaphors,* 150–52.

64. Aulikki Nahkola, "Amos Animalizing: Lion, Bear and Snake in Amos 5:19," 83–104 in Anselm C. Hagerdorn and Andrew Mein, eds., *Aspects of Amos: Exegesis and Interpretation* (London: T & T Clark, 2011).

law. In what follows, however, with some exceptions my comments focus on floral and faunal images in formal wisdom texts as well as wisdom-oriented passages (that is to say, texts with a discernible wisdom focus or themes). In each case I want to specifically investigate how the plant or animal functions to define the human moral struggle.

Human Domination Over Nature in Genesis 1:26-28

The Bible's most famous and seemingly programmatic statement regarding the relationship of humans to the natural world occurs in Genesis 1:26-28, when the deity speaks humankind into existence, charging that they "rule over the fish of the sea, and over the birds of the air, and over the cattle, and over all the wild animals of the earth, and over every creeping thing that creeps upon the earth."[65] The human self here is thus destined for mastery and defined (at least partly) by his/her separation above and beyond non-human nature. Though this passage is not typically considered as a "wisdom" text,[66] I want to begin this review with the famous statement from the opening chapter of Genesis, given the close connection between

---

65. Studies of Gen. 1:27 in particular are numerous; see George W. Ramsey, "Is Name Giving an Act of Domination in Gen 2:23 and Elsewhere?" *CBQ* 50 (1988): 24–35; David T. Williams, "'Fill the Earth and Subdue It' (Gen 1:28): Dominion to Exploit and Pollute?" *Scriptura* 44 (1993): 51–65;Bernard W. Anderson, "Human Dominion Over Nature," 27–45 in Miriam Ward, ed., *Biblical Studies in Contemporary Thought* (Somerville, MA: Hadden, 1975); James Barr, "Man and Nature: The Ecological Controversy and the Old Testament," *Bulletin of the John Rylands University Library of Manchester* 55 (1972): 9–32. Much of the reaction from biblical scholars and theologians came in response to the challenge set forth by Lynn White, Jr., "The Historical Roots of our Ecologic Crisis," *Science* 155 (1967): 1203–7.

66. Of course, the "tree of the knowledge of good and evil" in Gen. 2:17, 3:1-6 forges a connection between plants and wisdom (note the "tree of life" motif also in Prov. 3:18; 11:30; 13:12; 15:4). Note also the plant that Gilgamesh picks up from the bottom of the sea (and later loses by theft to a serpent) in the Gilgamesh Epic. Others have explicitly drawn the early chapters of Genesis into a discussion of wisdom; see, e.g., Luis Alonso-Schökel, "Sapiential and Covenant Themes in Genesis 2-3," 468–80 in Crenshaw, ed., *Studies in Ancient Israelite Wisdom*; Tova Forti, "The Polarity of Wisdom and Fear of God in the Eden Narrative and in the Book of Proverbs," *Biblische Notizen* 149 (2011): 45–57.

wisdom and creation and given the fact that it sets the narrative or canonical stage for everything that follows.

> (1:26) God said, "let us make humans (*'ādām*) in our image, according to our likeness; and let them rule over (*rādāh*) the fish of the sea, and over the birds of the air, and over the cattle, and over all the wild animals of the earth, and over every creeping thing that creeps upon the earth." (27) So God created humankind (*hā 'ādām*) in his image; in the image of God he created them, male and female he created them. (28) God blessed them, and God said to them, "Be fruitful and multiply, and fill the earth and subdue (*kābaš*) it; and rule over (*rādāh*) the fish of the sea and over the birds of the air and over every living thing that moves upon the earth."

Some environmentally conscious and well-meaning religious traditions have attempted to downplay the violence of the subjugation language in this passage,[67] but such interpretations founder on the well-known linguistic range for terms like *rādāh* and *kābaš*. *Rādāh* ("rule over") conspicuously refers to authority that could be exercised in the owner-slave relationship (Lev. 25:43, 46, 53), the rule of a military conqueror over a subjected population (Lev. 26:17; Num. 24:19; 1 Kgs. 5:4 [English 4:24]; Isa. 14:2, 6; Ezek. 29:15; Pss. 72:8; 110:2), or the unjust rule of the powerful over the weak (Ezek. 34:4). *Kābaš* ("subdue, conquer") refers to the subjugation of the land by military might (Num. 32:22, 29; Josh. 18:1; 2 Sam. 8:11; 1 Chr. 22:18), the authority exercised by a master over a slave (Jer. 34:11, 16; 2 Chr. 28:10), and divine conquest over military or spiritual foes (Mic. 7:19; Zech. 9:15). Other biblical texts also endorse this nature-under-human-control paradigm. Psalm 8, for example, puts the entire world of animals—both domestic and wild, as well as birds

---

67. See, e.g., Walter Brueggemann, *Genesis* (Interpretation; Atlanta: John Knox, 1982), 32, who claims that "the 'dominion' mandated here [in Gen. 1:26–28] is with reference to the animals. The dominance is that of a shepherd who cares for, tends, and feeds the animals. . . . It has to do with securing the well-being of every other creature and bringing the promise of each to full fruition."

and fish—under the command of humankind: "You have made them (humans) rule (*māšal*) over the works of your hands, you set all things under their feet" (Ps. 8:7 [6]).

Though this control certainly must involve care and concern for all living things, the model is human-centric: the righteousness and wisdom of the human ruler determines the order of the ecosystem in question. The primal human in Genesis 1–2 acts as a priest and king over the garden and its inhabitants—much like the role of the human king in ancient iconography such as the eighteenth-century BCE Mari palace wall relief, where Zimri-Lim stands at the center of a miniature cosmos, receiving the token of kingship amidst a world of flourishing plants, animals, and water (see Figure 2).[68]

Figure 2: Palace relief from Mari, with investiture of Zimri-Lim (18th c. BCE).

68. André Parrot, *Mission archéologique de Mari, II: Le palais. Peintures murals* (Paris: Geuthner, 1958), pls. VIII–XIV.

Figure 3: Glazed brick panel of Shalmanesar III (9th c. BCE).

In this ideology the initiation of wise rule in the form of divinely-ordained kingship energizes and fructifies the natural world. The king's wisdom and justice release the fourfold streams representing the earth's storehouses of water (compare Gen. 2:5-6, 10-14). Trees sprout up, and the animal world is alive. The Zimri-Lim investiture scene from Mari clearly embodies the theme of royal abundance, so common throughout the ancient Near Eastern literary record and prominent in the iconography of Neo-Assyrian empire (e.g., the "Tree of Abundance" motif; see Figure 3).[69]

Deuteronomy's Sapiential Nature Covenant

Cast as Moses' final speech in the Torah, the book of Deuteronomy is flush with plants and animals.[70] These nature images appear predominantly in the service of covenant-making language within the book; in its simplest form the covenant's relationship to natural flourishing amounts to a fairly straightforward rule: *obedience to covenant terms leads directly to plant and animal success, and disobedience leads to plant and animal failure*. In these texts, plants and animals are not singled out above or beyond any other category of human flourishing and failure, nor are the plants and animals used as actors in a fable. Rather, in Deuteronomy we find the natural world woven into the fabric of human moral activity. Plants fade and animals die as the nascent Israelites intermarry with Canaanites, while crops and wombs abound with produce when they worship the Lord alone. Deuteronomy 7:12-13 provides a typical example of this language; Moses assures the people that God will bless and multiply them, pending their obedience to divine commands. "He will bless the fruit of your womb and the fruit of your ground, your grain and new wine and oil, the offspring of your cattle and the issue of your

---

69. As expertly discussed by Irene J. Winter, "Ornament and the 'Rhetoric of Abundance' in Assyria," 163–83 in eadem, *On Art in the Ancient Near East*, Vol. I (Culture and History of the Ancient Near East 34.1; Leiden: Brill, 2010).

70. Opinion varies widely regarding the date and compositional strata of Deuteronomy, yet nearly all agree that the book was composed long after the putative time of Moses—most likely in various stages between the eighth and sixth centuries BCE. See a review of the question in Thomas Römer, *The So-Called Deuteronomistic History: A Sociological, Historical and Literary Introduction* (London: Bloomsbury T & T Clark, 2006).

flock" (7:13). The phrase "the fruit of your womb and the fruit of your ground" (pĕrî biṭnĕkā ûprî 'admāteka) demonstrates the parallel between human and earth, and the interdependence between crops, herd animals, and human life is as straightforward as it is significant.

Standard ancient Near Eastern treaty formulae—to which Deuteronomy has been often and helpfully (even if at times imprecisely) compared[71]—routinely employ similar promises and threats. The eighth-century BCE Old Aramaic Sefire inscriptions contain a treaty between a certain Bar-ga'yah and Mati'el of the royal family of neo-Hittite Arpad. The list of curses against Mati'el for violation of the treaty involves a long litany of plant and animal failures—animals will not give birth, locusts will devour the land, grass will not sprout, and desert animals will inhabit the desolate mound that was once Mati'el's fertile land.[72] The seventh-century Assyrian vassal treaties of Esarhaddon similarly list lengthy consequences for treaty-breakers, including failure of plants for food. Moreover, these Assyrian treaties contain poignant animal analogies to describe curses: "Just as a snake and a mongoose do not enter the same hole and do not live there, but plot of cutting each other's throat, so may you and your women not enter the same house, but plot of cutting each other's throat"; "Just as a butterfly does not fit into and does not return to its cocoon, so may you not return to your women in your houses"; "Just as a honeycomb is pierced through and through with holes, so may holes be pierced through and through

---

71. Among many other publications see George E. Mendenhall, *Law and Covenant in Israel and the Ancient Near East* (Pittsburgh: Biblical Colloquium, 1955); Klaus Baltzer, *The Covenant Formulary in Old Testament, Jewish, and Early Christian Writings*, trans. David E. Green (Philadelphia: Fortress Press, 1971); Moshe Weinfeld, *Deuteronomy and the Deuteronomic School* (Winona Lake, IN: Eisenbrauns, 1992), esp. 59–157.

72. Translation with references in Joseph A. Fitzmyer, SJ, "The Inscriptions of Bar-ga'yah and Mati'el from Sefire," *COS* II, 213–17, at Face A, ll. 14b–35a. Similar imagery appears in truncated form in a treaty from the same period between the Assyrian Ashurnirari V and Mati'el; see Erica Reiner, "Treaty Between Ashurnirari V of Assyria and Mati'ilu of Arpad," *ANET*, 532–33, part iv.

your flesh . . ."; "May they cause you, your brothers, your sons and daughters to go backward like a crab."[73]

The Hittite vassal treaties (fourteenth to thirteenth centuries BCE), once thought to be the closest parallels for the biblical materials, seem to lack significant reference to plants and animals, whereas these features are major components of the Sefire and Esarhaddon treaties, as well as in Deuteronomy. Of course, Deuteronomy is not exactly a treaty, and its differences from the other ancient Near Eastern materials are clear. Deuteronomy is a narrated piece, and contains an eclectic mix of materials and narrative expansions not paralleled in any ancient treaty. Whereas the appearance of floral and faunal failure (in the form of lurid curses) in the non-biblical Near Eastern treaties most often seems perfunctory (the striking animal analogies in Esarhaddon are exceptions), in Deuteronomy the *abundance* of the land takes center stage. This is due in part to the character of the document: Deuteronomy concerns itself precisely with the land Israel is to inherit. Still, as I will demonstrate below, floral and faunal images are woven into the core of Deuteronomy's vision of the moral universe, so that these common treaty elements are transformed into creative expressions of Israel's particular covenant thinking.

Some of the nature images in Deuteronomy embody a distinctly wisdom-oriented tone, and consequently the book can be properly discussed under the "nature wisdom" rubric in the Hebrew Bible. Moshe Weinfeld argues most forcefully that wisdom schools made distinct contributions to Deuteronomy—based on verbal and thematic parallels among Deuteronomy, Proverbs, and the Egyptian Amenemope wisdom text, as well as the inclusion of humanistic themes, concepts of agricultural reward, concern for land possession,

---

73. Text here from Erica Reiner, "The Vassal-Treaties of Esarhaddon," *ANET*, 534–41; crop failure imagery at section 47 (44); animal analogies quoted here at sections 71 (555), 79 (579), 84 (594), 92 (618).

and theodicy.[74] Even so, for Weinfeld, Deuteronomy's conception of wisdom was "entirely novel," as the book moves from seeing wisdom as "pragmatic talent" or "possession of extraordinary knowledge" to holding wisdom as "synonymous with the knowledge and understanding of proper behavior and with morality."[75]

Which of Deuteronomy's nature images can be isolated for this "wisdom" emphasis? Arguably all of them, since the Deuteronomic plant and animal universe is closely related to structures of affluence, abundance, and theodicy. Like wisdom literature in the Hebrew Bible generally, Deuteronomy views plant and animal thriving as a function of human righteousness, and in Deuteronomy these concerns are also primarily linked to questions of theodicy, righteousness, and divine provision. As Weinfeld notices, the possession-of-land motif is an important concern in Job (Job 9:24; 15:19; 22:8), and thus in a major portion of the Bible's formal sapiential literature.[76] At times, linguistic parallels even suggest (however tentatively) a distinct manner of wisdom speech, such as the use of the word 'āsām ("barn, storehouse") only in Deuteronomy 28:8 and Proverbs 3:10, or the phrase "houses full of good things"

74. Moshe Weinfeld, *Deuteronomy and the Deuteronomic School* (Winona Lake, IN: Eisenbrauns, 1992), esp. 244–74, 307–19; for a more concise treatment see the introductory remarks in idem, *Deuteronomy 1–11* (AB 5; New York: Doubleday, 1991). Others, such as Jean Malfroy, "Sagesse et Loi dans le Deutéronome," *VT* 15 (1965): 49–65, see wisdom influence in Deuteronomy. See a review of the question in Paul Sanders, *The Provenance of Deuteronomy 32* (Leiden: Brill, 1996), 81–84, and a comparison of ways of knowing between Deuteronomy and Wisdom literature in Ryan O'Dowd, *The Wisdom of Torah: Epistemology in Deuteronomy and the Wisdom Literature* (FRLANT 225; Göttingen: Vandenhoeck & Ruprecht, 2009), esp. 53–110. Even those who stridently criticize Weinfeld's method acknowledge the presence of distinct wisdom strata within Deuteronomy; e.g., Alexander Rofé, *Deuteronomy: Issues and Interpretation* (London: T & T Clark, 2002), 165 n. 58. The primary criticism seems to be that Weinfeld cast the Wisdom net so wide that virtually any theme or text could be called "Wisdom" (so Rofé, *Deuteronomy*, 222–23). Thus I tread lightly here regarding the "wisdom school" connection, bearing in mind the still-relevant methodological concerns raised by Crenshaw, "Method."

75. Weinfeld, *Deuteronomy and the Deuteronomic School*, 254–55. Weinfeld sees this fusion of Law and Wisdom as occurring particularly in the seventh century bce (see ibid., 255–56).

76. Ibid., 314.

with reference, in Deuteronomy, to the abundant state of the land's vegetation (see Deut. 6:11, *ûbāttîm mĕlē'îm kol-ṭûb*, and Job 22:18, *wĕ-hû' millē' bāttêhem ṭôb*).[77] It is possible that elements of Job rely on phraseology and ideology in Deuteronomy—precisely in order to counter it, or qualify it in some way—and thus our consideration of Deuteronomy here is at least appropriate insofar as Deuteronomy sets up a basis of covenantal "tradition" or "orthodoxy" vis-à-vis the Joban wisdom engagement.

In Deuteronomy, nature and the human self—indeed, also the national "self"—mirror each other, though the analogy runs predominantly in one direction: human to nature. But this is not the entire story. The land holds fruitful potential that exists before Israel arrives and allows for the possibility that people will succeed on the basis of the land's own properties. Upon arriving in the land the people will find wonderful, large cities not the product of Israel's own labor; houses will be filled with unearned goods, water cisterns carved out with hard labor not their own, vineyards and olive groves already planted and thriving (Deut. 6:10-11). The land flows "with milk and honey" (*ḥālāb ûdĕbāš*) in the famous idiom, conjuring an almost unreal paradise.[78] On this same theme, Deut. 8:7-9 has the land erupting in over-nature and total abundance before any Israelite arrives there:[79]

> (8:7) For Yhwh your God is bringing you to a good land, a land with torrents of water, springs and deep waters (*tĕhōmōt*) coming out of the valleys and hills, (8) a land of wheat and barley, of vines and figs and pomegranates, a land of olive oil and honey, (9) a land where you will

---

77. Ibid., 310.
78. In the Torah alone see Exod. 3:8, 17; 13:5; 33:3; Lev. 20:4; Num. 13:27; 14:8; 16:13-14; Deut. 6:3; 11:9; 26:9, 15; 27:3; 31:20. On Canaan as a natural paradise see Hans-Jürgen Zobel, "kena'an," *TDOT* VII, 211–28, at 220–22.
79. As Winter ("Ornament") notices, such references are to be considered within the context of the broader Near Eastern theme of the monarch vis-à-vis the abundant land.

eat bread without scarcity—you will not lack anything in it—a land where the very stones are iron and from its hills you will mine copper.

In the book of Numbers (13:23), spies into the Promised Land bring back a giant grape-cluster (perhaps meant to be miraculously huge, needing to be carried by two men), pomegranates, and figs to demonstrate the land's floral success.

Over-nature comes with its dark side, however. The land that produces giant grapes also produces giant humans who will be Israel's enemies in combat as they attempt to take the land by force (Num. 13:32-33; Deut. 1:24-28). Indeed, as the (maligned) Israelite spies frantically report, the land is not simply fruitful in the positive sense; it also "devours its inhabitants" (Num. 13:32). The beautiful cities and their produce, waiting to provide for the Israelites, are also fortified and guarded (Deut. 9:1-2). Nature may not be so easily controlled; rather than "have dominion" over such a place, Israel might be content merely to prevent it from eating them alive. On this theme we may compare Deuteronomy with the thirteenth-century BCE Egyptian "Craft of the Scribe" (Papyrus Anastasi I) document, which describes the road through Canaan as "overgrown with junipers and *alluna* [Semitic *'ln*, oak] and cedars (that) have reached the sky, where lions are more numerous than leopards and bears, and surrounded with Shasu on every side."[80] We must then be left with the impression that the natural provision of the land is not so straightforward—and we must not assume, given the wickedness that tradition imputes to the native population (e.g., Deut. 9:5), that natural flourishing can only be yoked to righteous Israelite possession. The land has its own force, even if under the Deuteronomic covenant Yhwh introduces new conditions for its blossoming.

---

80. James P. Allen, trans., "The Craft of the Scribe," *COS* III, 9–14, at 12 (18.7).

Several other examples of Deuteronomy's covenant language will suffice to show the book's engagement with these nature themes.[81] Nature must not be worshiped or involved in worship through the form of animals as divine images, nor must Israel turn toward sun, moon, or stars for inspiration in this regard (Deut. 4:17-19; 5:8, 23; 9:16; 17:3). Rather, God is to be "viewed" in abstraction, in pure darkness or in fire (Deut. 4:12-15, 33; 5:4, 22-24). One thinks of Egypt and its myriad animal deities, coupled with Deuteronomy's exhortation to remember God's deliverance from Egypt (Deut. 4:16-18; 17:16; 29:16-17). In fact, Deuteronomy seems to imply that the style of worship employed by the indigenous ("Canaanite") population is somehow nature-focused, distinct from what Israel's own worship is supposed to be, since this worship occurs on mountains, hills, and, in the common accusatory idiom, "under every green tree" (taḥat kol 'ēṣ ra'ănān, Deut. 12:2).[82] Israelites are not to plant any tree ('ēṣ) as an "Asherah" or "sacred pole" ('ăšērāh) beside the altar for their deity (Deut. 16:21). Elsewhere, hearts that turn away from Yhwh are metaphorized as poisonous and bitter plant roots, growing up in the midst of the otherwise righteous garden: ". . . lest there be among you a sprouting root, poisonous and bitter" (Deut. 29:17[18]). In Deuteronomy nature is bridled within the covenant,

---

81. A maximal list of nature images in Deuteronomy (some of which I have already mentioned and some of which I will discuss below) would include: 1:24-25; 1:44; 4:17-19; 4:26; 5:14, 21; 6:3, 11; 5:8; 7:13, 22; 8:7-9, 15; 9:16; 11:9-17; 12:2, 22; 13:15; 14:22-23, 28; 15:14; 16:13; 17:1; 20:6, 19-20; 21:22-23 (?); 22:6-7, 9-10; 25:4; 26:9-10, 15; 27:3; 28:4-5, 11-12, 17-18, 21, 31, 33, 38-40, 42, 51; 29:17 (English 29:18), 23 (English 29:22), 27 (English 29:28); 30:9; 31:20; 32:2, 11, 13, 24, 32; 33:14-17, 22. Moreover, many passages mention livestock (and sometimes plants) to be kept or not kept as property or plunder, to be eaten, to be offered as sacrifices, or used in festivals or rituals; see 2:35; 3:7, 19; 8:13; 12:6; 14:3-21; 15:19-23; 16:2, 9; 18:3-4;21:4; 22:1-4; 23:24-25; 24:20-21; 26:2; 27:6. However, I see these references to animals as distinct from my focus here.

82. See also 1 Kgs. 14:23; 2 Kgs. 16:4; 17:10; Isa. 57:5; Jer. 2:20; 3:6, 13; Ezek. 6:13; 2 Chr. 28:4. On the variants and origins of the phrase see William L. Holladay, "'On Every High Hill and Under Every Green Tree,'" *VT* 11 (1961): 170–76.

and yet must not be used illicitly; nature holds multiple possibilities: it is simultaneously charged, sacred, repulsive, and dangerous.[83]

Another statement of the standard Deuteronomic nature theme comes in 11:8-17. Here the speaker warns the audience against idolatry and points out that the land Israel will inherit is not like Egypt in the sense that it is not irrigated land.[84] Rather, God himself looks after this rugged new place full of hills and valleys—highlighting the precarious situation of natural flourishing or failure without divine blessing predicated on human righteousness (11:10-12). Irrigation implies human effort and agricultural control; the flat and predictable Nile floodplains are the counter-model for the rugged hill country and its droughts. Thus the author forcibly grounds plant success on God's own care. The new land is not an irrigated garden—it is a wild and craggy garden, to be tamed only by the covenant (Deut. 11:13-15):

> (13) If you surely listen to my commandments that I am commanding you today—to love Yhwh your God and to serve him with all your heart and all your being—
>
> (14) then I will give rain for your land in its season, early rain and late rain, and you will gather in your grain and your new wine and your oil.
>
> (15) I will give green grass for your field, for your animals, and you will eat and be satisfied.

These terms are repeated in routine language in the blessings of chapter 28 (28:4-5, 11-12). In Deuteronomy 31:10-13, the Festival of Booths—a distinctly agricultural celebration at the (autumn) new year—serves as the venue in which the people are to gather communally for reading the covenant. If Israel fails to uphold that

---

83. See Keith A. Stone, "Singing Moses's Song: A Performance-Critical Analysis of Deuteronomy's Song of Moses," PhD Dissertation, Harvard University (2013), 153–54.

84. See Victor Matthews, "Treading the Winepress: Actual and Metaphorical Viticulture in the Ancient Near East," *Semeia* 86 (1999): 19–32, at 24.

covenant, Moses promises, the people will be uprooted like a plant and cast out of the garden along with the poisonous weeds of idolatry mentioned earlier: "Yhwh will uproot (*nātaš*) them from upon their land . . ." (Deut. 29:27[28]).[85] In the "Song of Moses" (Deuteronomy 32), the climactic pedagogical treatise in the book, Moses returns to nature analogies at several points. His own sung words will rain upon the listeners "like rain upon grass, like showers upon green plants" (v. 2); Yhwh guides the people "as an eagle tends to its nest, and flutters over its young . . ." (v. 11); disloyalty to Yhwh will be met with animal attacks—"the teeth of beasts . . . the venom of things creeping in the dust" (v. 24);[86] and the foreign "plants" (= people) not worshiping Yhwh are like vines from Sodom and Gomorrah, their grapes and other produce poisonous and bitter (v. 32).

Other assorted images of plant and animal life in Deuteronomy do not at first seem to fit into the book's driving covenant themes, yet in some cases these images are closely related to the wisdom and abundance motifs discussed above. If a man has planted a crop but not yet harvested its produce, he is to be excused from battle to enjoy that produce—presumably on the grounds that experiencing natural abundance is a pivotal part of the fulfillment of the covenant promises to the nation (Deut. 20:6). The enigmatic decree in 21:22-23, which stipulates that a person hanged on a tree (*'ēṣ*) is cursed, relies on some notion of the defilement of the land, as if the land were a person defiled by a corpse (Leviticus 21; Num. 19:11).[87] Similarly, the land participates in codes of human purity and behavior through the

---

85. For *nātaš* as plant uprooting with regard to Israel, see 1 Kgs. 14:15; Ezek. 19:12; Amos 9:15; and many instances in Jeremiah (e.g., Jer. 1:10; 12:14, 15, 17; 18:7; 24:6; 31:28, 40; 42:10; 45:4).

86. Indeed, animal attacks for disobedience are a Deuteronomistic sub-theme; see 1 Kgs. 13:24-28; 20:36; 2 Kgs. 2:23-24; 17:25-26.

87. Compare with Num. 33:33-34. See Jeffrey H. Tigay, *Deuteronomy* (JPS Torah Commentary; Philadelphia: Jewish Publication Society, 1996), 198; Koert van Bekkum, *From Conquest to Coexistence: Ideology and Antiquarian Intent in the Historiography of Israel's Settlement in Canaan* (Leiden: Brill, 2011), 271–72.

prohibition against sowing with two kinds of seed or plowing with a mixed-animal team (Deut. 22:9-10, in the context of Lev. 19:19, or even Deut. 22:5). After an Israelite army besieges and invades a town they must not attack the trees of that place: "Are the trees of the field human, that you should besiege them?" (Deut. 20:19). Here the imagery *disentangles* human affairs from nature. Without the extra statement in the second half of the verse differentiating trees from humans, one might assume that the trees are merely to be kept standing for human food. Instead, the explanation forbids the siege on the grounds that an enemy's trees are not to be treated as enemy trees. Nature has its own status. So too the prohibition against muzzling the treading ox (25:4) and the exhortation against taking a mother bird and her eggs simultaneously (22:6-7) encourage the protection of animals with no explicit reference to human concerns.

As this review demonstrates, Deuteronomy offers striking nature motifs that are inextricably fused with concepts of human thriving or dying. These floral and faunal covenant images operate within the framework of a sapientializing ethos that focuses on a wide range of concerns: proper treatment of animals, theodicy, proper land possession, abundance, and the good life. Israel's relationship to the natural world is made a central part of the nation's political origins; the politics of the community not only include the growth of its plants and the breeding of its animals, but the community is both at the mercy of nature and in control of nature through its fidelity. Deuteronomy's repeated invocation of plant growth, rain and watering, ill-growing or poisonous plants, and the cycles of natural fertility at least prepare the reader to enter a world governed by nature metaphors; the audience enters a cosmos wherein the human moral self is inscribed on the very earth.

Plants and Animals as Parabolic Wisdom Actors

Throughout the Hebrew Bible, plants and animals serve as actors in what could rightly be called "parables" (Heb. *māšāl*; the verb *māšal* means "compare, be like")—that is, a genre defined as one in which a character within a narrative tells a story that explicitly relies on comparisons or correspondences between the elements of the story and the context of the audience.[88] A functional definition of this kind helps us categorize texts with similar elements irrespective of the varied terminology biblical authors use for their own purposes; in one instance a speaker marks a "parable" under the definition above by calling it a *māšāl* directly (Ezek. 17:2), though elsewhere *māšāl* describes any number of speech types, including sayings, lamentations, taunts, riddles, prophetic oracles, and songs.[89] Whatever terminology is used, prominent examples of the functional genre of the parable in the Hebrew Bible would include Jotham's tree speech in Judges 9, Nathan's condemnation of David in 2 Samuel 12, the Wise Woman of Tekoa's appeal in 2 Samuel 14, an unnamed prophet's story in 1 Kings 20, Isaiah's Song of the Vineyard in Isaiah 5, and Ezekiel's stories involving lions, plants, and eagles in Ezekiel 14 and 17.[90] Adherents to a formal "wisdom school" need not have authored these materials for us to consider them as forms of wisdom speech, for the parable is inherently wisdom-oriented, engaging with classic elements of the formal wisdom corpus: persuasion, theodicy, character formation, existential observation, ethics, and more.[91]

---

88. Jeremy Schipper, *Parables and Conflict in the Hebrew Bible* (Cambridge: Cambridge University Press, 2009), 2.
89. E.g., the following references demonstrate the variety of uses of *māšāl*: Num. 21:8, 27; chs. 23–24 (*passim*); 1 Sam. 10:12; 24:13; 1 Kgs. 5:1; 9:7; Isa. 14:4–5; Jer. 24:9; Ezek. 12:22; 21:15; Mic. 2:4; Hab. 2:6; Ps. 78:2; Job 13:12; 27:1; Prov. 1:1, 6; 10:1; 25:1; Eccl. 12:9.
90. All these texts are expertly treated in Schipper, *Parables*.
91. See the list of wisdom characteristics in James L. Crenshaw, *Old Testament Wisdom: An Introduction*, 3d ed. (Louisville: Westminster John Knox, 2010), 4–11, 27. Crenshaw is suspicious of attempts to draw disparate texts under the "wisdom" rubric as I do in this chapter. It might

Though much can be said about the parable genre as a wisdom motif generally, here we focus on texts that stand out through their use of plants or animals as the wisdom actors: Jotham's tree parable (Judg. 9:8-15), Jehoash's thornbush story (2 Kgs. 14:9 // 2 Chr. 25:18), Isaiah's vineyard song (Isa. 5:1-7), and Ezekiel's various nature stories (Ezek. 17:1-10; 19:1-14).[92]

Jotham's Tree: Judges 9:8-15. Plants serve as a wisdom motif in Judges 9:8-15, in what is often referred to as "Jotham's Parable,"[93] though the story, since it involves action narrated purely in the world of plants, could be rightly defined as a "fable."[94] The context in Judges 9 reveals a violent political situation: Abimelek attempts to eradicate seventy of his familial rivals to monarchic rule near Shechem, though one escapes—Jotham, the youngest son of Jerubbaal (Gideon). Learning of Abimelek's massacre, Jotham ascends Mount Gerizim and shouts down a fable involving various contenders for kingship in the world of trees (9:7-15). The opening line already bristles with shrewd implications (Judg. 9:8): "The trees went out to anoint a king for themselves . . . ." Do trees need a king? Why? Does Israel need a

---

be best to say that in some cases, such as those I discuss here, the parable has "sapiential significance," as is argued for certain parables in the New Testament by Grant Macaskill, *Revealed Wisdom and Inaugurated Eschatology in Ancient Judaism and Early Christianity* (JSJSS 115; Leiden: Brill, 2007), 22. See also Ronald M. Hals, *Ezekiel*, FOTL 119 (Grand Rapids: Eerdmans, 1989), 115–16 for links among fables, parables, and wisdom speech.

92. See, briefly, Oded Borowski, "Animals in the Literatures of Syria-Palestine," 289–306 in Collins, *History of the Animal World,* at 296–97.

93. Scholarship on the Jotham fable includes Schipper, *Parables and Conflict,* 23–40; Yassif, *The Hebrew Folktale,* 23–26; Silviu Tatu, "Jotham's Fable and the 'Crux Interpretum' in Judges IX," *VT* 56 (2006): 105–24; Karin Schöpflin, "Jotham's Speech and Fable as Prophetic Comment on Abimelech's Story: The Genesis of Judges 9," *Scandinavian Journal of the Old Testament* 18 (2004): 3–22; Wouter Cornelis Van Wyk, "The Fable of Jotham in its Ancient Near Eastern Setting," 89–95 in idem, ed., *Studies in Wisdom Literature* (Hercules, South Africa: N. H. W. Press, 1981). For commentaries see esp. J. Alberto Soggin, *Judges: A Commentary,* trans. John Bowden (OTL; Philadelphia: Westminster, 1981), 171–79; Victor Matthews, *Judges and Ruth* (Cambridge: Cambridge University Press, 2004), 100–7; Susan Niditch, *Judges: A Commentary* (Louisville: Westminster John Knox, 2008), 106–17; Robert G. Boling, *Judges* (AB 6A; Garden City, NY: Doubleday, 1975), 165–74.

94. Yassif, *The Hebrew Folktale,* 23.

king? The olive tree, offered the crown first, rejects it, worried that he will not have time to produce his coveted oil. The fig tree demurs for similar reasons, as kingship would prevent him from producing figs for consumption. The grapevine follows suit. Finally, the offer comes down to the lowly bramble (*'āṭār*), who accepts on condition that the offer is made in good faith (*be'ĕmet*, Judg. 9:14-15).

The last part of the fable provides the drama going forward. The bramble offers his shade if the kingship offer proves genuine: "but if not, may fire come out from the bramble and devour the cedars of Lebanon" (9:15). Jotham offers his own interpretation (9:16-20). His father, Jerubbaal, is the bramble who offered protection; Jerubbaal fought, risked his life, and rescued the people from the Midianites, and yet Abimelek dishonored that arrangement by killing the seventy other potential heirs (9:17). The fire from the bramble is then some kind of divine justice, flaming out against the wrongdoers, and the use of the word *'ĕmet* in verse 19 (parallel to the bramble's own words in 9:15) clinches the identification between Jerubbaal and the bramble. On the other hand, Jotham's declaration that the people have made Abimelek, "the son of his slave woman," king over and against presumably other, better options (corresponding to the olive tree, the fig tree, and the grapevine?) makes the ignoble bramble a cipher for the ignoble Abimelek.[95] Whatever the case, Jotham's words prove ominous, taking on the power of a spoken curse when, at the end of the incident, Abimelek is killed. Tree imagery frames the narrative: Abimelek is crowned king by a certain oak in Shechem (Judg. 9:6), Jotham curses Abimelek and the lords of Shechem through a tree fable, and Abimelek is killed while attempting to burn down a stronghold with trees he has cut down (9:48-57).[96]

---

95. See Schipper, *Parables and Conflict*, 30–31.
96. See the perceptive comments on the arboreal imagery in Schipper, *Parables and Conflict*, 35, and Matthews, *Judges and Ruth*, 106–7.

Albrecht Alt declared that this story "only constitute[s] a transferal of human conditions into an extra-human sphere in order ultimately to make some didactic point for humanity" (this contrasted, by Alt, with Job's plant and animal world, where the nature images are integral to the book's themes).[97] But this is not quite correct, for the elements of the story do not map very well onto the preceding narrative action in any simple way. Jerubbaal's sons do not receive offers of kingship as the trees do, the three tree candidates bear no numerical relation to the seventy slain relatives, and the bramble agrees to rule only by persuasion (Abimelek attains rule in no such way).[98] Moreover, the identity of the plant actors in Jotham's tale contributes significant elements to the story via the inherent qualities of the plants. As mentioned above, the notion that trees would want or need a king is absurd. In a landscape like that in ancient Israel/Palestine where real tree growth was relatively sparse, trees would appear quite stately and austere, the very opposite of an obedient, manageable crowd that would be amenable to rule (as opposed to, say, sheep: 2 Sam. 7:8; 1 Chr. 21:17; Ps. 78:52). So too, in the human landscape of the Judges we find only isolated poles of power. Soggin interprets the story to mean that political leadership is essentially a race to the bottom: only the basest individual will accept a leadership role. Those with real contributions to make (the olive tree, the fig, the grapevine) will make those contributions and refrain from wasting time in politics. The bramble is an apt symbol indeed for the power-hungry, as it produces only a fleeting blossom in the spring but ultimately is useful for nothing.[99] As Eli Yassif points out, the classic ancient Near Eastern plant dialogue—such as the tamarisk-versus-

97. Alt, "Solomonic Wisdom," 103.
98. See Yassif, The Hebrew Folktale, 24. One may reasonably conclude that the tree fable was a traditional tale, not originally crafted for use in the context of the Abimelek story. See Soggin, Judges, 174–76.
99. Soggin, Judges, 114–15.

palm debate—puts the bramble or thorn in the role of mediator between the warring plant brothers, providing opportunity for both tamarisk and palm to heap abuse upon the lowly bramble. Thus we must not see the bramble as a "negative" element in Jotham's fable. Rather, the three "useful" plants reject the leadership role because of selfish (and perhaps irrational?) concerns rather than using their talents for the good of the whole.[100]

Regardless of the pervasive (and probably correct) scholarly speculation that the fable functioned independently of its local narrative context, Jotham's storytelling is subtle and demanding within the book of Judges as a whole. Judges repeatedly engages the question of kingship: can Israel find appropriate, centralized leadership? The individual judges represent overwhelming failures on this front, punctuated by the unsubtle closing statement in Judges 21:25: "In those days there was no king in Israel; everyone did what was right in their own eyes." In Jotham's parable, problems of leadership are built into the structure of the natural world. Brambles and thorns make fleeting promises (flowers), only later to be burned. Trees remain through generations, but kingship, like scrub-brush, is transient. Trees observe coronations and burn enemies, but they also serve as wisdom actors, casting judgment on human pretense to rule.

Jehoash's Thornbush: 2 Kings 14:9 // 2 Chronicles 25:18. A second example of a plant fable comes in 2 Kings 14:9, with a parallel text containing differences not relevant to the fable in 2 Chronicles 25:18.[101] Euphoric after his slaughter of ten thousand Edomites (2 Kgs. 14:7), Amaziah of Judah sends a seemingly unprovoked military challenge to Jehoash of Israel. Jehoash's response comes in the form of a story that is blunt, short, and not particularly artful on the surface (v. 9): "The thorn (*haḥôaḥ*) of Lebanon sent word to the cedar (*'ĕrez*) of

---

100. Yassif, *The Hebrew Folktale*, 26.
101. Schipper, *Parables and Conflict*, 93–110, is the best treatment of this episode.

Lebanon, saying, 'send me your daughter as a wife for my son.' But a wild animal of Lebanon passed by and trampled the thorn." Jehoash's own application is straightforward (v. 10): stay home; do not incite trouble. Amaziah does not listen and suffers defeat and capture in battle against Israel.

Who is the thorn and who the cedar in this episode? And what is the meaning of the trampling animal? Perhaps the animal represents the unpredictable element of chance, sure to undercut the overconfidence of the thorn in the certainty of his arranged marriage plan. Stately trees of Lebanon, which often appear in reference to monarchic arrogance (see also Judg. 9:15, as well as 1 Kgs. 10:21; Ezek. 27:5; 31:3),[102] make grand plans, but even a nameless wild animal is enough to disrupt those plans in a random encounter. Schipper argues that Jehoash's fable escalates the conflict and does not constitute a genuine warning against Amaziah's attitude. Under this view Jehoash could be the cedar *and* the wild animal (just as several elements in the 2 Kings 12 parable could represent King David).[103] The narrative is ambiguous enough so that one cannot make confident identifications or point to motives. I would suggest that the saying is a simple (if not clumsy) attempt at a wisdom trope, one that is misunderstood by the overconfident Amaziah, to his own ruin. Perhaps von Rad summarized the episode best: "What a period, when kings, in diplomatic communications, wielded the intellectual weapon of the fable!"[104]

Isaiah's Vineyard Song: Isaiah 5:1-7. Recent scholarship has produced voluminous debate on the form or genre of the poem

---

102. Boling, *Judges*, 174.
103. Schipper, *Parables and Conflict*, 98.
104. Gerhard von Rad, *Wisdom in Israel*, trans. James D. Martin (London: SCM, 1972), 43. Parables as political correspondence also appear in letters from eighth-century bce Mari and seventh-century bce Assyria; see Mordecai Cogan and Hayim Tadmor, *II Kings* (AB 11; Garden City, NY: Doubleday, 1988), 156.

in Isaiah 5:1-7,[105] in which Isaiah sings a "song" (*šîr*) concerning a vineyard owned by "my beloved" (correlated with Yhwh in 5:7).[106] The action of the parable is brief, spanning just two verses (5:1-2). The viticulturist here takes exceedingly great care—indeed, the necessary care—to cultivate his field for growing, and expects grapes (*'ănābîm*). Instead, the land yields "wild grapes" (*bĕ'ušîm*; the root *b'š* denotes stink, foulness, and rot). Under the terms established here the story can technically be called a parable,[107] and for our purposes it is enough to notice the poem's agricultural imagery, focused on the relationship between human and land. The parable is of interest because of its combination of floral themes and theodicy. When the plant world does not yield what is expected, the response is not only human dismay at the loss of crops but also brooding about the meaning of the failure.[108]

Agricultural incompetence is one thing, but in Isaiah's parable the unexpectedly foul plant is the unexpectedly foul human. The farmer acted with all diligence: the hill itself is amply fertile (*bĕqeren ben-šāmen*), the land cleared of stones, the vine (*śōrēq*) is of high quality, a watchtower stands guard over the planting, the wine vats are ready, a hedge (*śôk*) protects the field (5:5). When the land misproduces, the farmer can only cry out in exasperation, as he does in 5:4: "What

---

105. Studies of Isaiah 5:1-7 are numerous; see, e.g., John T. Willis, "The Genre of Isaiah 5:1-7," *JBL* 96 (1977): 337–62; Gale Yee, "A Form-Critical Study of Isaiah 5:1-7 as a Song and a Juridical Parable," *CBQ* 43 (1981): 30–40; Francis Landy, "The Parable of the Vineyard (Isaiah 5:1-7), or What is a Love Song Doing Among the Prophets?" *Studies in Religion / Sciences religieuses* 34 (2005): 147–64; Schipper, *Parables and Conflict*, 111–17, and the detailed commentary in Hans Wildberger, *Isaiah 1–12*, trans. Thomas H. Trapp (Minneapolis: Augsburg Fortress, 1991), 175–87. For a specifically ecological reading see Jules Gomes, "The Song of the Vineyard in Isaiah 5:1-7: An Eco-Justice Reading Using Socio-Literary Methods," *Bible Speaks Today (United Theological College)* (2000): 181–98.

106. The Heb. root *dôd* in Isa. 5:1 can mean "uncle," "relative," and is related to the term *yādid* ("beloved") earlier in the same verse. See discussion in Wildberger, *Isaiah 1–12*, 180.

107. See Schipper, *Parables and Conflict*, 111–12.

108. Isaiah is not alone in his use of such themes; see, e.g., Ezek. 17:5–6; Hos. 9:8; 10:1; 14:8.

more could I do for my vineyard!" So, too, Israel remains planted in a fine land, but yields a crop of bloodshed, greed, and injustice (5:7-8).

The ancient (and modern) winemaking process involves intense effort and a multi-year buildup to a useful harvest (around four to six years).[109] The emotional letdown after such an effort would be extreme, as is Yhwh's disappointment at the crop of Israelites. The vintner will tear out the vineyard (Isa. 5:5-6). Wild thorns will overtake the once-arable land, an un-creation motif signaling a return to the desert wilderness and a foreshadowing of future exile outside the land, without a king.[110] Isaiah's poem also seems to have political implications, with significance for Isaiah's eighth-century BCE world. Marvin Chaney gives an intriguing analysis of the parable though a political lens, arguing that vineyards such as the one used for the image in Isaiah 5 were "at the vortex of a battle that convulsed Judahite and Israelite society." Under this view an eighth-century urban elite had taken land traditionally held by peasant farmers in order to process luxury goods, thus making these very elite a pointed object of attack when the vineyard fails to produce as expected (see also Isa. 3:12-15, as well as two other prophets of the same era, Amos 5:11 and Mic. 2:2, on similar themes).[111] If Chaney's interpretation has merit, and I think it does, we are reminded that nature metaphors may not be crafted out of thin air or for purely abstract, rhetorical purposes. Rather, nature is embedded in economic and historical contexts, and nature parables or allegories can reflect real geographical concerns. While it is true that Isaiah's imagery here plays on the audience's emotions by associating injustice with shared

---

109. Matthews, "Treading the Winepress," 24–28, and Carey Ellen Walsh, *The Fruit of the Vine: Viticulture in Ancient Israel* (Harvard Semitic Monographs 60; Winona Lake, IN: Eisenbrauns, 2000).

110. Matthews, "Treading the Winepress," 29. For other un-creation motifs focused on the reversal of nature see, e.g., Genesis 6–7; Job 3; Jer. 4:23-28; Hos. 4:3.

111. Marvin L. Chaney, "Whose Sour Grapes? The Addressees of Isaiah 5:1-7 in the Light of Political Economy," *Semeia* 87 (1999): 105–22, at 109.

concern over agricultural failure in a fictive literary form, here the "symbolic" merges with reality on the ground: for Israel in the north, their actual vineyards had been lost to the incursion of Tiglath-Pileser III, and for Judah, to whom the song is also directed (5:7), loss of land to the Assyrians (and later the Babylonians) was imminent.[112]

Ezekiel's Eagle, Lion, and Plant Fables: Ezekiel 17:1-10; 19:1-14. The fables in Ezekiel 17 and 19 presuppose the events of 597 BCE and following, when Nebuchadnezzar invaded Jerusalem and took Jehoiachin captive to Babylon.[113] The Babylonians placed Jehoiachin's uncle, Zedekiah (Mattaniah), on the throne as a puppet-king, hoping to secure the allegiance of the region. After years of intrigue and hand-wringing among the smaller Syro-Palestinian states, Judah decided on formal rebellion against Babylon (marked by cessation of tribute), opting to call for Egyptian military aid. Ezekiel 17 seems to refer to elements of this negotiation with Egypt, which would eventually result in another Babylonian incursion and the loss of Temple and monarchy in 586 BCE. The themes of moral instruction, social advancement, and a meditation on folly all point up the wisdom orientation of these fables. As Schipper rightly observes, Ezekiel's riddles solidify the prophet's identity as a wise interpreter of events, since the propounder of the riddle holds a powerful and, in Ezekiel's case, damning secret over the heads of the audience.[114]

---

112. As also cogently stated by Yee, "A Form-Critical Study of Isaiah 5:1-7," 38–39.

113. See 2 Kings 24–25, Jeremiah 27–29, and the review in J. Maxwell Miller and John H. Hayes, *A History of Ancient Israel and Judah*, 2d ed. (Louisville: Westminster John Knox, 2006), 468–77. For expanded commentary and a review of past research on Ezekiel 17 and 19 see esp. Walther Zimmerli, *Ezekiel*, Vol. I, trans. Ronald E. Clements (Philadelphia: Fortress Press, 1979), 354–68, 388–98; Moshe Greenberg, *Ezekiel 1–20* (AB 22; Garden City, NY: Doubleday, 1983), 307–24, 348–59; Walther Eichrodt, *Ezekiel*, trans. Cosslett Quin (Philadelphia: Westminster, 1970), 220–31, 249–58; as well as the brief remarks in Schipper, *Parables and Conflict*, 117–22.

114. Schipper, *Parables and Conflict*, 118.

In the fable of Ezekiel 17 (called both a *ḥîdāh* ["riddle"][115] and a *māšāl* ["parable, allegory"] in 17:2), Zedekiah's rebellion clearly appears within the "theopolitics" of sixth-century Judah as rebellion not primarily against Babylon but against Yhwh.[116] Rather than introducing pure clarity, though, Ezekiel does not explicitly identify the animals and plants in the fable so as to identify the humans in question.[117] Many seem to agree that the first eagle in Ezekiel 17 corresponds to Babylon, and Jehoiachin is the branch sent into Babylonian exile; the second eagle is then Egypt, the empire to which Judah appealed without success.[118] The material in chapter 19 (called a *qînāh* in Ezek. 19:1[119]) is also possibly about Zedekiah, but the images here are more ambiguous—the first lion cub may be Jehoahaz, the second Jehoaichin, and Zedekiah the third; the mighty vine stem (19:11) is possibly Zedekiah, though this is unclear.[120] In both fables there seems to be no organic connection between the plants or animals of the fable and the nature of the human actors,[121] and yet, as with Isaiah 5, reality blends seamlessly with the image—the "land of trade" and "city of merchants" in the parable of Ezekiel 17:4 is clearly a place like Babylon, and in 19:9 Ezekiel steps out of the fable genre and mentions the Babylonian king directly.[122]

Especially noteworthy in these chapters is the motif of plant height or overgrowth as a signal of human arrogance.[123] In Ezekiel 17:3-4

---

115. Compare with Samson's lion *ḥîdāh* in Judg. 14:13-14.

116. Hals, *Ezekiel*, 115–17.

117. See Schipper, *Parables and Conflict*, 117–18.

118. E.g., Zimmerli, *Ezekiel*, Vol. I, 362. Ezekiel himself seems to suggest this interpretation in Ezek. 17:12-21. Greenberg (*Ezekiel 1–20*, 321) points out that original hearers of the riddle in chapter 17 may quickly assume the first eagle is Yhwh (based on Exod. 19:4; Deut. 32:11), and the cedar is Israel (Num. 24:6); then the second eagle represents another deity.

119. In fact, Ezekiel 19 functions as an extended metaphor or analogy, not a fable, in that the speaker clearly identifies the humans in question with the animal and the plant (19:2, 10).

120. See Greenberg, *Ezekiel 1–20*, 355–56 for these and other positions. On this lion imagery see Strawn, *What is Stronger than a Lion?* 248–49.

121. See, e.g., Eichrodt, *Ezekiel*, 223; Greenberg, *Ezekiel 1–20*, 320.

122. See Zimmerli, *Ezekiel*, Vol. I, 360.

the plant is a "topmost shoot" (*ṣammeret hāʾārez*) of a Lebanon cedar, recalling the appearance of this same tree in the wisdom traditions previously discussed (within Ezekiel, note also Ezek. 27:5). This shoot, however, is not able to soar again—it becomes a vine (*gepen*), "sprawling out, but low in height" (*sōraḥat šiplat qômāh*, 17:6). Later in the chapter Yhwh promises to take up his own transplanting project (17:22-24):

> (22) Thus says Adonai Yhwh: I myself will take a sprout from the tall cedar, and I will situate it—I will pluck off a tender shoot from the top, and I myself will plant it upon a high and lofty mountain.
> (23) On a mountain of Israel, up high, I will plant it—so that it may produce branches and bear fruit, so that it will be a noble cedar, so that every winged bird may dwell beneath it, in the shade of its boughs they will dwell.
> (24) Then all the trees of the field will know that I, Yhwh, bring the exalted tree down low; I exalt the low tree; I dry up the green tree, and I make the dry tree sprout forth. I, Yhwh, have spoken, and I will do it.

In Ezekiel 19 this theme continues (vv. 10-12):

> (10) Your mother was like a vine in your vineyard, transplanted by the water, fruitful and full of branches from abundant water;
> (11) her strong stem (*wayyihyû lāh maṭṭôt ʿōz*) became like the scepters of rulers; its upper reach (*qômātô*) grew up to the leaves, and its height (*gābhô*) appeared among the multitude of branches.
> (12) But it was plucked up in a fury, it was tossed down to the ground; an east wind dried up its fruit, its strong stem (*maṭṭēh*) torn away and dried up—fire consumed it.

The plant-height imagery here may be inspired by the royal "ascent to heaven" myth, reflexes of which appear in Isaiah 14:12-20 and

123. In this context see Greenberg, *Ezekiel 1–20*, 356, 358, and on this theme more generally, Doak, *Last of the Rephaim*, 120–23; Gregory Nagy, "Theognis and Megara: A Poet's Vision of his City," 22–81 in Thomas J. Figueria and Gregory Nagy, eds., *Theognis of Megara: Poetry and the Polis* (Baltimore: Johns Hopkins University Press, 1985); Ann Michelini, "Hybris."

Ezekiel 28. Royal ambitions are marked by surging upward, but Yhwh brings down the lofty plant (compare also Isa. 2:12-14; Ps. 80:9-14[8-13]). One may also recall Nebuchadnezzar's dream in the book of Daniel, in which a giant tree growing out of the center of the earth represents the king's overreaching power (Dan. 4:10-12; see also Dan. 8:9-11). Arrogant humans build to the heavens, but the Lord scatters them down below (Genesis 11).[124]

Proverbial Nature Observation

The book of Proverbs frequently uses both plant and animal observations to make wisdom arguments.[125] Nature motifs appear throughout the book, in all of the major proverbial collections: in the sayings ascribed to Solomon in chapters 1–9; 10:1–22:16; the sayings of "the wise" in 22:17–24:34;[126] further words of Solomon copied by Hezekiah's men in 25:1–29:27; the Agur speech in 30:1-33; the words of King Lemuel in 31:1-31. One notices many conventional images, such as the "fruit" (*pĕrî*) of the mouth or actions (8:19; 13:2; 18:20; 31:31), but Proverbs engages in its own distinctive world of sapiential plant and animal comparisons. The righteous are a "tree of life" (*'ēṣ ḥayyîm*; 3:18; 11:30; 13:12; 15:4), the wrath of a king is that of a lion (19:12; 20:2; 28:15), the ant is a paragon of industrious strength (6:6; 30:25), and the lazy or foolish individual must live in fear of the

---

124. Doak, *Last of the Rephaim*, 144.

125. The authoritative treatment regarding animals here is Tova Forti, *Animal Imagery in the Book of Proverbs* (Leiden: Brill, 2008); see also eadem, "Animal Images in the Didactic Rhetoric of the Book of Proverbs," *Biblica* 77 (1996): 48–63; "Bee's Honey—From *Realia* to Metaphor in Biblical Wisdom Literature," *VT* 56 (2006): 327–41. A reasonably comprehensive list of Proverbs' use of nature imagery would include 1:17; 3:9-10, 18, 19-20; 5:19; 6:5, 6-11; 7:22; 8:19, 20-31; 11:22, 30; 12:10, 12, 14; 13:2, 12, 23; 14:4; 15:4, 19; 16:24; 17:12; 18:20; 19:12; 20:2; 22:13; 23:4-5, 32; 24:30-32; 25:14; 25:20; 26:1, 3, 11, 17; 27:8, 18, 23-27; 28:1, 15; 30:4, 15, 17, 18-19, 24-28, 29-31; 31:16, 31.

126. Portions of Proverbs 22–23 may well be an Israelite adaptation of the Egyptian "Wisdom of Amenemope" (and other Egyptian sources); see, e.g., Michael V. Fox, *Proverbs 10–31* (AB 18B; New Haven: Yale University Press, 2009), 710–33.

animal world (22:13; 26:13; 28:1). In the major treatment of animal imagery in Proverbs, Tova Forti surveys all of the Proverbial animals, finding faunal references spread across all the book's literary forms (comparisons; antithetical sayings; "better-than" sayings; metaphors; first-person address; admonition; exhortation; "biographical confession"; numerical sayings). Forti rightly notes that Proverbs never invokes baldly mythological animals or talking animals that can serve as revelators from God;[127] the Proverbial universe is a thoroughly "natural" one, though it is certainly one in which the commonplace (the ant, the leech, the goat) serves as a reminder of industry, order, and sobriety before the deity.

Plants in particular come off as straightforward and reliably-oriented metaphors for the Proverbialists, and the Proverbs audience must routinely inhabit an iron moral world in which the results of human action are as constant and reliable as the seasons.[128] Consider the following selected examples:

> (3:9-10) Honor Yhwh with your wealth, and from the first fruits of your produce; then your storehouses will be filled with plenty, and new wine will burst out from your wine vats.
> (25:23) The north wind whips up rain—a gossiping tongue, indignant looks.
> (28:19) One who works his land will be sated with bread, but one who pursues worthless things will be sated with poverty.

Any perversion of the moral order is as unexpected as unseasonable weather:

> (26:1) Like snow in the summer or rain in the harvest, so honor is not fitting for a fool.

---

127. Forti, *Animal Imagery in Proverbs*, 131.
128. The Proverbial moral scheme—that righteousness results in reward and prosperity while wickedness leads to poverty and ruin—is a repeated theme in Proverbs. See, e.g., Prov. 1:32-33; 3:9-10, 33; 10:3-4, 9, 27, 30; 11:8, 25, 31; 12:11, 28; 13:6, 21; 14:11, 14; 15:6, 19; 19:15, 23; 21:5; 24:33-34; 26:27; 28:18-19.

Of course, a fool may indeed receive honor, but the audience is to recognize such honor for what it is ("not fitting"). So too Proverbs 13:23 is willing to recognize plant failure for those who are not explicitly categorized as sinners, but here the exception proves the rule, since the plant loss actually comes through a denial of justice:

> (13:23) Even the fallow land (*nîr*) of the poor may yield much food—but it is swept away through lack of justice (*mišpāṭ*).[129]

True, the Proverbialist speaks of plant failure directly as the result of human laziness—and thus not as a mystical or automatic reflection of the human inner state—but laziness is one of the premier moral failures of the fool in Proverbs, and thus, in the Proverbial mentality broadly conceived, it is not so easy to separate a situation like that in Haggai 1:10-11 (discussed above) and the observation in Proverbs 24:30-32:

> (30) I passed by the field of the lazy one (*'îš 'āṣēl*), by the vineyard of the stupid man (*'ādām ḥăsar lēb*);
> (31) and look—thistles (*qimmĕśnîm*) grew up and covered all of it, the ground (lit. "its face," *pānâw*) covered with nettles (*ḥărullîm*), and its wall of stones destroyed.
> (32) I looked, and pondered (this); I saw, and I received instruction.

As far as plants are concerned, then, the Proverbial self must live within a specific ecological narrative: human moral activity plows deeply into the land, either poisoning its produce through ineptitude (laziness, iniquity) or guaranteeing its success through diligence and fear of God and sobriety. This eco-anthropology places quite a bit of pressure on the self for the quality of plant and animal; ecology is

---

129. Cf. the translation in Fox, *Proverbs 10–31*, 570. Fox's interpretation of the meaning of the passage is in line with my own, however: "The verse states a raw injustice. The sages of Proverbs were quite aware that life can be unfair, at least temporarily."

a subservient character in the drama, while the human orchestrator decides the yield by sheer force of moral will.

In the speech of Agur ben Yakeh (Proverbs 30), the animal world in particular serves as a site of inspiration and wonder. Here animals react to human moral states in parallel to the passages cited above involving plants:

> (30:17) The eye that mocks a father or despises obedience to a mother—ravens of the wadi will pluck it out and vultures will eat it.

Albrecht Alt points to Proverbs 30, citing several numerical-type statements there, some in relation to plant or animal observation, which he thinks are only a remnant of what must have existed as part of a *Gattung* of nature wisdom in Israel.[130] Fox disputes this point and asserts that these proverbs only revel in nature by way of arousing "a sense of wonder in the commonplace."[131]

Whether or not we can categorize these references under a nature *Gattung*, Proverbs' nature references are not merely ornamental. Sometimes the Proverbial animal is subtle or subversive. Consider Proverbs 30:27: "No king for the locust, yet he marches out in order" (or: by rank; *ḥōṣēṣ kūllō*). Here Agur ben Yakeh revels in the military order of this famously destructive insect, which elsewhere appears as an enemy of human thriving (Exod. 10:4-20; Isa. 33:4; Jer. 46:23, 51; Joel 1–2; Nah. 3:15-18).[132] The locust, along with the ant, the badger, and the lizard, receives praise for being small yet "exceedingly wise" (30:24-28). Ants are tiny, yet they provide vast stores of food. Badgers lack overwhelming societal power or individual strength,

---

130. Alt, "Solomonic Wisdom," 104.
131. Fox, "Egyptian Onomastica," 309–10.
132. See Forti, *Animal Imagery in Proverbs*, 7, 111–16. Compare this striking depiction of the locust with the positive estimation of the bee—usually indicated as a pest in the Bible (e.g., Deut. 1:44; Isa. 7:18)—in the LXX of Proverbs (discussed in Forti, *Animal Imagery in Proverbs*, 106–7).

yet they take up secure domicile in rocks. Lizards, though tiny, make their way into palaces. By suggesting these paradoxes of power and achievement Proverbs 30 offers a counter-narrative to the other nature references in the book, at least in its rhetorical tone (indeed, the book seems out of step with the rest of Proverbs generally). On this front, consider also the numerical list in Proverbs 30:29-31:

> (29) There are three things pleasing in their steps, four that are pleasing in their movement:
> (30) the lion, warrior among the beasts, who does not turn away before anything;
> (31) the strutting rooster (lit. "rooster of loins"), or the male goat, or the king parading (*'alqûm*)[133] before his people.

A saying like this may be read as taking its comparison much further than mere wonder at basic animal action; the insertion of the human king into the animal list is not only clever and perhaps unexpected but also a mockery of human power. The king is like a lion in his power or anger or magnificent stride, to be sure (see Prov. 19:12; 20:2), but even the Proverbial lion may become oppressive or excessive (Prov. 28:15: "A roaring lion or a rushing bear [is like] a wicked ruler over poor people"). The king is also like a strutting rooster or a male goat, two animals with markedly less power and prestige than the lion—yet both stride around like pompous kings nonetheless.

Plants and Animals in the Wisdom-Oriented Psalms

Of the several well-recognized psalm types (e.g., praise, lament, royal, creation), the "wisdom psalm" is one of the more elusive.[134]

---

133. Cf. Fox, *Proverbs 10–31*, 880.
134. See William P. Brown, "'Come, O Children . . . I Will Teach You the Fear of the Lord' (Psalm 34:12): Comparing Psalms and Proverbs," 85–102 in Ronald L. Troxel, Kelvin G. Friebel, and Dennis R. Magary, eds., *Seeking Out the Wisdom of the Ancients: Essays offered to honor Michael V. Fox on the occasion of his sixty-fifth birthday* (Winona Lake, IN: Eisenbrauns, 2005).

Roland Murphy offers the clearest set of criteria for identifying what we can fairly label "wisdom-oriented psalms," citing recognized sapiential features as markers of this category. Stylistic features include ʾašrê formulae, numerical sayings, better-than sayings, teacher to child address, acrostics, simple comparisons, and admonition language, and content features include a contrast between the rašaʿ and the ṣaddîq, discussion of the two ways, a preoccupation with retribution (theodicy), practical advice, and fear of Yhwh.[135] Through careful examination of the moth in Psalm 39 and the senseless horse and mule in Psalm 32, Tova Forti adds another criterion, animal imagery, as a category that can deepen a particular wisdom psalm's identity within the wisdom genre.[136] If indeed animals make effective markers of wisdom speech, as we have already noticed, then we might also consider the role of plants in the Psalter as wisdom tropes. It is admittedly true, as Gören Eidevall has observed, that rocks and rivers (not flowers and agriculture) dominate the Psalter's landscape, and Eidevall goes so far as to say that this poetic geography is "rather barren and desolate."[137] Where animals, flowers, grain, trees, and grass do appear, then, their symbolic value is enhanced.[138]

The Psalmists as a group do not consider plants or animals in isolation; their existence is viewed within a more or less coherently

---

135. Roland E. Murphy, "A Consideration of the Classification 'Wisdom Psalms,'" 157–67 in *Congress Volume, Bonn*; VTSup 9 (Leiden: Brill, 1962), at 159–60.

136. Forti, *Animal Imagery in Proverbs*, 160–68. Note also Katharine J. Dell, "The Use of Animal Imagery in the Psalms and Wisdom Literature of Ancient Israel," *Scottish Journal of Theology* 53 (2000): 275–91.

137. Gören Eidevall, "Metaphorical Landscapes in the Psalms," 13–21 in Pierre van Hecke and Antje Labahn, eds., *Metaphors in the Psalms* (BETL 231; Leuven: Peeters, 2010), at 17. Eidevall sees this putative lack of agricultural imagery in the Psalms as evidence of the urban- and Temple-oriented nature of the Psalms genre.

138. Significant nature imagery in the Psalms appears, e.g., in Psalms 1, 8, 9, 19, 37, 49, 65, 67, 72, 80, 85, 90, 92, 104, 107, 128, 129, 144, 147, 148. See Stephen A. Geller, "Wisdom, Nature and Piety in Some Biblical Psalms," 101–21 in Tzvi Abusch, ed., *Riches Hidden in Secret Places: Ancient Near Eastern Studies in Memory of Thorkild Jacobsen* (Winona Lake, IN: Eisenbrauns, 2002), esp. on Psalms 8, 19, and 104, and with some brief comparisons to nature wisdom in Job.

articulated "cosmic geography."[139] In its prominent use of nature themes Psalm 72 makes a helpful case study for examining this geography in order to understand how an author can build a political narrative by characterizing the interrelationship between human and plant selves.[140] Probably a coronation hymn for an Israelite king (whether contemporary with the monarchy or in later memory),[141] Psalm 72 appears to be a prayer of dedication or blessing, using a jussive-style invocation ("may he . . ." or "let him . . .") to suggest direct connections between the king's administration of divine *mišpāṭ* ("justice") and *ṣĕdāqāh* (v. 1) and the fructification of the land:

> (3) May the mountains yield prosperity (*šālôm*) for the people, and the hills, righteousness . . .
>
> (6) May he [the king] come down like rain upon the mown grass, like dripping showers upon the earth . . .

139. For cosmic geography and related concepts, see, e.g., Wayne Horowitz, *Mesopotamian Cosmic Geography* (Mesopotamian Civilizations 8; Winona Lake, IN: Eisenbrauns, 1998); Rachel Havrelock, "The Two Maps of Israel's Land," *JBL* 126 (2007): 649–67; Thorkild Jacobsen, "Mesopotamia: The Cosmos as a State," 125–84 in Henri Frankfort, et al., *The Intellectual Adventure of Ancient Man: An Essay on Speculative Thought in the Ancient Near East* (Chicago: University of Chicago Press, 1946); Lawrence Stager, "Jerusalem and the Garden of Eden," 183–94 in *Eretz-Israel* 26 (Frank Moore Cross Volume, ed. Baruch A. Levine, 1999); William P. Brown, *The Seven Pillars of Creation: The Bible, Science, and the Ecology of Wonder* (Oxford: Oxford University Press, 2010), 33–77.

140. Other instructive examples would be the image in Psalm 80 of Israel as a vine brought out from Egypt and later ravaged, as well as the parallels between Torah and natural cycles in Pss 147:7-11, 16-20; 148:3-10. On Psalm 72 see Hans-Joachim Kraus, *Psalms 60–150*, trans. Hilton C. Oswald (Minneapolis: Fortress Press, 1993; first published 1978), 74–81; Carmen Diller, "Er soll leben, solange die Sonne bleibt" (Ps 72,5): Die räumlichen und zeitlichen Dimensionen der Köningsherrschaft in Psalm 72," 1–26 in Carmen Diller, Kristinn Ólason, and Ralf Rotherbusch, eds., *Festschrift für Hubert Irsigler* (Herders Biblische Studien 64; Freiburg: Herder, 2010); on the solar imagery in the psalm see Uwe Becker, "Psalm 72 und der Alte Orient. Grenzen und Chancen eines Vergleichs," 123–40 in Angelika Berlejung and Raik Heckl, eds., *Mensch und König. Studien zur Anthropologie des Alten Testaments* (Freiburg: Herder, 2008); on the "economic code" of the psalm see David Jobling, "Deconstruction and the Political Analysis of Biblical Texts: A Jamesonian Reading of Psalm 72," *Semeia* 59 (1992): 95–127, esp. 111–13.

141. The psalm begins with the unique superscript *lišlōmōh* (to/for/by Solomon), though I am inclined to view this attribution with the same caution as scholars generally afford to the *lĕdāwid* superscript.

(16) May there be an abundance of grain in the earth, may it wave on the top of the mountains, its fruit like Lebanon; and may the city-dwellers sprout forth (wĕyāṣîṣû mēʿîr) like the green things of the earth.

Humans become a direct part of the nature narrative: the sky is raining righteous Solomons and the fields blooming forth with people. Reciprocally, mountains and hills act as purveyors of šālôm and ṣĕdāqāh.[142]

Nearly all of the generally-recognized wisdom psalms (Psalms 1, 32, 34, 37, 49, 112, 128) rely on striking floral and faunal analogies for the human self. Psalm 1 is most famous, standing as it does at the head of the Psalter.[143] Here the ṣaddîq

(3) . . . is like a tree, planted by streams of water, which yields its fruit in season; its leaves do not fade, and all that he does prospers.

Othmar Keel situates this type of tree imagery as Egyptian in origin, where the tree signifies the "true silent ones."[144] Frequently found in afterlife iconography, these trees serve as reward for the righteous, providing nourishment and shade.[145] One particular Egyptian funerary image, from the tomb of Amenakht at Deir el Medinah, serves as a striking point of reference for thinking about the analogical relationship between the human and the tree in Psalm 1 (Figure 4).

142. See Klaus Koch, "The Old Testament View of Nature," *Anticipation* 25 (1979): 47–52.
143. See Jerome F. D. Creach, "Like a Tree Planted by the Temple Stream: The Portrait of the Righteous in Psalm 1:3," *CBQ* 61 (1999): 34–46.
144. Othmar Keel, *The Symbolism of the Biblical World: Ancient Near Eastern Iconography and the Book of Psalms*, trans. Timothy J. Hallett (New York: Seabury Press, 1978; first German publication 1972), 354–55.
145. Christopher B. Hays, "'There Is Hope for a Tree': Job's Hope for the Afterlife in the Light of Egyptian Tree Imagery," presentation at the 2012 Society of Biblical Literature Annual Meeting (Chicago, IL, 19 November 2012); John H. Taylor, *Death and Afterlife in Ancient Egypt* (Chicago: University of Chicago Press, 2001), 127.

Figure 4. Painting on stucco; Deir el Medinah; Tomb of Amenakht (no. 218), ca. 14th–11th c. BCE.

The figure kneels beneath the palm, melding with the trunk of the tree so that the comfort and success of the human is in fact a part of the thriving tree. The human fuses into the ground, partaking of the same nourishment as the tree, fully integrated into the ecological narrative of floral abundance and natural success accorded to deities in the afterlife.[146] Plant thriving forms the basis for comparison again in Psalm 128:1-4, where the righteous family blossoms:

(1) . . . Happy are all who fear Yhwh, who walk in his ways;

(2) you will eat from the labor of your hands; you will be happy, and it will be good for you—

(3) your wife will be like a fruitful vine in the midst of your house; your sons will be like olive plants surrounding your table.

(4) This is how he will be blessed, the man who fears Yhwh.

Clearly, the metaphor is closely related to actual agricultural abundance—the family is not just "like" these plants; rather, the wise male who is the subject of admonition will work hard and enjoy the tangible fruit of the vine and the real products of successful olive cultivation. The good food and familial blessing are not the product of specific agricultural knowledge but instead, as indicated by the literary inclusion in verses 1 and 4, the "fear of Yhwh" (*yĕrē' yhwh*) produces all of this.

The flourishing tree as a wisdom motif is not univocal, however. In Psalm 37 the *wicked* are like vegetation—transient, marginal vegetation, low to the ground and about to die:[147]

(vv. 1-2) . . . Do not be dismayed because of the wicked, do not be jealous of the workers of iniquity; for like the grass (*ḥāṣîr*) they will quickly wither, and like the green herb (*yereq dešeʾ*) they will fade away.

---

146. This stands in contrast to Job's complaint in Job 14:7-12. In a recent study Amy Erickson, "'Without My Flesh I Will See God': Job's Rhetoric of the Body," *JBL* 132 (2013): 295–313, at 304, finds similarly incompatible notions of the "self" as corporeal body between Psalms and Job. On the body theme in Job see also Alec Basson, "Just Skin and Bones: The Longing for Wholeness of the Body in the Book of Job," *VT* 58 (2008) 287–99.

147. Compare with Ps 126:5-7: "May they be ashamed and turned back, all who hate Zion; may they be like grass on housetops that withers before it comes up, with which the one who reaps does not fill his hand . . ."

The wicked may also thrive like a tree, but again this success is only illusory; verse 35 has a difficult or possibly a corrupted reading in the Masoretic Text, but may read:[148]

> (vv. 35-36) I saw the wicked in a state of ruthless oppression (*'āriṣ ûmit'āreh*), like a cedar of Lebanon (MT: *kĕ'ezrāḥ ra'ănān*; lit. "like a local green tree" [?]). I passed by again, but he was no more—I sought him, but he could not be found.

The reference to the "cedar of Lebanon"—if this emendation is correct—invokes a very specific tree tradition within the Hebrew Bible, which we have already had occasion to explore above (Judg. 9:15; 1 Kgs. 10:21; Ezek. 17:3-4; 27:5; 31:3; cf. Ps. 72:16). In the earliest explicit interpretive tradition we know of for any Psalm, 4Q171 (commentary on Psalm 37 from Qumran), the tree here in 37:35 is none other than the *'iš hakkāzāb*, "the Man of the Lie" (the ultimate opponent of the speaker).[149]

Other wisdom-psalm nature analogies involve animals, mostly in simple negative terms with a Proverbial feel wherein the Psalmist compares himself to the brutishness or ignorance of animals. Psalm 32:9 advises the listener to avoid acting like a horse or mule, "without understanding, (who needs to be) restrained with bit and bridle ... ." Though not usually considered in the formal corpus of wisdom psalms, Psalm 73 exhibits clear wisdom themes (focus on theodicy, the fate of the wicked versus the righteous). The speaker compares himself to an animal in verse 22: "I was stupid, and without knowledge—I was like an untamed animal (*bĕhēmôt*) before you." Psalm 49:11-13, 21 (English 10-12, 20) uses an animal comparison refrain to speak of the inevitability of death:

---

148. Cf. Hans-Joachim Kraus, *Psalms 1–59*, trans. Hilton C. Oswald (Minneapolis: Fortress Press, 1988; first pub. 1978), 401–4.

149. See, conveniently, Florentino García Martínez and Eibert J. C. Tigchelaar, eds., *The Dead Sea Scrolls Study Edition*, Vol. I (Leiden: Brill, 1997), 346–47.

(11) For we look at the wise (ḥăkāmîm), and they die; together the fool and the ignorant perish, and they leave their wealth to others.

(12) Their grave is their home forever, their dwelling places from generation to generation, (though) their names are recited upon the earth [?].[150]

(13) Humans are fragile, they cannot remain (yālîn); they are like the animals that perish. . . .

(15) . . . Like sheep they are appointed to Sheol; Death will shepherd them, they go down straight to the grave,[151] and their form wastes away—Sheol is their abode . . .

(21) . . . Humans are fragile, they do not understand (yābîn); they are like the animals that perish.

In this world animals die and humans die; both are leveled as a marker of humility, as Qoheleth bitterly notices in Ecclesiastes 3:17-22. Indeed, this psalm shares many philosophical and linguistic features with Qoheleth, though in Psalm 49:15 the author (or a later redactor) holds out special hope for himself: "But God will ransom my soul from the power of Sheol—he will receive me. Selah."

Psalm 34:11(10) ventures into more complex realms, posing a juxtaposition that requires deeper reflection: "Young lions (kĕpîrîm) struggle in poverty (rāšû) and hunger—but those who seek Yhwh do not lack any good thing." The root here for "poverty, lack," rwš, is used twenty-three other times in the Hebrew Bible—mostly in Proverbs, and always with regard to human poverty.[152] The image thus invites reflection on shared notions of success between the human and animal world, and even introduces a conundrum of animal theodicy: how can such powerful creatures fail to provide food for their young? The main point here for the Psalmist is obviously that the fearers of Yhwh receive protection above and

---

150. Cf. Kraus, *Psalms 1–59*, 479: "they have called lands their own."

151. Emending *yĕšārîm labbōqer* to *yĕšārîm laqqeber*, though the combination of *yāšār* and *qeber* is admittedly awkward.

152. 1 Sam. 18:23; 2 Sam. 12:1-4; Ps. 82:3; Prov. 10:4; 13:7-8, 23; 14:20; 17:5; 18:23; 19:1, 7, 22; 22:2, 7; 28:3, 6, 27; 29:13; Eccl. 4:14; 5:7(8).

beyond even the mightiest predator, but the conflation of human economic terminology with the lion forges a narrative of human morality that can rise above the brutish failures of other life forms.

Qoheleth's Royal Garden and the Un-Created World

As a final stop on our selective tour through nature wisdom imagery in the Hebrew Bible and elsewhere in the ancient Near East we arrive at the book of Ecclesiastes. The speaking voice in the book, Qoheleth ("Preacher to the Assembly"), takes on the *persona* of Solomon but in fact represents a much later author, living as late as the fifth to third centuries BCE.[153] The Solomonic mask the author dons in the first verse of the book ("The words of Qoheleth, son of David, king in Jerusalem . . ."), as Peter Machinist aptly notes, does not cover the entire face of the narrator;[154] rather, the narrator uses Solomon's legendary achievements, wealth, and wisdom to craft a pointed criticism of all human endeavor.

Among his many forays into the meaningless or absurd state of existence (which he frequently labels *hebel*, "vapor, breath"), Qoheleth uses multiple nature images. In the opening address nature comes off as relentlessly cyclical—the water cycle goes round and round, the sun up and down, and so on. Such processes might have evoked happy wonder for Qoheleth, but instead natural cycles induce depression: "all things are wearisome" (Eccl. 1:8). Nature is dreary, predictable, and inevitable. Trees lie down where they fall, as for

---

153. This point is virtually undisputed; see, e.g., Choon-Leong Seow, *Ecclesiastes* (AB 18C; New York: Doubleday, 1997); Michael V. Fox, *Ecclesiastes* (JPS Bible Commentary; Philadelphia: Jewish Publication Society, 2004).

154. Peter Machinist, "The Voice of the Historian in the Ancient Near Eastern and Mediterranean World," *Interpretation* 57 (2003): 117–37, at 133–34. See also Machinist's "Fate, *miqreh*, and Reason: Some Reflections on Qoheleth and Biblical Thought," 159–75 in Ziony Zevit, Seymour Gitin, and Michael Sokoloff, eds., *Solving Riddles and Untying Knots: Biblical, Epigraphic, and Semitic Studies in Honor of Jonas C. Greenfield* (Winona Lake, IN: Eisenbrauns, 1995), and Brown, *Seven Pillars*, 178.

Qoheleth humans lie in the grave, without movement (Eccl. 11:3). The wind (*rûaḥ*) is an image of useless tantalization—"pursuit of wind" (*rĕ'ût rûaḥ*) is a frequent image of *hebel* (1:14, 17; 2:11, 17, 26; 4:4, 6, 16; 6:9). Human toil, evil, work, enjoyment, and everything else occur specifically "under the sun" (*taḥat haššemeš*; e.g., 1:3; 2:11; 3:16; 4:1; 5:13; 6:1; 8:9; 9:3; 10:5), a reminder of the droning or even oppressive constancy of nature, the sun burning above as a singular, judgmental, unblinking eye of remote cosmic or political leadership. There is a time to plant and a time to harvest (Eccl. 3:2), but there is little to gain from any of it (3:9). Such a world has no history to speak of, and perhaps even no future.[155]

In thematic parallel to Psalm 49, Qoheleth dares to suggest that God has created humans not for kingly rule over the created world but rather for the purpose of humiliation (Eccl. 3:18-22): God wants to "test" or "purge/purify" (*bārar*) them to show that they are merely animals (*bĕhēmāh*). Qoheleth does not definitively declare that humans, like animals, have no afterlife—rather, he says that he has heard of the idea of human spirits rising upward and animal spirits descending down and concludes that he simply doesn't know (*mî yôdēaʿ*; 3:22). An animal proverb points up the advantage to living a simple life in the face of anonymous, eternal death (Eccl. 9:4): "a living dog is better than a dead lion" (see also 10:1, 11). Fish are captured in nets and birds fly into snares, as humans too are snagged by calamities (9:12). No human can anticipate these snares, just as animals ignorantly swim or fly into them. Qoheleth saw corruption at every level of his society, perhaps that of the first few decades of Hellenistic rule in the Mediterranean (beginning in 333 BCE); power was felt to be so intrusive that even a little bird could tattle one's private thoughts to the paranoid king (Eccl. 10:20).[156] As opposed to

---

155. As noted by Brown, *Seven Pillars*, 180, 189.

the Proverbial emphasis on nature's success brought about by diligent human effort, Qoheleth encourages rising early and planting, yet is quick to point out that it may not work (11:6).

Two more of Qoheleth's engagements with nature imagery stand out for our purposes here. The first comes in Ecclesiastes 2:4-8, where the narrator takes up the literary genre of the ancient Near Eastern royal achievement inscription, commenting specifically in verses 4-6 on royal garden projects:

> (4) I raised up great works: I built houses for myself, I planted vineyards for myself,
> (5) I made gardens (*gannôt*) and parks (*parēsîm*) for myself, and I planted fruit trees of all kinds in them;
> (6) I made pools of water for myself, to water a forest of sprouting trees.

This passage bears the marks of the Mesopotamian royal inscription genre used by multiple Assyrian kings, and even more locally it resembles Northwest Semitic royal "résumé" inscriptions such as the Tell Siran bottle inscription (ca. 600 BCE) and the Mesha stela (ca. 840–830 BCE).[157] In the résumé style of this genre the repeated use of the perfect ("I built . . . I planted . . . I made . . .") emphasizes past achievements,[158] and the repeated use of the word *lî* ("for myself") centers attention on the king's own wisdom. Canals and irrigation projects (as in Eccl. 2:6) are of course practical economic achievements, but they also represent profound ideologies of abundance, mythic victory, and righteousness. Consider, for example, an inscription of the Assyrian Tukulti-Ninurta I (1244–1208 BCE) at the foundation of his self-titled Kar-Tukulti-

---

156. For the dating of the book here I follow Machinist in "The Voice of the Historian" and "Fate, *miqreh*, and Reason."

157. On the Tell Siran inscription see Douglas J. Green, *"I Undertook Great Works": The Ideology of Domestic Achievements in West Semitic Royal Inscriptions* (FAT 2/41; Tübingen: Mohr Siebeck, 2010), 266–81.

158. As pointed out by Choon-Leong Seow, *Ecclesiastes*, 128, 151.

Ninurta: "I opened up a *miṭirtu*-canal that ensured the life (*napultu*) of the land and bore prosperity (*nuḫšu*) for his city."[159] Here Tukulti-Ninurta I adds interpretive depth to his water-work: he not only digs canals as a mundane tactician; rather, his right rule creates and maintains a divinely ordained symbolic geography of abundance.[160]

This nature narrative of monarchic achievement can be "read" visually in striking examples from neo-Assyrian reliefs. A mid-seventh-century BCE panel has the Assyrian king proudly standing in a garden; a major aqueduct and its channels flow down from the top right, irrigating rows of many varieties of trees (Figure 5).[161] The composition places the king, housed in an elegant structure (possibly a Temple), atop a kind of "cosmic mountain," from which his military prowess and administration of justice implicitly form the pinnacle of natural abundance and control over nature's boundaries.[162] The altar, a reminder of cultic piety, sits below the king on a kind of axis along the near-center of the mountain, and the body of the king may be a cipher for the god Assur himself. Some of these same features appear in the garden scene of Sargon II at Khorsabad (8th c. BCE; Figure 6), though the king is not present.

---

159. Information here from Green, *"I Undertook Great Works,"* 52–53; see pp. 46–63 on the "king as gardener" motif, with ample documentation of the sources. See also William P. Brown, *The Ethos of Cosmos: The Genesis of Moral Imagination in the Bible* (Grand Rapids: Eerdmans, 1999), 248–52.

160. Green, *"I Undertook Great Works,"* 52; on the abundance theme in Mesopotamia see Irene J. Winter, "Representing Abundance: A Visual Dimension of the Agrarian State," 199–225 in eadem, *On Art in the Ancient Near East*, Vol. 2 (Culture and History of the Ancient Near East 34.2; Leiden: Brill, 2010), at 213–14, as well as eadem, "Ornament," 174–75.

161. Richard David Barnett and the British Museum, *Sculptures from the North Palace of Ashurbanipal at Nineveh (668–627 B.C.)* (London: British Museum Publications, 1976), pl. XXIII; see discussion of these images in Stager, "Jerusalem as the Garden of Eden," 183–86. Note also Izak Cornelius, "Paradise Motifs in the 'Eschatology' of the Minor Prophets and the Iconography of the Ancient Near East. The Concepts of Fertility, Water, Trees, and 'Tierfrieden' and Gen 2–3," *Journal of Northwest Semitic Languages* 14 (1988): 41–83.

162. Compare with Psalm 72, discussed above. The scene beneath the garden hill (see Barnett, *Sculptures*, pl. XIII) depicts subjugated Elamite soldiers; their subdued stance below the garden places the enemy in a state of subjugated tranquility on par with the natural world above it.

Figure 5 (left): Assyrian palace relief; irrigated garden (mid-7th c. BCE);

Figure 6 (right): Assyrian palace relief of Sargon II at Khorsabad (8th c. BCE).

Judean and Israelite royalty may well have cultivated official gardens in Jerusalem or Samaria, though we do not have the same kind of evidence for this that we have in Assyrian reliefs or in lavish later traditions of the "hanging gardens" of Babylon. The *šadmôt qidrôn* mentioned in 2 Kings 23:4 and Jeremiah 31:40 may, some suggest, be translated as "cascade of terraced gardens and parks,"[163] and archaeological evidence suggests a royal garden complex at Ramat Rahel in the seventh to fourth centuries BCE (with exotic plants imported during the Persian period).[164] For Qoheleth the motif here in 2:4-6 may be a literary reflection on 1 Kings 5:9-14 (English 4:29-34), in which the narrator presents Solomon as an extraordinary gardener in wise command of his kingdom. We do know that rulers in the ancient Near East took great pride in control over nature, especially through exotic excursions, harvesting of rare trees, and

163. Stager, "Jerusalem and the Garden of Eden," 183.
164. See Dafna Langgut, Yuval Gadot, Naomi Porat, and Oded Lipschits, "Fossil Pollen Reveals the Secrets of the Royal Persian Garden at Ramat Rahel, Jerusalem," *Palynology* 37 (2013): 115–29, and brief discussion in Geoffrey P. Miller, *The Ways of a King: Legal and Political Ideas in the Bible* (Journal of Ancient Judaism Supplements 7; Göttingen: Vandenhoeck & Ruprecht, 2011), 35.

prestige animal hunts.[165] Royal command over nature was certainly a native Israelite monarchic theme, though we do not yet know the extent to which these kinds of expressions correspond with any particular individual in Iron Age Israel.[166] For Qoheleth, however, what does all of this control really amount to? Futility. The adaptation of this royal accomplishment résumé serves in the end to criticize the value of royal achievement—the echoes of the royal inscription genre here in Ecclesiastes 2 are parody.[167] This mockery may even serve to criticize one example of the Bible's own creation tradition: the terms in Eccl. 2:4-6 for "plant," "garden," "tree"/"all"/ "fruit," "water," "sprout," and "make," though common enough in Hebrew generally, all appear clustered (sometimes repetitively) in the creation accounts of Genesis 1–2 to describe God's own gardening projects.[168] Insofar as the king reenacts God's control, then, meaninglessness can be the only result.

The second passage of interest comes in Qoheleth's final, haunting address (Eccl. 12:1-8), where the breakdown of the body finds analogy in natural decay and motifs of un-creation:

(1) Remember your creator (*bôrĕʾêkā*) in the days of your youth, before evil days come, and the years draw near when you will say, "I have no pleasure in them";

---

165. See the wealth of data on this front collected by Halpern, *David's Secret Demons*, 114–21.

166. See Ronald Simkins, *Creator and Creation: Nature in the Worldview of Ancient Israel* (Peabody, MA: Hendrickson, 1994), 39, 167–72; Hans H. Schmid, "Creation, Righteousness, and Salvation," 102–17 in Bernhard W. Anderson, ed., *Creation in the Old Testament* (Philadelphia: Fortress Press, 1984), part of which appeared earlier in Schmid's *Altorientalische Welt in der alttestamentlichen Theologie* (Zürich: Theologicher Verlag, 1974); Roland E. Murphy, *The Tree of Life: An Exploration of Biblical Wisdom Literature* (Grand Rapids: Eerdmans, 2002; first pub. 1990), 111–32.

167. I first began to think of this passage as a mockery of the ancient Near Eastern genre in a presentation by Peter Machinist, "Mesopotamian and Biblical Historiography: Comparisons, Models, Reflections," 2011 Society of Biblical Literature Annual Meeting (San Francisco, CA; 21 November 2011). Compare with Isaiah 10:5–15, 37:21–29 regarding elements of this genre.

168. Arian Verheij, "Paradise Retried: On Qoheleth 2.4-6," *JSOT* 50 (1991): 113–15.

(2) before the sun and the light and the moon and the stars go dark, and the clouds return with rain . . .

(5) . . . when they fear heights, and terrors in the road; the almond blossoms, the grasshopper is burdened down, and the caper-berry fails to satisfy (*wĕtāpēr hāʾăbiyyônāh*).[169] For all humans must go to their eternal home, and mourners circle up in the streets . . .

Taking up the notion of a "cosmopolis" (cosmos polis) as a totalizing system of meaning, Timothy Beal persuasively argues that Qoheleth longed for some new order beyond the existential breakdown he saw in his own system of values and in his society as a whole. Beal interprets the imagery of darkness in Eccl. 12:2 not simply as the silent sleep of death but more specifically as an "apocalyptic in-breaking of chaos" (with reference to the use of *ḥōšek* in prophetic texts of judgment; see Joel 2:2; Zeph. 1:15; Ezek. 32:7-8).[170] This darkness is a reversal of the "good" created order of Genesis 1, just as it is in Job's famous lament in Job 3 (*yĕhî ḥōšek*). Citing Jacques Derrida's reading of Hamlet in *Specters of Marx*, Beal sees Qoheleth here entering a "chaotic desert," bleakly hoping (yet still hoping) for some renewal.[171]

Conclusion

The invocation of nature (and specifically plants and animals) in wisdom sayings is a common motif within the ancient Near Eastern world, and I have gone to some length here to demonstrate the pervasiveness of these images in order to prepare us to hear the

---

169. Or possibly: "and desire fails . . ." Here I follow the translation of Timothy K. Beal, "C(ha)osmopolis: Qoheleth's Last Words," 290–304 in Tod Linefelt and Timothy K. Beal, eds., *God in the Fray: A Tribute to Walter Brueggemann* (Minneapolis: Augsburg Fortress, 1998), at 293. The reference to a "grasshopper" or "locust" here may be a symbolic reference to the penis—"the penis droops (in old age)"—and the caper-berry was used as an aphrodisiac (Seow, *Ecclesiastes*, 379–80).

170. Beal, "C(ha)osmopolis," 296. See also Brown, *Seven Pillars*, 182–83 on this imagery.

171. Beal, "C(ha)osmopolis," 303.

Joban plant metaphors and the struggle to define Job's narrative on those terms. At points in some of these wisdom traditions, plants and humans meld seamlessly together, growing and responding to one another—at other points authors are quick to point out the stark differences between humans and plants to make a didactic point. One cannot help but notice that nature is sometimes used almost willy-nilly in the Hebrew Bible; it has no clear, overarching "status" as a single theme, and creation itself is multiply narrated (through peaceful speech acts in Genesis 1 or violent struggle in Psalm 74). Other than the basic and vague conviction that God is in control of nature, there is no single "biblical view" of nature or nature's consequences for humankind.

That being said, we do find Israel inevitably in contact with the environment, as plant and animal actors play roles in its national drama. Perhaps in a most loaded manner in Deuteronomy, nature is charged with multiple possibilities—nature is truly "natural," but sometimes it is a type of punishment, like a lightning bolt in God's hand. When we use the word "nature" with reference to the biblical world generally we may erroneously load nature down with secularist notions of non-"religious" causation, a concept that had no meaning in the ancient Near East. Rather, in the Hebrew Bible at least, the land of Canaan has a numinous quality before Israel or any Davidic king arrives there. Israel's nature wisdom materials participate in an act of Israelite self-making as they forge narrative possibilities for considering natural failure or success vis-à-vis individual or national success. These narratives, like all narratives, are inherently ambiguous and multivocal. With this in mind, we now turn directly to the book of Job, where Job, the Friends, and God all make distinct and competing attempts to characterize the plant and animal world.

3

Eco-Anthropologies in the Joban Dialogues

Approaching Job

Job's Friends are infamous for their attempts to comfort Job, and the broad strokes of their arguments are well known: righteous behavior produces a life of harmony and prosperity while wickedness causes sure ruin. In truth, however, the notion that the Friends represent a single viewpoint or argumentative strategy is not exactly borne out by a close reading of the text.[1] Rather, the Friends offer a storm of conflicting viewpoints. Here are two of them: First, there is the "Deuteronomistic,"[2] or "Proverbial" strategy—life is a type of cosmic

---

1. See, e.g., some comments on this in Urmas Nõmmik, *Die Freundesreden des ursprünglichen Hiobdialogs: Eine form- und traditionsgeschichtliche Studie* (BZAW 410; Berlin: de Gruyter, 2010), esp. 140–58.

2. In twentieth-century biblical scholarship the term "Deuteronomist" and "Deuteronomistic History" became popular shorthand for discussing the author and the literary product that is, roughly speaking, the books of Deuteronomy, Joshua, Judges, Samuel, and Kings, which tell a story of Israel's rise as a nation in the land, the rise of the monarchy under David and Solomon, and then the decline and eventual destruction of the nation. This literary work operates under a certain assumption about human disobedience and divine punishment, namely, that human disobedience prompts divine punishment. Some had speculated that this storyline was compiled by an individual in ancient Israel (even in the mid-6th c. BCE, specifically) who attempted to

math equation (framed as a covenant) in which excellent moral choice results in excellent results, while poor choices result in destruction (see, for example, Job 4:7-8, or Proverbs 10:2-4). A second option is what we might call the "Mysterious God Strategy." Here the comforter evokes great empathy for the sufferer, ultimately throwing hands in the air and proclaiming—both for the specific case and in general—the incomprehensible movements of blessing or punishment (see, for example, Job 4:17, or Eccl. 7:15, 9:2).

Even though speakers may roll out these two rhetorical angles in the same speech (as in Job 11:7-8, 13-20), they seem to be deeply at odds with one another—just as they were, hundreds of years before Job was written, in the so-called "Babylonian Theodicy" (possibly composed around 1000 BCE), a story very much like the book of Job in that it tells of a man in the throes of grievous suffering who engages in a back-and-forth argument with a friend. At certain points the Friend asserts that the Sufferer's predicament is the clear result of impiety. He makes accusations such as the following:[3]

> You have let your subtle mind wander,
> [. . .] you have overthrown wisdom.
> You have spurned propriety, you have besmirched (every) code. (XX.1-3)
> Unless you serve the will of a god, what will be your profit?
> He who bears a god's yoke shall never want for food, though it may be meager. (XX.5-6)

Alternatively, other flights of speculation from the Friend appear to sow doubt regarding the straightforward purposes of the deities and the righteousness-reward schema:

justify God's deeds in light of Israel's long march into apostasy and subsequent exile in 586 BCE at the hand of the Babylonians. See the classic formulation of this theory by Martin Noth, *The Deuteronomistic History*, trans. J. Doull, J. Barton, M. D. Rutter, and Daffyd R. Ap-Thomas (JSOTSS 15; Sheffield: JSOT Press, 1981; an edition of this book was first published in German in 1943).

3. "Babylonian Theodicy," translation from Benjamin R. Foster, *COS* I, 492-95.

> You are a mere child, the purpose of the gods is remote as the
>   netherworld. (VI.3)
> The strategy of a god is [as remote as] innermost heaven,
> The command of a goddess cannot be dr[awn out].
> Teeming humanity well understands trouble . . . . (VIII.4-6)

Such flailing in the face of suffering is to be expected. Even in
tranquil times, as recent neuroscientific research has demonstrated,
the human psychological experience is chaotic, fragmented, and
contradictory.[4] The isolated self would seem not to approach
suffering with a coherent strategy, by default—only organized,
culturally managed systems (such as those traditionally provided by
religions, for example) can construct a consistent worldview that
persists through suffering and pain. Returning to Ricoeur's assertion
that "in many narratives the self seeks its identity on the scale of an
entire life," we try to understand the struggle in these narratives. To
be sure, the tension among efforts to understand the self in Job is even
encoded in the book's attempt to marry differing literary genres (at
minimum, prose and poetry) to narrate these selves. Before moving
into a reading of the text itself, with its narratives of plant and animal
lives, I want to briefly examine some of the historical-critical issues
evoked by the relationship among Job's Prologue, poetic debates, and
Epilogue. Because I begin my analysis with the Prologue, and treat
it as an organic part of the ecological narratives that follow, some
history of the debate and justification for my own approach must be
given.

Scholars have most often viewed the prose tale that launches the
primary action in the book as either a late addition to the "core"
poetic debates in chapters 3–41 or as a preexisting folktale adopted
by the poet as a framing device for the argument. Already in the

---

4. Patrick McNamara, *The Neuroscience of Religious Experience* (Cambridge: Cambridge
University Press, 2009), 32–38.

late seventeenth century Richard Simon said perhaps all that can be said confidently about the question of multiple authorship: it "is easy to be known by the diversity of the style of the two first Chapters of Job, which have been put at the beginning of this Poem by way of Argument or Prologue."[5] In Simon's wake, modern scholarly opinions on the topic are legion, following the usual path of basically convincing nineteenth-century German studies by the likes of Karl Budde, Bernhard Duhm, and others, who pointed out not only differences in language and style between Prologue and Dialogues, but also striking divergences in the religious rhetoric of the separate sections.[6] Recent attempts to address the question have almost universally acknowledged a plurality of authorship, though it is increasingly popular for investigations to focus on the literary meaning of the book as it stands—Prologue and Dialogue together as a meaningful whole.[7]

There are instances within the poetic dialogues that assume and refer directly to the Prologue, suggesting that even if the Prologue and Dialogues are of separate genre and authorship they have been fused together in a thoughtful and meaningful way. In the first place, the discussion in chapters 3–41 simply does not make sense without the Prologue, and thus the Prologue's logic (whether any individual speaker affirms or opposes it) is everywhere presumed.

---

5. Richard Simon, *A Critical History of the Old Testament*, trans. "A Person of Quality" (London: Jacob Tonson, 1682), 1.iv, 34. I have updated the spelling in this quotation.

6. E.g., Karl Budde, *Das Buch Hiob übersetzt und erklärt*, 2d ed. (Göttingen: Vandenhoeck & Ruprecht, 1913); Bernhard Duhm, *Das Buch Hiob* (Freiburg: J. C. B. Mohr, 1897); see the extended discussion in Hans Peter Müller, *Das Hiobproblem: Seine Stellung und Entstehung im Alten Orient und im Alten Testament*, 3d ed. (Darmstadt: Wissenschaftliche Buchgesellschaft, 1995), and also, more recently, Konrad Schmid, "Das Hiobproblem und der Hiobprolog," 9–34 in Manfred Oeming and Konrad Schmid, eds., *Hiobs Weg. Stationen von Menschen im Leid* (Biblisch-theologische Studien 45; Neukirchen-Vluyn: Butzon & Berker Kevelaer, 2001), and other literature cited there. On the language of the Prologue see Avi Hurvitz, "The Date of the Prose-Tale of Job Linguistically Reconsidered," *HTR* 67 (1974): 17–34.

7. See the overview of positions in Carol Newsom, *The Book of Job: A Contest of Moral Imaginations* (Oxford: Oxford University Press, 2003), 4–10.

Comparable wisdom materials from the ancient Near East, such as the "Babylonian Theodicy," usually provide some sort of context or implicit narration to describe the suffering under debate. Even though the "Babylonian Theodicy" does begin with dialogue directly, the first speech tersely and cleverly provides the equivalent of a Prologue, as the Sufferer recounts his woes in summary fashion. The Sufferer is addressing his companion in the dialogue, but of course the *narrator* is primarily telling the *audience* of his woes so as to frame the debate. More directly, in what is arguably a closer formal parallel to the book of Job, an eighteenth-to-seventeenth-century BCE Egyptian work entitled "The Eloquent Peasant," we find a framing narrative around the "poetic" complaints of the eloquent peasant himself, explaining how he arrives at his situation of complaint and how that situation is resolved.[8] My point here, then, is that comparable ancient works contain either a direct narrative prologue or a functional prologue, and Assyriologists and Egyptologists seem not to frequently discuss these introductions as secondary. We might best situate ourselves as readers—even while mindful of historical-critical concerns—by first assuming a basic continuity between Prologue and Dialogue, as opposed to viewing the Prologue through the lens of alien composition and disjunction.

Moreover, specific examples of the fusion between Prologue and Dialogue are not hard to locate. Bildad's opening volley against Job in chapter 8 contains a rather brusque reference to the death of Job's children in the Prologue: "If your sons sinned (ḥāṭ'û) against him (= God), then he delivered them over to their transgression" (compare Job 1:5). In 11:15 Zophar may well be referring to Job's painful skin ailments (see 2:7-12) when he promises that, upon Job's repentance,

8. Nili Shupak, trans., "The Eloquent Peasant," *COS* I, 98–104. I am not in a position to judge the "prose" qualities of the framing stories as opposed to the "poetry" of the complaints section on a linguistic level in the Egyptian text, though in English one can certainly appreciate the change in tone from the frame to the poetic complaints.

God will "restore your face from blemishes (*mimmûm*)."[9] True, the poet could easily have added a minimum number of such references to the Dialogue to create continuity. But the point remains: the fusion of the Prologue and the Dialogue is not the result of hapless "editors," but rather an intentional literary creation wrought by the Dialogues' author.[10] While the Prologue itself is hardly a simplistic narrative, the notion that it could have formed a self-sufficient story of any kind, treasured as a *Volksbuch* in anything like its present form,[11] is odd.

And what of the book's prose Epilogue (chapter 42), which not only returns to the prose style but does so in a way that seems to comically undercut—or even threaten to obliterate—the philosophical and moral heart of the book? Here one cannot help but agree with those who have found the Epilogue to be cut from a different cloth than either the Prologue or the Dialogues.[12] There are convincing

---

9. *Mûm* may refer to a ritual defect that is not necessarily a skin problem; see, e.g., Leviticus 21–22, 24. A skin problem like this would have signified moral degradation for an ancient audience; see Amy Erickson, "'Without My Flesh I Will See God': Job's Rhetoric of the Body," *JBL* 132 (2013): 295–313, at 299.

10. Alternatively, one may assume that the Dialogues were inherited by the Prologue author, who appended them to his prose story. This view seems less attractive, perhaps on the basis that the Dialogues appear to be the more sophisticated literary and theological expression, and thus we assume that this more sophisticated voice must be responsible for something like the book's final form.

11. See Budde, *Das Buch Hiob*, viii.

12. See the basic review of problems here with bibliography in Choon-Leong Seow, *Job 1–21*, Interpretation and Commentary (Illuminations; Grand Rapids: Eerdmans, 2013), 27–39. Seow's commentary is exemplary of the best available linguistic, text-critical, theological, and literary commentary on Job; the author pays ample attention to nature within Job, and thus his work makes a helpful dialogue partner for at least chapters 1–21. The following works, also in the commentary genre, deserve close attention by those interested in the scholarly debate over these texts. For linguistic issues see esp. Édouard Dhorme, *A Commentary on the Book of Job*, trans. Harold Knight (London: Thomas Nelson & Sons, 1967; French orig. 1926), and Marvin H. Pope, *Job* (AB 15; Garden City, NY: Doubleday, 1965); for literary and theological readings see David J. A. Clines, *Job 1–20* (WBC 17; Dallas: Word Books, 1989), *Job 21–37* (WBC 18A; Nashville: Thomas Nelson, 2006), and *Job 38–42* (WBC 18B; Nashville: Thomas Nelson, 2011); Gerald J. Janzen, *Job* (Interpretation; Atlanta: John Knox, 1985); Samuel E. Balentine, *Job* (Smith & Helwys Bible Commentary; Macon, GA: Smith & Helwys, 2006). For a thorough examination of the forensic imagery in the dialogues see Norman Habel, *The Book of Job*

methods of reading that would meaningfully incorporate the Epilogue into the book as whole, such as Newsom's Bakhtinian interpretation,[13] but the fact is that scholars have felt forced to adduce some theoretical construct or simply leave the book in historical-critical shambles (and then see the editorial layers as "the meaning" of the book itself) to redeem the book's three parts. My own view is that the Epilogue is historically secondary and represents a profound disjunction from the logic of the preceding chapters; we should have an easier time integrating the Prologue with the Dialogues—even the Elihu speech, almost universally considered a total flop, coheres better with the book's other materials than does chapter 42. Therefore, on the historical levels of the book's composition, I posit three layers of "belonging," with the Prologue and Dialogues (different as they may be from one another) as both a historical and thematic core:

Prologue—Dialogues (chapters 1–31)
   Elihu speeches (chapters 32–37)
     Epilogue (chapter 42)

This is hardly an original scheme, but I offer it as a starting point for thinking about the relationship among what are universally debated as extraneous or secondary parts of Job. Not only does each of these sections contain differing narrative logics, but we also find conflicting types of argumentation, imagery, and moral reasoning *within* each section. These intra-genre conflicts have been underappreciated in past analyses,[14] and my task in this chapter is to interrogate these narratives on the basis of their sometimes differing,

---

(OTL; Philadelphia: Westminster, 1985). Other fine works include Naphtali H. Tur-Sinai, *The Book of Job, A New Commentary* (Jerusalem: Kiryath Sepher, 1957); Francis I. Andersen, *Job. An Introduction and Commentary* (TOTC; London and Downers Grove, IL: InterVarsity, 1976); Robert Gordis, *The Book of Job: Commentary, New Translation and Special Studies* (Moreshet 2; New York: JTS Press, 1978).

13. Newsom, *Book of Job*, 20, 258, etc.

14. The notable exception here is Newsom's work in *The Book of Job*.

sometimes complementary strategies for analyzing Job's problem. In what follows I trace one of these strategies in particular, the argument from the natural world, and I present a series of moments in the book, *ad seriatim*, to demonstrate competing strategies for fusing or disassociating the human self from plant and animal selves.[15]

Prologue: Cattle, Slave, and Hedge (chapters 1–2)

Before the dialogue proper begins in chapters 3–31 we must first make note of the floral and faunal imagery in the Prologue (chs. 1–2). Job's personal introduction in the first few verses of the book reveals a flourishing domestic animal world (Job 1:3): seven thousand sheep (small cattle, *ṣōʾn*), three thousand camels (*gĕmalîm*), five hundred yoke of oxen (large cattle, *bāqār*), and five hundred donkeys (*ʾătônôt*). The large, even numbers of the animal herds—all multiples of ten—may be a reflection of the supposedly perfect number of children Job and his wife bear, ten (seven sons and three daughters, Job 1:2).[16] Nature thus bears witness to Job's righteousness. The cycles of human and animal reproduction suggest harmonious breeding and economic success, and math proves his status. Human success and animal success are already mirrors.

A herd of such animals is most appropriate for the quasi-patriarchal lifestyle Job appears to live, though the enormous quantity would be difficult to maintain without the "many slaves" also present (literally

---

15. On animals and dialogical argument in Job see Peter Riede, *Im Spiegel der Tier: Studien zum Verhältnis von Mensch und Tier im alten Israel* (OBO 187; Fribourg: Universitätsverlag, 2002), esp. 107–52.

16. Pope, *Job*, 7, points to several echoes of the number ten and the ratio of sons to daughters: When the lost children are replaced in 42:15 the same number and proportion are retained; we find the same ratio between Job's sheep and camels in 1:3, as well as between Solomon's wives and concubines in 1 Kgs. 11:3; 1 Sam. 2:5 mentions seven children, and Ruth 4:15 speaks of seven sons as ideal; in the Ugaritic Baal Epic, Baal has seven sons and three daughters (*CTU* 1.14.I.8-9; 15.II.23). See also Steve A. Wiggins, "Pidray, Tallay and Arsay in the Baal Cycle," *Journal of Northwest Semitic Languages* 29 (2003): 83–101.

"very much service," *waʿăbŭddāh rabbāh mĕʾōd*). Indeed, slaves are a kind of animal in such a list, an afterthought that becomes personal for Job when, after disaster strikes, he reflects on his own position as a "slave (*ʿebed*) longs for shade, and as a hired worker (*śākîr*) waits for his wages" (7:2; see also 3:19). Job will later speak of having to plead with his servants (19:15-16) in situations that were, before the disaster, presumably straightforward interactions of power. The rhetoric of the *ʿebed* in Job takes on further nuance when Yhwh repeatedly calls Job "my slave (*ʿabdî*) Job" in his dialogue with the Adversary (*haśśāṭān*) in the Prologue to the book (1:8; 2:3), and also in the book's conclusion (42:7, 8 [3x]). A fascinating and specific connection between animals and the rhetoric of slavery in Job comes in the grand Divine Speech in 41:4, which I will discuss in detail later. For the moment, suffice it to say that when Yhwh asks Job if it seems right that the animal Leviathan would enter into a covenant (*bĕrît*) with Job, or serve as Job's own *ʿebed*, Yhwh starkly relativizes the human place among the hierarchy of animals.

During the Adversary's initial tête-à-tête with Yhwh in 1:10, Job's material wealth takes center stage. The Adversary suggests that Yhwh has rigged the system; if Job's animals are allowed to remain safe and numerous, this is only because Yhwh has provided a "hedge" around him (*śaktā baʿădô*) and the whole lot. This hedge is itself a distinctly agricultural image, a structure used to guard a field one hopes will thrive in its protective midst.[17] What few other biblical references to hedges we have speak in terms of thorns or scrub brush (Judg. 9:49; Hos. 2:8 [English 2:6]), and the prophet Isaiah's "Song of the Vineyard" in Isaiah 5 identifies a "hedge" (*mĕśûkkāh*) that Yhwh

---

17. With regard to animals this kind of "hedge" would more appropriately be a "corral" or "sheepfold." However, see Paul Kruger, "'I Will Hedge Her Way with Thornbushes' (Hosea 2,8): Another Example of Literary Multiplicity?" *BZ* 43 (1999): 92–99. I thank Victor Matthews for pointing me to this source.

will remove from the Vineyard (= Israel; Isa. 5:5). Thus the notion that Yhwh would indeed hedge in his favored nation or person is not a strange one—but hedges can come and go. Alternatively, God may use a hedge to *imprison* the disobedient, as in Hosea 2:8, where the adulterous woman will find herself hedged in with thorns (*hinnĕnî śāk 'et darkēk bassîrîm*). Hosea's metaphor in this passage is rife with comparisons between the state of nature and human morality, as the Deity promises to punish the woman's adultery by transforming her into a "wilderness" (*midbār*) and a "parched land" (*'ereṣ ṣiyyāh*).[18] Moreover, the Adversary specifically claims that Job's cattle have "burst forth out into the land" (*pāraṣ bā'āreṣ*); the verb *pāraṣ* tellingly describes the abundance of children and cattle for the patriarchs in Genesis (28:14; 30:30, 43; compare Isa. 54:3), a fact that sets the Joban narrative scene during an imaginary ancestral period and simultaneously draws attention to the blessings associated with Israel's primal covenant. As Seow points out in his commentary, *pāraṣ* also specifically describes breached fences (2 Kgs. 14:13; Pss. 80:13[12]; 89:41[40]; Isa. 30:13),[19] and the prophet Isaiah uses this term in Isaiah 5:5 to describe the ruin of the "hedge" around the vineyard.

Thus the hedge and the cattle are deeply ingrained metaphors of Job's moral status; the first Joban animals are the tangible markers of Job's morality and the first Joban plant is God's own hedge that guards—or creates—the system. The success of the plant hedge stands in mystical union with Job's own success, and we may appropriately wonder which is the primal, driving force: the righteousness or the prosperity.[20] Reading against the grain of the narrative, one could

---

18. Given Hosea's use of exodus and wilderness imagery throughout the book (e.g., 2:16 [English 2:14], 11:1-10), one must see the reference to the *midbār* here as a direct allusion to Israel's forty-year wilderness sojourn before entering the Promised Land.

19. Seow, Job *1–21*, 276.

accuse Job of impiety at some substrate level. Perhaps buried in the reference to his children's death in 1:13, in which the narrator casually tells us that the sons and daughters were "drinking wine in the eldest brother's house," one could detect a hint of the children's overly decadent lifestyle—implicating Job and his failure to properly atone for them.[21]

Of course, the presence of the children eating and drinking in Job 1:13 is (at least) a simple plot device, meant to gather the brood under one roof so as to have them killed in the same cave-in disaster in 1:19. The house collapse in 1:19 is, however, affected by nature, a "great wind" from the desert (*rûaḥ gĕdôlāh bāʾāh mēʿēber hammidbār*), as opposed to, say, a structural collapse or fire. Presumably the children could have died from any number of causes, for example, murder associated with the animal plunder. From the perspective of the human actors in the story such events only heighten the ambiguity of the deaths—the harsh desert wind could easily suggest to an onlooker that nature has reacted badly to some wicked deed. The notice about the sons and daughters in 1:13 is separated from the actual account of their death by several verses, during which the animals are mysteriously burned (by a "divine fire" [*ʾēš ʾĕlōhîm*] in 1:17) or taken by raiders, prompting us to wonder why the disaster is framed in this exact way, that is, by drawing attention back to Job's frantic efforts to pre-save the children in 1:4-5. Alternatively, one may simply

---

20. Balentine, *Job*, 47, cites the "*waw* consecutive" grammatical construction beginning the phrases in Job 1:2-3 as meaning: "*and so* there was born . . . *and so* he had . . ." i.e., *for this reason* (= his righteousness) there were born . . ."—though Balentine is only willing to aver that "the grammar invites consideration" of the relationship between Job's piety and prosperity. See also Clines, *Job 1–20*, 13. But this grammatical cue is not decisive; see Ronald J. Williams, *Williams' Hebrew Syntax*, 3d ed., revised and expanded by John C. Beckman (Toronto: University of Toronto Press, 2007), 76–77; Paul Joüon, *A Grammar of Biblical Hebrew, Part Three: Syntax*, trans. and revised by T. Muraoka (Subsidia Biblica 14/II; Rome: Pontifical Biblical Institute, 2005), 390–95.

21. Here we may wonder whether the reference to Job in Ezek. 14:14, 20 in fact refers to a different version of the narrative, one in which Job's righteousness *does* save his children (parallel with the examples of Noah and Dan[i]el that Ezekiel lists in these same verses).

agree with the Adversary that Job's perfection is predicated on his safety; notably, God never explicitly refutes the Adversary on this front. Whatever the direction of influence, animal flourishing and the floral hedge have already become inextricable from Job's moral position, and the book begins by raising tantalizing questions about the definition of human righteousness in the face of animal and agricultural imagery.

Misery Does Not Come From the Earth

Eliphaz the Temanite, first to venture a word with the stricken Job, immediately offers a statement that will become programmatic for the response of the Friends—though it is by no means their only response (4:7):

> Remember (*zĕkōr*): who that was innocent ever perished? And where have the upright (*yĕšārîm*) been destroyed?

It is important that we translate the initial imperative specifically as "remember" and not generically as "think" or "consider," since the appeal here is a covenantal one. The root *zkr*, as verb and noun, usually indicates a situation of covenant, invoking the history of divine promises to Israel that God must remember or Israel is asked to remember; see, for example, Yhwh's "remembrance" of Noah and the covenant with him in Genesis 8:1 and 9:15-16, the repeated references to "remembering" the Abrahamic covenant (Gen. 19:29; Exod. 2:24; Lev. 26:45), and the constant refrain in Deuteronomy for Israel to "remember" the period of slavery in Egypt and the divine rescue from that condition (Deut. 5:15, 7:18, 8:2, 15:15).[22]

---

22. Many other examples could be adduced here; see, e.g., Gen. 30:22; Exod. 6:5; 13:3; 17:14; 20:8; 32:13; Num. 15:40; Deut. 8:18; 16:12; 24:18, 22; 25:17; Josh. 1:13; Judg. 8:34; 1 Sam. 1:11, 19; 2 Kgs. 20:3 // Isa. 38:3; Isa. 17:10; 44:21; Ezek. 16:60; Mal. 4:4; Pss. 20:3; 98:3; 103:18; 105:8, 42; 106:45; 119:49; Neh. 1:8; 5:19; 13:14. See Yosef H. Yerushalmi, *Zakhor: Jewish History and Jewish Memory* (Seattle: University of Washington Press, 1996), esp. 1–26.

In this microcosm of Eliphaz's anthropology humans are not merely defined by their relationship to God in some abstract way; they are specifically defined by *covenant*. The human self is a self that is, by definition, in league with God. The self is a character in a narrative, and the truth here, which inspires the Friends against Job, is not only mathematical or empirical but also mythic—it is a narrative truth to inspire attempts at retelling the story.[23] For those who preach this story, narratives that fail to conform to the covenant pattern (such as Job's) are aborted, false narratives.

Eliphaz's reference to the *yĕšārîm* ("upright") in the second part of 4:7 prefigures, in one sense, some of the floral imagery he will come to employ in this chapter and elsewhere in the book and thus stands as a fitting introduction to the definition of the human subject within the natural world. Etymologically, *yāšār* refers to what is *level, straight,* or *pruned* within boundaries.[24] Perhaps the most striking instances of such images come in Second Isaiah's soaring rhetoric (Isa. 40:4; 42:16; 45:2), where the prophet speaks of leveled mountains and the straightening of "rough/twisted places" (*maʿăqaššîm*, 42:16) needed to facilitate Israel's return to the land after exile.[25] Proverbs 15:19 offers the pruning metaphor clearly: "The way of the sluggard is like a thorny hedge (*mĕśūkat ḥēdeq*), but the path of the upright (*yĕšārîm*) is level (*sĕlūlāh*; lit., 'built up')." Outside of the specific use of *yāšār*, we find other striking images of nature in need of pruning or straightening. In Isaiah 2:12-14 the prophet speaks of Yhwh's wrath against all that is *rām*, "lifted up," and calls for the

---

23. See Newsom, *Book of Job*, 122 on this point, and also William P. Brown, *The Ethos of Cosmos: The Genesis of Moral Imagination in the Bible* (Grand Rapids: Eerdmans, 1999), 325–27.
24. See L. Alonso-Schökel and Helmer Ringgren, "*yāšar*," *TDOT* VI: 463–72, esp. 465–66. Compare the Mesopotamian concept of *mīšaru* (*CAD* 10.2, 116–18).
25. See also Isa. 26:7; Jer. 31:9; Hos. 14:9, and the noun *mīšōr*, "tableland, plains"; Brian R. Doak, *The Last of the Rephaim: Conquest and Cataclysm in the Heroic Ages of Ancient Israel* (Ilex Foundation; Cambridge, MA: Harvard University Press, 2012), 122.

leveling (*šāpēl*) of every "elevated" thing (*kol niśśāʾ*)—namely, the "lofty and elevated cedars of Lebanon" (*ʾarzē hallĕbānôn hārāmîm wĕnniśśāʾîm*), the "oaks of Bashan," lofty mountains (*hehārîm hārāmîm*), and elevated hills (*haggĕbāʿ ôt hanniśśāʾôt*).[26] In Joshua 17:15-18 the military confrontation with the fearsome, native, and putatively gigantic Rephaim (among other Canaanites) is mentioned in parallel with the need to clear out agriculturally inhospitable forestland (*yaʿar*) in the hill country.[27]

The combined political and floral connotations of *yāśār* can, in this respect, be instructively considered by analogy to the ancient Greek terminology of *dikē* and *hybris*.[28] As Gregory Nagy has shown, in ancient Greek literature *hybris* can be strategically connected with plant overgrowth, and other political language, such as *koros* ("instability") and *ethunō* ("straighten, regulate"), serves as technical terminology for the state of plant life or the control of vegetation.[29] Since, in Greek botanical thinking, plants had infinite potential for

26. Compare Isa. 37:24 on this theme. Of course, phrases like "high mountains" and "elevated hills" seem redundant; "high" and "elevated" here indicate what is *too* high and *excessively* elevated, what elevates itself arrogantly before God.

27. E.g., Josh. 17:15: "Go up to the forest, and clear ground for yourselves." See discussion in Doak, *Last of the Rephaim*, 94–96, 119–23; on nature and confrontation see Ronald Simkins, *Creator and Creation: Nature in the Worldview of Ancient Israel* (Peabody, MA: Hendrickson, 1994), 170–72.

28. Doak, *Last of the Rephaim*, 119–23. For the applicability of the *dikē-hybris* concept to the Hebrew Bible see Paul Humbert, "Démesure et chute dans l'Ancien Testament," 63–82 in *Maqqél shâqédh. La branche d'amandier. Hommage à Wilhelm Vischer* (Montpellier: La Faculté Libre de Théologie Protestante de Montpellier, 1960). In Greek literature see Matthew W. Dickie, "*Dike* as a Moral Term in Homer and Hesiod," *CP* 73 (1978): 91–101, and Gregory Nagy, *Greek Mythology and Poetics* (Ithaca: Cornell University Press, 1990), 64–69.

29. Specifically, *koros* can describe the overproduction of wood and leaf products at the expense of fruit, while the verb *ethunō* can refer to the pruning of plants. See Theognis 40; Theophrastus *Historia plantarum* 2.7.6-7; Aristotle *De generatione animalium* 725b35; discussion in Gregory Nagy, "Theognis and Megara: A Poet's Vision of his City," 22–81 in Thomas J. Figueria and Gregory Nagy, eds., *Theognis of Megara: Poetry and the Polis* (Baltimore: Johns Hopkins University Press, 1985), 22–81 (specifically §§49–50 in the online publication of this essay at the Center for Hellenic Studies website, http://chaptersharvard.edu, from which I cite this article). See also the ample documentation of this imagery in Ann Michelini, "Hybris and Plants," *HSCP* 82 (1978): 35–44.

expansion, wild growth had to be confronted by force; in moral and political terms this is *dikē*. So too in the Hebrew Bible, wild, crooked, or overgrown natural space must be checked. Not only is the innocent human self aligned with God's purpose, the righteous self is straight and pruned as a symbol of obedience on par with the natural world that can be made to reflect God's own deliverance.

Having shot this rhetorical question, with resonances of natural pruning, into the discussion, Eliphaz answers it in 4:8-11 with a strong dual invocation of agriculture and animals:

> (8) It is just as I have seen: the plowers of iniquity (*ḥōršê ʾāwen*) and sowers of trouble (*zōrʿê ʿāmāl*)—they reap it (*yiqṣĕrūhû*).
> (9) By the breath of Eloah they perish, and from the wind of his anger they are consumed.
> (10) The roar of the lion (*ʾaryēh*), the voice of another lion (*šaḥal*)—but the teeth of the young lions (*kĕpîrîm*) are broken.[30]
> (11) The father lion (*layiš*) perishes for lack of prey, and the sons of the lioness (*lābîʾ*) are scattered.

In a famous fit of poetic bombast in verses 10-11 the author employs five different terms for "lion." The most frequently attested biblical term for "lion" is *ʾaryēh*, but it is not clear what a *šaḥal* is as opposed to an *ʾaryēh*, or then whether the *layiš* and *lābîʾ* represent some meaningful expansion on these other lions here in Job.[31] A frequently invoked predator in the Hebrew Bible, the lion travels with a pride, and lion-words are often mentioned in tandem with other lion-words,[32] sometimes due to the poetic requirements of Hebrew parallelism. In his rich study of lion imagery in the Bible and the

---

30. I translate the *wĕ-* here as adversative, hoping to solve the grammatical problem in the first clause of the verse (the lack of a verb), which others have noted; cf. Seow, *Job 1–21*, 397.

31. See Brent A. Strawn, *What is Stronger Than a Lion? Leonine Image and Metaphor in the Hebrew Bible and the Ancient Near East* (OBO 212; Fribourg: Academic Press, 2005), esp. 294–307, 314–17, 322–26, 330–31, 340–41, 344–45; note also the caution expressed in Seow, *Job 1–21*, 397–98. Clines, *Job 1–20*, points to several interpreters who see this section as "the work of an inferior poet" and thus deem the passage secondary.

ancient Near East, Brent Strawn asserts that an ʾaryēh is a single, male lion, but the other terms are too ambiguous for clear identification. For Strawn, Job 4:10-11, along with the various lions mentioned in Nahum 2:12-13, give us "at best a list of lion terms" with no clear order or purpose.[33]

However, we should not be too quick to write off these multiple references as merely lists or formal contrivances.[34] In Nahum 2:12-13, for example, the specific pairing of (male) lion (ʾaryēh), lioness (lābîʾ), and cubs (kĕpîrîm; gûr) depicts a lion *family* in the act of defending its den and providing food for the young lions. So too in Ezekiel's lion parable in Ezekiel 19:1-9, the entire passage depends on the familial connection between the lĕbiyyāʾ and her cubs (kĕpîrîm). In an obscure "oracle of the animals of the Negev" (maśśāʾ bahămôt negeb) in Isaiah 30:6, the prophet invokes a pair of lions (lābîʾ walayiš), perhaps a male-female duo, to illustrate the threat of the desert; a few verses later the prophet uses human familial imagery (30:9) to speak of Isaiah's rebellious audience, thus juxtaposing lion and human families. The repeated references to lions in their grouping of pairs and cubs in these passages and others could be read as a kind of primitive ethnography of lions. Lions are to be found in families; they are relational and provide food for cubs; they are fierce and not easily subdued as a group;[35] they live in steppeland regions.

In Job 4:10-11, then, we should read the multiple lion terms in context—specifically, I would suggest, with the familial imagery invoked for lions elsewhere in the Bible and within the familial

---

32. As in Gen. 49:9; Num. 23:24; 24:9; Isa. 5:29; 30:6; Ezek. 19:2; Hos. 5:14; Joel 1:6; Nah. 2:12-13 [English vv. 11-12]; Ps. 91:13; Prov. 26:13.

33. Strawn, *What is Stronger Than a Lion*, 300.

34. See James Kugel, *The Idea of Biblical Poetry: Parallelism and Its History* (Baltimore: Johns Hopkins University Press, 1981), 7–8 on the nuances that can be missed by assuming parallelism is crass or obligatory repetition (as opposed to meaningful expansion).

35. Even the defeat of a single lion, as in the contest in 1 Chr. 11:22, is lauded as a great achievement.

context of Job, his wife, and his children. The lions do not appear haphazardly after the attempt at an agricultural-moral lesson in verses 8-9; rather, for Eliphaz the plant and animal lessons are intimately connected. Sowing and reaping plants is the equivalent of human spiritual states. On the surface the relationship would seem straightforward enough: plow *in* a certain kind of seed (iniquity) and reap *out* the trouble that springs forth. The most obvious problem with this reasoning is, of course, its bald inapplicability to Job's own situation. He has sowed righteous acts and reaped trouble.

But audiences of any era may detect other, subtler problems buried within such an analogy. Do plants really grow up so easily or automatically when they are sown? Not always; and what person familiar with planting is not familiar with the mystery of failing plants, even when one provides all proper care? Perhaps one should not be too hard on Eliphaz; he intends to speak a maxim that is generally true, even as he may recognize that is not always the case. The point is that he asserts its applicability for Job in the moment. Job and the floral body are one, growing in the same moral universe. By connecting the animals, then, with the plant lesson, Eliphaz suggests that *the lion family equals Job's family*. Lions may roar, but suddenly (and without explanation) the young lion-children's teeth are broken (v. 10); the lion-lioness pair loses its young by failing to gather food (v. 11). The connections among the lion family's behavior, the breaking teeth, and the food shortage is not directly stated, but the implication of the plowing and reaping scheme in verses 8-9, combined with the lion references, can only be that parental negligence results in injury and the loss of family cohesion.[36] By raising the question of Job's situation in terms of lions Eliphaz recognizes that Job's family had functioned in the protective world

---

36. See Riede, *Im Spiegel der Tiere*, 134–37, on the lions here as reflections of the destiny of the wicked.

of regal animal selves, but failures occur even in that world. Also, the invocation of the lion prefigures Job's own complaint later, in 16:9, when Job will accuse God of mauling and mangling his body as a wild beast mangles prey.[37]

Eliphaz follows up on his harvesting and lion examples by recounting an odd visionary experience (4:12-21) about which we will have more to say later. For the moment we may observe that through this vision Eliphaz claims to receive a distinct, mysterious, and direct spiritual revelation (spoken to him by some kind of ghost) to the effect that *no one* is righteous before God; God doesn't even trust angels, humans lack wisdom, and all life is just one big misery-fest. Already in the first round of response to Job's conundrum, then, we see appeals to what have become, in the long history of (at least Christian) theology, two distinct—and traditionally incompatible—categories of divine disclosure: nature and revelation. These categories already appear at odds with one another, since Eliphaz has, of course, just finished telling us that those who plow iniquity sow trouble. If humans suffer just because they are humans, then Eliphaz need not lecture on with nature analogies that rely on the contingency of human behavior—raising the question of whether Eliphaz has, ironically and disastrously, misunderstood his own vision.

And yet he does lecture on, as if perhaps not quite believing in the vision. The rest of the speech (5:1-27) is interlaced with references that take us deeper into the complexity of the book's floral theologies. In 5:1-7 a new speech begins, the conclusion of which offers a strong and explicit anthropological pronouncement.

---

37. See Jürgen van Oorschot, "Beredte Sprachlosigkeit im Ijobbuch: Körpererfahrung an den Grenzen von Weisheit und Wissen," 239–53 in Angelika Berlejung, Jan Dietrich, and Joachim F. Quack, eds., *Menschenbilder und Körperkonzepte im Alten Israel, in Ägypten und im Alten Orient* (Tübingen: Mohr Siebeck, 2012), at 248.

(1) Respond, please:
   is there anyone who can answer you?
   To which of the Holy Ones (*qĕdōšîm*) can you turn?
(2) Anger slays the fool, and jealousy kills the simple;
(3) I have seen (*'ănî rā'îtî*) the fool taking root (*mašrîš*),
   but I cursed his pasture suddenly (*wā'eqqôb nāwēhû pit'ōm*).
(4) His sons are far from rescue,
   they are crushed at the gate and there is no deliverer.
(5) The hungry man eats from his harvest (*qĕṣîrô*),
   he takes it from the thorns (*wĕ'el miṣṣinnîm*),
   he pants after his wealth amidst snares.[38]
(6) For trouble (*'āwen*) does not spring forth from the dust (*'āpār*),
   and from the earth (*mē'ădāmāh*) problems (*'āmāl*) do not sprout up
   (*yiṣmaḥ*).
(7) For man (*'ādām*) was born for problems (*lĕ'āmāl*),
   as sparks (*bĕnê rešep*) fly up high.

Here we find the same philosophical tension detected between the appeal to nature and reason in Eliphaz's earlier speech. Verse 2 lays out the first theme: jealousy and anger—negative deeds and emotions—are the cause of death, and the following selection of musings on plant life, eating, and agriculture must somehow prove this point. The fool may begin to take root, but something happens "suddenly"—the plant in the garden grows initially, taking root, but the process fails. In the second half of verse 3, as translated above, the Masoretic Text has *wā'eqqôb*, "I cursed," seemingly from the root *qābab*, though other options are possible.[39] Seow, for example, takes the root to be *nāqab*, "take note, identify," so that Eliphaz claims to have noted the rapid root establishment.[40] The parallel concept of "seeing" in both halves of verse 3 is a compelling reason for this latter reading, though the translation given above provides better

38. The reading here is not at all clear; see the long notes in Seow, *Job 1–21*, 432–36.
39. Here I follow the MT; Seow, *Job 1–21*, 429–30, reviews several options for emendation.
40. Seow, *Job 1–21*, 430.

continuity with the next few verses, where we find the *consequence* of this loss of pasturage (which would not follow from mere observation on Eliphaz's part?). Moreover, against Seow's reading we must ask whether the adverb *pit'ōm* modifies the verb (the cursing or the seeing) or the noun (the pasturage, *nāwēhû*). In none of the other instances of *pit'ōm* in the Hebrew Bible does *pit'ōm* characterize a noun in the way that Seow would have it function here, "sudden [place of] habitation"; rather, *pit'ōm* describes a verb: God appears unexpectedly (Num. 12:4; Josh. 12:9; Isa. 29:5-6), or disasters come suddenly (Isa. 47:11; Jer. 4:20; Ps. 64:5[4]; Job 9:23; 22:10; Eccl. 9:12). If one chooses to read the verb as *nāqab*, "take note, identify," then it would seem that the syntax indicates that Eliphaz's *perception* is "sudden" ("I suddenly perceived . . .").

In either reading Eliphaz's claim to have personally observed natural truth is a central concept. His emphatic claim that he has himself observed the fool beginning to take root (v. 3, *'ănî rā'îtî* . . .) is significant, and finds a parallel in the rumination on agriculture and human success in Proverbs 24:30-32: "I passed by the field of the lazy one, by the vineyard of the stupid man; and look—thistles grew up and covered all of it, the ground covered with nettles, and its wall of stones destroyed. I looked, and pondered (this); I saw, and I received instruction."[41] Other examples of "initial rootage" followed by failure form the basis of Jesus' wisdom-oriented teaching in Matthew 13:5-6 // Mark 4:5-6 and serve to create a political theodicy in Second Isaiah (Isa. 40:24).[42] Here in the Job passage the plant drama is accessible to all who can truly see—the *observable* universe holds the key to interpreting suffering, negligence, and growth.

---

41. Note also ibid., 415–16.
42. As pointed out by Seow, ibid., 416.

Job 5:5 resumes the agricultural theme of harvesting and its problems; the "hungry" pluck food out from thorny places and gather what little wealth they can find through snares.[43] Apparently those even worse off than the fool and his cursed or suddenly-inhabited arable space will come in to plunder land. But how does one become so destitute in the first place? Eliphaz may already be assuming a full-blown version of his quasi-Deuteronomistic or Proverbial scheme in verses 4-5: the mere mention of the children who are crushed and the "hungry" is to lead us to assume that the subject is hungry precisely because of *moral fault*.[44] The children died for a reason. After all, as he then says, trouble does not come from the ground (v. 6). This is perhaps not quite the same as saying that trouble does not come from *nowhere*; specifically, he asserts that there is no *inherent* trouble in the ground, and perhaps by extension in the natural world. Nature is benign, or at least neutral. If the ground does not offer one enough food, it is not the ground's fault. This physical living space, as noted above, is indicated by the noun *nāweh*, the most basic meaning of which is "pasture," an agricultural plot or space of land for animal grazing.[45] Along with this wild pasturage, however, *nāweh* also refers to a secure human dwelling—even, particularly, the safety of God's chosen space for God's people as indicated by Jerusalem, the complex of imagery associated with Zion, and the Temple (e.g., Exod. 15:13; 2 Sam. 15:25; Isa. 33:20). As Seow perceptively notices, this dual meaning of *nāweh* allows the speaker in Job 5:1-7 to move fluidly between plant and human realms: "Eliphaz speaks of the fool's children being far from *yeša'* (verse 4a), a term implying success,

---

43. Habel, *The Book of Job*, 131, wonders whether "the hungry one" (*rā'ēb*) in v. 5 could refer to Death (Mot) as "the Hungry One," along the lines of Ugaritic materials that speak of Mot this way.

44. See, e.g., Ps. 37:25; Prov. 10:3-4.

45. E.g., 2 Sam. 7:8; Isa. 34:13; Jer. 23:10; Ps. 23:2, among many other examples.

including the successful growth of plants (Isa. 45:8; compare Isa. 17:10)."[46]

The conclusion in 5:7, however, introduces ambiguity into the rant. Here Eliphaz provides a sort of summary that undercuts any of the cause-and-effect rhetoric in verses 2-6: humans are simply born for problems. Two issues stand out. First is the allusive word for "man" or "humankind," 'ādām. In just the previous verse, the "earth" from which problems do not sprout up is the 'ădāmāh. Verses 6-7 thus evoke the famous wordplay from Genesis 2:7: God creates 'ādām from the 'ădāmāh; more specifically, Genesis 2:7 has God fashioning 'ādām from the 'āpār, the "dust" that is itself "from the 'ădāmāh." Whatever the case, humans appear in Genesis 2 as an organic part of the ground, and the first three chapters of Genesis are quite concerned with the question of the human place vis-à-vis plants and animals and the consequences of human disobedience—just as Eliphaz has been so far in Job 4–5.[47]

If Eliphaz is offering an allusion to, or commentary on, the Creation and Garden episodes in Genesis, then what is the message? Whatever the nature of the trouble Adam and Eve get into in Genesis 3, the Yahwist does not clearly present this trouble as springing forth from the earth itself with no provocation, but rather as the result of a curse placed on the 'ădāmāh (if anything, the trouble comes from an animal, the serpent [nāḥāš]). Trouble does not spring forth from the ground, but rather the ground is cursed because of the fruit-eating. Thus Eliphaz's assertion in Job 5:6 could be an appeal to the Garden narrative: the strife between humans and the ground is the

46. Seow, Job 1–21, 416, 431.
47. In viewing Job 5:6-7 as a direct, intentional allusion to Genesis 2:7 one certainly runs the risk of over-subtlety; can one simply speak about 'ādām and the 'ădāmāh without reference to the canonical creation story? This problem is of course inherent in all discussions of inner-biblical allusion. See comments on Job 5 and Genesis 2 in Habel, The Book of Job, 131–32; Seow, Job 1–21, 417.

result of the fruit-eating, not chance—and certainly not a divine setup (Gen. 3:17-19). The stark pronouncement in Job 5:7, following this view, could suggest a Christian style of interpretation of the Garden Narrative in which humans are now born for trouble, predicated on that fateful early human experiment with disobedience. The human self ('ādām) is differentiated from the ground ('ădāmāh), even forever separated from it. Trouble springs forth from human actions, not from the dust—even if the human self is entrapped by birth in the cycle of trouble.[48] There is truly no way out.

Regarding this image of what "sprouts up" from the earth, we might also consider a related statement in Psalm 85:11-13[10-12]:

> (11) Faithfulness (ḥesed) and Truth ('ĕmet) will meet,
>   Righteousness and Peace will kiss;
> (12) Truth ('ĕmet) will sprout forth (tiṣmāḥ) from the earth ('ereṣ),
>   and Righteousness will drop from the heavens.
> (13) For Yhwh will give what is good,
>   and our land ('arṣēnû) will bring forth its produce.

All of this bounty will come about, in the world of the psalm, when Yhwh's saving acts arrive. For the moment, apparently, they are only *near* (qārôb, v. 10), as the first half of the psalm (vv. 1-7) speaks of deep pain, indignation, and death for the speaker and his community. Later, when the salvation at hand is realized, the agricultural images represent hope: an earth sprouting (ṣāmaḥ) truth like healthy plants (instead of problems), and a fertile land as the parallel for Yhwh giving the people "what is good."

The second provocative issue here is the choice of the sparks analogy. Scholars have seized upon the phrase bĕnê rešep, literally "sons of Resheph," with Resheph being a well-known Semitic and Egyptian deity associated with plagues and other mayhem.[49] In the

---

48. Cf. Habel, *The Book of Job*, 132.

Hebrew Bible the word *rešep* has largely become a personification of some plague or fire element first associated with the deity Resheph (as in Deut. 32:24; Pss. 76:4[5]; 78:48; Song 8:6), though in at least one instance, Habakkuk 3:5, Resheph appears alongside another otherwise-attested Northwest Semitic deity, Deber (*debār*), as part of Yhwh's divine retinue in battle. The connection here in Job 5:7 with fire can be associated with at least one other biblical reference, Song 8:6: ". . . for love is as strong as death, jealousy (or: passion) as fierce (lit.: hard) as Sheol; its arrows (*rĕšāpêhā*) are arrows of fire (*rišpê*), flaming." This, of course, does not mean that *bĕnê rešep* in Job 5:7 should be translated "sparks," but at least Song 8:6 demonstrates that a biblical author could have understood Resheph's popular association with arrows in tandem with fire imagery for whatever reason.[50]

John Day suggests reading the first two clauses in Job 5:6-7 as rhetorical questions:[51]

> For does not affliction come from the dust
> and does not trouble sprout from the ground?
> For man is born to trouble
> and the sons of Resheph fly upwards [from the underworld].

This rendering reverses the meaning from the way I have translated the lines above, so that now Eliphaz offers perhaps a more straightforward commentary on Genesis 3, with a mythological flair: the ground (*'ădāmāh*) is cursed, and man (*'ādām*) with it. The "sons

---

49. See, e.g., Izak Cornelius, *The Iconography of the Canaanite Gods Reshef and Ba'al: Late Bronze Age I Periods (c 1500–1000 BCE)* (OBO 140; Göttingen: Vandenhoeck & Ruprecht, 1994); Martin J. Mulder, "*rešep*," *TDOT* XIV: 10–16; John Day, *Yahweh and the Gods and Goddesses of Canaan* (Sheffield: Sheffield Academic Press, 2000), 199–208, esp. 201–3, 207–8 on Job 5:7; Mark S. Smith, *The Origins of Biblical Monotheism: Israel's Polytheistic Background and the Ugaritic Texts* (Oxford: Oxford University Press, 2001), 47.

50. Additionally, some have tried to translate the Egyptian plague recitation in Ps. 78:48 with reference to "lightning" or "thunderbolts": "He gave their beasts over to hail, and their cattle to lightning (*rĕšāpîm*)."

51. Day, *Yahweh*, 202–3.

of Resheph" would thus represent demonic forces flying upward, and the reference to Resheph's status as a chthonic deity would cohere with the references to the *'āpār* and *'ădāmāh* as physical indicators of the Underworld.[52] Usually, however, it is specifically the *'ereṣ* that is most often mentioned as a euphemism for the land of the dead in the Hebrew Bible (e.g., Exod. 15:10-12; Isa. 26:19; Ps. 88:13; Job 10:21-22),[53] and Day's underworld-focused solution removes the *běnê-rešep* reference from the realm of the cause-and-effect nature imagery employed in the statements leading up to it. The idea of sparks inevitably flying upward from a fire, however, is very much in line with the types of appeals Eliphaz has already made to this point: natural forces behave in specific, observable patterns. One may even find allusion to the running plant-human comparison theme in the Resheph imagery. Drawing on mythological tropes in Deuteronomy 32:23-24 and Psalm 127:4-5, Resheph's arrows can be viewed as some kind of natural pestilence of pollen that rains down on the earth and sows misery for humans.[54]

Eliphaz moves on in 5:8 to suggest full-blown repentance as the solution to Job's problems. After all, God can do marvelous things (*niplā'ôt*, v. 10), so perhaps forgiveness for the presumed iniquity is the miracle Job needs. Again, the natural order of rain and plant growth provides a fitting image of the human moral self before the deity in 5:9-12, when God is

(9) the one who does great things, unsearchable (*'ên ḥēqer*),
    wonders that cannot be counted.
(10) The one who gives rain upon the face of the earth (*'ereṣ*),
    and sends water upon the face of the fields (*ḥûṣôt*);
(11) to place (*lāśûm*) the lowly up high,

52. Day, *Yahweh*, 203.
53. Compare also the cognate Akkadian term *erṣētu* (*CAD* 4, 310–11).
54. As suggested by Seow, *Job 1–21*, 437–38.

and those who mourn are exalted, given salvation (*śāgĕbû yeša'*),
(12) breaking the plots of the crafty,
so their hands have no success.

The close juxtaposition of God's rain provision for plant growth and the divine power to exalt the lowly and frustrate the schemers blends together the paths of success and the miracle of plant growth. Indeed, God's ways in either growing or leveling the human self are as miraculous for the speaker as falling rains: "great things, unsearchable, wonders that cannot be counted." In a land distressed by constant drought, the notion that God alone can provide the precipitation needed for nature's success is a strong theological appeal; the prophet Hosea also uses the agricultural imagery of plowing and reaping to encourage a return to Yhwh for his audience in Hosea 10:12-13. Indeed, an integral part of Deuteronomy's sapientially-themed covenant for nascent Israel discussed in the previous chapter involves the provision or withholding of rain: showers and crops for the righteous, parched land and death for the wicked (see Deut. 11:14, 17; 28:12, 24; 1 Kgs. 8:35-37).[55]

The preposition at the start of 5:11, *lĕ-* ("to, for"), is grammatically a bit odd in this position; one might have expected a continuation of the so-called "hymnic participle" style here,[56] as in the preceding statements in verses 9-10 (*'ōśeh*, "doer, one who does"; *hānnōtēn*, "giver, the one who gives"; *śōlēaḥ*, "sender, one who sends"), so that verse 11 would begin: "setting" (*śām*) the lowly up high . . ."[57] The

---

55. Seow, *Job 1–21*, 419–20; to Seow's examples here I would add 1 Kings 18, where the drought Elijah declares on the Northern Kingdom reverberates with themes of rain as blessing and lack of rain as covenant punishment.

56. On the "hymnic participle" see, e.g., James L. Crenshaw, *Hymnic Affirmation of Divine Justice: The Doxologies of Amos and Related Texts in the Old Testament* (SBLDS 24; Missoula: Scholars Press, 1975).

57. The repeated vowel pattern of the strong-verb participle, *pōʿēl*, creates a repeating poetic cadence that cannot be duplicated by the (middle-weak) verb *śwm* (the participle for which would be *śām*), so, admittedly, the switch to the infinitive construct *lāśûm* may be nothing more

lĕ- preposition and infinitive form in verse 11 (*lāśûm*) disrupt the participles and introduce a kind of consequence, a pointing arrow that not so much continues the preceding list as it proclaims the results of God's unsearchable mighty acts: God enacts miracles and sends rain upon the earth *as a method of* raising up the lowly or flattening the proud.[58] Fertility and morality are subtly fused here; rain falls to water righteous fields or to correct an upside-down social order. Provision, or lack thereof—disaster, or lack thereof—correspond to natural cycles of cause and effect. Still, one may argue, the specter of the mighty acts or "wonders" (*niplāʾōt*) in 5:9, qualified as they are with phrases like "unsearchable" and "without number," introduces uncertainty of outcome into such cycles, for what pattern could not be disrupted by the miraculous? Moreover, the appearance of the wondrous or miraculous fosters not only comfort or respect but also fear and uncertainty. Such power may be unpredictable.[59] Eliphaz's strategy here, though, is not to highlight the philosophical problem of miraculous disruption (for good or ill), but rather to place himself within the boundaries of an "ecology of wonder."[60] The ordered system is itself a miracle, divinely created and divinely maintained. Rain and growth thus become an analogy for social, political, and spiritual states.

Recall that, in 5:8, Job was advised to "seek God," which could only be interpreted as a call for repentance in light of preceding elements in the speech (most prominently 4:7: "who that was innocent ever perished?"). Now Eliphaz narrates Job's potential repentant future by

---

than a mundane way for the poet to continue the list of divine deeds in this passage. Cf. Seow, *Job 1–21*, 439–40.

58. So also the translation in Dhorme, *Job*, 64.

59. A point made compellingly in Laura Feldt, *The Fantastic in Religious Narrative from Exodus to Elisha* (Sheffield: Equinox, 2012).

60. Borrowing a phrase from the title of William Brown's *The Seven Pillars of Creation: The Bible, Science, and the Ecology of Wonder* (Oxford: Oxford University Press, 2010).

casting things more positively, highlighting the instability of divine action (5:17-18):

> (17) Happy is the man whom Eloah reproves!
>   Do not reject the instruction of Shaddai.
> (18) For he wounds, but then he heals;
>   He strikes, but his hands will heal.

The motif of inscrutable twists and turns in the divine attitude was the focus of early Mesopotamian wisdom literature, such as the famous work known as *Ludlul bēl nēmeqi,* "I Will Praise the Lord of Wisdom."[61] Early in this poem the speaker declares the polarities of the deity at whose hands he has suffered (Tablet I, ll. 5-10):

> Whose anger is like a raging tempest,
> But whose breeze is sweet as the breath of morn.
> In his fury not to be withstood, his rage the deluge,
> Merciful in his feelings, his emotions relenting.
> The skies cannot sustain the weight of his hand,
> His gentle palm rescues the moribund.

For the speaker of *Ludlul bēl nēmeqi* one does not really seek to *understand* God as much as one just wallows in lurid descriptions of pain—which can, if things turn out all right, be followed by the jubilation of healing. It just depends. If Eliphaz means to endorse this

---

61. See the most recent edition by Amar Annus and Alan Lenzi, *Ludlul Bēl Nēmeqi: The Standard Babylonian Poem of the Righteous Sufferer* (Helsinki: Neo-Assyrian Text Corpus Project, 2010), as well as the translation by Benjamin R. Foster, "The Poem of the Righteous Sufferer," *COS* 1: 486–92 (I quote from this latter version below). The presence of this literary work in Assurbanipal's 7th-c. BCE library means that it must have been composed before this time, but how much earlier is not known. In one of the Bible's primal affirmations of God's character, in Exod. 34:6-7, this same wild swing of hurting and healing appears central to Israel's understanding of Yhwh, who proclaims that Yhwh is slow to anger and abounding in love, and yet ready to punish the guilty—even the children of the guilty. See the quotation and tweaking of the Exod. 34:6-7 theme in Nah. 1:2-3 and Jon. 4:2, to give examples of two authors who grasp hold of tellingly different parts of the affirmation: Nahum knows that God must punish, and Jonah knows God will forgive.

view, he does so in direct contradiction to his attempts at pinning the blame for suffering on Job himself.

But surely he does not mean to endorse it; he returns to his nature theme, and the argument is made more explicit and polished in the final words of the address, as the speaker masterfully lays out a vision of Job's potential (re-)flourishing in the realm of animals, stones, and grass:

> (5:22) You will laugh at destruction and famine;
>   and you will not fear the animals of the earth;
> (23) for you will have a covenant (*bĕrîtekā*) with the stones of the field,
>   and the animals of the field will be at peace with you.
> (24) You will know that your tent is at peace,
>   and you will inspect (*pāqad*) your pasture and find no sin;
> (25) and you will know that your descendants will be numerous,
>   and your offspring like the green things of the earth (*kĕʾēśeb hāʾāreṣ*);
> (26) you will come to the grave with vigor (*kelaḥ*),[62]
>   as standing grain (*gādîš*) ascends at the right time (*bĕʿittô*).
> (27) We have now investigated this: so it is.
>   Listen, and know it for yourself.

Eliphaz hopes to close the argument here, turning to a harmonious vision of humans and nature. And indeed, this description is among the most moving the Friends have to offer. The animals of the earth are, in this view, entities to be feared indeed—*for those on the wrong side of nature's story.* Job can escape this fear when God's hand turns toward healing, a turning that, it seems, would be predicated on Job's repentance. The world that, in Job's famous curse in chapter 3, had become all darkness and bitterness—the opposite of light and goodness (Genesis 1)—could now re-emerge in the grand Edenic vision of Isaiah of Jerusalem in Isaiah 11:6-9:[63] wolves and lambs,

---

62. For discussion of the problematic term *kelaḥ* here see Dhorme, *Job*, 73; Pope, *Job*, 47; Seow, *Job 1–21*, 447–48.

leopards and kids, calves and lions, all sleep near one another without fear; children play with snakes, and the mountain of the Lord, Zion, stands as a safe haven for a renewed nature. In Hosea 2:20 (2:18), another putatively eighth-century BCE prophet explicitly imagines repentance in terms of a new covenant with nature:

> On that day I will make a covenant with them, with the animals of the field and with the birds of the air, and the creeping things upon the ground, and I will abolish (lit. "break") the bow and sword and warfare from the earth, and I will make them lie down in safety.

The arrangement Eliphaz lays out here involves not only animals and plants but also the stones of the ground itself.[64] As it stands, Job does not have a covenant with the stones of the field. The very ground on which he currently resides—in the state of suffering—is out of league with destroyed humanity. The suffering human self may re-flourish like greenery, and this is an optimistic anthropology. The results of suffering are not permanent. When Eliphaz asserts in 5:25 that Job's offspring could be "like green things," or "like grass" he is using a common comparative trope in the Hebrew Bible, comparing humans to grass or other assorted green growth (ʿēśeb, "grass," or "green plants"; ḥāṣîr; dešeʾ).[65] But what is grass like, exactly? Comparisons between grassy green things and humans can break in several directions:

(1) Grass as harmonious flourishing. In one of the more vivid expressions of nature in harmony with human righteousness in the Hebrew Bible, Psalm 72, the speaker prays that people "from the city may blossom like the grass of the earth" (v. 16, wĕyāṣîṣû mēʿîr

---

63. See discussion in Seow, *Job 1–21*, 425–26.

64. Here Seow, *Job 1–21*, 415 (and sources cited there) envisions a restoration of Eden, a time before stones came to hinder agricultural work (see Gen. 3:17-18; 2 Kgs. 3:19; Isa. 5:2).

65. Lytton John Musselman, *A Dictionary of Bible Plants* (Cambridge: Cambridge University Press, 2011), 70–71.

kĕʿēśeb hāʾāreṣ). Likewise, a prophet in Isaiah 66:14 speaks in a soaring vision of the bones of the faithful that will "sprout forth like green grass (*kāddeśe*)," and in Micah 5:6[7] the rain upon flourishing grass (*kirbîbîm ʿălê-ʿēśeb*), unconditioned by human effort, is an image of the "remnant of Jacob" surviving in the midst of surrounding nations.

In each of these instances the human as flourishing grass is a deeply political metaphor. Psalm 72 seems to be a prayer for monarchic blessing, or even an inaugural performance piece for the ascendency of a new ruler; the last ten chapters of Isaiah (culminating in chapter 66, where intra- and inter-community polemics reach fever pitch), are rife with contested religious identities in the land after the return from exile,[66] and Micah 5 makes explicit reference to the eighth-century Assyrian threat, against which the prophet assures deliverance and human flourishing. Invading armies trample grass, and the green things of the world mark victory for rulers or communities who need economic (i.e., agricultural) success to validate their legitimacy. One does not often see a single blade of grass, but rather clumps or fields of sprouting things, and thus growing grass represents righteous community, multiplicity, and sudden growth.

(2) Grass as unrighteous transience. But it is not only the righteous who can experience this plant-like growth. In Psalm 92:8(7) the speaker laments the success of the wicked who sprout like grass and flourish like prosperous green things (*biprōaḥ rĕśāʿîm kĕmô ʿēśeb wayyāṣîṣû . . .*). Here, however, the image is turned on its head and exploited on the other end of the spectrum of grassy properties: such plants fade quickly. Grass thus stands as an excellent theodicy metaphor since its properties are a helpful natural complement to the Psalmists' often-invoked solution to the classic theodicy conundrum

---

66. See Brian R. Doak, "Legalists, Visionaries, and New Names: Sectarianism and the Search for Apocalyptic Origins in Isaiah 56–66," *BTB* 40 (2010): 9–26.

in the wisdom-oriented psalms (God is completely just; God is all-powerful; yet the righteous suffer terribly at the hands of the wicked). The wicked only *appear* to succeed, *temporarily*, just as rapidly sprouting grass or green weeds give an appearance of abundance but ultimately cannot last.

Psalm 37:1-2 provides another fitting example of this type of theodicy metaphor: "Do not be dismayed on account of the wicked, do not be jealous of the doers of iniquity; for like the grass (*ḥāṣîr*) they will quickly wither, and like a green plant (*kĕyereq deše'*) they will fade." In other places within the Psalms the speaker complains of being struck down or withering like grass, such as Psalm 105:5(4), 12(11), or ruminates on the entire human condition, for the righteous or the wicked, in terms of grass-like transience (Ps 103:15-16): "As for humans (*'ĕnôš*), their days are like grass (*kĕḥāṣîr*); they flourish like a flower of the field, then a wind comes and passes over it, and it is no more; its place no longer recognizes it." The fickle state of grass can even provide an agricultural lesson (which is, of course, a moral lesson on multiple levels) in Proverbs 27:23-26. Since specific forms of wealth cannot last forever, the speaker advises his audience to diversify investments in various kinds of flocks, to provide for the times when the "grass (*ḥāṣîr*) is gone and new growth (*deše'*) appears, and the green things (*'iśśĕbôt*) of the mountain are gathered up" (27:25). In the poetic introduction to Second Isaiah (40:6) the speaker expresses lack of confidence in human ability to proclaim any message, the reason being that "all flesh is grass (*ḥāṣîr*), and all their faithfulness (*ḥesed*) is like the flower of the field" (*kĕṣîṣ haśśādeh*).

(3) Grass as outright wickedness. At other points the transience of grass—specifically green things growing on rooftops—is only the background for an outright hope that one's enemies will be burned to death like grass. Such is the message of the prophet in Isaiah 37:27

// 2 Kings 19:26, who assures Hezekiah that the enemy (presumably the Assyrians here, in their "fortified cities") will be like "plants of the field" ('ēśeb śādeh) and "tender shoots" (wiyraq deśeh), "grass on a rooftop, scorched before it is grown." Psalm 129:6-7 sounds a similar note, wishing that enemies would be burned "like grass on a housetop" (kaḥăṣîr gaggôt). Grass is also directly related to disobedience in Jeremiah 12:4 (see also Jer. 14:6), where withering grass is included within a broader vision of a fading, devastated ecology—all the result of human wrongdoing.

As this review demonstrates, the grass-as-transience or grass-as-unrighteousness motif is prominent in many locations, more so than the grass-as-righteous-abundance theme. Thus within a canonical context, at least, the grass analogy carries with it connotations that are less straightforward than Eliphaz suggests. The hope that Job's children will sprout forth "like grass" is something of a mixed or ironic blessing, for hidden within the grass image are implications of transience, enemy threats, and sudden death. Of course, by wishing for descendants like grass Eliphaz surely means that they will sprout up plentifully and not that they will quickly wither away, yet this premature withering is exactly what has already happened to Job's children.

The reader is thus invited to recall the book's opening narrative and the question of fidelity raised there by Job's wealth and by the discussion between God and the Adversary. In 5:23 Eliphaz says: "For you will have a covenant with the stones of the field, and the animals of the field will be at peace with you." This question of "covenant" (běrît) has already become a loaded one up to this point in the argument; recall Eliphaz's initial attack in 4:7, when Job is called upon to "remember" (zākar) with language bristling with covenantal implications of the Deuteronomic blessing-and-reward scheme. More specifically, the notion of a covenant with the animals evokes the question of whether Job's material flourishing in Job 1, marked specifically by animal abundance, was also a marker of his righteous covenant status before God: the flourishing natural world, its potency and fertility, is a refraction of Job's own fertility. Currently Job is not at peace with nature. Nature has turned against him (see 1 Kgs. 13:24; 20:36; 2 Kgs. 17:25-26) and not yielded produce in accordance with the fertile human self (Isa. 33:8-9; Jer. 23:10; cf. Psalm 72).

Here Eliphaz's words participate in a type of analogy or metaphor through which the speaker not only points out the reality of nature's relationship to the human as he sees it but also forges what we might call a counterintuitive ontology of beings[67]—nature is not discrete from the human self but rather participates in the world of moral fear, covenant making, and the politics of personal peace (Job 5:22-23). The human future and the grass future may rise and fall together (5:25). If the human can become unsynchronized with the cycles of natural flourishing, presumably the stones of the field, animals, and plants can languish in their places. For Eliphaz, natural analogy provides the solution to suffering: not only can the self flourish with the grass and walk peacefully with animals but, in a striking twist in 5:26, Job will find his completion as in a moment of harvest: "You will come to the grave with vigor, as standing grain ascends [i.e., *for harvest*] at the right time (*bĕ'ittô*)." Regarding the theme of seasonality here, one is reminded of Deuteronomy 11:13-15, where covenant obedience will produce "rain for your land in its season (*bĕ'ittô*) . . . I will give green grass for your field, for your animals, and you will eat and be satisfied" (vv. 14-15). Time and nature are fused with the human life narrative before God (on this theme see also Deut. 28:12;

---

67. Recall the discussion in chap. 2 above; Justin L. Barrett, *Cognitive Science, Religion, and Theology: From Human Minds to Divine Minds* (Templeton Science and Religion Series; West Conshohocken, PA: Templeton Press, 2011), 68.

Jer. 5:24; Ezek. 34:26; Hos. 2:11[9]). Clearly, the "harvest" of standing grain in Job 5:26 is *death*, as Job's life and prosperity are, in this view, only in the past; Job can come back into moral synchronicity with nature in one final act that is essentially, to quote Nietzsche, to *die at the right time*. Thus spake Eliphaz.[68]

As Newsom rightly contends, in his speech Eliphaz (and the other Friends after him) seek to restore narrativity to Job's life, where narrative has been lost.[69] Job had intended to roll back time in his birth-lament (ch. 3), to erase story where life is concerned—a kind of erasure that could border on erasure of the entire cosmos, for all humans. The declaration in Job 3:4, *yĕhî ḥōšek* ("let there be darkness"), is the ritual opposite of God's famous first words in Genesis 1: *yĕhî 'ôr* ("let there be light").[70] "Let there be light" marks the Hebrew Bible's canonical narrative beginning, the first actor's first sentence; what can *yĕhî ḥōšek* represent but Job's attempt to become the Bible's final character, at the very end of biblical narrative? Eliphaz's nature story, while obviously congruent with aspects of the Deuteronomic and Proverbial visions, is unlike the fatalistic march toward exile prefigured by Deuteronomy's lurid curses.[71] Eliphaz holds out real hope for Job. His narrative is not

---

68. Here I invoke Nietzsche's famous advice through Zarathustra in *Thus Spoke Zarathustra* (1883): "Many die too late and some die too early. Still the doctrine sounds strange: 'Die at the right time.' . . . Die at the right time: thus Zarathustra teaches." Not incidentally to our theme, in the same passage Nietzsche compares humans to overripe fruit on trees: "Many too many live and they hang on their branches much too long. I wish a storm would come and shake all this rottenness and worm-eatenness from the tree! I wish preachers of *speedy* death would come! They would be the fitting storm and shakers of the trees of life!" Friedrich Nietzsche, *Thus Spoke Zarathustra*, trans. Walter Kaufmann (New York: Modern Library, 1995).

69. Newsom, *Book of Job*, 101–5.

70. On this see Abigail Pelham, *Contested Creations in the Book of Job* (Leiden: Brill, 2012), 225–29; Brian Britt, *Biblical Curses and the Displacement of Tradition* (The Bible in the Modern World 34; Sheffield: Sheffield Phoenix Press, 2011), 80–105, and Valerie Forstman Pettys, "Let There be Darkness: Continuity and Discontinuity in the 'Curse' of Job 3," *JSOT* 98 (2002): 89–104.

71. See also Clines (*Job 1–20*, 153), who notices the "strikingly positive" nature of Eliphaz's death speech.

the scripted theater of *post facto* theodicy but participates in creative possibilities, even if only for a fruitful death.

Flourishing Without Water?

In chapters 6–7 Job lets loose with what sounds to the next Friend to enter the debate, Bildad the Shuhite, like a very impious speech indeed. Raising the specter of the monstrous in 7:12 ("Am I the Sea [*yām*], or a Serpent Monster [*tannîn*], that you set a guard over me?"), Job ruminates on the apparently ridiculous divine effort to punish him, which involves treating a simple mortal as though he were a mythological enemy. Job does make one other ambiguous reference to nature in 6:5 ("Does the wild donkey bray over grass, or the ox low over his fodder?"), apparently using the analogy from animals to argue that even the donkey and the ox should be able to accept their food, while Job himself cannot (6:6-7). To return to Ricoeur's language of self-making, we may say that Job has not yet entered the appropriate place of vulnerability that could lead toward proper self-recognition; his reference to nature has not yet properly engaged with the human others (the Friends) or the embodied physical world around him.[72]

Bildad forges his rebuke in chapter 8 by invoking the authority of history (the views of the ancestors; v. 8, *dōr rîšôn*, *'ăbôtām*), and moves directly into rumination on plant life and the human body in 8:11-20. For centuries interpreters have debated the nature of the plant imagery in these verses;[73] some contend that the entire description speaks of one failing plant (= human = Job), while others see in 8:16-20 a distinct second plant metaphor.[74] Despite offering

---

72. Paul Ricoeur, *Oneself as Another*, trans. Kathleen Blamey (Chicago: University of Chicago Press, 1992).

73. Part of the confusion here, as Habel, *Book of Job*, 177 notices, comes from the diversity of images the speaker employs throughout the plant discussion. See the expanded discussion in Seow, *Job 1–21*, 520–25.

several different kinds of images throughout 8:11-20 and even within each specific plant section (vv. 11-13, 16-19), Bildad develops a clear contrast: beginning with the plant that fails, moving to a counter-example of the successful plant, and then offering Job the hope that he can be like the second plant example ("He will yet fill your mouth with laughter . . ." v. 21a).

The first plant metaphor, in 8:11-13, reads as follows:

(11) Will papyrus (gōme') sprout up (yig'eh) where there is no marsh
     (biṣṣāh)?
     Will reed-grass ('āḥû) flourish (yiśgeh) without water?
(12) Still in its early stage of growth (bĕ'ibbô), will it not be cut down,
     and wither before any other foliage (ḥāṣîr)?[75]
(13) Such are the paths of all who forget El,
     and the hope of the impious (ḥānēp) perishes!

The opening four lines of this address pose three questions: the first two elaborate a simple riddle-question involving plant growth while the third moves into a partial answer to the riddle (by way of another, rhetorical question). Indeed, the riddle format and the nature imagery here, combined with the motif of the "two ways" developed throughout 8:11-22, mark the address as classic and straightforward wisdom speech.[76] The final couplet in verse 13 then "solves" the riddle through a direct application of its terms to the impious human, Job. The logic of the riddle's two parts is not exactly straightforward, however. The first two questions prompt an answer in the

---

74. Two popular English translations, for example (the NIV and the NRSV), follow the former interpretation of a continuous (not contrasting) plant narrative in this chapter; see also Dhorme, *Job*, 122–23; Pope, *Job*, 64–65.

75. I carry the sense of the question (hāyig'eh) from 8:11 here into 8:12. Alternatively, one may translate: "While still in its early stage of growth, not picked (for profitable use), it will wither before any other foliage."

76. As various commentators point out (e.g., Habel, *Book of Job*, 176–77), the words here for "papyrus" (gōme') and "reed grass" ('āḥû) are Egyptian loanwords, thus enhancing the exotic, cosmopolitan wisdom orientation of Bildad's address.

negative—papyrus will *not* sprout up outside its proper habitat, and reed grass will *not* flourish without water—while the second part, which prompts an answer in the *affirmative*, operates on the assumption that these plants have *already failed* and now must be removed prematurely. The phrase *bĕʾibbô* in 8:12, "in its flourishing," or "in its green/new/fresh state,"[77] most likely suggests that these waterless plants in verse 11 have never even flourished at all; they never got off the ground, and thus they would be cleared out to make way for thriving, watered flora. The sense of prematurity—of plants being "plucked up" (*yiqqāṭēp*)—haunts the example, for Job's suffering has come at what should be the pinnacle of his enjoyment as a rich patriarch and father.

Noteworthy is the fact that the word *gāʾāh*, "rise up, exalt," used in verse 11 in what at first seems to be a neutral sense of plant growth or flourishing, takes on a decidedly *negative* connotation in nearly all its other uses in the Hebrew Bible (especially the adjective *gēʾeh*, "pride," but also verbal forms).[78] In Job 10:16, Job accuses God of rising up (*yigʾeh*) like a lion to hunt him, and in Job 40:11-12 Yhwh challenges Job's own ability to put down the proud (*gēʾeh*; see also Jer. 48:29; Pss. 94:2; 140:6[5]; Prov. 8:13; 15:25; 16:19). In Isaiah 2:12 *gēʾeh* refers to what is proud and elevated, specifically in relation to hubristic plant-thriving—the cedars of Lebanon and the oaks of Bashan have grown up too high and must be mowed down as rivals to Yhwh's own height (i.e., Mt. Zion).[79] Along these lines, consider also Ezekiel 17:24, "All the trees of the field will know that I am Yhwh—I bring

---

77. From the root *ʾbb*, "fresh, new"; see also Song 6:11, *ʾibbê hannāḥal* ("blossoms/shoots of the valley"); note *ʾābîb*, the month name associated with Passover, and a term for "first fruits; fresh, young barley" (e.g., Exod. 12:2; 13:4; Exod. 9:31; Lev. 2:14), and *ʾnb*, "fruit; foliage" (Dan. 4:12, 11[14], 18[21]).

78. As Clines (*Job 1–20*, 207–8) notices, if a *gōmeʾ* is a "perennial aquatic rush that grows to a height of ten or fifteen feet" the language of rising up high (*gʾh*) is particularly relevant.

79. See discussion of the Isaiah passage *supra* for Job 4:7.

down (*hišpaltî*) the tall tree (*'ēṣ gābōah*) . . ." and the vine stem in Ezekiel 19:10-12: "Your mother was like a vine in your vineyard ... her strong stem became like the scepters of rulers; its upper reach (*qômātô*) grew up to the leaves, and its height (*gābhô*) appeared among the multitude of branches. But it was plucked up in a fury, it was tossed down to the ground . . . ." In fact, the only positive use of *gā'āh* in the Hebrew Bible comes in the jubilant "Song of the Sea" in Exodus 15, describing Yhwh's great triumph over his enemies. Pride or triumph (insofar as it is described as *gā'āh*) is apparently Yhwh's own privilege.

Bildad's words are quite clear on their own terms, and again, as with the grass example above, we see the intersection of plant and human selves in the attempt to build a theodicy for Job. For Bildad humans live in the moral universe of dying and thriving inhabited by papyrus and reed-grass. But, as Newsom notices regarding this kind of dialogue in Job, "[n]o one thinks it relevant to ask if an ox or a stone can be *ṣedeq* [righteous]."[80] And it is true, no one does ask; there is an assumption everywhere in the exchange about the relationship between humans and nature. Plants are not neutral; nature tells a story about justice—and Job is on the losing side of this story. However, we also see that these plant images are shot through with double meanings and ominous or ambiguous tones. Not only does no one think to ask—so far in the dialogue—whether plants or animals can be impious or righteous, but Bildad and Eliphaz invoke nature as a single story with a single meaning, a story whose center we can know. Job is not flourishing. He has wilted like an impious plant.

In Bildad's speech, as in Eliphaz's address about harvest (death) in 5:26, the issue of *timing* is all-important. Growth may be cut off at the

---

80. Newsom, *Book of Job*, 145.

early stage (*bĕʾibbô*) instead of the mature stage; withering is relative, for all things wither. The imperative is to avoid withering *too soon, before other foliage.* Questions of seasonality and timing, often a focus of wisdom rumination (Eccl. 3:1-8 comes immediately to mind), are thus central and intimately related to agricultural discourse. To be sure, part of the Friends' psychological drama involves their own current flourishing vis-à-vis Job's failure in light of the fact that the four men are all regal, wealthy patriarchs of similar status. The Friends inhabit the same austere Eastern geography of desert wisdom as Job—for example, they come from Teman, in the southeastern desert, and the land of the "Shuhites," presumably nearby (Job 2:11)[81]—and they presumably share in Job's general socio-economic status of wealth, righteousness, and privilege. These miserable comforters (Job 16:2) are deeply haunted by Job's sudden loss, for without the implication of unrighteousness what veil now separates them from becoming waterless plants, too?

A brief animal reference, sandwiched between the dueling plant analogies in 8:11-19, yet again fuses the natural world with Job's predicament. 8:14 continues to address the "impious" forgetter of El from verse 13:

> (14) . . . His confidence is flimsy,[82]
> his security the house of a spider;[83]
> (15) he leans upon his house, and is not able to stand;
> he grasps it, but it will not hold.

---

81. On the gentilic *šûḥi* compare Abraham's son *Šûaḥ* in Gen. 25:2, alongside Midian, etc.

82. MT might seem to read "He loathes (*yāqôṭ*) his confidence," or even "his confidence is loathed" (from the root *qwṭ*, "loathe"), but the sense of the imagery here requires a different interpretation. Most suggest *qṭṭ/qwṭ*, as in something slight, flimsy, or fragile, which coheres with the following image of the spider web.

83. Cf. Riede, *Im Spiegel der Tier*, 133–52.

As many have noticed, the reference here to a "house" (*bayit*) not so subtly recalls the Prologue, in which Job's children die beneath a wind-toppled house (1:19). In general the "house" here indicates all that Job had and lost, blown down or removed as easily as a spider's web. Was Job's house destroyed without much effort? Spiders build back their webs rather quickly, though, without suffering a total loss. On the one hand, one might say that Job's downfall involved quite a bit of wrangling—recall the initial discussion between powerful heavenly beings—and on the other the whole affair may appear flippant and brief, highlighting God's insouciance. The spider metaphor throws us back into the problem without solving anything. We may come to expect this kind of metaphorical instability, but the instability is important to notice nonetheless, since the arguments from nature Job's Friends offer rely on their supposedly stable rhetorical appeal. The Friends are those offering up a particular vision, of a supposedly reliable narrative of nature and the self.

Bildad's address continues in chapter 8 and turns to the second, flourishing plant. While plant failure, on the one hand, seemed relatively simple for Bildad in 8:11-13, in verses 16-19 the successful plant-man comes off as precariously situated, on the edge of destruction but flourishing despite obstacles:

(16) As for the freshly watered plant (*rāṭōb*),
   it (grows) before the sun, and its shoots spread out in its garden;
(17) its roots are tangled upon a heap,
   he sees its house (*bēt*) of stones.
(18) If he swallows it up from its place,
   then he has deceived (*kiḥeš*) it—"I didn't see you!"
(19) So this is the pleasure of his way (*darkô*),
   and from the dust others sprout up afterward (*ûmēʿāpār ʿaḥēr yiṣmāḥû*).

This passage is particularly enigmatic; neither the translation provided here nor the following interpretation can be secure.[84] The "he" mentioned in verses 17-19—unidentified by proper noun—may very well be God. The plant is flourishing on its own terms, on the basis of natural cycles of water, sunshine, and its garden setting. The image of roots growing tangled upon a heap, housed in by stones, introduces a problem with the "garden" setting, suggesting hindered or problematic growth and perhaps tenacity in the face of obstacles. All of this quickly transitions into a problem for the plant—the God problem. God enters the fray, disrupting the narrative of natural survival, even survival by tenacious clinging. Bildad's deity is a harsh one here, even engaging in subterfuge.[85] Verse 18 is particularly troubling on this front: God "deceived" or "denied (knowing about)" the plant, claiming not to see it while devouring it nonetheless.[86] These are not merely God's detached ways (*derek*); rather, this is God's *choice*, in Bildad's reckoning, the joy of the divine moral decision-making process.[87] Unlike expressions of God's "joy" (*śwś*) in situations of reward for covenant fidelity (notably in Deut. 28:63; 30:9), here God's pleasure (*měśôś*; v. 19) is unhitched from any clear behavior on the part of the plant.[88] The plant in verses 16-17 certainly seems to be doing the right thing.

---

84. For example, see the very different rendering by Dhorme, *Job*, 121–22; Habel, *Book of Job*, 168 translates "he" as "its" (= the plant's) in vv. 17-19.

85. Compare with deception (*kiḥēš*) as a divine tool in 1 Kgs. 13:18, as well as 1 Kgs. 22:20-23 (using different terminology). Note *kiḥēš* as plant failure in Hab. 3:17.

86. So Seow, *Job 1–21*, 515, 535–36; "If one should destroy it from its place, But disclaims it—'I did not see you!' . . . ."

87. The term *derek*, "way," is a wisdom-oriented moral decision-making term, used repeatedly throughout Job and Proverbs and elsewhere in the Hebrew Bible (e.g., Gen. 6:12; Deut. 11:22; Mic. 4:2; Ps. 1:6; 25:8; 27:11, etc.).

88. See also the "joy" (*śwś*) of nature flourishing in Isa. 35:1; 66:14; Jer. 32:41. *Pace* Gordis, *Book of Job*, 93, there is no reason to think that the "joy" here in Job is ironic or that we should prefer a different reading of *měśôś* in order to avoid the moral implications here.

For Bildad, then, failure for the immoral seems guaranteed and for the upright failure still happens, willy-nilly, at God's (in)discretion. The question of God's pleasure in violent, unpredictable, or strange creation will reappear meaningfully later in the book (Job 38:7, 39:21). For now it is enough for Bildad to assert the possibility of human success, even if yoking that success to the instability of the plant world. Bildad's story in chapter 8, however, is not finished. Verses 20-22 provide an odd dénouement in which Bildad concludes by asserting God's straightforwardly moral system of rewards: the blameless will not be rejected; the wicked will disappear. Newsom is surely correct to characterize Bildad's words here as discordant, at least in the sense that sure moral schemes do not comport with the divine insouciance on display in Job 8:18-19.[89] Historically minded interpreters face an intractable choice—to attribute the discordance to the hands of frantic editors who might insert a phrase here and there as an ongoing engagement with the book's meaning, or to view this ambiguity as built into the text itself from its inception.

In the end, as it stands, the plant discourse in Job 8 refutes the notion of a completely simple, unidirectional nature narrative; the nature metaphors are garbled enough to undercut their use as a kind of primitive, singular wisdom science. The trope of "survival" is still the dominant theme here, and indeed this theme permeates the plant imagery generally in the Friends' nature narrative. In this instance it is precisely the resilience of plants that provides hope for the future—they will sprout up again from the dust. Job's story is truly unfinished for Bildad, in the sense that Job's experience could be viewed as one part of a natural cycle of flourishing and wanton destruction.

---

89. Newsom, *Book of Job*, 105.

Ask the Plants of the Earth, and They Will Teach You

Having now reviewed the majority of the Friends' most meaningful arguments from plant and animal analogies (with a few more to come *infra*), I turn to Job's own responses in chapters 9, 12, and 14. Before Job engages in the true dialogue of self-making, however, he offers a bitter lament in chapter 3 that contains some striking nature imagery.[90] Through his curses, "let the day on which I was born perish" (3:3) and "let there be darkness" (3:4), Job attempts to reverse or break the calendar, throwing nature's goodness as well as its brutality into an abyss. Gloom and clouds and dark days are the metaphors here (3:5); blackness is the void out of which no green plant will grow. The sun will not shine on the earth, for now there is no sun, and nurturing domestic animals will not creep about on that earth, grazing on its produce. No rejoicing can be found here, no joy-shouts (*rĕnānāh*, 3:7).

Though we are left without plants, what we *do* still have in Job's cursed, dismal world, is an animal: Leviathan (*liwyātān*, 3:8). For the moment let us be content to identify this creature as something chaotic and awful, to be considered on parallel with another sea monster, Yamm:

> (3:8) May those who curse Yamm curse it [= the day of Job's birth],
> (9) those skilled to call up Leviathan . . .[91]

In the Ugaritic Baal epic, Yamm is a malevolent deity who stands in opposition to the warrior god Baal's attempts to establish an orderly house for himself. Cursing plays a role in Baal's engagement with

---

90. On these speeches see Leo G. Perdue, "Metaphorical Theology in the Book of Job: Theological Anthropology in the First Cycle of Job's Speeches (Job 3; 6–7; 9–10)," 129–56 in Willem A. M. Beuken, ed., *The Book of Job* (BETL 114; Louvain: Peeters, 1994).

91. Here I follow a common emendation, reading the MT's *'ōrrê yôm*, "day cursers," as *'ōrrê yam*, "Yamm cursers." Even the concept of a "day curser" would of course make sense here, since Job had been referring to the day of his birth in 3:1–7.

Yamm, as the weapons forged for the warrior deity take their power from the oral incantation of their names: Yagrušu, "drive out," and 'Ayyamurru, "expel."[92] Later in the story a creature named Lôtan, etymologically and mythically equivalent to the biblical Leviathan,[93] appears in a context of battle:

When you [= Baal] smite Lôtan, the fleeing serpent,
finish off the twisting serpent,
the close-coiling one with seven heads . . .[94]

Job's imagery here evokes not nature covenants or affirmations of nature's divine goodness, but rather black magic and violence. Given their prefacing with this kind of narrative disjunction in Job 3, we can situate the Friends' floral and faunal metaphors in Job 4 and following as story-building, life-affirming, and covenant-rooting. But Job has already journeyed deeply into the pre-creation desert—a place Genesis 1:2 calls *tōhû wābōhû*, "barren and unlivable"[95]—and, as we will see later, he can only be reintroduced back into a different kind of world.

Job's own nature narrative, then, as it unfolds in his bitter responses in chapters 9, 12, and 14, reads as a quite logical extension of a cursed and ecologically unfriendly cosmos. Whereas earlier the Friends pointed to plants and animals, invoking a familiar domestic sphere, Job turns to stars, cosmos, and rock—all elements of "nature," of course, yet distant from the organic intimacy of gardens and goats. For Job, God is

---

92. See the edition by Dennis Pardee, "The Ba'lu Myth," *COS* I, 241–74, at 248–49. See comment on the role of the spoken curse as weapon in Seth L. Sanders, *The Invention of Hebrew* (Urbana: University of Illinois Press, 2009), 51–52.

93. See, e.g., Smith, *Origins*, 36–37.

94. Pardee, "Ba'lu Myth," 265.

95. For *tōhû* as desert and uninhabitable land see Deut. 32:10; Isa. 34:11; 45:18; Jer. 4:23; Ps. 107:40; and Job 12:24 (discussed below).

(9:5) . . . the one who uproots mountains,
>they do not know when he will overturn them in his anger;

(6) he is the one who rocks the earth out of its place,
>and its pillars shake;

(7) he is the one who merely speaks to the sun,
>and it does not rise;
>he seals up the stars;

(8) he alone is the one who stretches out the skies,
>he the one who treads upon the heights of the sea;

(9) he is the one who made Bear and Orion,
>Pleiades and the Chambers of Teman . . .

The images here are not generic pictures of chaos or unpredictability, standard though such language may be in the Hebrew Bible.[96] More specifically, Job has, in effect, compared *himself* to a mountain, or the sun—perhaps even arrogantly—in that he has been likewise uprooted without warning. Job is the sea that has been trod upon; he is the earth shaken out of its place. Nature is off-kilter precisely because an injustice has been done. We may compare this state of affairs with the relationship between justice and the cosmos in Psalm 82, a startling scene in which Israel's God is depicted as one among a divine council.[97] For the moment, in the world of this psalm, other deities are truly in charge, but their lack of knowledge and failure to execute justice (*špṭ*) for marginalized human communities disqualifies them from their putative rule. These ethical failures have clear cosmological (and thus ecological) implications (Ps. 82:5): "all the foundations of the earth (*môsdê 'āreṣ*) are shaken."

96. See, e.g., the verb *rāgaz* ("shake") with regard to the divine (and destructive) shaking of the cosmos in 2 Sam. 22:8; Isa. 5:25; 13:13; 23:11; Joel 2:10; Pss. 18:8(7); 77:17-19(16-18).

97. See the detailed review of issues in Psalm 82 by Peter Machinist, "How Gods Die, Biblically and Otherwise: A Problem of Restructuring," 189–240 in Beate Pongratz-Leisten, ed., *Reconsidering the Concept of Revolutionary Monotheism* (Winona Lake, IN: Eisenbrauns, 2011).

So too, for Job, moral and ethical implications characterize his own framing of the cosmos in 9:5-9. In this upside-down ecology of thrown-down mountains and wantonly blackened stars, humans act out nature's amoral drama:

> (9:22) Therefore, I say: it is all the same (*'aḥat hî'*)—
> > he finishes off the blameless (*tām*) and the wicked (*rāšā'*)!
> (23) When the flood (*šôṭ*) brings sudden death,
> > he mocks the despair of the innocent!
> (24) The earth is given over into the hands of the wicked (*rāšā'*);
> > he covers up the eyes (*pĕnê*) of its judges—
> > if not, then who does it?

Such statements—and especially their further development in Job 12:13-25—comprise some of the more devastating accusations against God made by any character in the Bible. To be sure, no outright *enemy* of God in the Bible makes a speech like this anywhere. One can find instances in which Israel's deity is said to be vaguely responsible for the entire spectrum of moral activity, ranging from "good" to "bad." Consider two verses: Isaiah 45:7, "the one who forms light and creates darkness, the one who makes peace and the one who creates *rā'* (evil, woe, destruction)—I, Yhwh, do all these things"; Amos 3:6, "Is a horn blown in the city, and the people do not tremble? Is there *rā'āh* (evil, destruction) in a city, and Yhwh has not caused it?" In these oft-cited passages the terminology for "evil" (*rā'*, *rā'āh*) could easily be translated or understood as "destruction," as in "Yhwh brings *destructive judgment* on the wicked."

In Job 9, however, the implications are made chillingly clear: Yhwh laughs at victims; his ecology is unpredictable and disaster-ridden; he is indiscriminate, but not necessarily indifferent—he actively works *against the righteous* to obfuscate the judicial process and collude with the wicked. The reference to a "flood" (*šôṭ*) in 9:23

briefly but effectively highlights the problem inherent in the Friends' floral and faunal analogies:[98] water is not just for gently watering the gardens of righteous gardeners but also for drowning the innocent. This, too, represents a legitimate biblical narrative of nature, creation, uncreation, and suffering (as in Genesis 6–7). Moreover, Job attacks the Friends' notion of the *visibility* of wisdom (4:8; 5:3, 24; compare Prov. 24:30-32), by asserting that God covers up the eyes (lit. "faces," *pĕnê*) of human judges. One cannot simply observe God's ways in nature under a rigged system like this.

Perhaps this pillorying of the traditional "Good God" is to be excused in light of Job's suffering; he is in the midst of lament, a tradition in which one speaks not of proper theology but of the human situation in the world.[99] Even through his general laments, though, Job turns to address specifically his relationship to the plants and animals that Eliphaz and Bildad have so far evoked in order to understand his position before God. In another major speech in chapter 12, Job produces a little "natural theology" of his own, and asks his audience to consider what the earth may teach us:

> (7) By all means, ask the animals, and they will teach you,
>   the birds of the air, and they will inform you.
> (8) Or speak to the earth, and it will teach you,
>   and the fish of the sea will instruct you.

Such injunctions may appear to set up an attempt at a full-blown counter-narrative on Job's part, and yet the speech descends into hopeless futility, even sarcasm:

---

98. The root *šwṭ* most often refers to "disaster" or "scourge" more generally, but I translate the term here as "flood" in anticipation of Job's comments later in 14:18. See also Ezek. 27:26 for *šwṭ* in the context of water/flood imagery. Seow, *Job 1–21*, 566, notes that Maimonides interpreted *šwṭ* here as a flood.

99. As elsewhere in the Bible; see, e.g., Walter Brueggemann, *Spirituality of the Psalms* (Minneapolis: Fortress Press, 2002).

(9) Who does not know all these things—
   that the hand of Yhwh has done this?
(10) In his hand is the life (*nepeš*) of all living things,
   and the breath (*rûaḥ*) of all human flesh.

The reference to the "hand of Yhwh" (*yad yhwh*) in verse 9 is clever because, like so many words in Job, it is profoundly multivalent: the hand is powerful to defend or guide the people (Num. 11:23; Josh. 4:24; 1 Kgs. 18:46; Ezra 7:6), and yet the phrase *yad yhwh* also indicates sickness, insanity, plague, and burden (Exod. 9:3; Judg. 2:15; 1 Sam. 5:6, 9; Jer. 15:17; Ezek. 3:14).[100] Moreover, this is the only place in the Joban dialogues where the tetragrammaton (Yhwh) appears; but unlike the use of the full identical phrase in Isaiah 41:20 ("the hand of Yhwh has done this") to praise Yhwh's acts of deliverance, here Job characteristically and bitterly turns the formulation into an advertisement for God's acts of humiliation against humans and nature.[101]

What is it exactly, Job asks, that we can learn from the animals and birds and fish? The picture Job proceeds to lay out in 12:13-25 is a dystopian vision of a broken world, a devastated un-created earth upon which humans stagger like drunkards (12:24-25): "He takes away understanding (*lēb*) from the heads of the people of the earth, and he makes them wander in a wasteland (*tōhû*)[102] without roads; they grope around in the dark, and there is no light—he makes them stagger like drunkards." Job's use of multiple terms in 12:7-8

100. J. J. M. Roberts, "The Hand of Yahweh," *VT* 21 (1971): 244–51; note Roberts's discussion (esp. pp. 246–48) of the "hand upon me" motif when related to illness and suffering in *Ludlul bēl nēmeqi* and related ancient Near Eastern texts.

101. Kathryn Schifferdecker, *Out of the Whirlwind: Creation Theology in the Book of Job* (HTS 61; Cambridge, MA: Harvard University Press, 2008), 42–43.

102. On the reversal of creation here signified by *tōhû*, note Gen. 1:2, *tōhû wābōhû*, mentioned above with relation to Job's lament in Job 3.

for animals, the reference to *nepeš* and *rûaḥ* in 12:10, and the use of *tōhû* in 12:24 all clearly mark the author's direct familiarity with the creation tradition of Genesis 1 (or an independent and similarly worded story), indicating that the repeated concern with the created world of nature and its relationship to suffering is an intentional focus of this text. God reserves the power to withhold rain for himself, but when he does send forth the waters "they overwhelm the land" with flood (12:15).[103] Ecological wisdom and creation power surely fall into God's hands—but the moral implications of this control, for Job, lead us away from the garden and into a wasteland, and then from desert back to flood. God works at the extremes.

Job's most extended natural comparison comes in chapter 14, where he takes up the theme of the tree as a narrative of human fate. Most famously, Psalm 1 uses the tree as a wisdom trope; there, those who delight in the Torah of Yhwh are

(3) . . . like a tree (*'ēṣ*) planted by streams of water, which bears his/its
fruit in season (*bĕʿittô*);
his/its leaves do not wither, and all he/it does will prosper.

Here we find a concentration of themes we have been considering throughout our study of the intersection of floral imagery and the human self: a direct comparison of the human to a plant; a reference to seasons of flourishing for the man-plant (*bĕʿittô*; compare Job 5:26; Deut. 11:13-15); and even grammatical features, the masculine singular verb (*yaʿăśeh*) and masculine singular suffix -*ô* (he/it), which allow one to think of either the tree or the man (from Ps. 1:1, *hāʾîš*) with reference to the fruit, leaves, and actions. The Friends, of course, had been laboring to draw Job's experience into a Psalmic narrative of nature and self-making: Job is out of sorts, but he can re-grow

---

103. See the perceptive comments on this by Norman C. Habel, "Earth First: Inverse Cosmology in Job," *ESWT*, 65–77, at 73.

himself and offer produce at the right time (death; Job 5:26). Even so, his lack of success points to a lack of water for his plant-self (Job 5:3, 10, 25-26; 8:11-13).

Job's own plant metaphor confronts the identity-experience narrative directly in 14:1-2, further developing the tree image specifically in 14:1-2, 7-12:

(1) Humankind, born of woman,
　　few of days and full of trembling—
(2) like a flower comes forth and then withers (*wayyimmāl*),[104]
　　flees away like a shadow and cannot stand . . .
(7) But there is hope for a tree (*'ēṣ*)—
　　if it is cut down, it can be renewed (*yaḥălîp*),[105] and its shoots do not
　　altogether cease.
(8) Even if its root grows old in the earth,
　　and its stump expires in the dust,
(9) at the scent of water it will sprout up,
　　and make branches like a (new) plant.
(10) But mortals die, and they go down;
　　humans expire, and where are they?
(11) Water disappears from the sea,
　　and rivers waste away and dry up—
(12) and man lies down and does not rise up,
　　until the heavens are no more they will not wake up,
　　they will not be aroused from their sleep.

The marked shift between the flower in verses 1-2 and the tree in verses 7-12 may suggest a new type of speech or editorial layer here, and these kinds of source-critical solutions abound in the secondary literature. Alternatively, the rumination on two different kinds of plants may represent wisdom discourse on different kinds of

---

104. Compare with plant withering (*mll*) as a wisdom trope in Pss. 37:2; 58:8(7); 90:6; Job 18:16; 26:24.
105. The basic sense of the verb *ḥlp* is "change" or "pass along"; with reference to plants we should understand this as replanting or renewing. See Isa. 9:9 and Ps. 90:5-6.

ecologies, as if Job might say: I am like a flower—beautiful for a moment but quickly doomed—but I am *not* like a tree, for which there is hope even in dire circumstances. The references to root and stump in verse 8 echo combative plant language employed in the dialogues so far. Recall that Eliphaz (5:3) claimed to see the fool "taking root" (*maśrîš*), only to fail, and Bildad (8:17) observes the freshly watered plant thriving with its roots tangled up in a heap, still living but perhaps on the verge of sudden calamity. The verb Job uses to characterize the tree root "growing old" in the ground in 14:8, *zāqan*, does not appear anywhere else in the Bible, at least not with reference to a non-human subject, making this particular use of *zāqan* an unsubtle cue linking together the experience of the tree to that of Job.[106] The tree may grow old, but it will rise again; Job will become a *zāqēn*, an elder, but he has no future once he dies in his state of suffering.

One may wonder to what extent Job's afterlife analogy here should be taken as representative of some particularly ancient Jewish view about (the lack of) life after death, or whether, out of his pain, Job simply cannot see beyond the scandal of his own mortality.[107] Biblical wisdom literature does straightforwardly deny at least certainty regarding the afterlife; most famously in Ecclesiastes 3:18-21, Qoheleth ("the Preacher") expresses skepticism about rising souls, and in Proverbs, where there is no such meditation at all, we find no threat of punishment or promise of afterlife reward—prompting readers to wonder why the proverbial authors would not have discussed these options if indeed they were truly options.[108] It is not advisable to categorize afterlife views in the Hebrew Bible or the

---

106. Cf. Gen. 18:11; 27:2; Josh. 13:1; 23:2; 1 Sam. 8:5; 12:2; Ruth 1:12.

107. See Dan Mathewson, *Death and Survival in the Book of Job: Desymbolization and Traumatic Experience* (London: T & T Clark, 2006), 103–4 on chapter 14; Aron Pinker, "Job's Perspectives on Death," *Jewish Bible Quarterly* 35 (2007): 73–84; and the perceptive review of imagery in Job 14 by Janzen, *Job*, 108–13.

traditions developed afterward as a generic whole, since in fact we find a spectrum of possibilities expressed in different ways. Daniel 12, historically late as far as the Hebrew Bible is concerned (2d c. BCE), enigmatically embraces some type of resurrection, while Isaiah 26:14-19 seems to simultaneously deny and affirm resurrection, and whole swaths of other texts in the Hebrew Bible (e.g., the Torah, most of the prophets, and various narrative material) simply do not address the issue at all. Later Jewish authors would go so far as to say that resurrection can be inferred from every passage of the Torah (*Midr. Sifre Deut.* 306; see also *Sanh.* 90b), and in the Christian New Testament, Jesus, acting as a standard Jewish interpreter, in Mark 12:26-27 finds resurrection through wordplay and non-obvious reading strategies.[109] In Job 14:9 the "scent of water" at which a dead or nearly dead tree root may come alive again could offer the reader some promise, but the contrast Job draws between this scenario of natural revivification and his own situation

108. Compare also the statements in Eccl. 9:4-10; Isa. 26:14; 38:18; Pss. 6:6(5); 30:10(9); 88:6(5), 11-12(10-11); 115:16-17, all of which seem to indicate no afterlife. On wisdom and death in the Hebrew Bible see Roland Murphy, "Death and Afterlife in the Wisdom Literature," 101–16 in Jacob Neusner and A. J. Avery-Peck, eds., *Judaism in Late Antiquity*. Part 4: *Death, Life-After-Death, Resurrection and the World-to-Come in the Judaisms of Late Antiquity* (Leiden: Brill, 2000). Later Wisdom authors in the Jewish tradition would in fact affirm heavenly rewards for the righteous and punishments for the wicked; see David Penchansky, *Understanding Wisdom Literature: Conflict and Dissonance in the Hebrew Text* (Grand Rapids: Eerdmans, 2012), 97–109.

109. The most cogent argument for recognizing resurrection on a symbolic spectrum throughout the Hebrew Bible, and then carried forward into normative Jewish tradition, is Jon D. Levenson, *Resurrection and the Restoration of Israel: The Ultimate Victory of the God of Life* (New Haven: Yale University Press, 2006). Other major works on afterlife in the Hebrew Bible include Theodore J. Lewis, *Cults of the Dead in Ancient Israel and Ugarit* (HSM 39; Atlanta: Scholars Press, 1989); Brian Schmidt, *Israel's Beneficent Dead: Ancestor Cult and Necromancy in Ancient Israelite Religion and Tradition* (Tübingen: J. C. B. Mohr, 1994); Klaas Spronk, *Beatific Afterlife in Ancient Israel and the Ancient Near East* (AOAT 219; Neukirchen-Vluyn: Neukirchener Verlag, 1986); Rachel Hallote, *Death, Burial, and Afterlife in the Biblical World: How the Israelites and Their Neighbors Treated the Dead* (Chicago: Ivan R. Dee, 2001); Philip S. Johnston, *Shades of Sheol: Death and Afterlife in the Old Testament* (Downers Grove: InterVarsity, 2002); Karel van der Toorn, *Family Religion in Babylonia, Syria, and Israel* (Leiden: Brill, 1996), esp. 206–35; and, from an archaeological perspective, Elizabeth Bloch-Smith, *Judahite Burial Practices and Beliefs about the Dead* (JSOTSS 123; Sheffield: Sheffield Academic Press, 1992).

could not be clearer (v. 10, but mortals die . . ."; v. 14, "but man dies ..."). Whatever the case, the point here in chapter 14 is, for Job, similar to that in Job 7:9 (also through natural analogy): "A cloud vanishes and goes away—so too those who go down to Sheol do not come up."

Job's speech descends into further bleakness. Nature provides more appropriate metaphors for human experience than trees: barren seas and dried-up rivers (14:11). Where is God's covenant in the face of such reversals? Job asks that God "remember" him (*tizkĕrēnî*, "remember me," 14:13; see also 7:7; 10:9), recalling the covenantal language Eliphaz employed to frame his floral analogies in 4:17. Eliphaz's covenant memory moves in the direction of Deuteronomic blessing and curse—both are options. Now, for Job, a purely entropic principle sets in:

> (14:18) Indeed, a mountain falls and withers away,
>   and rock is removed from its place;
> (19) waters grind rocks down,
>   its flood torrents wipe away the dust of the earth—
>   this is how you destroy the hope of humanity.

The *waw* of apodosis (*wĕ*) in verse 19—*wĕtiqwat 'ĕnôš he'ĕbadtā*—links the divine destructive tendency to the movements of natural breakdown. Plants are lively, changeable, renewable. Trees spring up from death. But Job asks: what about the flood? These images of disintegrating earth evoke not seasonal changes—which the Friends mention with hope of repentance—but rather long geographic history and thick inevitability. If Job speaks of any change here it is the sudden change that comes from flash flooding, not the managed, seasonal world of carefully tended crops. However harsh this language may be, however, it is finally a direct engagement with the physical world and with the arguments of the Friends, and thus it is a journey into narrative self-making that can form an actual, embodied basis for further exploration.

Old Hills and Dead Branches

Eliphaz will not be outdone in the argument and comes back one more time in Job 15 with a series of rejoinders. The tone of the discussion turns increasingly frantic and personal as Eliphaz accuses Job of impiety on every level, including effrontery toward God. Job has condemned himself (15:6); he drinks iniquity like water (15:16); Job has threatened God, but he will lose (15:25). Eliphaz evokes his own notion of deep geological time against Job in 15:7-8:

> (7) Are you the firstborn of the human race?
>   Were you born before the hills?
> (8) Did you listen in on the secret council of God?
>   Do you limit wisdom to yourself?

The hills are older than Job, and thus their example must teach him in the priority of age (see also 15:10: "the grey-haired and the aged are with us [= the Friends], those mightier in days than your father"). Of course, neither Job nor the Friends have listened in on God's secret council (*sôd*),[110] which is precisely the grounds for their disagreement; had any of them listened, they would have heard a scenario perhaps more monstrous or strange than any of them imagined, rendering their entire discussion meaningless. For Eliphaz all humanity and all of the heavens are tainted—and how much more so Job (15:19): "He (God) does not even trust his Holy Ones [*qĕdōšāw*, possibly angelic or divine beings], and the very heavens are not pure in his eyes." In fact,

---

110. The term *sôd* often refers to God's secret decision-making capacity, which he reveals to his prophets. See Jer. 23:18, 22; Amos 3:7; Pss. 25:14; 89:8(7). See Habel, *Job*, 253–54 for perceptive comments on the "primal human" tradition here and the secret council of God.

of course, God does trust his angelic court enough to make the kinds of deals he has already made regarding Job (1:6-12; 2:1-7).

In the remainder of the speech (15:17-35) Eliphaz lays out a terrifying moral vision of his own, not so different in character from Job's own musings in chapters 9 and 12. For Job, however, the dystopic earth on which humans wander blindly like drunkards is amorally administered (see 9:22 and 12:16); for Eliphaz the wicked (*rāšāʿ*) experience the terrors of a desolate land (15:20). Eliphaz endorses the possibility of a scorched human existence, but he frames it within the narrative of a contingent covenant. Why does one suffer? "Because he stretched out his hand against God, and tried to prevail over Shaddai" (15:25). Predictably, by this point Eliphaz must include a vision of the natural world that mirrors the narrative of human experience (15:28-31):

> (28) (The wicked one) will reside in desolate cities,
>> in houses where no one can live,
>> which are fit to be ruinous heaps;
> (29) he will not be rich, and his wealth will not endure;
>> his possessions will not stretch down into the Underworld (*'ereṣ*);[111]
> (30) he cannot turn aside from darkness;
>> flames dry up his shoots (*yōnaqtô*),
>> and he will be removed by the breath of his mouth.
> (31) Let him not trust in emptiness—he is in error,
>> for emptiness will be his reward.
> (32) Before his time (*yômô*) it will be fulfilled,
>> and his branch will not be green.
> (33) As one destroys (*yaḥmōs*) sour grapes from his vine,
>> so too he will cast off his blossom like an olive tree.
> (34) For the counsel of the impious (*ḥānēp*) is barren,
>> and fire consumes the tents of bribery;

---

111. For this sense of *'ereṣ* ("earth") here see, e.g., Pope, *Job*, 107, 112. Compare the use of *'ereṣ* with Job 10:21-22; Isa. 26:19; Exod. 15:10,12, among many other examples in the Hebrew Bible, as well as the Akkadian *erṣētu* (*CAD* 4, 310–11).

(35) They conceive violence and give birth to trouble,
    and they prepare deceit in their bellies.

Though Eliphaz's routine has become obvious, the floral imagery in this portion of the poem creatively resonates with themes developed throughout the dialogues. The word *yôneqet* ("shoot, outward spreading plant-growth") in 15:30 indicates the expansive possibility for future growth (see Ezek. 17:22; Hos. 14:6[7]; Ps. 80:12[11]; compare the verb *yānaq*, used for the child's act of suckling), again highlighting the contingency of potential. There is no iron determinism at play here for Eliphaz; humans can thrive or fail depending on their produce. Just a chapter earlier, in Job 14:7, Job had claimed the "shoots" (*yôneqet*) of the tree signal hope, in opposition to his own position as a human. Now Eliphaz drags Job back into the realm of nature. Humans have a "time," a life-cycle space that signals true potential, and ultimately fulfillment. The shoots race toward maturity, reaching out and looking for water, but alas, they may be cut off: the impious loses out "before his time" (*bĕlō᾽ yômô*, v. 32). Everything depends on cultivation.

Humans are Maggots

The shortest speech in the dialogues, Bildad's in Job 25, may be an accident of textual transmission. Many commentators on chapters 25–26 see the speech in 25:1-6 as well as 26:5-14 as Bildad's, whereas the Masoretic (traditional) Hebrew text attributes only 25:1-6 to Bildad and the following material in chapter 26 to Job (26:1: "Then Job answered and said . . .").[112] There are two main reasons for emendation here. First, Bildad's speech in chapter 25 simply looks too

---

112. See, e.g., Nømmik, *Die Freundesreden*, 65–68; Pope, *Job*, xviii, 163–64; Dhorme, *Job*, 368–75; Robert Alter, *The Wisdom Books* (New York: W. W. Norton, 2010), 106–10; David Wolfers, "Job 26: An Orphan Chapter," 387–91 in Beuken, ed., *The Book of Job*.

short. None of the other speeches is this length, though admittedly it is also the case that no two of the other speeches are *exactly* the same length. The dialogue characters speak in rounds, perhaps with each speaker taking an intended three turns: Eliphaz beginning in 4:1; 15:1; and 22:1; Bildad in 8:1; 18:1; and 25:1; Zophar in 11:1 and 20:1 (Job's many responses come scattered among those of the Friends). Notably, Zophar does not get a third turn, leading some to suspect that his third speech was lost or accidentally transposed out of place (e.g., 27:7-23, put in the mouth of Job, is a candidate for Zophar's lost speech). Problems of this kind seem real and pervasive in chapters 25–27. Second, interpreters have turned to questions of content and argumentation—the speaker at the beginning of chapter 26, particularly in verses 2-4, sounds very much like Eliphaz in his opening taunt (Job 4:3-4). Alternatively, Job here could be speaking sarcastically to the Friends, chiding them for unwise words in the face of his innocent suffering.

Chapter 25, at any rate, seems clearly to be from Bildad's mouth, as he takes up a rather negative anthropology reminiscent of earlier elements of the argument:

> (4) How can a mortal be righteous with El?
>   And how can one born of woman be pure?
> (5) Even the moon has no protection,
>   and the stars are not pure in his eyes!
> (6) What then of a mortal—a maggot!—
>   and the son of man—a worm!

This is a blunt identification of humans with the basest of animals. Job had earlier spoken of the worm (*rimmāh*) in terms of his lowly estate: the worm was his family member in 17:4, both in terms of emotional lowliness but also with reference to the earthy physicality of the grave, and in 24:20 the worm graphically eats the dead (= soon

Job himself). In Isaiah 41:14, Jacob/Israel is called a worm (*tôlaʿat*) in a moment of national weakness, but God promises to help Israel; in Psalm 22 the human identification with a worm is an appeal toward piety and humility on the part of the faithful sufferer. For Bildad, however, this worm language is "an almost philosophical teaching on anthropology."[113] The entire cosmos is a failure before God—there is the naked moon and the impure stars, and then just worms all the way down.

The Monstrous Animal

The speaker in Job 26 turns to a creation scene of immense power to describe the way of God in relation to nature. As discussed above, though Job is explicitly made the speaker here in the traditional text, evidence of textual corruption in chapters 25–27 generally provides enough warrant for skepticism regarding the content of the words in chapter 26. Would Job really speak forth these images at this point? Though Job 26:2-4 sounds like Eliphaz in 4:3-4, Job may be turning those very words back on the Friends—and the actions of God in 26:5-14 speak of a violent deity from whose actions no aspect of heaven or earth is safe (note especially 26:5-6). This would be very much in line with what Job has been saying so far, though, as we have seen, the Friends have also pointed to God's profound unfathomability as one argument for why Job has suffered. All parties in the argument seem open to the idea that God is unpredictable, though the Friends paradoxically add to this many affirmations of God's covenant predictability as well. Job has been the only one so far to speak of monstrous animals (recall Leviathan and Yamm in 3:8 and then later in 26:12-13), and Job the only one to invoke the word *tōhû*, a desert or void, to speak of God's moral universe (6:18, 12:24,

---

113. Newsom, *Book of Job*, 142.

and then again in 26:7, if this is Job). Thus it would not be completely unreasonable on thematic grounds to see him as the speaker here again.[114] We can profitably read this poem through Job's voice as a working concept, aware of the textual problems and also that the Joban poet represents through the voices of the characters a variety of discrete viewpoints (even from the same character).

In Job 26:7-13 the speaker offers a stark vision of creation:

(7) He stretches out Zaphon upon the void (*tōhû*),
  he hangs the earth upon nothing;
(8) he binds up the waters in his clouds,
  and the cloud is not torn apart by them;
(9) he obscures the face of the full moon,[115]
  and spreads his cloud over it;
(10) he decreed a circle (*ḥōq ḥāg*) upon the face of the waters,
  at the limits of light and darkness;
(11) the pillars of the heavens tremble,
  they are astounded at his rebuke;
(12) by his strength he stilled the Waters (*hayyām*),
  and by his understanding he struck Rahab;
(13) by his breath he made the heavens beautiful,
  his hand pierced the Fleeing Serpent (*nāḥāš bārîaḥ*) . . .

As attentive readers of the Hebrew Bible know, creation stories come in various forms, and Genesis 1 represents only the first of many accounts.[116] These creation scenes can be considered roughly under two headings: peaceful creation and violent creation. In the ancient Near East broadly, both creation types are attested—the parade example of violent creative acts comes in the Babylonian *Enuma Elish*, while more peaceful scenes, like those in the thirteenth-century

---

114. Also Schifferdecker, *Out of the Whirlwind*, 44–46, and sources cited there.
115. Following the common emendation here for *kissē* ("throne"), read as *kēse'* ("full moon"; see Prov. 7:20; Ps. 81:4), as in Pope, *Job*, 165.
116. See William P. Brown, *The Ethos of Cosmos: The Genesis of Moral Imagination in the Bible* (Grand Rapids: Eerdmans, 1999).

Egyptian "Memphite Theology," depict creation through thought and speech. Of this peaceful kind, Genesis 1 is the exemplar, and Psalm 104 also participates in a world of serene, sovereign mastery. True, Genesis 1 offers a glimpse of a threat—the pre-creation world broods with "darkness," saltwater depths (*těhôm*), waters, and the *tōhû wābōhû* ("uninhabitable wasteland")—but the nearly immeasurable space between God's first command in Genesis 1:3, *yěhî 'ôr* ("let there be light") and the direct result, *wayhî 'ôr* ("and there was light"), openly mocks the very notion that God can be opposed.[117] In Psalm 104 a similar plot unfolds, with an emphasis on boundaries, limits, and stability (Ps. 104:5, 9); God does offer a rebuke to the waters (v. 7), but the waters scurry off with nary another word. As if to provide a brief but tantalizing demythologization of an *Enuma-Elish*-like monster threat, Psalm 104:26 mentions Leviathan (*liwyātān*), only to immediately domesticate him as a plaything in a mundane sea meant for mundane human seafaring.[118] The story of peaceful creation is, to borrow a phrase from Walter Brueggemann, a narrative of *orientation*—all is well with the world, for the Divine Master is in control.[119]

The violent creation scene, on the other hand, represents a different world—a narrative of *disorientation*. The violent creation scene comes to life in times of distress and political change. Presumably, the *Enuma Elish* represents just such a world: Babylon is newly ascendant and periods of political distress or novelty (represented by Hammurapi's rise to the throne or the Babylonian revival under Nebuchadnezzar I in the late twelfth century BCE) find

117. Mark S. Smith, *The Priestly Vision of Genesis 1* (Minneapolis: Fortress Press, 2010), 64–69.

118. Jon D. Levenson, *Creation and the Persistence of Evil: The Jewish Drama of Divine Omnipotence* (San Francisco: Harper & Row, 1988), 17, 53–65. On the relationship between Psalm 104 and Genesis 1, see Ronald A. Simkins, "Anthropocentrism and the Place of Humans in the Biblical Tradition," *Journal of Religion & Society*, Supplement Series 9 (2013): 16–29, esp. 23–25.

119. Brueggemann, *Spirituality of the Psalms*.

expression in Marduk's rise to power over chaos. So too, in Psalm 74:12-17 the creation recitation explicitly occurs within a context of national despair at the destruction of the Temple in 586 BCE. In this context of disorientation, the violent creator God comes forth:

> (12) But God my king is from of old,
>   doing wonders of salvation in the midst of the earth;
> (13) you divided the sea (*yām*) in your strength,
>   you broke the heads of the monsters (*tannînîm*) upon the waters;
> (14) you crushed the heads of Leviathan (*liwyātān*),
>   you gave him as food to the people of the desert;
> (15) you split open spring and torrent,
>   you dried up the mighty rivers . . .

After the cracking of skulls, ecological ordering begins:

> (16) . . . yours is the day, and also the night,
>   you established light and sun;
> (17) you set up a limit for all the territories of the earth;
>   summer and winter—you fashioned them.

In passages like this the monster takes on the role of similar creatures in a wide range of world literature: the monster is the *Unheimliche*, the Not-at-Home, threatening what is safe, domestic, and tranquil.[120] Foreigners invaded God's house (= Temple, the *bêt yhwh*), and now the divine warrior must rise up to defend the house.

Norman Habel claims that the creation imagery in Job 26 "deviated from the major Israelite tradition" in that the world is hung upon

---

120. For the imagery of the monster as the *Unheimliche* see Timothy K. Beal, *Religion and Its Monsters* (New York: Routledge, 2002), 4–5, where Beal argues that monsters are "personifications of *unheimlich*. They stand for what endangers one's sense of at-homeness . . . one's sense of security, stability, integrity, well-being, health, and meaning. . . . They are figures of chaos disorientation *within* order and orientation, revealing deep insecurities in one's faith in oneself, one's society, and one's world." In this conception monsters may threaten "one's confidence in the meaning, integrity and well-being of the entire cosmos (the world ecology as 'house')." See ch. 4 below and the discussion of Job 40–41 there for more reflection on the "monster" category.

emptiness, in mid-air, while elsewhere one finds a solid earth resting on pillars (as in 1 Sam. 2:8).[121] However, in Job 26 house and temple imagery does appear—verse 11 reminds us of this architecture through reference to the structure's "pillars" ("the pillars [ʿammûdê] of the heavens tremble"; compare Job 9:6; Ps. 75:4[3]). The phrase ḥōq ḥāg ("he decreed a circle") in 26:10 bespeaks a tangible process of carving out the divine will upon the face of the habitable world, and this combination of legal language (ḥōq = "statute, decree") with creation imagery fuses priestly notions of the Tabernacle/Temple with the order of nature. Similarly, Psalm 147:17-19 also conflates the natural order with God's own decrees:

> (17) He throws down his hail like crumbs;
>   who can stand upright in the face of his freezing blasts?
> (18) He sends forth his word (dābār) and melts them;
>   he blows forth his wind, and the waters flow;
> (19) he declares his word (dābār) to Jacob,
>   his statues (ḥūqqāw) and his rules (mišpāṭāw) to Israel.

If Job is meant as the speaker in chapter 26 one may notice a subtle but powerful connection between the way Job speaks of God's (a)moral direction of human political activity and the divine domination over nature: just as God "covers up the eyes of [the world's] judges" (9:24), God also "obscures the face of the full moon" (26:9). It is not that the moon merely "has no protection," as Bildad argued in 25:5, but rather that God is *actively* involved in acts of obfuscation concerning the natural world. Job has thus plunged deeply into a narrative of humans and nature, one that is at odds with the tradition of the Friends. Newsom characterizes Job's debate with the Friends in terms of acceptance or rejection of narrativity—the Friend arguing to *restore* narrative and Job *resisting*.[122] This line of

---

121. Habel, *Job*, 371.

thinking takes us a long way into understanding what is taking place here, but I would push this contrast more strongly; in light of Job's comments here in chapter 26, but also in chapters 9 and 12 discussed above, we must understand Job as offering a compelling *alternative* narrative. Job is now brought back into the Ricouerian self-making project of recognizing the Other and seeing his material existence. Eventually Job's words are not mere resistance but also *new meaning-making*. The animal monster comes forward as a figure of ecological disorientation, and only a divine act of overwhelming violence makes things "right" (though they are clearly not right for Job). Job has finally come around to offering at least the beginning of a new narrative—no longer is he vainly attempting to reverse creation completely (as in Job 3, which would be total narrative resistance), but he is now coming to face nature's true story. The bracing juxtaposition in 26:11-12 of acts of power, beauty, violence, and wisdom prepares us for the natural drama to come in chapters 38–41.

Job's Final Address

In the concluding chapters of the Joban dialogue (Job 27–31), comprising the longest speech in the book so far, Job seems to speak in a different voice from the rest of his discourse.[123] Again we return to questions of authorship, editing, and so on: can such incongruence be written off as the result of slapdash editing, secondary authors, or the composition history of the book in general? Perhaps, and many interpreters have pursued this route.[124] In a sense the meaning of the book would then merge with the history of its composition, such that

---

122. Newsom, *Book of Job*, 132–36.
123. On this see ibid., 183–86.
124. E.g., Bruce Zuckerman's "historical counterpoint" model in *Job the Silent: A Study in Historical Counterpoint* (Oxford: Oxford University Press, 1991).

the putative literary journey taken by perhaps dozens of authors over decades or even hundreds of years stands with and alongside of and over the book itself as a testament to an experience of the ongoing Joban community.

Carol Newsom's approach in *The Book of Job: A Contest of Moral Imaginations* (2003), which I have cited and highlighted at various points in this chapter and the spirit of which I endorse for my own reading, recognizes these editorial tensions and layers as real and yet asks how the clash of genres and the chorus of voices forms meaning. For Newsom the Job who speaks in these last chapters is committed to "monologic" truth, in which speech is "complete" and "logically self-consistent."[125] Job-the-battered-down is now Job-the-self-righteous, and he comes out swinging with a new attempt at covenant in chapter 31. Whatever narratives Job has forfeited in the process of the debate, he comes around to offer a doubled-down narrative of nature covenant fidelity: I used to flourish in righteousness as a well-watered plant (29:18-23), and I would flourish again if the natural world would react appropriately to my moral state (31:38-40). As he makes these claims, however, the contents are so strange (given what Job has already said in the book) and the tone becomes so shrill as to suggest continuing deep problems with even this rejuvenated narrative. If a secondary author sidled in and painted over Job's character with a new identity, he has done so only with massive anxiety.

They Waited For Me Like Rain (29:18-23)

In his opening address (27:1-23) Job still affirms God as the source of the trouble (v. 2), but he quickly turns to characterizing the wicked and the assured results of wickedness (vv. 13-23). These evildoers

---

125. Newsom, *Book of Job*, 27, 198

admittedly have a "portion" (*ḥēleq*) and "land inheritance" (*naḥălāh*), only to lose it immediately (v. 13). They are born to die. They can build a house like a nest and watch over their vineyards all they like (v. 18; compare Isa. 5:1-10), but the flood stands in the wings to wash it all away (v. 20). The flood is specifically *for them* in their wickedness, and not for the righteous (cf. 9:23; 14:19).

In Job 29:18-23, Job launches into a reverie, imagining his pre-disaster life in terms of thriving plants:

> (18) I said, I shall expire in my old age,
>   and like sand (*ḥôl*) I will extend my days.[126]
> (19) My root (*šorši*) was spread out to the water,
>   and dew lodged upon my branch . . .
> (21) . . . They listened to me, and waited,
>   and they kept silent during my counsel;
> (22) after I spoke they did not respond,
>   and my speech dropped upon them like showers (*tiṭṭōp*);[127]
> (23) they waited for me like the rain (*māṭār*),
>   and they opened their mouths for me like spring rain (*malqôš*).

For Job, social and floral worlds should be synched to one another; as in the Solomonic prayer of Psalm 72, the words of human justice drop like rain upon a parched land, sparking the ecological process into motion. So, too, even the human body, itself a part of animal nature, should automatically react to injustice (Job 31:21-22):

---

126. This verse presents several difficulties. In this translation I follow the emendation in the venerable commentaries of Pope (*Job*, 189–90) and Dhorme (*Job*, 426–27): instead of the MT's *qinnî* ("my nest") in the first half of the verse we read *ziqnî*, "my old age." This allows a more natural interpretation of the word *ḥôl* as "sand" in the second half, rather than attempting to read *ḥôl* as some type of phoenix or regenerating bird from Egyptian myth (compare Ps. 103:5; Isa. 40:31).

127. The root *nṭp* describes rain or other liquids dripping; see, e.g., Judg. 5:4; Joel 3:18; Ps. 68:9(8); Job 36:27. Compare Deut. 32:2: "May my teaching drop (*'rp*) like water (*māṭār*), my words like flow like dew (*ṭal*)—like rain upon grass, like showers upon green plants."

(21) If I have raised my hand against an orphan,
  because I saw I had support at the city gate—
(22) then let my shoulder fall out of its socket,
  and my arm be broken like a reed (*miqqānāh*).

This former situation for Job, marked by the fusion of the flourishing self and the flourishing land/body, has given way to a different landscape in chapter 30. Peter Riede strikingly characterizes Job's transformation within his natural environment when he points out that Job comes to occupy "an alternative world" (*eine Gegenwelt*).[128] Job has certainly died a kind of "social death," but the worms and maggots (7:5) associated with Job's condition remind us of actual death—the body burrowing deep underground in burial.[129] In this alternative world we find not plants but a desert. Here dwell the creeping, uncontrolled creatures of the steppe, not the cattle of Job's domestic flourishing; Job now speaks of those driven from society, using language describing what is dry, parched, peripheral, dead, dusty, and thorn-ridden:

(30:5) They are driven out from the center (*gēw*),
  others shout at them as after a thief;
(6) they dwell in treacherous wadis,
  in holes in the ground and in rocks;
(7) they moan out like animals (*nhq*) among scrub brush (*śîḥîm*),
  they dwell under prickly plants (*ḥārûl*);
(8) fools and without good reputation,
  they are beaten out of the land.

Job comes to embrace familial identity with the animals of this outer geographical zone in 30:29: "I am a brother to jackals (*tannîm*), and a relative of ostriches (*běnôt ya'ănāh*)."

---

128. Riede, *Im Spiegel der Tiere*, 132. See also Pelham, *Contested Creations*, 60, 167–69 on this theme.
129. Riede, *Im Spiegel der Tiere*, 132.

The Mine (28:1-28)

Job's speech in chapter 28 about the mine—called a "source" (*môṣā'*) and a "place" (*māqôm*) (28:1)—is often treated in its own right as a distinct composition.[130] Suggestions for the genre of this chapter vary, including "hymn," "meditation," and "speculative wisdom poem."[131] Some would remove chapter 28 from its place in the text and from Job's mouth altogether; Edward Greenstein, to choose one articulate representative of this view, thinks (on the basis of some thematic and linguistic cues) that the chapter actually belongs with the Elihu speech in Job 32–37.[132] Newsom reads the poem in terms of the book's "endless argument" as a whole; put in Job's mouth, the wisdom poem about the mine highlights the function of the wisdom dialogue genre, to revel in many solutions and unfinalizability, and one can still "trace dotted lines" of emphasis between chapter 8 and the themes in Job's further speeches (chapters 29–31).[133] Others read the poem as a natural literary and theological continuation of Job's speeches throughout the book. Gerald Janzen, for example, views the dialogic argument by analogy to the Garden of Eden story in which the snake, through persuasive speech, sways humans toward wrong

130. The most comprehensive and authoritative review of literature and overall study on this chapter is now Scott C. Jones, *Rumors of Wisdom: Job 28 as Poetry* (BZAW 398; Berlin: de Gruyter, 2009).

131. For this last categorization see Newsom, *Book of Job*, 171–72 (and 174–75 for alternative suggestions); for the others, with references, see Edward L. Greenstein, "The Poem on Wisdom in Job 28 in its Conceptual and Literary Contexts," 253–80 in Ellen van Wolde, ed., *Job 28: Cognition in Context* (Leiden: Brill, 2003), at 263–64. In this same volume edited by van Wolde readers will find a number of other pertinent essays on Job 28, discussing the text from a variety of angles. For another strong analysis of the chapter, exploring themes similar to those I pursue below, see Katharine Dell, "Plumbing the Depths of the Earth: Job 28 and Deep Ecology," *ESWT*, 116–25.

132. Greenstein, "The Poem," 269–76. See also Zuckermann, *Job the Silent*, 142–45, who reads this "Hymn to Wisdom" (as he calls it) as a "counterpoint" to some of the other materials in the book.

133. Newsom, *Book of Job*, 179–81. On the Bakhtinian "unfinalizability" theme see now Seong Whan Timothy Hyun, *Job the Unfinalizable: A Bakhtinian Reading of Job 1–11* (Leiden: Brill, 2013).

action—except that Job is not persuaded by the Friends' words but remains true to his own conscience. The result, for Janzen, is that "[b]y a strange paradox, the confession of 28:28, rightly heard, may betray the presence in Job of the very wisdom which he believes to be inaccessible to him."[134] One may want to ask Janzen why it is, however, that God comes down so hard on Job in chapters 38–41, if indeed Job had come so close to understanding (or outright understood) the true nature of wisdom.

To be sure, this chapter is unique in the Hebrew Bible in its description of mining practices and terminology and, as elsewhere in Job generally, the poet revels in arcane descriptions and obscure terminology. In 28:2-6 the speaker opens with many terms emphasizing the remote character of the mine: miners go into darkness (ḥōšek), to the extreme limits (taklît), peering into gloom ('ōpel) and deep darkness (salmāwet) (v. 3); like Job (see 30:5-8) they travel far from human footsteps, wandering away from human lands (v. 4). In the terranean realm, on the visible earth, grain may grow, but the subterranean produces fire and reveals treasure. The earth writhes in upheaval:

> (5) The earth above ('ereṣ)—from it comes bread,
>   but its underbelly churns like a fire (wĕtaḥtêhā nehpak kĕmô 'ēš).

The verb in the second half of this verse, hāpak, indicates overthrowing, turning, reversing, and churning, and Job uses this exact term repeatedly to describe his experience before God (9:5; 12:15; 19:19; 30:15, 21; see also 28:9). The only other (human) characters who use the word hāpak in the book, Zophar in 20:14 and Eliphaz in 34:25 (cf. 37:12), speak of the change of fate that comes *for*

---

134. Janzen, *Job*, 191.

the wicked: their food will turn over in *their* stomachs, and God will reverse the trajectory of the arrogant, mighty rulers.

Wisdom is real for the speaker in chapter 28, but it is remote; one might find it by the same odds that one might find a giant sapphire lying on the ground on a pathway outside one's house. Wisdom is not just there for the taking, like an apple or shrub grass or a goat. The entire mine image metaphorizes wisdom within the purview of the mine and mineworkers, but within that metaphor we must recognize the physical location of wisdom: wisdom is *in the earth* (*'ereṣ*). Wisdom is perhaps not completely detached from livable nature, but the spatial terms here are striking. One might contrast the image of the mine, for example, with the spatiality of wisdom in the opening address of the book of Proverbs. In Proverbs 1:8-9 the instruction of the father and the teaching of the mother are to be a "graceful garland" for the head and a "necklace" for the neck. Such learning is displayed, not hidden. In Proverbs 1:20-21 the speaker offers a veritable roll call of open, public spaces in which wisdom (*ḥokmāh*) cries out with a shout: in the street (*ḥûṣ*), in the public marketplaces (*rěḥōbôt*), in the main pathway (*běrō'š*, "at the head"), and in the entrances to the gates of the city (*pitḥê šě'ārîm bā'îr*), the symbolic (and sometimes literal) seat of public economic and social activity. The voice of wisdom shouts in such locations, as indeed she must, since they are already noisy to begin with, crowded with competing voices (note the location of the anti-wisdom voice in Prov. 7:6-23; 9:14-15).

True, the Proverbialist will speak of seeking wisdom as one searches for silver (e.g., Prov. 2:4; cf. 3:13-15, where wisdom is even better than jewels), and yet at no point is this wisdom as elusive as it seems to be in Job 28. Verses 7-8 emphasize the contrast between knowledge down in the mine and observation of animals up above:

(7) The path (leading into the mine)—no bird of prey knows it,
    and the eye of the falcon (*'ayyāh*) has not gazed upon it;
(8) proud ones (*běnê šāḥaṣ*) have not walked upon it,
    the lion (*šāḥal*) has not ventured over it.

Visible nature cannot access this deep, haunted mine-world. Dark though it may be, however, this mine also contains treasure, setting up both a possibility and a danger: sapphires, gold, and silver do exist, but to excavate them the miner must leave the familiar world. If the author of this passage knew about actual mining practice in his own time, as perhaps he did, he surely knew it was a deadly occupation (just as it often is today). Job's journey down into this mine represents an echo of a classically heroic journey, the *katabasis*, during which the hero traverses the Underworld in order to learn the true experience of death or to rescue a loved one (consider, famously, Odysseus in *Odyssey* book 11, or Gilgamesh's journey in the "Gilgamesh, Enkidu, and the Netherworld" poem).[135] As the speaking character in chapter 28, at least, Job finally gestures toward a descent into nature that might lead to ruby-like understanding, but truly this descent is beyond the capability of normal people.

Many interpreters focus on the supposed culmination of the speech in either the creation language of 28:24-27 or the "fear of the Lord" theme in 28:28 as a resolution or summary of the situation. In 28:24-27 God is perched on high, seeing everything, controlling the wind, decreeing (*ḥōq*) the rain,[136] and so on. Wisdom comes through the brute knowledge that God is creator (28:25-27)—you

---

135. See the review in Ken Dowden, "The Myth that Saves: Mysteries and Mysteriosophies," 283–300 in Ken Dowden and Niall Livingstone, eds., *A Companion to Greek Mythology* (Malden, MA: Blackwell, 2011) and, more technically, Walter Burkert, "Parmenides' Proem and Pythagoras' Descent," trans. Joydeep Bagchee, 85–116 in Vishwa Adluri, ed., *Philosophy and Salvation in Greek Religion* (Berlin: de Gruyter, 2013); for the Gilgamesh story see Andrew R. George, *The Babylonian Gilgamesh Epic: Introduction, Critical Edition, and Cuneiform Texts*, Vol. I (Oxford: Oxford University Press, 2003), 43–50.

136. See discussion above for this language of nature, creation, and legal decree in Job 26:10.

see it and you know, and that is it—but this knowledge may not be commonsensical or praxis-oriented. Or, as Greenstein puts it, "wisdom is not located in a place but is rather situated in time, bound up in the primordial act of creation."[137] In 28:8 the speaker resolves the creation discourse with a direct command from God to humans: "And he (God) said to humankind, 'the fear of the Lord (*yirʾat ʾădōnāy*), that is wisdom (*ḥokmāh*)—and to turn from evil is understanding (*bînāh*).'"[138] Newsom argues that here the wisdom piece "takes sides with the prose tale against the dialogue, for in verse 28 it echoes the words of the prose tale when it advises that for human beings 'fear of the Lord' and 'turning from evil' are the effective equivalents of the transcendent wisdom that remains inaccessible to humans."[139] In this sense the poem grinds against itself, since this simplistic advice cannot cover over the pessimism and complexity of the mine image.

As "ending" or "moral," Job 28:28 provides as much comfort as Qoheleth's moral at the end of his book (Eccl. 12:13-14)—which is to say, not much comfort at all. Ecclesiastes 12:13-14 reads: "The end of the matter, all has been heard: fear (*yĕrāʾ*) God, and keep his commandments, for this is (the duty of) all humanity. For God will bring every deed into judgment, including all hidden things—whether good or evil." Those who attempt to find easy comfort in these final verses in the face of all Qoheleth had been saying throughout his book clearly have not come to terms with the divine character as Qoheleth imagines it. So, too, we should pause before accepting this last statement in Job 28 as an easy or clear conclusion for any of the nature problems throughout the dialogue.

---

137. Greenstein, "The Poem," 274.
138. The "fear of the Lord" is a common wisdom trope; see, e.g., Eccl. 5:7; 8:12; 12:13; Prov. 1:7, 29; 2:5; 8:13; 9:10; 10:27; 14:27; 15:16, 33; 16:6; 19:23; 22:4; 23:17; Job 1:9; 6:14; Pss. 19:10(9); 34:12(11); 55:20(19); 66:16; 111:10; and Sirach 1–2, etc.
139. Newsom, *Book of Job*, 26.

For those who look to the mine as nature analogy, the rejection of plant and animal knowledge—a rejection initiated by Job in chapters 12 and 14—is now complete. Wisdom is subterranean, not with plants, not with animals, and not with humans. Wisdom is not even alive, in the world of the mine metaphor; it is hard and dead and bizarre, like a rare jewel one has heard of but never seen.

The Words of Job are Now Complete (31:38-40)

Job's final case in chapter 31 comes in the form of a covenant (*běrît*), and the nature imagery he uses seems to adopt the Friends' perspective on suffering and then doubles down on the very nature analogy he had previously rejected for his own situation. Job's simple and stunning final words take us directly to the heart of the nature debate in the book, leading us again to the world of plants as the final arbiter of truth and pointing up the centrality of nature's witness in the dialogue. If I have made missteps, Job declares, "let me sow and another eat, and let what grows for me be uprooted (*yĕśōrāśû*)" (31:8); if I have been enticed by my neighbor's wife, he vows, let fire come down and "consume all my harvest, to the root" (31:12). Job's case ends in 31:38-40 with words that could almost have been quoted from Deuteronomy's covenant nature curses:[140]

(38) If my land has cried out against me,
    and together its furrows have wept;
(39) if I have consumed its produce without payment,
    and cut off the breath (?) of its owners—
(40) then let thorns come forth instead of wheat,
    stink-weeds instead of barley.
    The words of Job are now complete.

---

140. Because of the perceived incongruity here with Job's earlier words or for other reasons, some interpreters have simply removed these verses (at least in this location); see, e.g., Dhorme, *Job*, 470–71; Pope, *Job*, 199.

Marvin Pope saw this oath as "a rather weak ending to Job's eloquent deposition," which "markedly weaken[s] the rhetorical effect."[141] A judgment like this obviously depends on how one views the intended or possible "rhetorical effect." On one plane the final nature oath marks Job's largest concession to the system espoused by the Friends, but at the same time the oath challenges the Friends and the God of the Friends on their own terms: if the Deuteronomic covenant is the standard, then let its results come forth. If loss of land, children, and cattle signals moral failure in the world of covenant (Deut. 11:13-15; 28:15-68), and if Job has lost these things and yet cannot admit moral failure but still cannot bring himself to completely deny some sense of reciprocity and justice, then he is forced back to the iron terms of the land—either it produces or it does not. In the final form of the book, then, Job comes around to the side of covenant, to tradition, and to his Friends. Even so, the oath can only haunt us with a sense of mockery or parody, given what Job had already said (9:22-24; 12:7-10; 14:7-12) about the unreliability of nature to mete out decisions in accordance with justice and the impossibility of comparing human and natural flourishing.

Excursus: Elihu and Nature

Nearly all modern critical scholars of Job have viewed the Elihu speech cycle in Job 32–37 as later material, appended to the heart of the dialogue by some disturbed reader in the history of the tradition who wanted to craft an adequate response to Job's devastating rants (assuming, as the Elihu-author may have assumed, that the Friends had not yet won the argument).[142] In this view the Elihu speeches

---

141. Pope, *Job*, 202.
142. See any of the major commentaries for this view, as well as more specific studies such as David J. A. Clines, "Putting Elihu in his Place: A Proposal for the Relocation of Job 32-37," *JSOT* 29 (2004): 243-53; David Noel Freedman, "Elihu Speeches in the Book of Job," *HTR* 61 (1968): 51-59.

are something like the work of a good-hearted but inferior artist who sidles up to a Rembrandt and attempts to paint in a background character. He does a very bad job, of course. So, too, the Elihu character ends up spewing forth uninspired material upon the Joban canvas, which otherwise contains what many agree is the most elevated poetry of any kind in the Bible. Under a purely final-form, literary view, one may read the speeches as a natural part of the book;[143] Elihu comes off as that awful, uninformed voice, interrupting the conversation to add his own bombastic, repetitive views. By making him the youngest of the interlocutors (32:6-10), the grand Joban author is able to insert unsubtle snide remarks about zealous but unwise youth. This literary perspective does not solve the problem of why Elihu is not mentioned along with the three main Friends at the end of Job 2 (or throughout chapters 3–31), nor does it address Elihu's absence from the divine rebuke in 42:7.

In terms of our investigation Elihu has little real substance to contribute, though he does make reference to God's work as creator in 37:14-18 (see also 36:24), invoking language that Greenstein, at least, sees as continuous with the address about the mine in chapter 28.[144] Job 35:5-14 is more intriguing, as Elihu urges Job to turn toward nature: "Gaze upon the heavens and see, observe the clouds, since they are high above you" (35:5). What would Job learn specifically from the observation of nature? Elihu never really says how or what nature would teach him. Job simply suffers, in Elihu's opinion, because he is no better and no worse than anyone else (35:8). Humans may cry out to God because of the oppressive nature of life, but, Elihu says (35:10-11):

---

143. E.g., Clines, *Job 1–20*, lviii–lix.
144. Greenstein, "The Poem," 269–72.

(10) . . . no one says, "Where is Eloah, the one who made me,
    the one who gives songs (?) in the night,
(11) who teaches us more than the animals of the earth,
    and makes us wiser than the birds of the air?"

Or rather, Elihu goes on to state, they do cry out, but God does not answer because he is upset with the pride of the wicked (35:12). Are humans then to be considered above nature, in Elihu's view? If we are wiser than birds and beasts, can or should we even look to the animal world for wisdom analogies? When Elihu argues that "no one says . . ." in verse 10, does he mean that no one should ask whether God has taught humans more than animals, or that no one should even need to ask, or that he is upset that humans do not turn to God who has taught humans more than animals? Might God teach humans through nature or creation if we were not so corrupt? Elihu does not seem to know.

Conclusion

Throughout this chapter—as in this study as a whole—I have sought the precise intersection among the human self, plant and animal selves, and the narrative of wisdom within which these relationships are metaphorized and organized. These identities, we have found, are sometimes elusive and seem to shift often. Indeed, the ancient Near Eastern dialogue genre—which can be compared to or contrasted with the Greek Platonic dialogue model in various ways—more clearly resists the triumph of a single voice within any given dialogue.[145] This genre is indeed *dia-logos*, the words of two: and

---

145. See Newsom, *Book of Job*, 84–85, citing Sara Denning-Bolle, *Wisdom in Akkadian Literature: Expression, Instruction, Dialogue* (Leiden: Ex Oriente Lux, 1992), 70. However, it is not exactly the case, as Newsom implies, that the Mesopotamian dialogue genre does not allow "the clear triumph of one perspective over another" *as opposed to* Greek models (which allegedly did). Rather, we find ancient Greek authors using different styles or approaches (as in the distinction among early, middle, and late Platonic dialogues), and later classical authors (such as Cicero)

not only two; rather, we have a multi-logos, first the narrated words of past tense story in Job 1, within which we already find dialogue between God and the Adversary, giving way to a quadrilogue among Job and the three Friends (Job 3–31), followed then by the Elihu speech (Job 32–37). Still more voices stand ready to speak. The sum of the book to this point forms a macro-narrative of plot: Job is righteous and prosperous, in tune with all of nature and justice, after which he suffers as the result of a divine gamble, and after that Job and his Friends engage in bitter debate. Our focus in this chapter has been on what we might call micro-narratives of nature crafted by human characters within the book.

These micro-narratives are shaped through a process similar to what Ricoeur (following Robert Alter) calls "refractory human nature"; the Joban speakers contend for differing visions of God's "ineluctable" ways with nature—and all do agree that they are ineluctable—but they can only see this plan through competing narratives. Ricoeur argues for the "narrative mode" as the only major hermeneutical project that can confront the Divine Plan: narrative provides the point of collision, of conflict.[146] One could even say that the Friends' attempts to lay down nature as a final law (when in fact they do this, which is not always) are doomed the very moment their vision is cast as a nature *narrative*, for that narrative is bound to be contested and at any rate cannot function as a law. Given the inevitable collisions and new meaning that narrative generates, we should not be surprised to find that Job's attempt to obliterate narrative in chapter 3 cannot succeed—not just against the Friends, but even for himself, as Job proceeds to offer not non-narrative but

were fond of laying competing positions side by side without the clear triumph of one voice (e.g., *De finibus bonorum et malorum*, "On Moral Ends").

146. Paul Ricoeur, "Interpretive Narrative," in idem, *Figuring the Sacred: Religion, Narrative, and Imagination*, trans. David Pellauer, ed. Mark I. Wallace (Minneapolis: Fortress Press, 1995), 181–99, at 182, 184.

rather a competing nature narrative. True, Job's alternative world in chapters 12 and 14 presents us with a malicious environment, but the story of the chaos-world is truly a story, even if it is an unresolved story and even if it is a story that no one can bear to hear.

The simplest conclusion we can draw from the analysis of materials in this chapter is an affirmation of the centrality of the animal and plant world as the primary idiom of debate among Job and the Friends. Nature is the referee, deciding or demonstrating God's handiwork in the world, and it is surprising to see just how frequently and deeply these characters invoke nature. They argue about the behavior of grasses and lions to the point of obsession, as if the minutest shades of meaning to be extracted from grasses or lions constitute the exact stakes of the argument. They invoke nature so often that they run the risk of abandoning Job himself as the sole focus of suffering and instead drawing attention to an entire cosmos of living things. Do these plants and animals reflect the human, or vice versa, or does everything reflect everything else in mystical union? We have heard representatives argue for several nature narratives—if not outright, then at least in echo or allusion:

1. nature is obvious, straightforward, and predictable—we reap what we sow, and nature's lessons are visible (4:8; 5:1-7);
2. nature is miraculous, even mystical, and as such potentially unpredictable—but this is a source of wonder, and humans must hold on for the ride (5:17-27; 8:16-19);
3. nature is wild and dangerous; animal and human children may die suddenly, despite all possible protection (4:10-11);
4. nature is unhitched from morality (9:22-24);
5. humans are like plants (8:11-13);
6. humans are not like plants (14:1-12).

Appeals to the supposedly thoroughgoing "negative anthropology" of the Friends are not exactly a helpful or accurate way to categorize the moral universes in which these characters dwell,[147] since in fact the Friends offer competing attempts to characterize nature. Some of them offer soaring hope for humans. Moreover, I have argued, these plant and animal analogies are not mere decoration, even though they are wielded at times in rather arbitrary ways (indeed, the multivocal potential in nature precisely contributes to the unfinalizability of the dialogue when nature is invoked). Rather, they point the reader toward broader visions of God's work in the world; they gesture toward other narratives of nature in Proverbs, Deuteronomy, and elsewhere in the tradition. Speaking of God: the deity has said nothing about plants or animals to this point in the book; he has said very little about anything, except to boast about his favorite son, Job the Righteous. The Adversary alone has dared to make anthropological statements. Will God provide a resolution for the many nature narratives? And what could such a resolution look like?

---

147. See Newsom, "Models of the Moral Self," 13. Newsom does say that the "negative theology" of the Friends "is specifically generated by a contextual desire to emphasize the ontological difference between the divine and the human," and thus their words are not to be taken as programmatic.

4

Eco-Anthropologies in the Joban God-Speech

Approaching the Joban Storm God

Since his own assent to the Adversary's acts of torture in Job 2, God has not spoken—a haunting silence. As Paul Ricoeur explains, the process of narrativization can proceed with two distinct effects: (1) The narrative interprets by way of amplification or explanation, by providing a "why" (God did this *because* . . .), or (2) the "inverse of amplification," or "reticence."[1] Opacity has its own power—the longer the Joban characters have argued about Job's personal relationship to nature and wrongdoing, the longer God is silent, and the more intensely the characters must wonder about the divine perspective. After thirty-five long chapters, however, and to the

---

1. Paul Ricoeur, "Interpretive Narrative," in idem, *Figuring the Sacred: Religion, Narrative, and Imagination*, trans. David Pellauer, ed. Mark I. Wallace (Minneapolis: Fortress Press, 1995), 181–99, at 186–87. Here Ricoeur echoes and cites the work of Robert Alter in *The Art of Biblical Narrative* (New York: Basic Books, 1981).

apparent surprise of all parties, God enters the fray and addresses Job and Friends. The divine method of entry complements the address that follows (Job 38:1): "Yhwh answered Job out of the whirlwind (*min hassĕʿārāh*), and said . . ."

One grammatical issue of note is the presence of the definite article (*ha-*), "*the* whirlwind."[2] Why not *a* whirlwind? Which whirlwind? One that had already been raging? One we are already supposed to know about? Poetic Hebrew routinely omits the definite article where one might expect it, and sometimes grammatical definiteness in Hebrew seems not to mean very much.[3] Still, the semantic range of *ha-* overlaps very closely with "the" in English, raising the question of why God does not speak here from *a* whirlwind, or in the *form of a* whirlwind, but rather from *the* whirlwind. "The" draws more explicit attention to the whirlwind, making this type of theophany notable as an expression of God as a violent nature-force. A "whirlwind," if that is the best translation for *sĕʿārāh*, is a technical atmospheric phenomenon, an overarching category including tornadoes, waterspouts, and other wind vortices. In the high desert setting that is the stage for the book of Job, "dust devils" would be a common occurrence, but the minor and mostly ephemeral nature of these squalls would seem not to indicate the force and terror congruent with God's speech in chapters 38–41. Perhaps we would better understand *hassĕʿārāh* here as a full-blown dust storm (or sandstorm), the kind that can derail trains, engulf cities in a debris cloud, and kill humans.[4]

---

2. This "whirlwind" appears again in a nearly identical opening statement in Job 40:6, though in this latter case without the definite article (*min sĕʿārāh*).

3. E.g., Paul Joüon, *A Grammar of Biblical Hebrew*, Part 3: *Syntax*, trans. and revised by T. Muraoka (Subsidia Biblica 14/II; Rome: Pontifical Biblical Institute, 2005), 102, 473–81.

4. See, e.g., the descriptions and images in Xiaojing Zheng, *Mechanics of Wind-blown Sand Movements* (Berlin: Springer, 2009), 6–11. Given the language of the storm here, as well as the "divine warrior" motif discussed below, and not to mention the content and bombast of the divine speech in chapters 39–41, one is hard pressed to understand how Yhwh's speech could

Earlier in the book of Job, windstorms had already marked God's activity—or at least activity God will allow—when a "great wind (*rûaḥ gĕdôlāh*) came blowing across the desert" (1:19), killing Job's children. In the report of the death of cattle in 1:16 the servant described the destruction as a "fire from God" (*'ēš 'ĕlōhîm*); in Job 9:17, Job claims that God whipped him around in a "whirlwind" (*śĕ'ārāh*). Thus before Job 38:1 God had already been identified in some manner as meteorological phenomena. The image of God as storm or whirlwind, specifically with the term *sĕ'ārāh* (or the bi-form *śĕ'ārāh*), occurs frequently in the Hebrew Bible in contexts of visceral theophany and divine punishment.[5] The prophet Ezekiel sees God in a *sĕ'ārāh* carrying a frightening zoomorphic structure (Ezek. 1:4), and the *sĕ'ārāh* embodies divine wrath against the wicked in several prophetic books (Isa. 29:6; 40:24; 41:16; Jer. 23:19; 30:23; Ezek. 13:11, 13; Zech. 9:14). Notably, with the possible exception of Isaiah 29:6, all instances of the use of *sĕ'ārāh* in the Bible's prophetic corpus are from putatively sixth-century BCE (or later) texts, perhaps contemporaneous with the final form of the book of Job, suggesting that this storm image was perceived to be particularly relevant during this time period.

More broadly, meteorological and geological upheavals regularly accompany the deity in his capacity as divine warrior,[6] and these

---

be read as *lacking* "the fearful elements that caused Israel to tremble at Sinai," or how one could claim that, in these speeches, "God does not display immeasurable power. Rather, Yhwh utters 'please'" (as recently claimed by T. C. Ham, "The Gentle Voice of God in Job 38," *JBL* 132 [2013]: 527–41, at 541).

5. See Hans Lugt, "Wirbelstürme im Alten Testament," *BZ* 19 (1975): 195–204.

6. On Yhwh and divine warrior motifs see the overview in Patrick D. Miller, *The Divine Warrior in Early Israel* (Atlanta: Society of Biblical Literature, 1973), as well as Mark S. Smith, *The Early History of God: Yahweh and Other Deities in Ancient Israel*, 2d ed. (Grand Rapids: Eerdmans, 2002), esp. ch. 2, "Yahweh and Baal." Most American scholarship on this topic follows in the wake of the pioneering and influential treatment by Frank Moore Cross, *Canaanite Myth and Hebrew Epic: Essays in the History of the Religion of Israel* (Cambridge, MA: Harvard University Press, 1973). For a view of the Joban speech in light of divine warrior imagery see Randy Klassen, "Taunts of the Divine Warrior in Job 40:6–14," *Direction* 40 (2011): 207–18. On the

upheavals comprise one of four classic components typically appearing in descriptions of this broadly shared ancient Near Eastern trope:[7]

(1) the war march;
(2) an upheaval of nature at the display of divine power;
(3) victorious return to the divine above (mountain) for recognition of kingship;
(4) focus on the voice of the deity, with provision of rain for the earth.

On at least a symbolic or notional level all four of these elements appear in Job 38–41, but more specifically the storm in Job 38:1—coupled with a plethora of other nature images in chapters 38–41—indicates the upheaval-of nature-theme, and the focus on divine provision of rain and sustenance for nature (e.g., 38:25-34; 39:5-6) reflects the deity's crowning achievement as king.

This image of God is very much in line with God's revelation as divine warrior elsewhere in the Bible. In prophetic literature, for example, one finds natural cataclysm as a prominent idiom of divine war.[8] The oracle against "all the nations" and eventually Edom in Isaiah 34 speaks the clear language of natural and cosmic upheaval: after a massive slaughter mountains will flow with blood, the "host of heaven" rots away, the skies roll up like a scroll, and the cosmos withers away "like leaves withering off the vine, like the withering of a fig tree" (Isa. 34:3–4). Isaiah's seamless combination of "cosmic"

---

iconography of the divine warrior with reference to Job, see Izak Cornelius, "The God of Job: Iconographic Perspectives *after* Keel," 21–33 in Izaak J. de Hulster and Rüdiger Schmitt, eds., *Iconography and Biblical Studies*, Proceedings of the Iconography Sessions at the Joint EABS/SBL Conference, 22–26 July 2007, Vienna, Austria (Alter Orient und Altes Testament 361; Münster: Ugarit-Verlag).

7. See the helpful overview by Smith, *Early History of God*, 80–81. For these four characteristics of the divine warrior Smith explicitly relies on Cross, *Canaanite Myth*, 151–63.

8. See Corrine Carvalho, "The Beauty of the Bloody God: The Divine Warrior in the Prophetic Literature," 131–52 in Julia M. O'Brien and Chris Franke, eds., *Aesthetics of Violence in the Prophets* (Library of Hebrew Bible/Old Testament Studies 517; London: T & T Clark, 2010), 131–52.

and "local" natural imagery probably indicates a lack of totally clear conceptual boundaries between "cosmic" and "local," though we may notice that in the Joban dialogues (chapters 3–37) the nature imagery is largely local, while the scale of the divine speech in God's discourse becomes cosmological and strikingly exotic. The prophet Nahum's opening onslaught of rage works very much in this same tradition (Nah. 1:3–5): Yhwh comes in a great storm (*sûpāh*) and whirlwind (*śĕʿārāh*), treading upon clouds, rebuking the sea (*yām*), drying up rivers, melting mountains, drying up vegetation, and throwing the world's inhabitants into dismay. The archaic hymn in Habbakuk 3 engages with these same themes,[9] as does a host of other literature in the divine warrior tradition (e.g., in Exodus 15 the seas congeal to defeat the enemy and God's people are subsequently "planted" [*nātaʿ*] on the divine mountain, and in Psalm 68 the heavens convulse, rain pours down, and wild animals are rebuked in the presence of the warrior deity).

Thus the divine warrior motif nearly always connects the deity with the natural world in some way, and in most cases the connection is integral to the theophanic presentation overall. The primal relationship between Israel's deity and the natural world takes on richer meaning when we consider the divine epithet "Shaddai" (*šadday*), one of the most frequently used terms for the deity in Job. We have reason to think that the El Shaddai epithet represents an archaic tradition—perhaps employed by pre-Israelite groups in Canaan to describe El or other leading deities (see also the ninth- or eighth-century BCE Balaam inscription from Deir ʿAlla), and later biblical authors strategically revived its use in post-exilic texts, perhaps as a direct appeal to earlier periods.[10] Though we will deal with questions of providing a date for the book of Job as a whole

---

9. On this see Theodore Hiebert, *God of My Victory: The Ancient Hymn in Habbakuk 3* (Harvard Semitic Monographs 38; Atlanta: Scholars Press, 1986).

in the next chapter, for now it is enough to assert that Job very likely belongs to this later (archaizing, not archaic) stratum of Israelite literature.

To be sure, of the forty-one occurrences of *šadday* in the Hebrew Bible, 75% (31 total) are in Job (including God's own self-identification as *šadday* in 40:2), suggesting that the explosion of the term in this particular book has some significance, even if there seems to be no clear way to explain the particular use of *šadday* in Job as opposed to other common divine names in the book (such as Eloah or Elohim).[11] Perhaps that significance is purely poetic or verisimilitudinous and represents the author's way of presenting these elegant speakers debating about a non-personal deity in a non-Israelite land. Given the extreme focus on nature in the Joban dialogues, and given the character of God's own speech in chapters 38–41, however, we must take into account the fact that many now agree that *šadday* indicates some nuance of geographical or nature-related power.[12] More specifically, the leading etymologies of *šadday* connect the term with either "mountains" (thus El Shaddai would

10. See Frank M. Cross, "'ēl," *TDOT* I, 242–61; idem, *Canaanite Myth*, 59–60. The Bible itself attempts to deal with the problem of identifying Yhwh with other names for the deity (such as El or El Shaddai) in the famous assertion at the burning bush (Exod. 6:3), where God claims that he had revealed himself specifically as El Shaddai to the ancestors and not as Yhwh (see Gen. 17:1; 28:3; 35:11; 43:14; 48:3; but cf. the clear use of Yhwh to/by the ancestors and others in Gen. 4:26; 14:22; 15:7-8; 16:2; 18:14; 19:14; 22:14; 24:7; 26:22; 27:7; 28:13; 29:32; 30:24; 31:49; 32:9; 49:18, among many other instances).

11. The fuller phrase '*ēl šadday*, by contrast (and not counted in the statistics here), occurs only seven times in the Bible (and never in Job). "Eloah" ('*ĕlôah*) seems to be the book of Job's preferred term for the deity (used slightly more frequently than *šadday*), with the tetragrammaton (*yhwh*) and *šadday* coming a close second and third, respectively (*yhwh* is used 33 times in Job, but only once in the dialogues [12:9]), and "Elohim" ('*ĕlōhîm*) a distant fourth (only about a dozen times). For *šadday* in Job see: 5:17; 6:4, 14; 8:3, 5; 11:7; 13:3; 15:25; 21:15, 20; 22:3, 17, 23, 25, 26; 23:16; 24:1; 27:2, 10, 11, 13; 29:5; 31:2, 35; 32:8; 33:4; 34:10, 12; 35:13; 37:23; 40:2. The prologue and epilogue author(s) clearly preferred *yhwh*, as opposed to the Dialogues, in which *šadday*, '*ĕlôah*, and '*ĕlōhîm* clearly predominate.

12. See the helpful overview with a summary of past research by Ernst Axel Knauf, "Shadday," *DDD*, 749–53, and Georg Steins, "*šadday*," *TDOT* XIV, 418–46, at 437–41 on *šadday* in Job specifically.

be "El [God] of the Mountains," or "El [God], the Mountain One"), or with untamed forestland more generally (as if *šadday* were related to the word *śādeh*, "field").[13] In short, though I find the "mountain" etymology most convincing on linguistic and comparative grounds, the connection of the Joban deity with wild animals and uncultivated fields takes on great thematic power in the divine speech, and we will have further occasion to explore the "master of animals" motif below. The point here, then, is that the deity who self-identifies as storm theophany in Job 38:1 also self-identifies as *šadday* (40:2), God who will control fierce animals, God who rains on deserts and measures mountains. This divine self is enmeshed in nature, speaking through nature, melting nature, revealed in nature, and named by nature.

In what follows, as we approach the Joban God's relationship to nature in chapters 38–41, we will continue to explore the interconnections among animals, plants, humans, and God. It is now God's own self that becomes the focus, trouncing the other characters in the book. From a traditional theological perspective it would of course be difficult not to privilege this divine self as somehow the ultimate expression of meaning in the book. However, we should not be quick to make such an assumption when exploring the Joban world of nature and the self. The plurality of voices in the book—and the plurality of voices even within those voices—makes singular interpretations very difficult, and not even desirable for this dialogical wisdom genre.[14] The specific focus on nature images in the book's final speech offers readers an extended opportunity to continue thinking about the themes raised in chapters 1–37, and we will find

---

13. The former interpretation was most forcefully argued by Cross, *Canaanite Myth*, 56–60, and endorsed by many others, e.g., John Day, *Yahweh and the Gods of Goddesses of Canaan* (London: Sheffield Academic, 2000), 32–34. For the "fields" view see Knauf, "Shadday."
14. As Carol Newsom has shown so well in *The Book of Job: A Contest of Moral Imaginations* (Oxford: Oxford University Press, 2003), 30, 234–35.

that the implications of these images were either implied or stated explicitly in the purely human dialogues that preceded God's speech.

Moreover, just as we discovered that Job and the Friends were obsessed with acting out the most important terms of their debate on the battleground of reed grasses, lions, crops, and so on, in chapters 38–41 we find a deity whose majestic self-revelation amounts to a kind of zoological lecture and a meditation on the earth's physical wonders. The secondary literature is already replete with analyses of the divine speech, and several of these studies appropriately highlight the Creator's relationship to the natural world. William Brown's incisive work, for example, considers the divine speech as ideologically generative (as opposed to God's mere attempt at overwhelming rhetoric), and specifically focuses on the contrast between domestic ecologies and nature at the margins.[15] Carol Newsom also pays appropriate attention to the role of wild animal life in this speech, and considers the animal menagerie in terms of aesthetic categories such as tragedy, sublimity, and the unfolding of the Bahktinian genre-clash that forms the book's moral drama and literary challenge.[16]

My intention in what follows is not to repeat the good work others have already done, but rather to offer some analysis of the exact nuances of the three main nature categories in the divine speech—the geography of creation, marginal animals, and monstrous animals—in the language of narrative and self-making that I have been developing throughout my study so far. Through this analysis we will see that the ecological significance of God's speech is far more profound and far more troubling than many interpreters have been willing to acknowledge: God is not "above" the system as a distant

---

15. William P. Brown, *The Seven Pillars of Creation: The Bible, Science, and the Ecology of Wonder* (Oxford: Oxford University Press, 2010), esp. 116–30.

16. Newsom, *Book of Job*, esp. 234–58; eadem, "The Moral Sense of Nature: Ethics in the Light of God's Speech to Job," *Princeton Seminary Bulletin* (1994): 9–27.

ruler or as the creator of beautiful natural phenomena—rather, God is *intimately involved in* the danger, violence, and broken moral narrative that nature tells through its multiple dramas.

God's Geography (38:1-38)

The non living physical cosmos—rock, water, precipitation, sky—resides at the foundation of Yhwh's self-revelation in Job. The very first question Yhwh poses to the beleaguered sufferer invokes the cosmic structure at its base: "Where were you when I laid the foundations of the earth?" (38:4). For the deity, creation = mastery = knowledge = intimate access = control, and Job is simply out of control and out of power. He is out of options and out of imagination at this point in the drama. The narrative stream has run dry. Yhwh must now verbally rebuild the cosmos from scratch for Job and the Friends, teaching them about the polarities of joy and horror as he does so. The first round of lectures in 38:1-38 has cosmic geographies and meteorologies as its focus—though reference to a plant does creep in at 38:27—but these hard, putatively nonliving elements are by no means impersonal. Rather, language of family, birth, worship, and the home permeates the speech.

The first cluster of images (38:5-6) employs imagery of the master craftsman in control of the cosmic house, laying down foundations (actually "declaring" [*haggēd*] the foundations), setting down measurements, stretching out measurements, sinking down bases,[17] and throwing down the cornerstone. The cosmos responds to the divine work (38:7)—reversing the language of Job's bitter grieving in Job 3[18]—as morning stars release a joyous shout (*rānan*) and divine

17. For *ṭābaʿ* as "sink" in terms of creation acts see also Prov. 8:25; otherwise *ṭābaʿ* refers to a gritty process involving mud and grime—perhaps here enhancing the personal aspects of God's involvement with nature (see Jer. 38:22; Ps. 69:3[2]; Lam. 2:9, etc.).

18. Many have noticed these reversals; see, e.g., the notes in Robert Alter, *The Wisdom Books* (New York: W. W. Norton, 2010), 158–75.

beings (*bĕnê 'ĕlōhîm*) exult. Perhaps the poet means here to conflate stars with the *bĕnê 'ĕlōhîm*, thus suggesting a divinely infused cosmos; whatever the case, the reference to the *bĕnê 'ĕlōhîm* here clearly gestures back to the *bĕnê 'ĕlōhîm* who present themselves before Yhwh back in the Prologue (1:6). The suggestion, as it already seems to be shaping up, is that, from the perspective of heaven, nature is a source of pure wonder and joy and the only response to its mysteries is the shout of worship. Readers may of course wonder, as Job must, whether the suggestion that one must worship in the face of destruction is a kind of divine coverup, the overpowering command of a dictator rather than the gentle leading of a loving God. (As Virginia Woolf famously quipped in a letter, "I read the book of Job last night—I don't think God comes well out of it.") Whatever the case, the shape of the cosmos is something for which the Joban deity takes explicit, personal responsibility.

The language of intimacy with regard to natural elements intensifies with a series of images throughout the rest of chapter 38. The sea (*yām*), potentially an element of chaos or fear, emerges as a tender baby at birth (38:8-9):

> (Or who) covered over the sea with doors,
>> when it burst forth from the womb (*reḥem*) and came out?
> (Where were you) when I clothed him with clouds,
>> made thick darkness his swaddling blanket (*ḥătūllāh*)?

Earlier in Job's own address the Sea was to be cursed, or confronted by God, or pummeled at the creation event (recall 3:8-9; 7:12; 26:12-13). The image of *yām* here can only come across as a stunning reversal of the one-sided consideration of nature. On the one hand God is supremely in control of the Sea; the birthing metaphor is nothing if not an image of complete parental jurisdiction and infant vulnerability. True, the sea has "proud waves" (38:11, *big'ôn gallêkā*),[19] but everything here is under control; God says to the waves, "this far and no more . . . ." This ruling idea comes in contrast to Job's lack of control over the Sea or other chaotic nature elements. On the other hand the Sea is simultaneously demythologized and remythologized—or perhaps better, demythologized and radically *personalized* under God's own care—through this birth and swaddling metaphor. In other words, the Sea is not taken out of Job's world of discourse without being offered back to him, even if on different terms.[20]

Yhwh pushes this type of language further still, evoking the notion of a personal tour of the deep (*těhôm*, 38:16), "gates" in the darkest places of the earth (38:17), a "road" (*derek*) and "paths" for the "house" (*bayit*) of light (38:19-20), and snow or hail piled up in a "storehouse" (*'ôsār*, 38:22), as though God is a farmer of extreme meteorological phenomena. Whatever else these images offer us, they do serve to make nature part of an intimate divine process. As we know from the variety of creation stories in the Hebrew Bible, creation can come off as rather abstract and impersonal (e.g., in Genesis 1), or the deity can forge elements through an earthy, physical process (e.g., in Gen. 2:7-8), not to mention visceral scenes of creation violence (e.g., Ps. 74:12-17; Job 26:11-12). Granted, this kind of domestic nature metaphorizing is common throughout the Hebrew Bible and in many other literatures (both ancient and modern) as well, but things can be more or less personal. The Joban God speaks of seemingly impersonal elements (sea, rock, earth, stars) in deeply personal terms.

19. See Newsom's comment here in *Book of Job*, 244, and my discussion in ch. 3 of this book on plant height and the language of *gāʾāh*, "rise up, exalt."
20. See the perceptive comment of Rebecca S. Watson, *Chaos Uncreated: A Reassessment of the Theme of "Chaos" in the Hebrew Bible* (BZAW 341; Berlin: de Gruyter, 2005), 278: "the depiction of God's protective care of the newborn sea represents the antithesis of the *Chaoskampf*, both in its appreciation of the need to nurture this great body of water and in the assumption of God's unchallenged parenting and ordering of the world, before which the sea stands not in antagonism but in infantile dependence."

However, this is not to say that any of these images offers clear "answers" for the problem of nature's meaning or non-meaning in Job that we have been discussing so far. At the beginning of the Divine Speech, God comes off as personally involved in the natural process, acting as midwife to the Sea at its birth, tending to the snow, strolling at the bottom of the sea, and so on. However, many interpreters detect an ironic, depersonalizing tone in 38:25-29, a passage that introduces many enigmas into the Joban nature narrative:

> (25) Who divided out a pathway for flood torrents (*šeṭep tě'ālāh*),[21]
> or a way for peals of thunder—
> (26) to bring rain upon a land without people,
> upon a wilderness (*midbār*) with no one in it?
> (27) To feed a desolate wasteland (*šō'āh ûmĕšō'āh*),
> to cause green grass to sprout forth there?
> (28) Does the rain have a father?
> Or who gave birth to the drops of dew?
> (29) From whose womb did ice come forth?
> And the frost of heaven—who gave birth to it?

At first the reference to divine acts of gushing water in 38:25 will remind the reader of the debate earlier in the book as it concerns well-watered plants—analogous to righteous humans—and natural destruction. In opposition to the Friends' domestic plant watering schemes, Job turned to the specter of floodwater (9:23; 12:15; 14:19; 27:20) as evidence of an amoral nature (and therefore an amoral God, especially in 9:13-24 and 12:13-25). What, then, is the divine response to all of this? What is the sense of this string of rhetorical questions? The "where-were-you" and "who-do-you-think-did-all-of-this" nature of the chapter, combined with the strong first-person

---

21. As opposed to other terms for running water, *šeṭep* indicates water that is overflowing, or destructively raging (as in a flash flood); compare Isa. 28:18; 30:28; Jer. 47:2; Ezek. 13:11; Ps. 69:3[2], among other examples.

opening in 38:4 ("Where were you when *I* laid the foundations
…"), suggests that the implied answer to the rain's fatherhood and
the identity of the one who provides rain on the uninhabited land
can only be God. This poet reiterates this same first-person speech
in God's mouth in verses 9 and 23, as signposts confirming God's
personal knowledge and involvement with all of the creative and
geographical processes mentioned in the speech.

In a programmatic essay Matitiahu Tsevat rejects a prominent line
of interpretation that scholars offer at this point: "education through
overwhelming."[22] Since Job had never doubted whether God could
indeed be overwhelming and wise, the content of God's response
cannot merely provide evidence of that overwhelming and wise
status. To those (like Gordis), who see beauty as "anodyne to man's
suffering," Tsevat asserts that "the beauty surrounding the tortured
may in its contrast intensify the pain."[23] He goes on to argue that
the Divine Speech serves to prove the ultimate point of the book: the
world is amoral, and "Divine justice is not an element of reality."[24]
The passage under consideration here in 38:25-27 forms what Tsevat
calls "the least conspicuous but the most interesting" proof of his
thesis.[25] "Wasted" rain proves that humanity is not central to the
world design. Phrases like "without people" (*lō' 'îš*) and "no one" (*lō'
'ādām*) in 38:26 can only point up the lack of purely or centrally
human meaning in the natural cycles of ecological provision.

Building on Tsevat's insights, and against the typical view of the
rhetorical outburst in Job 38, Alan Cooper argues that God's
questions here "should not be misconstrued as *statements* about what

---

22. Matitiahu Tsevat, "The Meaning of the Book of Job," 1–37 in idem, *The Meaning of the Book
of Job and Other Biblical Studies: Essays on the Literature and Religion of the Hebrew Bible* (New
York: Ktav, 1981), at 23–25.
23. Ibid., 25; for the view critiqued here see Robert Gordis, "The Lord out of the Whirlwind: The
Climax and Meaning of 'Job,'" *Judaism* 13 (1964): 48–63.
24. Tsevat, "The Meaning," 31.
25. Ibid., 30.

God actually does."[26] In this view it is not God who is "Father" to rain—rather, this kind of language is mere "literary fancy";[27] for Tsevat and Cooper, in the supposedly demythologized Joban worldview God scorns any notion of rain as Baal-semen or some such magical process. God does not infuse Job with beauty or wonder but rather mocks Job's insistence that he should be rewarded or punished as an individual on the basis of some set morality. In other words, in 38:28 God says: the rain has no father. Powerful though both Tsevat's and Cooper's essays are, their conclusions ignore God's relatively straightforward language in this chapter, as well as in chapters 39–41. God presents his geography and affirms: *I did this.* True, one may find oneself in a position of sheer embarrassment at God's involvement in the blunders and horrors of the created order, but such embarrassment cannot be so easily assuaged through simply flipping the statements in chapter 38 on their head.

What are we to make of the fact that some elements of the Divine Speech in chapter 38 already seem to echo or reassert things already argued by Job and the Friends? Both Tsevat and Cooper argue, in similar ways, that God should not come on the scene and reassert, piecemeal, things that we have already heard.[28] In fact, unavoidable references to previous arguments in the book appear at several points. Consider, for example, statements in 38:12-15 and 38:22-23 that seem to endorse the iron system of divine punishment and reward so often invoked by the Friends:

> 38:12-15: Have you commanded (*ṣiwwîtā*) the morning . . . so that it might reach the edges of the earth, and the wicked (*rĕšāʿîm*) would be shaken out from it? . . . Light is withheld from the wicked (*rĕšāʿîm*), and the uplifted arm is broken.

26. Alan Cooper, "The Sense of the Book of Job," *Prooftexts* 17 (1997): 227–44, at 240–41.
27. Ibid., 240.
28. Tsevat, "The Meaning," 23–24; Cooper, "The Sense," 240.

38:22-23: Have you come into the storehouses of snow, or have you seen the storehouses of hail, which I kept for a time of distress, for a day of battle and war?

The first passage in question here is more explicit: God's "commands" (ṣwh) do not make too many appearances in Job (see 36:32 and 37:12), but, combined with stock language about the rĕšāʿîm, God's musing at least recalls Psalmic affirmations of conventional wisdom regarding the fate of the wicked who disobey divine decrees (e.g., Psalm 1). Apparently, for the Joban poet, scattering the rĕšāʿîm for their wicked acts is in fact something God does. We should notice the fact that in 38:22-23 God stores up destructive elements for times of distress and battle and war.[29] Perhaps the meaning here is only idiomatic, or perhaps God signals the visible results of the divine interaction with nature—and, strikingly, the divine participation in this poetic moment involves only retribution, only violence.

A few other echoes of nature reasoning in the Dialogues appear in chapter 38. In 38:21 Yhwh gives the birth-order argument—not unlike Eliphaz in 15:7—to undermine Job's position vis-à-vis the created order. For both Eliphaz and Yhwh, Job cannot trump nature's ways because he is simply too young. Throughout the book of Job the term ḥēleq usually refers to land allotment for humans. In fact, the organizational promise of ḥēleq as land portion plays a large role in priestly texts and in the Deuteronomistic History and other texts that probably took their final form as written documents sometime during or shortly after the sixth century BCE.[30] In the Dialogues the language of ḥēleq appeared during intense discussion of punishment or reward from God (Job 20:29; 21:17; 27:13, 17; 31:2; 32:17), just as the term

---

29. Cf. the notion of a divine "storehouse" of blessing in Deut. 28:12; Mal. 3:10.
30. See, for example, Num. 18:20 and Numbers 26; Deut. 10:19; 12:2; 14:27, 29; 18:1, 8; 32:9; Joshua 18; 2 Kings 9; Isa. 53:12; 57:6; 61:7; Jer. 37:12; 51:19; Ezek. 45:7; 47:21; 48:8, 21. Notice also the clearly post-exilic concern for (re-)establishing a land portion (ḥēleq) in Ezra 4:16; Neh. 2:20; 9:22; 13:13.

frequently appears in other wisdom discourse (most specifically Eccl. 2:10, 21; 3:22; 5:18, 19; 9:6, 9; 11:2). Following the statement about doling out snow and hail as punishment, in 38:24 God hints at the distribution of light (for whom or what?), though without explicit reference to blessing: "Where is the place where light is apportioned (*yēḥāleq*). . . ." As we have already noticed throughout the Dialogues, the idea of seasonality and right agricultural timing has played an important rhetorical role (e.g., 5:24-26). Now, in 38:32-33, the roll-call of constellations marks out time, another cosmic movement Job cannot understand: "Can you lead out the Mazzaroth in its season (*bĕʿittô*) . . . do you know the statutes (*ḥūqqôt*) of the heavens? Can you establish its rule upon the earth?"[31]

Throughout chapter 38 God marks out geography through the refrain: *where?*[32] An argument about the suffering self has turned into questions of place, of lived location within a massive scale. Whatever these references mean, they at least suggest a personal system with an involved deity ready to declare war. Even if the physical cosmos is "personal" for God, however, there are enigmas built into the universe that depersonalize things away from relationship with a discrete human self. The riddle of rain on empty land is the surest example of a natural process detached from human needs or deeds, but the reference to snow and hail as weapons to punish the wicked is the surest sign that the cosmos can become personally destructive for people on the wrong side of divine commandments. God can go either way; all extremes are possible in this cosmic economy.

31. On the Joban constellations see Baruch Halpern, "Assyrian and pre-Socratic Astronomies and the Location of the Book of Job," 255–64 in Ulrich Hübner and Ernst A. Knauf, eds., *Kein Land für sich allein. Studien zum Kulturkontakt in Kanaan, Israel/Palästina und Ebirnâri für Manfred Weippert zum 65. Geburtstag* (OBO 186; Göttingen: Vandenhoeck & Ruprecht, 2002), which I discuss at greater length in the next chapter.
32. See comments on this in Brown, *Seven Pillars*, 125.

God's Menagerie (38:39–39:30)

The book of Job begins with animals in chapter 1 and nearly ends with animals in chapters 38–40, suggesting that animals have something important to say about the meaning of this experience of suffering and the God who orchestrates or allows it. Job's domesticated animal and hedge world in the Prologue of the book had posed no serious challenge to proverbial nature schemes, just as the depiction of non-human life in Genesis 1, incidentally, had no role independent of the imagined perfect state of human domination over the created world. Indeed, "nature" and "animal" can function as singular or blanket terms in the Joban prologue; animals act as a simple cipher for economic prosperity, which both drives Job's righteousness and serves as the reward for prosperity (the Adversary argued for prosperity driving the righteousness, while God remained noncommittal). Animals are under control in the prosperity dreamworld; they are, in that sense, anonymous and faceless, without personality or qualities of any kind apart from the plot set-up. In order for one to conceive of material prosperity along traditional Proverbial or Deuteronomistic lines (on biblical terms), animals would have to remain in this place, and humans, controllers of the moral drama, would master them as long as they (the humans) are righteous. In the Joban God's scheme, however, the animals will provide living evidence of what it is like to live vulnerably, on the edge of what one can take, in a position that can evoke something like Ricouer's notion of attestation, the "assurance" one can find in the midst of acting and suffering.[33] The animals of the Divine Speech are not ideas; they are animals, in dynamic relation to the suffering human.

---

33. Paul Ricoeur, *Oneself as Another*, trans. Kathleen Blamey (Chicago: University of Chicago Press, 1992), 22 (italics in original).

Master of Animals

An outburst of contemporary philosophical work has now challenged this "faceless," subservient character of animals generally for contemporary audiences, a move prefigured by God's own zoological outburst in Job 38–40.[34] The animals of the divine speech are loaded with pathos, strength, independence, arrogance, failure, and beauty—features that place these creatures outside human control, to be sure, but that also identify nature's drama with the predicament of human suffering. What is it about Job's problem, exactly, that calls for a long, zoologically-oriented lecture from the deity? When Carl Jung refers to the animals of the Divine Speech as a "prehistoric menagerie" in his famous *Answer to Job*, he does so with some bewilderment at the divine tactic.[35] The term "menagerie" is really quite appropriate, however, invoking as it does eighteenth-century notions of animal collections as a category of exotic prestige, a practice already known within the ancient Mesopotamian world.[36] The focus on the curious, the uncontrollable, and the abnormal is prominent; as others have noted, the speech takes its readers into a reverse creation story in which, instead of chaos moving toward order, God begins with order and measured space and presses outward or downward into chaos and the monstrous.[37]

34. See, e.g., Jacques Derrida, *The Animal That Therefore I Am*, trans. David Wills, ed. Marie-Louise Mallet (New York: Fordham University Press, 2008), especially on the question of "gaze" and animal anonymity; along similar lines see Giorgio Agamben, *The Open: Man and Animal*, trans. Kevin Attell (Stanford: Stanford University Press, 2003); Matthew Calarco, *Zoographies: The Question of the Animal from Derrida to Heidegger* (New York: Columbia University Press, 2008).

35. Carl Jung, *Answer to Job*, trans. Richard F. C. Hull (Bollingen Series XX; Princeton: Princeton University Press, 2010; orig. 1952), 19.

36. See Karen P. Foster, "The Earliest Zoos and Gardens," *Scientific American* 281 (1999): 64–71, and Allison K. Thomason, *Luxury and Legitimation: Royal Collecting in Ancient Mesopotamia* (London: Ashgate, 2005).

37. Brown, *Seven Pillars*, 126.

This movement has a corollary elsewhere in the Hebrew Bible, where the movement from city to wasteland is a trope of punishment (Ps. 107:33-38; Isa. 34:8-15; Hos. 2:5, 14; Lam. 2:8, 4:3); "characteristically eerie and uncanny animals" live in these wastelands (Isa. 13:19-21; 34:8-15; Jer. 50:39-40; Zeph. 2:13-15), dallying in places distant from home.[38] In a discussion of "domesticated" animals versus "monsters" as they are associated with deities in theriomorphic union, Mark Smith maps out an expected but insightful set of correlations: "benevolent deities" are anthropomorphic, associated with the domestic sphere, and take on emblems of bull, calf, bird, or cow, while "destructive divinities" are themselves "animal gods" who inhabit undomesticated space (desert, wasteland). Proper deities inhabit "near places," while monsters and demons stand outside (note Azazel in Lev. 16:8).[39] In the Ugaritic Baal cycle—stories rife with nature symbolism—Baal's climactic battles with Death (Mot) occur in the wilderness; as Smith points out, "the outback [Ugaritic *dbr*; compare Hebrew *midbār*] marks a marginal or transitional zone and the site of human activities such as grazing and hunting . . . here begins the area of dangerous forces."[40]

The danger associated with wild animals presents the heroic, benevolent deity with an enemy to overcome. In a very widely known set of iconographic examples from the ancient Near Eastern and Mediterranean worlds, the "master of animals" motif (for both male and female deities) indicates divine domination over wildness.[41] These depictions have a central figure grasping the throats or tails of

---

38. Newsom, *Book of Job*, 245.
39. Mark S. Smith, *The Origins of Biblical Monotheism: Israel's Polytheistic Background and the Ugaritic Texts* (Oxford: Oxford University Press, 2001), 28–33; see also John B. Geyer, "Desolation and Cosmos," *VT* 49 (1999): 49–64, at 58–59.
40. Smith, *Origins*, 29.
41. See ample images and discussion in Othmar Keel, *Jawhes Entgegnung an Ijob. Eine Deutung von Ijob 38–41 vor dem Hintergrund der zeitgenössischen Bildkunst* (Göttingen: Vandenhoeck & Ruprecht, 1978), 86–101.

animals on either side—typically a caprid (wild goat-antelope), horse, scorpion, lion, or steppeland bird such as an ostrich (discussed further below; for the general iconographic motif see Figure 7).[42]

Figure 7: "Master of animals" stamp seals.

In some examples it is unclear whether the anthropomorphic figure is "mastering" the animals or reaching out to them in some gesture of veneration.[43] In at least some cases, though, we know that this motif displayed a deity in association with a particular kind of animal; presumably the animal served as a symbolic token of that deity's presence (which could be signaled even without the anthropomorphic figure in the depiction), or the deity comes to conquer what is wild in the animal itself (as in cases involving lions, crocodiles, or the ostrich). Either way, in this iconography (whether visual or evoked by text) the deity and the animal cannot be separated; the deity's association with the animal is a picture of the cosmos, that is, of the ongoing status of divine control and the divine attributes needed to achieve that control.[44]

42. See Othmar Keel and Christoph Uehlinger, *Gods, Goddesses, and Images of God in Ancient Israel*, trans. Thomas H. Trapp (Minneapolis: Fortress Press, 1998), 141–52, 182–94.

43. Moreover, it is not always clear whether the anthropomorphic figure is a human or a deity (or something hybrid); see Keel and Uehlinger, *Gods*, 182, 184. In situations with clear (human) heroic motifs in play, as in Greek iconography, the assumption of a human master of animals is often made; see, e.g., Angeliki Kosmopoulou, *The Iconography of Sculptured Statue Bases in the Archaic and Classical Periods* (Madison: University of Wisconsin Press, 2002), 37.

44. Keel, *Jawhes Entgegnung an Ijob*, 125. As Keel and Uehlinger (*Gods*, 182) point out, we can observe a move from anthropomorphic depictions to animal-only icons; does this suggest that

When the Joban God rolls out wild creatures in the way he does (Job 38:39–39:30), what are we to assume about that deity's status? Using the taxonomy Smith suggests for benevolent and malevolent deities, what are we to make of the fact that, as Newsom and Brown rightly affirm in similar ways, God's own identity is bound up with the existence of these animals in a positive—even thrilling—manner?[45] Equally striking, and less often emphasized, however, is the notion that Job's failures—and God's own triumphant violence—are to be viewed in concert with harsh depictions of animal failures and nature violence. A review of the specific animals at the end of chapter 38 and throughout chapter 39 will help us locate God's presence and Job's situation within the animal world. Some of these animals warrant more attention than others in terms of our analysis here, though all work together in concert to narrate wisdom scenarios of the natural world.[46]

Lion (38:39-40)

In seamless transition from the cosmic geography, God moves to animals: "Can you hunt prey for the lioness (*lābî'*), or satisfy the desire of the lion cubs (*kĕpîrîm*) . . . ?" (38:39). Readers here will recall the lion riddle in 4:10-11, posed to Job by Eliphaz: "The teeth of the young lions (*kĕpîrîm*) are broken. The father lion (*layiš*) perishes for lack of prey, and the sons of the lioness (*lābî'*) are scattered."[47] Both passages take up the concern of food for the lion, among the most fearsome and regal of animals an ancient Near Eastern person might

---

the animal does not need to be "dominated" for the visual point to come across—i.e., that the visual point here has to do with divine identity with the animal?

45. Newsom, *Book of Job*, 245; Brown, *Seven Pillars*, 129–30.

46. On the rhetorical structure of the animals here see James E. Miller, "Structure and Meaning of the Animal Discourse in the Theophany of Job (38,39–39,30)," *ZAW* 103 (1991): 418–21.

47. On this and other lion imagery in the Hebrew Bible see Brent A. Strawn, *What is Stronger Than a Lion? Leonine Image and Metaphor in the Hebrew Bible and the Ancient Near East* (OBO 212; Fribourg: Academic Press, 2005), and my discussion of Job 4:10-11 in the previous chapter.

encounter. God makes no clear assertion here; if 38:39-40 provides a rejoinder to 4:10-11 one could only discern it by an interpretive leap. God only asks: can you feed these animals? The implication, in continuity with the creation-oriented questions in the rest of chapter 38, is that only God could provide. But even God may not provide. If Job cannot satisfy the hunger of lion cubs, perhaps he cannot protect his own children—a particularly harrowing suggestion, given the fact that God had personally signed off on their death.

Whether by literal hunting or as a political concept, the death of the lion symbolized monarchic power and control over unconquered space in the ancient Near East.[48] Assyrian monarchs took advantage of the lion in this role most enduringly, as the lion hunt motif formed the Assyrian royal glyptic symbol for almost 450 years (from the ninth to the late seventh centuries BCE); in grand bas relief, Assyrian kings—often cloaked in priestly attire (highlighting the cultic significance of the acts)—hunted lions on foot and from chariots, with a variety of weapons, as a reflex of mythological battles.[49] Lest one regard the Assyrian reliefs as merely chauvinistic displays of monarchic power, viewers should notice the depiction of suffering at the hands of the hunter: in many examples the lions grimace and writhe in pain and bleed profusely (see Figure 8).[50]

---

48. See the pioneering study of Keel, *Jawhes Entgegnung an Ijob*, 61–66, 76–81, as well as Michael B. Dick, "The Neo-Assyrian Royal Lion Hunt and Yahweh's Answer to Job," *JBL* 125 (2006): 243–70.

49. As thoroughly reviewed by Dick, "Neo-Assyrian Royal Lion Hunt," 246, 249–50, 252–55.

50. See Richard David Barnett and the British Museum, *Sculptures from the North Palace of Ashurbanipal at Nineveh (668–627 B.C.)* (London: British Museum Publications, 1976), pls. V–XV.

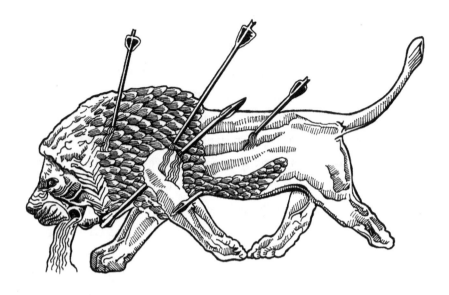

Figure 8: Scene from Assyrian lion hunt relief; palace of Assurbanipal; seventh century BCE; British Museum.

The sheer number of arrows stuck in the animal suggests the kill was not immediate or easy; the lion vomits blood as a last act of pain. The reason for this sensitivity toward the pathos and power of the lion, as explained by Michael Dick, is quite significant, and takes us deeper into the meaning of the "master of animals" motif in the iconography generally and in Job 38–40: in defeating the lion, the king becomes the lion (or he already is the lion, made manifest in the figure of the lion). The identities of hunter and prey fuse together; the king now governs the steppeland ruled by the lion. As examples of this dual identity Dick points to four Mesopotamian deities—Ninurta, Nabu, Nergal/Erra, and Ishtar—who engage in the lion hunt and yet take on leonine appearance themselves.[51]

51. Dick, "Neo-Assyrian Royal Lion Hunt," 244–45, 252 n. 52.

Lest these descriptions of the royal lion hunt lead us to believe that somehow Yhwh is a lion hunter in these chapters, we must admit the opposite: if anything, the deity functions in a role of care or provision.[52] However, we must also acknowledge notable points of contact between the iconographic register of the Job 39–40 text and the visual lion-hunt motif. First, the identities of hunter and hunted fuse together in the hunting narrative, an observation that illuminates the creeping suspicions many interpreters have entertained: Yhwh is to be somehow *identified with* the character of these animals as "wild," and Yhwh is at least equally at home in the outback and with the sheep behind Job's hedge. Second, various cues in the Divine Speech point to the fact that Yhwh stands in a position not just of "care" (in the tender sense of the word) over these animals but also domination, to the point where his cruel will determines an animal's cruel fate. Eliphaz suggested that lion-teeth could suddenly break—who is the breaker? If young ravens cry out in starvation, to whom do they cry out—and who might provide the solution, or not (38:41)? Who deprives creatures of abilities that might help them preserve their young (39:16-17)? Who ordained the blood culture of predation, by which animals must survive (39:29-30)?

The ambivalence with which some animals in Job 38–39 are portrayed turns these passages into a kind of textual rival or counterpart to the Assyrian reliefs; wounded, needy animals in Job 38–40 find some parallel in Assurbanipal's wounded, puking lion—an image that points further toward Job's own experience with God: God has hunted him (Job 10:16). The paradoxical yet necessary combinations of beauty and terror, suffering and triumph, and so on in the Assyrian relief lions accurately tell the story of the Joban God's

---

52. As noticed by Leo G. Perdue *Wisdom in Revolt: Metaphorical Theology in the Book of Job* (Bible and Literature Series 29; Sheffield: Almond Press, 1991), 215; Dick, "Neo-Assyrian Royal Lion Hunt," 266, 269.

animals and of Job's own journey between the poles of prosperity and near-death.

Raven (38:41)

"Who provides for the raven its prey, when its young cry out to God, and wander about for lack of food"? Job 38:41 gives only a quick glance at the raven family but, like all these images, this one is loaded with meaning. The repeated themes of birth, animal children, and food provision serve to highlight Job's lack of control over the natural world, just as they point out God's potential role in all situations of provision or starvation or suffering generally. Young ravens "wander about" (*tāʾah*) for lack of food; the verb here suggests not purposeful searching but wounded wandering—just as Job uses the term to describe the results of God's activity in his bitter, heterodox rant in 12:24-25: " . . . he (God) makes them (humans) wander (*tāʾah*) in a wasteland without roads; they grope around in the dark, and there is no light—he makes them stagger (*tāʾah*) like drunkards." Humans and animals struggle in the same world.

Mountain Goats, Deer (39:1-4)

In his thorough iconographic analysis of the Joban Divine Speech, Othmar Keel offers a mid-second-millennium Assyrian seal impression illustrating a spear-wielding warrior figure in battle with a deer-like creature, a lion, and an ostrich—notably, three of the animals appearing in Job 38–39.[53] Whether or not such animals formed a known grouping of wild animals for the purposes of the "master of animals" trope (adopted as a wisdom motif in Job), in 39:1-4 the deity cites mountain goats and deer as further examples of animals Job has not mastered. The potentially tender description of

---

53. Keel, *Jawhes Entgegnung an Ijob*, 74 Abb. 3.

the mystery of animal birth (animals knowing the "time" [*'ēt*] of birth by instinct and crouching to deliver [39:2]), accomplished without human assistance, prayers, midwives, or technology, is undercut by the poet with a straightforward analysis, its concluding line again suggesting the mystery of lost children: "Their children grow strong, they multiply in the open field (*bār*)[54]—they leave, and they never come back (*šwb*) to their parents" (Heb. *lāmô*, "to them"). The act of birth represents one pivotal transition: things come through the birth canal and change state. Birth is the beginning of life, but how does the animal parent know the time when such care will end, either through maturity of the children or death?

Wild Ass/Donkey (39:5-8)

The "wild ass" (*pere'*) or "wild donkey" (*'ārôd*) serves as God's explicit example of an animal thriving in harsh lands, away from cities. This animal is marked by *freedom*—"Who set the wild ass free (*ḥopšî*)? Who loosed the bonds of the wild donkey?" (39:5)—and this freedom specifically opposes the trappings of urban life: "He laughs at the bustle of the city, he does not hear the shouting of the taskmaster" (v. 7). Rather, his territory is in the wild: the steppe (*'ărābāh*), the salt-land (*mĕlēḥāh*), the mountains (*hārîm*). He must find green things (*yārôq*) to eat, but he must search for them (*dāraš*). Food provision is no act of righteous farming, but rather a function of the animal's free status in the wilderness. The term here for the wild ass's freedom, *ḥopšî*,appears only elsewhere in the Bible with reference to humans, and most often as a technical term for a freed slave (Exod. 21:2-5, 26-27; Deut. 15:12-18; Jer. 34:9-16).

Once again the Divine Speech takes a point of departure in Job's lament in chapter 3, when he had wished for rest in the land of

---

54. See Dhomre, *Job*, 599.

the dead or the never-even-born: "small and great are there" in that place, Job claimed, "and the slave (*'ebed*) is free (*ḥopšî*) from his masters." Yhwh's animal logic could refute Job's assertion, since the wild ass possesses clear freedom in the land of the living. In order to acknowledge this state of living *ḥopšî*, however, Job would have to recognize a sphere of existence outside his hedged-in success world. In other words: human success is frankly incompatible with Job's notion of "freedom."

Wild Ox (39:9-12)

The manner in which Yhwh describes the wild ox (*rêm*) again harks back to Job's domestic animal world in chapter 1. "Is the wild ox willing to work as your slave (*'ābad*)?" (39:9). Such an animal would not eat at the keeper's feed crib, plow valleys, or submit to ropes.

Two potentially archaic poetic descriptions of God in the poems of Balaam (Num. 23:22; 24:8) and Moses (Deut. 33:17) describe Israel's deity as a "wild ox" (*rĕʾêm*) who gores enemies, distinct from the generic, tamed cattle (*bāqār*) of Job's peaceful existence. This wild ox in Job 39 is admittedly very strong (*kî rab kōḥô*, v. 11), but its instincts prove a liability for human use: if you cannot tie it down with ropes, or keep it in a barn, then "can you trust (*'mn*) that it would return (*šwb*), and gather your seed to your threshing floor?" (v. 12). Themes of "return" (*šwb*) now reverberate through the animal speeches (recall 39:4, and see 39:22), as Job is asked to consider the prospect of restoration as well as the pain of permanent exile. This notion of return is linked to "trust" or "faith," raising the question whether humans should expect or even hope for control over or restoration from the brokenness of their situations (compare Eliphaz's description of the wicked in 15:22: "He cannot trust [*'mn*] that he will return [*šwb*] from darkness . . .").

Ostrich (39:13-18)

In the account of the bird in Job 39:13-18 we arrive at one of the more perplexing and revealing animals in the divine menagerie. Most translators take the term *rĕnānîm* in 39:13 to mean "ostrich," based on the non-domestic geography of the animals in chapters 38–39 generally and because of the references to flight inability (39:13) and laying eggs on the ground (39:14).[55] *Rĕnānîm* is a *hapax legomenon*, with no clear cognates (as an animal) in other ancient languages (the root *rānan* means "singing aloud joyously"). Elsewhere in the Bible ostriches are called *bĕnôt ya'ălāh* (*bāt hayya'ănāh*), "ones who cry out" (?).[56] Ostriches do emit various kinds of distinct noises, and their sounds are often perceived as peculiar. During mating season noises come most often at night and exhibit an aural character that makes the source of the sound hard to identify. During the day the sounds are "uncanny and ferocious," often involving hissing and yelps and associated with aggressive behavior.[57] In the wild, ostriches are known as careful protectors of their nests (males and females alternate sitting on the eggs),[58] which makes the Joban poet's depiction of this animal as careless in this regard striking.

55. For previous analyses of Job 39:13–18 see Izak Spangenberg, "Who Cares? Reflections on the Story of the Ostrich (Job 39.13–18)," *ESWT*, 92–102; Clines, *Job 38–42*, 1124–27; Jürgen van Oorschot, *Gott als Grenze. Eine literar- und redaktionsgeschichtliche Studie zu den Gottesreden des Hiobbuches* (BZAW 170; Berlin: de Gruyter, 1987), 176–78; Habel, *Book of Job*, 46–47; Robert Gordis, *The Book of Job: Commentary, New Translation and Special Studies* (Moreshet 2; New York: JTS Press, 1978), 458–60, 565; Geyer, "Desolation," 58–59. Against the "ostrich" translation see the cogent challenge of Arthur W. Walker-Jones, "The So-Called Ostrich in the God Speeches of the Book of Job (Job 39,13-18)," *Biblica* 86 (2005), 494–510.

56. This etymology is only speculation, based on taking the root *'nh* in one of its less common meanings, "revel; wail; cry out"; see, e.g., Ludwig Koehler and Walter Baumgartner, *Hebräisches und Aramäisches Lexikon zum Alten Testament*, III (Leiden: Brill, 1983), 808. For other ostriches in the Bible see Lev. 11:16; Deut. 14:15; Isa. 13:21; 34:13; 43:20; Jer. 50:39; Lam. 4:3; Job 30:29. See discussion of the Isaian ostriches along with other desert animals of this type in Geyer, "Desolation," 58–59.

57. Ingvar Ekesbo, *Farm Animal Behaviour: Characteristics for Assessment of Health and Welfare* (Wallingford: CABI, 2011), 184.

58. Ibid., 185.

In ancient Near Eastern iconography the "master of ostriches" scene forms a distinct sub-category of the "master of animals" motif (see Figure 9).[59] These scenes are surprisingly common, and took their symbolic currency from the fact that ostriches are notoriously difficult animals to control; according to Othmar Keel and Christoph Uehlinger in their instructive study of "lord of animals" iconography, ostriches present us with a "deserted, dangerous and sinister world." They embody "a numinous power that commands respect and honor because [the ostrich] can survive mysteriously at the edge of hospitable land . . . Fear and respect for numinous powers that are demonic is not far distant from fascination with such creatures."[60]

Figure 9: "Master of ostriches" motif on seals.

Indeed, Yhwh himself seems fascinated with this creature in Job 39:13-18, and the "lord of ostriches" scene and other attribute-animal depictions largely replace other motifs in Israel/Palestine during the

59. See Keel, *Jawhes Entgegnung*, 104–6.
60. Keel and Uehlinger, *Gods, Goddesses, and Images of God*, 182. See further discussion with ample images in Keel, *Jahwes Entgegnung an Ijob*, 66–68, 84–86. In his *Reste Arabischen Heidentums, Gesammelt und Erläutert*, 2d ed. (Berlin: Georg Reimer, 1897), 152–53, Julius Wellhausen spoke of the ostrich (*Strauss*) specifically, claiming that, for Muslims, "zoology" and "demonology" were intertwined. In his *The Book of Job: A Biography* (Princeton: Princeton University Press, 2013), 177–79, Mark J. Larrimore cites the ostrich passage in Job as an example of the type of *mysterium* Rudolf Otto saw (in his famous 1917 book *The Idea of the Holy*) in the divine speeches.

Iron IIA period (late-eleventh to tenth centuries BCE). Yhwh's connection with the desert lands of the southwest Levant, where ostriches would certainly have been more common than in the central country, appears in some of the allegedly archaic poetic materials (Deut. 33:2; Judg. 5:4; Hab. 3:3; Ps. 68:8; see also Isa. 63:1-2), an association that coheres with possibly the earliest texts to mention the name Yhwh in some form (from Egypt in the fourteenth and thirteenth centuries BCE) and the so-called "Midianite hypothesis," which posits that the Yhwh religion originated in this southwest region.[61] At any rate, such associations between deities and ostriches in the desert regions near Israel/Palestine persisted for many centuries, as evidenced in a sixth-century BCE desert shrine at Hurvat Qitmit (10 km south of Arad) where distinct and numerous terracotta figurines of ostriches turned up.[62]

---

61. An early fourteenth-century text from Amenophis III of Egypt refers to "Yahu [Egyptian *yhw*; others vocalize Ya-h-wi, or Ya-h-we; see Cross, *Canaanite Myth*, 62] in the land of the Shosu-bedouins." See Raphael Giveon, *Les bédouins Shosou des documents égyptiens* (Leiden: Brill, 1971), 26–28, 74–77. This reference comes up again, along with Seir, in a 13th-century list of Ramses II. Among the early studies of the "Midianite hypothesis" idea see Eduard Meyer, *Die Israeliten und ihre Nachbarstämme: alttestamentliche Untersuchungen* (Halle: Max Niemeyer, 1906); more recently see the summary in Lawrence Stager in "Forging an Identity: The Emergence of Ancient Israel," 90–129 in Michael D. Coogan ed., *The Oxford History of the Biblical World* (Oxford: Oxford University Press, 1998), at 105–11, as well as Frank Moore Cross, "Reuben, the Firstborn of Jacob: Sacral Traditions and Early Israelite History," 53–70 in idem, *From Epic to Canon: History and Literature in Ancient Israel* (Baltimore: Johns Hopkins University Press, 2000); J. David Schloen, "Caravans, Kenites, and *Casus belli*," *CBQ* 55 (1993): 18–38.

62. See brief discussion and image in Keel and Uehlinger, *Gods, Goddesses, and Images of God*, 382–85, and the excavation reports of Itzhaq Beit-Arieh, "The Edomite Shrine at Horvat Qitmit in the Judean Negev: Preliminary Excavation Report," *Tel Aviv* 18 (1991): 93–116; Itzhaq Beit-Arieh and Pirhiya Beck, *Edomite Shrine: Discoveries from Qitmit in the Negev* (Israel Museum Catalogue 277; Jerusalem: Israel Museum, 1987). The ostrich played a role in Egyptian religion as well, with an ostrich feather serving as a token of the goddess Maat: Spangenberg, "Reflections," 97. Though the counter-case against the "ostrich" translation in this passage in favor of the "sand grouse" by Walker-Jones ("The So-Called Ostrich") is formidable in some respects, I still believe the ostrich reading makes as much sense as any other option. In the end, the lesson to be learned is not so different whether one chooses a sand grouse or an ostrich. Moreover, Walker-Jones does not adequately account for the iconographic depictions of ostriches I review here, and some other points of his argument are as debatable as the points in favor of the ostrich.

With all of this in mind, the Joban *rĕnānîm* takes an expected place among the animals of the Divine Speech, yet offers surprises and riddles of its own:

> (39:13) The wings of the *rĕnānîm* flutter jubilantly (*ne'ĕlāsāh*),[63]
> even though she lacks (*ḥăsîdāh*) pinions or the right kind of feathers for flying (*nōṣāh*).[64]
> (14) She leaves her eggs on the ground,
> and upon the dust they grow warm;
> (15) she forgets that a foot might crush them,
> or a beast of the field might trample them.
> (16) She acts harshly against[65]
> her sons, as if they were not her own;
> her labor is for nothing (*lĕrîq*), but not to worry (*bĕlî pāḥad*);[66]
> (17) Eloah made her forget wisdom, he gave her no share of understanding.
> (18) But another time comes—she rises up on the height,
> she laughs at horse and its rider.[67]

---

63. The verbal root here (*'ālas*, "rejoice") is uncommon, appearing only here and Job 20:18; Prov 7:18.

64. I have taken two liberties with the translation of this second half of the verse: (1) The MT has the adjective *ḥăsîdāh*, often translated "stork" elsewhere in the Hebrew Bible (Lev. 11:19; Deut. 14:18; Jer. 8:7; Zech. 5:9; Ps. 104:17). However, the presence of a "stork" here is hard to understand, and the Heb. *dalet* (*d*) may simply be a scribal mistake for *resh* (*r*), thus giving us *ḥăsîrāh*, "lack, want" (compare *ḥāsēr*, *ḥeser*). See Marvin H. Pope, *Job* (AB 15; Garden City, NY: Doubleday, 1965), 260, and Édouard Dhorme, *A Commentary on the Book of Job*, trans. Harold Knight (London: Thomas Nelson & Sons, 1967; French orig. 1926), 603–4 for some of the more difficult translation issues in this passage. (2) The meaning of *nōṣāh* is not clear, but in parallel with *'ebrāh* ("pinion"), *nōṣāh* probably refers to some kind of feather or plumage. I interpret the verse here to mean that, although the bird is happily flapping its wings, it does not have the *right kind* of feathers to fly. The root *nṣr* usually means "keep, watch," though a *nēṣer* is the "shoot" of a plant in Isa. 60:21 and Dan. 11:7—thus I venture to interpret *nōṣāh* as what might cause the bird to spring forth.

65. The form here is actually masculine: "he hardens" (*hiqšîaḥ*). In parallel with the *hiphil* perfect at the beginning of the next verse, it may be that the "he" who hardens (= acts cruelly) is, in fact, God (as in 39:17).

66. Lit. "there is no fear."

67. This line, *kā'ēt bammārôm tamrî*, is incomprehensible as it is currently written. *Kā'ēt* could mean "in due season," "at a certain time," or "in the course of time" (e.g., Gen. 18:10; 2 Kgs. 4:16-17), or some unspecified time in the future or a given moment (Num. 23:23; Judg. 13:23). If we understand the verb *mārā'* with the meaning "rise up"—for which there is no real Hebrew evidence—we might literally translate the phrase as "like the time she rises up on the height." I

The bird's title here, *rĕnānîm*, could perhaps be translated loosely as "joy bird." As mentioned above, the usual biblical nomenclature of the ostrich probably alludes to noise (*bāt hayyaʿănāh*), but probably not *joyous* noise. Here the ostrich maintains its identity as a proud bird, difficult to control, with a harsh character, but the *rĕnānîm* title and the description of her odd behavior paint her with conflicting colors. In a short essay incorporating some research on the behavior of ostriches, Izak Spangenberg points to some of the bird's paradoxical qualities, which are not limited to the flightless wings: additionally, the wings are not waterproof, making them doubly useless during a downpour.[68] Nevertheless, the bird flaps these wings "jubilantly" (*neʿĕlāsāh*), which goes well with her name as *rĕnānîm* and yet provides additional tensions. Strikingly, the only use of the verb *ʿls* outside of Job, in Proverbs 7:18, describes the sexual delight of a temptress. Our bird is powerless but happy, able to procreate but then unable to protect her young, yet filled with a pretense of military might ("horse and rider" is a traditional phrase marking major battles in the Hebrew Bible; see Exod. 15:21; Jer. 51:21; Nah. 3:2).

The fact that the ostrich lays eggs *on the ground* presents yet another difficulty. Even though ornithologists can now affirm the ostrich's great care in protecting eggs, the poet here may have perceived that such eggs were particularly vulnerable in this position (as opposed to their being laid in trees or bushes, in nests), thus suggesting another paradox.

---

interpret this to mean that, in spite of the bird's inability to protect her own young, she is all too ready to rise up arrogantly (see 39:13) against a military force (not that the ostrich could access a "height" through flying as does the eagle in 39:27-29, discussed below).

68. Spangenberg, "Reflections," 98–99. As Spangenberg (p. 100) further points out, the "ostrich" here must be of the variety *Struthio camelus syriacus* (the "Arabian ostrich"), now extinct. After some (admittedly casual) reviews of scientific literature on the ostrich, I know of no reason to see the behavior of the *Struthio camelus syriacus* as distinctly different from that of other types that would be more familiar to contemporary audiences. Clines, *Job 38–42*, 1124–27 has a review of ornithological insight on ostrich behavior.

We need not take the behavior of the bird here as biologically normal or paradigmatic. Even if we did not have examples from the Hebrew Bible itself to show us that ancient Israelites could engage in "magical" or "folk" thinking about animals (see, e.g., Jacob's breeding tactics in Gen. 30:37-43, and Jeremiah's folk wisdom about a bird hatching eggs it did not lay in Jer. 17:11), we might very well guess that the author here could not give us a proper study of the ostrich. Still, the author knew enough to evoke the paradoxes such an animal could embody—paradoxes that are simply part of the bird's own body. The symbolism here continues themes introduced by the other animals so far: reproduction, freedom, and provision. The ostrich cannot, or does not, protect her young. But why? We cannot accept Habel's contention that the bird is to serve as an example to Job of poor moral judgment,[69] nor can we endorse Spangenberg's argument, as he states that the ostrich is not concerned with rewards; such matters are to be left up to God, he asserts, and the creature should merely enjoy life.[70] Jürgen van Oorschot's subtle view, that the ostrich in fact trumps the reader by her ability to rise up against horse and rider, while the reader had assumed she was ridiculous, is perhaps too subtle.[71]

A more obvious reason for the bird's behavior is stated baldly as a terrifying admission in 39:17: *Eloah made her forget wisdom, he gave her no share (ḥeleq) of understanding.* As elsewhere in Job and other wisdom literature in the Hebrew Bible, this notion of one's "share" or "portion" (ḥeleq) plays a key role. What kind of reward does one expect, and in return for what kind of behavior? Yhwh now takes some slanted ownership of Job's accusatory words about the divinely blinded eyes of the judges (9:24) and earth's power to hurt

---

69. Habel, *Book of Job*, 546–47.
70. Spangenberg, "Reflections," 101.
71. Van Oorschot, *Gott als Grenze*, 176–78.

humankind through flood-torrents (9:23, 12:15, 14:19, 27:20). There is intentional negligence *built in* to the entire created order (before the fact, for no given reason). What is anyone going to do about it? Nothing. Regarding the ongoing trope of provision for children in the animal examples, readers can hardly fail to notice the bracing analogy between the crushed bird eggs and Job's own brood. God removes wisdom, as well as the hedge (Job 1:12; 2:6).

Horse (39:19-25)

The example of the war horse comes off as a fairly straightforward example of animal power and violence.[72] To appreciate this we need to think not of a tranquil pet horse grazing in a field, or of genteel equestrian sports, but rather of war and chariotry. In this battle role the horse appears often enough in the Bible, and Keel has shown the close relationship between the horse and human as a team to pursue animals (particularly the ostrich) in hunting scenes.[73] Of course, in war the human warrior does indeed control the horse, and the hunting scene is a trope of control over nature. The author conceivably imagines the war horse in this role, but the intensity of the animal here is striking and perhaps even threatens the illusion of control the warrior may have over it: the horse snorts and paws the ground (39:20-21), laughing at all fear (v. 22), rushing into battle (v. 22) when perhaps even the rider might shrink back, straining against the bit at the sound of the battle horn (v. 24-25).

Hawk and Vulture (39:26-30)

The final example in chapter 30, involving hawk (*nēṣ*) and vulture (*nešer*), reaches a stunning, violent climax. Robert Alter goes so far

---

72. See comments on the horse's lust for battle in this passage in Abigail Pelham, *Contested Creations in the Book of Job* (Leiden: Brill, 2012), 27–29.
73. Keel, *Jawhes Entgegnung an Ijob*, e.g., 72–75, 79, 84–86.

as to call it "one of the most unsentimental poetic treatments of the animal world in the Western literary tradition," and at least initially the images come as a surprise from God's mouth.[74] The hawk does not soar by Job's wisdom (39:26), and the vulture does not build inaccessible nests at Job's command (v. 27). The height image, of the vulture's nest upon towering crags, directs our gaze up out of the mine metaphor in Job 28. The animal possesses vision (a true "bird's eye view"), as opposed to Job's own limited perceptual range—limited both physically and morally. From this altitude the vulture spies out food for its young, and the chicks eat in a stark manner: "they lap up blood; in the place of the corpses, there he is." These animals are scavengers, thriving off of pure death. They drink blood, surviving in a harsh land through what would appear harsh tactics to a sheltered outsider. They survive nonetheless, unmindful of Job, though, in Yhwh's opinion, their lives deserve Job's notice.

In summary, what have we learned about these animals and their relationship to other living things? The animal selves of Job 38–39 are certainly *providers*. Humans cannot provide for all animals, and in that sense control over the order of movement and food (the world animal economy) is not part of the scheme of human existence. Animals find ways to become self-sufficient; they resist servitude; desert animals live as alien creatures in strange lands, but they are *survivors*. The animals of the divine speech are *parents*—they are reproducers who carry on in their own ways. Their abilities are sometimes stunted at the level of their very bodies, at God's whim. One fears stretching the correspondence too far, but the connection among these themes and Job's initial dilemma—the loss of animals (property), the death of

---

74. Robert Alter, *The Art of Biblical Poetry*, revised and updated (New York: Basic Books, 2011), 127.

the ever-feasting children, and the dismantled cosmos of hedged-in power—suggests that the human moral universe interacts with and can be compared to animal failures, negligence, and alienation. If this is true, however, then another possibility offers itself: humans may also take up the power to survive in an alternative universe not unlike the wildest desert. Job's situation is fully within the purview of what is real.

God's Monsters (40:1–41:34)

Although I have already discussed some aspects of Joban animal-monster imagery in the previous chapter, a few remarks are in order concerning God's own hymn to the "Leviathan" (*liwyātān*) and the "Behemoth" (*bĕhēmôt*), arguably the crowning poetic achievement of the book of Job. These creatures have received a massive amount of attention in the secondary literature, so much that any adequate review in this space is, fortunately, impossible.[75] Text critical and philological problems beyond the boundaries of what we can address here abound as well.[76] The last few decades of the twentieth century in particular saw an explosion of articles bent on identifying these

---

75. For short and helpful overviews with bibliography on Leviathan see Christoph Uehlinger, "Leviathan," *DDD*, 511–15, and Edward Lipiński, "liwyātān," *TDOT* VII, 504–9; on Behemoth see, e.g., Bernard Couroyer, "Behemoth = hippopotamus ou buffle," *Revue Biblique* 94 (1987): 214–22; Bernard Batto, "Behemoth," *DDD*, 165–69. One of the better summaries of opinions over the past few centuries (up to 1975) is J. V. Kinnier Wilson, "A Return to the Problems of Behemoth and Leviathan," *VT* 25 (1975): 1–24; other useful treatments include Habel, *Book of Job*, 548–61; Clines, *Job 38–42*, 1141–1203; Keel, *Jahwes Entgegnung an Ijob*, 127–56, with ample iconographic comparisons; Michael V. Fox, "Behemoth and Leviathan," *Biblica* 93 (2012): 261–67; Pelham, *Contested Creations*, 127–37; David Wolfers, "The Lord's Second Speech in the Book of Job," *VT* 40 (1990): 474–99; John Day, *God's Conflict with the Dragon and the Sea: Echoes of Canaanite Myth in the Old Testament* (Univesity of Cambridge Oriental Publications 35; Cambridge: Cambridge University Press, 1985), 75–84; Robert Gordis, "Job and Ecology (and the Significance of Job 40:15)," *Hebrew Annual Review* 9 (1985): 189–202, esp. 196–98; idem, *Book of Job*, 467–90; Alter, *Art of Biblical Poetry*, 132–38; Newsom, *Book of Job*, 234–58.

76. On this see especially Wolfers, "The Lord's Second Speech"; Gordis, *Book of Job*, 467–90; Pope, *Job*, 265–87; Dhorme, *Job*, 616–44.

creatures as either "real" (a hippopotamus and crocodile, usually) or "mythological," as in the "Leviathan" Job invokes in 3:8 or the allusion to a creature like the Ugaritic Lotan, whom Baal smote.[77] Indeed, the fact that Leviathan has already appeared in Job in a mythological context means that readers of Job can hardly think first of Leviathan as anything but a wild sea monster beyond the bounds of anything we would call a "real" animal today.[78] However, the fact that it is *Job* who spoke of Leviathan, combined with the fact that much of the Divine Speech seems slanted against Job's and/or the Friends' arguments in sum, might suggest that we are to seek a subversive identity for Leviathan in Job 41.

Animal, Myth, and Monster

Almost every interpreter of these animals' identities is now quick to point out that ancient audiences would not have distinguished between "real" and "mythical" animals,[79] though it is not clear whether we mean that ancient people did not know or suspect that some creatures did not in fact exist. Perhaps more accurately, ancient audiences had no resources with which to know one way or the other whether remote, strange animals did truly exist, and thus they were willing to engage in speculation about non-obvious beings beyond what readers today could tolerate.[80] Even the venerable King James Bible—in its original 1611 version as well as in updates in the nineteenth century and in all (Old) King James Bibles

---

77. See my discussion in the previous chapter, and the passage in Dennis Pardee, "The Ba'lu Myth," *COS* I, 241–74, at 265.

78. A point also made by Habel, *Book of Job*, 560.

79. E.g., Watson, *Chaos Uncreated*, 333; Fox, "Behemoth and Leviathan"; Alter, *Art of Biblical Poetry*, 132.

80. Then again, a 2012 Angus Reid public opinion poll found that around one-third of Americans believe in the existence of "Bigfoot," a fact that would complicate an overly strong dichotomy between ancient and modern humans on this front (http://www.angusreidglobal.com/polls/44419/americans-more-likely-to-believe-in-bigfoot-than-canadians/; accessed 5 January 2014).

today—mentions unicorns about a dozen times, apparently prompted in at least some instances by the Greek translation of *rĕ'ēm* ("wild ox") by *monókerōs* ("single-horn"; the Latin Vulgate has *rinoceros*), thus preserving the spirit of ancient animal thinking (even if by erroneous translation).[81] Other translations actively delete "mythological" animal thinking where it may exist in the text, such as the NIV 2011, which translates *śārāp mĕ'ôpēp*, "*flying* serpent," twice as "*fiery* serpent" (Isa. 14:29; 30:6; compare Isa. 6:2). Other animals, such as Jonah's "large fish," dwell at some borderline between what, for an ancient Israelite, is biologically feasible and a mysterious unknown realm of sea creatures or desert predators.

Nothing about the Behemoth (40:15-24) needs to be read as particularly non-realistic for a biological animal, leading most interpreters to identify the creature as a hippopotamus, though the Leviathan (40:25–41:26)[82] pushes boundaries in at least two respects: (1) Leviathan poses a threat to divine world. Pending a common emendation in 41:1(41:9), the text would read "the gods were thrown down (or: dismayed) at its appearance,"[83] though, as it stands, the Hebrew *'el mar'âw yūtāl* could be translated "at its appearance he was/will be thrown down," the "he" being the fisherman alluded to in 40:31-32(41:7-8). However, in 41:17(41:25) the *'ēlîm* clearly react in terror at the Leviathan: "at his majesty the deities (*'ēlîm*) are in fear, at his crashing (*miśĕbārîm*) they are thrown amiss (*yithattā'û*)." In either or both cases Leviathan would be best imagined as a Sea Monster in opposition to the divine world, such as in the Baal Epic, *Enuma Elish*, or any number of references to the *Chaoskampf* in the

---

81. In the KJV see Num. 23:22; 24:8; Deut. 33:17; Job 39:9-10; Pss. 22:21; 29:6; 92:10; Isa. 34:7.

82. Hebrew and English verse numberings diverge at the Leviathan; Hebrew continues the ch. 40 verse numbering through 40:32, while the English-language tradition begins with Leviathan in 41:1 (Heb. 40:25); each time I cite a Hebrew verse here I give the English reference in parentheses.

83. See the reasonable explanation of Pope, *Job*, 282.

Hebrew Bible (e.g., Ps. 74:14; Isa. 27:1).[84] (2) Leviathan breathes fire in 41:11-13(41:19-21).

One could excuse either of these references within the bounds of poetic hyperbole, as the rest of the description fits reasonably with the common assertion that Leviathan here is a crocodile, or even a whale.[85] Keel's iconographic analysis demonstrates the common occurrence of both hippopotamus and crocodile hunt scenes on Egyptian seals and tomb art, which itself makes reasonable a suggestion that the poet saw these two animals as at least inspiration for the grand examples in Job 40–41.[86] The overall presentation of these creatures reminds us that Israelites did not think in Linnaean terms,[87] and thus words like "biology," "myth," and so on cannot take us to the heart of what is happening in Job 40–41, just as we could not assume biological knowledge of the behavior of ostriches as a strict foreground for Job 39:13-18 above.

Perhaps the most productive approach to these animals, then, is to view them as "monsters," a type of non-human animal in many cultures both ancient and modern.[88] Though etymologies of words are not always particularly relevant for ongoing function, "monsters" live out their etymology in revealing ways: "monster" apparently comes through the Old French *monstre*, from the Latin *montrer*, "to

---

84. Most interpreters (e.g., Newsom, *Book of Job*, 248) speak of these creatures in terms of "chaos," though cf. Watson, *Chaos Uncreated*, 366, who disputes this connection.

85. For the crocodile interpretation see Keel, *Jawhes Entgegnung an Ijob*, 141–56, and for the whale see Fox, "Behemoth and Leviathan."

86. Keel, *Jawhes Entgegnung an Ijob*, 127–41 on the hippo and 141–56 on the crocodile. See also Tryggve N. D. Mettinger, "The God of Job: Avenger, Tyrant, or Victor?" 39–49, 233–36 in Leo G. Perdue and W. Clark Gilpin, eds., *The Voice from the Whirlwind: Interpreting the Book of Job* (Nashville: Abingdon Press, 1992), at 46, who compares the Joban animals to animals and animal-deities in Egyptian mythology.

87. As Scott C. Jones cogently argues with regard to lion and serpent imagery in "Lions, Serpents, and Lion-Serpents in Job 28 and Beyond," *JBL* 130 (2011): 663–86.

88. A growing body of contemporary theory on monsters and their roles now exists; see, e.g., Marina Levina and Diem-My T. Bui, eds., *Monster Culture in the 21st Century: A Reader* (London: Bloomsbury: 2013); Jeffrey Jerome Cohen ed., *Monster Theory: Reading Culture* (Minneapolis: University of Minnesota Press, 1996).

show, reveal."[89] The monster *demonstrates*. The monster points to otherness or fear or the viewer through its own body; zombies in film are never only about a quick scare, but rather always gesture toward contemporary cultural notions of what is perceived as foreign or invasive.[90] This is not to say that the monstrous demonstration is straightforward; as Marie Hélène Huet shows, monsters are "doubly deceptive" in that their odd appearance can be "a misleading likeness to another species." Monsters can present "similarities to categories of beings to which they are not related," but this can be "a *false* resemblance."[91]

Few descriptions of this false resemblance would be better than William Blake's famous 1826 engraving of Behemoth and Leviathan (first in black and white, but then colored by Blake himself; see cover of this book).[92] God directs Job and Friends downward to a revelation of a cosmos-in-miniature, as if to say: *this* is the true nature of things. The Behemoth creature at the middle of the cosmos certainly does resemble a biologically real hippopotamus, but something of the face (especially the eyes, ears, and fangs), the back, and the coloring is suggestively amiss—this is no ordinary animal, though it stands on human ground, among the reeds mentioned in Job 40:21-22. On the lowest tier, of course, the coiling Leviathan comes forth as straightly mythological, representing watery depth as opposed to land. Blake's image of the Behemoth in particular takes us deeply into the feeling of the passage and, I would argue, represents what

89. For some discussion (including the uncertainty of the etymology) see Robert Burch, "Frames of Visibility: Si(gh)ting the Monstrous," 74–97 in Wilhelm S. Wurzer, ed., *Panorama: Philosophies of the Visible* (London: Continuum, 2002) at 87–88; Marie Hélène Huet, *Monstrous Imagination* (Cambridge, MA: Harvard University Press, 1993), 6.

90. See the readings in Joshua David Bellin, *Framing Monsters: Fantasy Film and Social Alienation* (Carbondale: Southern Illinois University Press, 2003).

91. Huet, *Monstrous Imagination*, 4 (italics in original).

92. See William Blake, *Illustrations to the Book of Job*, The Butts Set (Morgan Library and Museum; 1805–06 and 1821–27); online at http://www.blakearchive.org/exist/blake/archive/work.xq?workid=but550 (accessed 6 January 2014).

the poet of Job 40–41 attempted to do in textual form with these animals. Behemoth is a hippopotamus and takes its point of departure from the hippopotamus, but it is also more than a species that could be controlled by definition. So too, Leviathan is a scaly, toothy reptile, a crocodile, but then evokes more terror and dominance than a crocodile could show—even demonstrating the power of chaos control and creative power that the Lord God lords over Job.

Biblical scholars have already made helpful forays into the interpretation of these creatures as "monsters," though usually not in any technical sense. In a perceptive essay Rebecca Raphael argues that the monsters of Job show Job something about himself; monsters metaphorize the torn human body and reveal to Job what an invincible body would truly look like (in response to what Job wished his body could be—strong as stones or bronze [Job 6:11-12]).[93] Timothy Beal injects his reading of monsters in his *Religion and Its Monsters* with a range of comparative and theoretical sophistication, and takes up a consideration of Behemoth and Leviathan on these terms. Beal asserts that the Joban creatures here are "dangerous otherness within creation," as God eventually "out-monsters" Job.[94]

Reading Behemoth and Leviathan as Joban Nature Images

God offers a fairly clear prologue in Job 40:7-14 as an interpretive key to the presentation of Behemoth and Leviathan. Not satisfied with Job's first backdown in 40:4-5, Yhwh responds with crushing bombast and a challenge: *try to overpower me if you can.* Height imagery appears again, but no longer are we to consider how high the man-plant might grow, watered by his righteousness—recall

---

93. Rebecca Raphael, "Things Too Wonderful: A Disabled Reading of Job," *Perspectives in Religions Studies* 31 (2004): 399–424, at 404–9, 415–21, and also Alec Basson, "Just Skin and Bones: The Longing for Wholeness of the Body in the Book of Job," *VT* 58 (2008): 287–99.

94. Timothy K. Beal, *Religion and Its Monsters* (New York: Routledge, 2002), 47–55; quotations here from 50 and 48, 55, respectively.

Bildad's plant allegory in 8:11: "Will papyrus sprout up (*yigʾeh*) where there is no marsh?" Yhwh challenges Job to truly "see," to observe nature as Eliphaz had claimed to be able to do in his own nature musing (5:3).

> (40:11b) ... See (*rĕʾēh*) everyone who is lifted up (*gēʾeh*), and bring him down;
> (12) see everyone who is lifted up (*gēʾeh*), and make him kneel.
>   Stamp down the wicked (*rĕšāʾîm*) where they stand;
> (13) Hide them together in the dust . . .

Humans cannot make the world right; the proud tower over everyone, and that is where they will stay.

The first animal, Behemoth,[95] appears as an example of this thesis. The Behemoth is neither good nor bad: terms of morality or justice are completely lacking, replaced only by the vocabulary of raw power. Along these lines it is important to notice the fusion of plant, animal, and human here. The animal is clearly Behemoth, and his relationship to the earth's produce is frank but also provocatively ambiguous, with a lack of any moral rubric to guide that interrelationship:

> (40:20) The mountains yield produce for him,
>   and all the living things of the field play there;
> (21) under lotuses (*ṣeʾĕlîm*) he lies down,
>   in the hiding place (made by) reed and marsh;
> (22) lotuses surround him in their shadow,
>   water willows surround him;
> (23) even if the river rages, he is in no hurry;
>   he is confident, though the Jordan flows right into his mouth.

---

95. The word *bĕhēmôt*, which appears only here in the Hebrew Bible, seems to be a plural of *bĕhēmāh*, a term used very frequently for any sort of large land animal. The plural here is perhaps truly a *pluralis majestaticus*, marking the beast's exceptional status.

Undoubtedly the poet revels in the description of the hippo's natural environment, but we must consider the animal's relationship to the floral worlds around it. In terms of provision, this animal is set up within the cosmos of the righteous king of Psalm 72: "May the mountains yield prosperity for the people, and the hills, righteousness" (v. 3); "May there be an abundance of grain in the earth, may it wave on the top of the mountains, its fruit like Lebanon . . . " (v. 16). Lest this connection between Behemoth and Job seem too understated as the poet's program, consider the opening statement in 40:15: "I made him along with you (*'immāk*)," Yhwh asserts. "He eats grass (*ḥāṣîr*) like the cattle . . . " The deity explicitly compares Behemoth's status as a created thing, benefiting from the nurture of the earth, with Job's position.

More than that, even, Yhwh calls Behemoth the "first" (*rēʾšît* = in the sense of "preeminent") of creation. There could be no clearer statement about rank as the result of sheer power than what Yhwh offers here. Yet what kind of power? It is physical power, to be sure, but it is also the power of leisure and the power of laughter; in this place of natural mountainous provision for Behemoth, other animals "play" (*yĕśaḥăqû*, 40:20). Whereas Job would have to feed his plants with his own good deeds, which the Friends suppose are lacking, the land provides for Behemoth. Whereas Job fears the deleterious force of rushing water (Job 9:23; 12:15; 14:19; 27:20), the hippo opens his mouth wide.[96] These are very different narratives of thriving within nature. Indeed, they are ultimately incompatible. And the human self in conversation with the animal is, of course, none other than Job.[97] He is the one who had wished for flesh of bronze (6:12) and,

---

96. Note Pelham's interpretation here (*Contested Creations*, 133): when faced with Behemoth, Job is to see that he is "stronger than he thinks he is."

97. Many have noticed correspondences or disjunctions between Job and the Behemoth; see, e.g., John G. Gammie, "Behemoth and Leviathan: On the Didactic and Theological Significance of Job 40:15–41:26," 217–31 in idem, et al., eds., *Israelite Wisdom: Theological and Literary Essays*

in lament after lament, discusses the state of his degraded bones or wishes for better bones (4:14; 10:11; 19:20; 21:24; 30:12; 33:19, 21).[98] Behemoth is different: bones like bronze tubes, limbs like iron bars (40:18).

Leviathan, too, has a body made of everything Job's is not.[99] The poet spends a major part of the long Leviathan poem (40:25 [41:1]–41:26[41:34]) telling of the animal's indestructible, sharp body, detailing every scale and tooth (which would be odd if the animal were conceived as a purely "mythological" creature). These scales (Hebrew "rivers of shields") are Leviathan's point of "pride" (*ga'ăwāh*, 41:7[41:15]);[100] he is airtight, and nothing comes through (41:8-9[41:16-17]); his flesh is liked a poured out molten statue (41:15[41:23]), his heart as hard as stone (41:16[41:24]; compare Job in 6:12); and even bronze, for him, is like "rotted wood" (41:19[41:27]).

The fact that a creature like this exists *at all* as part of the created order is disorienting in its own right and pushes Job to the edge of the habitable cosmos; one does not need to retreat into myth to find this kind of creature: the "normal" world is frightening enough. Oddly, though, God never directly claims to have created Leviathan as he does Behemoth; one can assume, but the silence leaves open the possibility that the poet is stretching out toward a description of what is completely out of reach. The one reference to Leviathan's nature as "created" at all, in 41:25(41:33), makes use of a passive

---

in Honor of Samuel Terrien (Missoula: Scholars Press, 1978), and Ferdinand Ahuis, "Behemot, Leviaton und der Mensch in Hiob 38–42," *ZAW* 123 (2011): 72–91.

98. Raphael, "Things Too Wonderful," 414–15 also notes that the other conspicuous appearance of metals in the book comes in the Mine poem of chapter 28, where again hard lessons are to be learned. See also Pelham, *Contested Creations*, 133.

99. For Leviathan elsewhere in the Bible see Job 3:8; Pss. 74:14; 104:26; Isa. 27:1, and allusion in Job 26:13. Note also 2 Esdr. (4 Ezra) 6:49-52, where Behemoth and Leviathan are two creatures God preserves at creation—they will one day be eaten (presumably by the righteous), a motif that made its way into later Rabbinic traditions.

100. Newsom, *Book of Job*, 251–52, on the "pride" theme in these speeches.

construction, *he'āśû liblî ḥāt*, "he is created without fear." If anything, Yhwh forges a strange identity with Leviathan in 41:2-3(41:10-11), where the Masoretic Text reads:

(2) No one is fierce enough to rouse him—
   who then can stand before me?
(3) Whoever confronts me, I will pay them back;
   everything under the heavens is mine.[101]

Some emend object suffixes to the third masculine singular here so that the poem continues on unproblematically with Leviathan: "who then can stand before *him* . . . who can confront *him*, and be safe ..." (see NRSV).[102] One interpretation of the Masoretic Text as it stands would be that if Job cannot confront Leviathan, how could he oppose God? But what then would verse 3 imply? That God will pay Job back with the speech itself (given that he is restored to health and wealth at the end of the book)? Or that God does operate with strict retribution after all? Alternatively, does the poet claim that opposing Leviathan is tantamount to opposing God, and Leviathan's acts and status are essentially God's own acts and status?

Perhaps the most striking aspect of Leviathan's presence near the end of the book has to do with Job's reference to Leviathan in 3:8-9: "May those who curse Yamm curse it (= the day of Job's birth), those skilled to call up Leviathan . . . ." Leviathan, for Job, is an element of curse, a creature whose black magic could be "called up" by human experts of incantation. Those who compare Leviathan here to the "tamed" Leviathan of Psalm 104 have some grounds for their case, as both Leviathans are animals that sport about in waters; both are part of God's economy of animal meaning.[103] But the Leviathan

---

101. I take the following verse (41:4[41:12]) as belonging to the next section, describing the body of Leviathan.
102. See, e.g., the note on this in Habel, *Book of Job*, 555; Pope's highly conjectural emendations (*Job*, 280–83) should be rejected.

of Psalm 104:26 is a playful afterthought, truly demythologized out of meaning for human travails. In Job's world, despite all his pain and all that had gone wrong, Job remained king, with slaves at hand. In bitterness of soul Job complained that his slaves would no longer respect him (19:16), and he seems more than a little defensive regarding his treatment of slaves (31:13). For a patriarch like Job, slaves and animals alike populate one's fields in obedience to covenant schemes—and the terrible truth of Job's deep solidarity with the arguments of the Friends is revealed, despite his protests. So, too, the Friends' own fear of becoming like Job at a moment's notice (i.e., totally within the bounds of what is right, yet torn to the ground, losing everything) is revealed. All characters end up telling the truth.

In this context the ludicrous nature of the wild ox (39:9) or Leviathan becoming Job's "slave" ('ebed) can be known. Can Job make a "covenant" (běrît) with Leviathan (40:28[41:4])? Surely the world of covenants is long gone. The closing lines of the hymn in Job 41, at any rate, crown Leviathan as king over all elevated things, including Job himself:

> (41:26[41:34]) He sees all that is lofty,
> he is king over all that are proud.

Among the many other gestures backward into the Dialogues that the Divine Speech provides, Leviathan's subjects here, "all that are proud" (běnê šāḥaṣ, lit. "sons of pride"?), appear as such only one other time in the Hebrew Bible—in a couplet of the Mine poem in 28:7-8: "The path—no bird of prey knows it, and the eye of the falcon has not

---

103. These issues are discussed further by Jon D. Levenson, *Creation and the Persistence of Evil: The Jewish Drama of Divine Omnipotence* (San Francisco: Harper & Row, 1988), 49, 53–65, and Watson, *Chaos Uncreated*, 367. Cf. Leo G. Perdue, "Cosmology and Social Order in the Wisdom Tradition," 457–78 in John G. Gammie and Leo G. Perdue, eds., *The Sage in Israel and the Ancient Near East* (Winona Lake, IN: Eisenbrauns, 1990), at 475, who speaks of Yhwh's interaction with Leviathan in Job in terms of a "battle."

gazed upon it; proud ones (*běnê šāḥaṣ*) have not walked upon it, the lion has not ventured over it."[104] Whatever is inaccessible, elevated, or remote, this is Leviathan's monarchic territory. Job now sees all the way down, to the base of Blake's miniature cosmos of monsters, and thus we have almost reached the end of the Joban nature narrative.

Conclusion

The intervention of God's voice in Job 38 offers a type of resolution at the right time in the book's nature narrative. The Friends had taken their metaphors as far as they could reasonably go, and Job had offered scattered claims, ranging from accusations against a malevolent nature world and a malevolent nature deity to affirmations of Deuteronomic nature-covenant thinking in the end.[105] In the speeches here God builds the cosmos back up from the ground. Animals teach Job how to be human, though the lessons are not always crystal clear; he is not to become like a covenant plant in danger of wilting, but rather like a laughing and roaring and devouring animal. This is the new starting point. In this way nature teaches humans how to be human.

Once again adopting Ricoeur as a guide for our movement through narrative and the self that is forged through narrative, this time through his famous exposition on stages of naïveté in *The Symbolism of Evil*, we can detect a clear movement through phases of perceptual interaction in Job's nature narrative:[106] *first naïveté*, a

---

104. See Jones, "Lions," 681–83 on the translation of *šāḥaṣ*; he thinks the term means something like a cross between a lion and serpent, a dragon-like associate of Leviathan. I translate *šāḥaṣ* here simply as "proud," based on the presumed parallelism with *gābōah* (as do many others, such as Pope, *Job*, 281, 287; Gordis, *Book of Job*, 472, 490).

105. Carol Newsom (*Book of Job*, 19) puts the matter this way: ". . . whether by intent or by accident of transmission," by the time the third round of speeches by Job and the Friends has arrived the discussion "disintegrates, with only a short speech by Bildad and none by Zophar, and with Job's own speeches rife with incongruities. What promised to be a search for truth via the mutual examination of expert sages ends in fragmentation and incoherence."

childlike unawareness of the power of the symbol; *critical distance*, wherein one is alienated from one's self and tradition at the discovery that the world is difficult; then the coveted *second naïveté*, a place beyond criticism and despair but one that does not leave criticism behind entirely. In this new naïveté one leans into the symbol and lives into a new view that is still naïve in the sense of openness, or even playfulness, but in which one is appropriately broken by the realizations of criticism and distance. Job's nature journey can be helpfully charted along these lines. In the Prologue nature is the simple righteousness-wealth covenant—indeed, the narrator gives us no explicit cue that the hedge, the animals, and the family that lives in righteous symbiosis are a problem at all (though one may detect problems lurking beneath the surface). The Adversary introduces the problem and the Dialogues represent a fractured moral distance in which the participants cannot truly figure out whether they will retreat back into the naïveté of Job's former life by way of untransformed plant analogies or whether some strange new territory stands beyond them. At moments, though, we see the inbreaking of the new view: nature is violent, the covenant is no longer in place. The Divine Speech represents the transition point into second naïveté, during which Job learns of cosmic secrets that can be interpreted as both horrifying and, eventually, reassuring. While in a recent essay the cultural theorist Slavoj Žižek wonders why God could not, in the end, simply tell Job "the truth," we might see, instead, that more has been revealed than withheld—God has, in fact,

---

106. Paul Ricoeur, *The Symbolism of Evil*, trans. Emerson Buchanan (Boston: Beacon Press, 1969; first published as *La Symbolique du mal*, 1960), 349–53. See other uses and explications of Ricoeur's scheme in Dan R. Stiver, *Theology After Ricoeur: New Directions in Hermeneutical Theology* (Louisville: Westminster John Knox, 2001), 64–66; Mark I. Wallace, *The Second Naiveté: Barth, Ricoeur, and the New Yale Theology*, 2d ed. (Studies in American Biblical Hermeneutics 6; Macon, GA: Mercer University Press, 1995), esp. 51–86. David J. A. Clines also uses the language of "naïveté" (with parallels to Ricoeur's use, but not explicitly), in "False Naivety in the Prologue to Job," *Hebrew Annual Review* 9 (1985): 127–36.

told Job the truth, or at least a series of truths, or at minimum set him on ground from which he could reach outward and learn the truth.[107]

Throughout this chapter I have variously affirmed what previous interpreters have concluded about Yhwh's nature speech: for the deity, the cosmos is a place of dizzying beauty yet also danger, and the animals that inhabit the cosmos include not only the familiar stock of human wealth but also an array of exotic creatures who thrive on the weirdness of their situations. Beyond this affirmation, however, we learn much about the Joban God. He has now become detached from the nature covenant. The poet of Job 38–41 had as much space and freedom as any biblical author to engage in the weighty task of forging the Divine Self, and the presentation shines or glowers with shocking freedom and, we can only conclude, a completely new direction regarding plants, animals, earth, and humans (at least vis-à-vis so much of the other nature wisdom in the Hebrew Bible). God is not primarily "above" or "Other" or "abstract" or "strong" in this grand speech; stranger, actually, God is directly menacing for the human world, and problems of the menacing sort Job has faced are built into nature's leaves, animal bodies, and rocks. In this respect God confirms Job's suspicions, while at the same time refuting the Adversary (who posited a rather mechanical, one-sided scheme). This is the shock of the book. It is not shocking to think that God is a creator, or that God is high above us, with ways not our ways, and so on. It is shocking to think that we might look at nature's fractures and see God's pleasure.

As James Kugel and others have rightly emphasized, it is the "God of Old," who acts with intense emotions, arrogance, regret, and anthropomorphic contingency at various points in the Bible—and

---

107. Slavoj Žižek, "The Fear of Four Words: A Modest Plea for the Hegelian Reading of Christianity," 24–109 in Slavoj Žižek and John Millbank, *The Monstrosity of Christ: Paradox or Dialectic?*, ed. Creston Davis (Cambridge, MA: MIT Press, 2009), 104 n. 78.

perhaps nowhere more powerfully than with Job, who remains a compelling figure for readers.[108] For the Joban God, righteousness and assumptions about God's own being are no longer a form of control; nature enters the scene as its own set of confounding variables. This is not the polite, armchair theology of airtight, handcrafted gods. If anything, God's answer in Job is that the security nature brings (both economic and emotional) does not come through covenant guarantees but through a different way of *seeing*. In this sense morality is not mechanical or abstract, but rather a function of one's own ecology—that is to say, a function of one's peculiar place.

108. James Kugel, "Two Models of God and the 'God of Old,'" 107–18 in idem, *How to Read the Bible: A Guide to Scripture Then and Now* (New York: Free Press, 2007); see Kugel's more robust treatment of this theme in *The God of Old: Inside the Lost World of the Bible* (New York: Free Press, 2004).

5

Natural Theologies of the Post-Exilic Self
in Job

In this final chapter I turn to the intersection of ecology, politics, and the role of the specifically Joban "self" in the creation of new possibilities for Israel's existence in the sixth to fifth centuries BCE. In the previous two chapters I have argued that this Joban "self" is a rather insecure entity, torn among several competing fragments of ancient Israelite self-making projects. The Friends' alluring nature-response covenant posited that Job's suddenly stunted economic life and blistered body came by way of a morally disobedient self. Job had sinned, and the world reacted. They attempted to restore Job from the brink of death to the world of the living with metaphors of life—the plant can grow again if it is watered with repentance. The Friends augmented this appeal to Proverbial plant and animal analogies, however, with other strategies, more ambiguous and in fact contradicting the "traditional" language of nature and covenant. Perhaps God acts for his own purposes and we cannot know what these are. If you are living rigorously in the world of the nature covenant, however, you surely *do* know. One could certainly settle on an outlook that is poised somewhere in the middle—covenants at the center and some mystery as necessary around the edges—but the Friends and ultimately Job himself (see Job 31) attempt to cling to obvious signals of nature success as a self-making narrative. At this precise impasse, between the lurking mysteries of the failures of airtight covenant thinking and the complete loss of all narrativity, the Divine Storm blows in and charts a new course for the human animal within the greater world of animal selves, unhitched from obvious moral schemes but nonetheless with an order and beauty of its own violent genius.

Job as an individual, even seeming to live in a historical no-man's-land as he does, can certainly reflect on the changed perspective for his own life. But how would an entire nation live, die, or change through the story the book of Job tells? In his justly celebrated essay, "The Meaning of the Book of Job," Matitiahu Tsevat places Job at a significant juncture in the history of Israel's ideas: the earlier doctrines of "collective retribution" had fallen by the wayside but no new ideas of "individual retribution" (say, in the afterlife) had emerged. As Tsevat notices, these schemes can be combined so that a doctrine of retribution can be applied to the individual. Clearly this happens in Job at some points, though one is then faced with the awkward situation of righteous suffering.[1] In the collective situation the "righteous individual" could be swept away with the crowd, provided we do not adhere to a modern, separate version of the self as one who can show detached, pure commitment apart from any other consideration.[2] It is feasible that collective retribution or even some

---

1. Matitiahu Tsevat, "The Meaning of the Book of Job," 1–37 in idem, *The Meaning of the Book of Job and Other Biblical Studies: Essays on the Literature and Religion of the Hebrew Bible* (New York: Ktav, 1981), at 31–32.

notion of a "generational curse" could have continued to function in the post-exilic world, and no doubt it did in some quarters; two major sixth-century prophetic voices—Ezekiel and Jeremiah—voiced stern opposition to such a curse and thus canonized a different view (see, e.g., Exod. 20:4-6; 34:6-7; cf. Deut. 7:9-10; Jer. 31:29; Ezekiel 18).[3]

Following Tsevat's notion of Job in a period of transition, and returning to the world of the Joban nature metaphors, I want to ask what Job's "transitional ecology" might have looked like in light of what almost all interpreters assume is the date of the book's composition and earliest reception history, in the sixth or fifth centuries BCE.[4] It is no secret that the book of Job is evidence of some kind of crisis. What I want to explore in this chapter are the specifically ecological dimensions of that crisis and the implications of that ecology for understanding whatever new system of nature, God, and humans Job seems to offer. Moreover, how do Job's nature metaphors stack up against other biblical materials that are widely alleged to have been produced or finalized in the same time period? Given the importance of the (re-)inheritance of land in the exilic and immediate post-exilic periods, not to mention the reinstitution of the Temple (and all that it could represent ecologically), we might take an opportunity here to conceive of this lived space in very visceral terms: how did the early post-exilic audiences in Judah/Yehud experience the very land on which they lived?

Phraseology such as "author(s)" and "audience" and "reception" in biblical studies scholarship evoke a disturbing cloud of ambiguity, and with good reason: we simply do not have what in other fields

---

2. See Charles Taylor, *Sources of the Self: The Making of the Modern Identity* (Cambridge: Cambridge University Press, 1989), 185.

3. Tsevat ("Meaning," 32) avers that the Pentateuch "represented" this doctrine of collective retribution, though in fact it seems to represent the opposite as well (Deut. 7:9-10).

4. Obviously I do not want to confuse "composition" and "reception history" but, as we will see, both topics are debated for Job and are not easily traced in the time period I wish to speak of.

might count as good evidence for any of these things for almost any biblical book. The best we can do is to make suggestions based on the texts we have, supported by any archaeology or theoretical construct available, to help make sense of the texts. We will always need more evidence. My argument here, in brief, is that while the book of Job offered its audience a range of creative options for thinking about nature's meaning and movement, it had an important ecological function in reorienting its audience toward a new view of both individual and divine freedom in the face of a changed land, specifically in the late sixth to early fifth centuries BCE. The post-exilic period is the ecological time of the Divine Voice, pronouncing the terror of empire and charting a way forward for a small community in its land, a place still laden with cosmic significance.

The Joban Context

A Date for Job

The book of Job makes no claim to historicity for itself (at least not in the way that some of the narratives of Samuel or Kings adduce written sources or claim a chronological succession of kings and so on leading up to climactic national moments). This fact made it all the easier for early interpreters to assert that Job was a parable of some sort (see *b. Baba Batra* 14b–16b, which suggests various settings for the book, Mosaic authorship, and its status as a *māšāl* [parable]), though for some the mere fact of the book's existence, coupled with a view that demanded a "literal" or "historical" reading of all such stories, seemed to suggest historicity in a vaguely archaic period.[5] The wide range of theories for the book's setting and authorship

---

5. Martin Luther seemed to believe the story of Job was a "fable," though he apparently also believed that Job was a real, historical person. Critics of Theodore of Mopsuestia, a fourth- to fifth-century ce Syrian Christian theologian, claimed that Theodore found the book to be a demonic distortion and wished it removed from the canon (though assertions about Theodore's

reflects the lack of clear, datable material within Job. Though this situation has been frustrating for scholars, the lack of context gives Job a "timely" and "timeless" feel and thus has made the book easily adaptable to many communities of interpreters.[6] This being said, there is no reason to think the book is archaic (as opposed to archaizing) or that it represents any single individual living in the putative era of a patriarch like Abraham or Jacob. On the contrary, many indications point toward a sixth or fifth century BCE date for the book, and this date is now a basic consensus (though not without dissenters), based on internal references within the book and language.[7] Five typical considerations warrant review:

(1) Many have noticed dozens of close phraseological parallels between Job and other well-established sixth-century literature, especially Jeremiah, Lamentations, and Isaiah 40–55.[8] The sheer number of these parallels is too long to be easily brushed aside, and the fact that Job echoes so many different books from this time period suggests that Job is secondary to the other works. The only other reference to the name "Job" in the Hebrew Bible comes, strikingly, in

---

position are disputed; see Choon Leong Seow, *Job 1–21, Interpretation and Commentary* [Illuminations; Grand Rapids: Eerdmans, 2013], 174).

6. Seow, *Job 1–21*, 39–46; Ernst A. Knauf, "Hiobs multikulturelle Heimat," *Bibel und Kirche* 59 (2004): 64–67; and now Mark J. Larrimore, *The Book of Job: A Biography* (Princeton: Princeton University Press, 2013).

7. The presence of a copy of Job at Qumran (4QPaleoJobc) indicates that the book cannot have been written later than the third to second centuries BCE, though this fact hardly fixes a date in any particular earlier period. In my treatment of dating evidence here I follow Seow's reasonably comprehensive review (*Job 1–21*, 30–37). See also Kathryn Schifferdecker, *Out of the Whirlwind: Creation Theology in the Book of Job* (HTS 61; Cambridge, MA: Harvard University Press, 2008), 13–20; Rainer Albertz, "Der sozialgeschichtliche Hintergrund des Hiob-Buches und der 'Babylonischen Theodizee," 349–72 in Jörg Jeremias and Lothar Perlitt, eds., *Die Botschaft und die Boten: Festschrift für Hans Walter Wolff zum 70. Geburtstag* (Neukirchen-Vluyn: Neukirchener Verlag, 1981); David Wolfers, *Deep Things out of Darkness: The Book of Job: Essays and a New English Translation* (Grand Rapids: Eerdmans, 1995), 51–75.

8. E.g., Job 3:3, 10-11, 10:18-19 is similar to Jer. 20:14-18, along with about a dozen other correspondences like this between Job and Jeremiah; Lam. 3:7-9, 14, seems to be echoed in Job 6:4, 19:7-8, and 30:9; and Isaiah 40–55 finds many prominent parallels in Job (compare Isa. 44:24; 41:20; 53:9; 51:15 with Job 9:8; 12:9; 16:17; 36:12). See the longer list in Seow, *Job 1–21*, 41–42.

a sixth-century book, Ezekiel (14:14, 20), where the prophet cites the figure of Job in the context of a theodicy argument about whether righteous ancestors or parents can save their children. One can easily imagine why the story of Job would have been pertinent in such a context, and if the parallels with this sixth-century corpus are indeed real, then we have evidence that the author of Job was a learned reader of an emerging corpus of biblical texts as well as a wide range of literature in the realms of ancient Near Eastern history and myth.

(2) Until the discovery of the trilingual Behistun inscription of Darius I (probably around 515 BCE), Job's outburst in 19:24 seemed to make little sense, as he wishes his words would be written down "with a stylus of iron, and with lead, permanently . . ." (*bĕʿēṭ barzel wĕʿōpāret lāʿad*). The Persian text, notably, was a metal-inlaid inscription, the only known example of this technique from the time period. Moreover, the text of the Behistun inscription achieved wide circulation in the ancient Near East, from Babylon (on a stele) to Elephantine (on papyrus, in Aramaic). Knowledge of the Behistun inscription by Job's author seems almost certain, as the wide publication of the Persian text (even in Aramaic) makes a perfect example for Job's wish that his own situation of injustice be equally famous.[9] Job has gotten his wish, of course, since most educated people know about him, and incidentally now almost no one thinks about the Behistun inscription.

(3) The reference to Sabaen raiders in Job 1:15 would make the most sense in the sixth century BCE, as by that time the Babylonian Nabonidus (ruled 556–539 BCE) had exerted control over Tema, forcing the Sabaeans to raid other territories. Moreover, a fascinating short text recording a prayer of Nabonidus from Qumran (4QPrayerofNabonidus) mentions a "terrible inflammation" from

---

9. Seow, *Job 1–21*, 43.

which the king wishes to be healed—the terminology for which is identical to the description of Job's skin disease in Job 2:7 (*biṣḥin rāʿ*).[10] The conflation of these two facts may lend credence to the speculative idea that the Joban author (or, at least, some layer of the Joban authorship in the history of the book's compilation) knew of the regional political geography of the sixth century BCE, and that the author knew of some Jewish adaptation of the Nabonidus tradition in which the king went out into the desert, suffered, but was healed (not unlike the macro-plot of the book of Job).[11]

(4) The *haśśāṭān* ("the Adversary") figure in Job 1–2 plays no independent role anywhere else in the Bible except in Zechariah 3, a prophecy dated to the second year of Darius (I), who ruled from around 521 to 486 BCE. Though we do find *śāṭān* figures elsewhere (Num. 22:22; 1 Sam. 29:4; 1 Kgs. 11:14), the sense is usually of a very generic, limited role (but see 1 Chr. 21:1). Of course, later periods would engage in full-blown discussions about Satan as an independent figure, but Job's *śāṭān* (as well as Zechariah's) seems to fall at some early stage in this development.

(5) Though this is not the place to make a detailed analysis of the language in which Job is written—certainly Hebrew, but with Aramaic coloring and possibly a mixture of various dialects—there is a reasonable case to be made on linguistic grounds that Job is post-exilic.[12] In an often-cited study Avi Hurvitz demonstrates that

---

10. Seow, *Job 1–21*, 40. But see also Exod. 9:8-11; Deut. 28:27, 35.

11. Some see the Nabonidus prayer tradition from Qumran (4QPrayerofNabonidus) as predating and inspiring Daniel's treatment of a suspiciously similar motif (Daniel 4) involving Nebuchadnezzar; if the court tales in Daniel are earlier than the apocalyptic portions of the book, dating to the Persian period (sixth to fourth centuries), then the Nabonidus tradition could be genuinely sixth to fifth century. See, e.g., George W. E. Nickelsburg, "Stories of Biblical and Early Post-Biblical Times," 33–87 in Michael E. Stone, *Jewish Writings of the Second Temple Period* (Compendia Rerum Iudaicarum ad Novum Testamentum, Section Two; Philadelphia: Fortress Press, 1984), at 36–37.

12. Avi Hurvitz, "The Date of the Prose-Tale of Job Linguistically Reconsidered," *HTR* 67 (1974): 17–34.

Job's Prologue (chapters 1–2) and Epilogue (chapter 42) exhibit clear "deviations" from "standard Biblical Hebrew," as evidenced both within the Bible and in extrabiblical sources, indicating that the final form of the book as we now have it must be relatively late (e.g., the sixth to fifth centuries BCE). This linguistic meter provides at least a semi-objective control on the other factors, making the overall case much stronger. Though the evidence presented here can never be "certain" enough to make arguments based on dating, most readers should be able to appreciate the relative specificity of the data we do have, impressionistic though they are in some cases.

A Land for Job

Even though in the narrative Job famously lives "in the land of Uz," presumably a steppleland southwest of Israel proper, in a recent assessment of the Joban social and geographic context Michael Coogan persuasively argues that Job's author everywhere assumes the domestic confines of a simple agricultural setting within Israel: Joban characters live in permanent houses situated in or near towns with gates and squares and markets; they raise typical Israelite crops such as wheat, barley, olives, and grapes, and, as we saw in Chapter Three of this book, they discuss all kinds of marsh grasses, reeds, and so on; they herd large and small cattle and they plow their land with oxen.[13] If the book of Job really was produced in the sixth to fifth centuries BCE, and if, as I hope to have shown in the previous two chapters, ecological concerns are so central to the book's symbolic world and its anthropological arguments, then we would do well to pay attention to the *actual land* on which the author of Job would have lived.[14] What happened to the ecological setting of the land

13. Michael D. Coogan, "The Social Worlds of the Book of Job," 77–81 in J. David Schloen, *Exploring the Longue Durée: Essays in Honor of Lawrence E. Stager* (Winona Lake, IN: Eisenbrauns, 2009).

during the exilic and early post-exilic periods, and how might this ecology be uniquely reflected in literary products from this period? True, natural disasters, the desolation of war, droughts, and problems with the land were constant, and could play a role in many different periods and places, but ancient Israel did experience specific crises of ecology, as any society does, and those crises were occasions for deeper-than-usual reflection on the human relationship to the rest of the living world. The Babylonian destruction and attempts at resettlement decades later proved to be one such crisis, which prompted a variety of responses in the Bible (including, perhaps, Job's).

Very few attempts have been made to bring concerns of historical geography or economy to bear on the book of Job; Karel van der Toorn's essay exploring the position of Job as a transition between a "natural theology" and a "theology of revelation" represents a notable exception.[15] By "natural theology" van der Toorn means the notion that God and humans are alike, and he sees the "doctrine of retribution" at the center of this natural theology: the visible world

---

14. Recall several examples cited in chap. 2, wherein political reality mirrored the state of the natural world (and vice versa); e.g., Marvin L. Chaney, "Whose Sour Grapes? The Addressees of Isaiah 5:1–7 in the Light of Political Economy," *Semeia* 87 (1999): 105–22. Moreover, many scholars affirm various ways by which the geography of the central highlands of the Iron I period shaped Israelite theology; as Frank S. Frick puts it, "ecological potential" was translated into "sociopolitical change" (*The Formation of the State in Ancient Israel* [The Social World of Biblical Antiquity 4; Sheffield: Almond Press, 1985]), 100. See also Lawrence E. Stager, "The Archaeology of the Family in Ancient Israel," *Bulletin of the American Schools of Oriental Research* 260 (1985): 1–35; David C. Hopkins, *The Highlands of Canaan: Agricultural Life in the Early Iron Age* (Sheffield: Almond Press, 1985); and Howard Eilberg-Schwartz, *The Savage in Judaism: An Anthropology of Israelite Religion and Ancient Judaism* (Bloomington: Indiana University Press, 1990), 118, on nature metaphors and one's experience of the land.

15. Karel van der Toorn, "Sources in Heaven: Revelation as a Scholarly Construct in Second Temple Judaism," 265–77 in Ulrich Hübner and Ernst A. Knauf, eds., *Kein Land für sich allein. Studien zum Kulturkontakt in Kanaan, Israel/Palästina und Ebirnâri für Manfred Weippert zum 65. Geburtstag* (OBO 186; Göttingen: Vandenhoeck & Ruprecht, 2002), at 265. Note also Leo G. Perdue, "Cosmology and Social Order in the Wisdom Tradition," 457–78 in John G. Gammie and Leo G. Perdue, eds., *The Sage in Israel and the Ancient Near East* (Winona Lake, IN: Eisenbrauns, 1990), at 460, who situates Job at a "crisis" between "faith" and "reason."

can show us the results of impiety.[16] The Joban theological squabble, in van der Toorn's estimation, reflected economic concerns: new taxation and coinage circulation meant that a class of *nouveaux riches* supplanted the "old money" and reversed the regnant social situation. Job reflects this dynamic generally, and various references in Job may indicate this upheaval (Job 9:24; 15:19; 20:18-19).[17]

As the Bible has it, the Babylonian destruction of 586 BCE leveled both temple and monarchy. Despite this, 2 Kings 25:8-12 // Jeremiah 52:15-16 (cf. 39:9-10) gives a short reference to the state of the land in the immediate aftermath: the "poorest of the land" (*middallat hāʾāreṣ*) remained in order to "be vine-dressers and farmers" (*lĕkōrĕmîm ûlĕyōgĕbîm*). These remaining caretakers of the land were probably not an element of an organized Babylonian plan (for which there is no evidence), but rather a desperate group of survivors.[18] Quietly, almost out of view of the political upheaval and solemn description of the end in the Deuteronomist's tale of monarchy, there is the land, which endures beyond the worst of destructions. The status and ownership of this land would apparently become a matter of fierce debate, at least as evidenced within the Bible itself—the drama of reestablishing the temple in Ezra 1–6 involves opposition from the "people of the land," and Jeremiah's vision of the good and bad figs in Jeremiah 24 has the exilic community as "good figs" that God himself will "plant" (24:6) back into the land. Those left over in Jerusalem are the "bad figs" to be plucked up. Through

---

16. Van der Toorn, "Sources," 266–67.

17. Ibid., 268–69. Others had posited such a model; see Albertz, "Der sozialgeschichtliche Hintergrund," as well as the brief reference in Perdue, "Cosmology and Social Order," 478.

18. Oded Lipschits, "Achaemenid Imperial Policy, Settlement Processes in Palestine, and the Status of Jerusalem in the Middle of the Fifth Century B.C.E.," 19–52 in Oded Lipschits and Manfred Oeming, eds., *Judah and Judeans in the Persian Period* (Winona Lake, IN: Eisenbrauns, 2006), at 23–24. See now Roger S. Nam, "'The Poorest of the Land': Perception and Identity of the Remnant in 2 Kings and Jeremiah," 61–69 in Ronald A. Simkins and Thomas M. Kelly, eds., *The Bible, the Economy, and the Poor* (Journal of Religion & Society, Supplement 10 [2014]).

this imagery Jeremiah offers floral language to describe the floral drama of land ownership and political leadership in the sixth-century context, whereas Ezra and Nehemiah are nearly devoid of ecological imagery.[19] Instead, Ezra-Nehemiah are filled with human names, lists of names, and an explicit focus on aspects of rebuilding, human-to-human conflict, administration, and so on. The status of the land lurks in the background, however.

Exactly what happened in the land between 586 BCE and the time of Ezra-Nehemiah in the mid-fifth century has been a matter of considerable debate. We at least know that after the conquest of Babylonia under Cyrus the Great in 539 BCE and subsequent organization of the Persian empire the former Judean capital become one small but important district in the Persian territory "across the river" ('ăbar nahărāh, mentioned repeatedly in Ezra 4–7).[20] Early returnees apparently reestablished the Temple, with Persian support, around 515 BCE (see Ezra 1–6), and by the time of the Ezra-Nehemiah missions around the 450s BCE, Egypt was in a state of revolt against the empire (ca. 464–454 BCE), perhaps enhancing Persian interest in an organized Yehud.[21]

What can we say about the physical status of the land itself—its arability, its plants, and its animals—in the wake of the Babylonian destruction and into the early era of the Second Temple?[22] First, it

---

19. This is, of course, not to suggest that Ezra-Nehemiah are not sophisticated in other ways; see, e.g., Mark McEntire, *Portraits of a Mature God: Choices in Old Testament Theology* (Minneapolis: Fortress Press, 2013).

20. For an overview see Pierre Briant, *From Cyrus to Alexander: A History of the Persian Empire*, trans. Peter T. Daniels (Winona Lake, IN: Eisenbrauns, 2002), esp. 487–90.

21. The dating of Ezra and Nehemiah is a matter of debate; see, e.g., Miller and Hayes, History, 528–38; on the Egyptian revolt in this period see Briant, *Cyrus to Alexander*, 573–79; Muhammad A. Dandamaev, *A Political History of the Persian Empire*, trans. Willem J. Vogelsang (Leiden: Brill, 1989), 178–87. But cf. Lipschits, "Achaemenid Imperial Policy," 35–38.

22. For a reliable summary of textual and some archaeological sources for the Babylonian and Persian periods see J. Maxwell Miller and John H. Hayes, *A History of Ancient Israel and Judah*, 2d ed. (Louisville: Westminster John Knox, 2006), 478–540. The basic archaeological summaries for this period are Ephraim Stern, *Material Culture of the Land of the Bible in the*

seems clear that the Babylonian destruction of Jerusalem was serious and decisive; some participants in the "Babylonian gap" debate (was the land completely depopulated, or was there continuous occupation?), as represented by Joseph Blenkinsopp and Ephraim Stern, seem to agree that much damage had been done by the Babylonians, involving "considerable ecological degradation."[23] The results of this destruction echoed through the sixth and fifth centuries, as the reduced size of what had been "Judah" now included the central hill region around Jerusalem, and nearly half the land of the new province was unsuitable for any kind of growing.[24] The central hill country proved to be as rugged and difficult for farming as it

Persian Period, 538–332 B.C. (Warminster: Aris & Phillips, 1982); idem, *Archaeology of the Land of the Bible*, Vol. 2: *The Assyrian, Babylonian, and Persian Periods, 732–332 B.C.E.* (ABRL; New York: Doubleday, 2001), 353–582. See also Charles E. Carter, *The Emergence of Yehud in the Persian Period: A Social and Demographic Study* (JSOTSS 294; Sheffield: Sheffield Academic Press, 1999), and Carter's summary of this material, "Syria-Palestine in the Persian Period," 398–412 in Suzanne Richard, *Near Eastern Archaeology: A Reader* (Winona Lake, IN: Eisenbrauns, 2003); and various essays in Oded Lipschits and Manfred Oeming, eds., *Judah and Judeans in the Persian Period* (Winona Lake, IN: Eisenbrauns, 2006), esp. Charles E. Carter, "Ideology and Archaeology in the Neo-Babylonian Period: Excavating Text and Tell," 301–22, and Oded Lipschits, "Achaemenid Imperial Policy," and "Demographic Changes in Judah between the Seventh and the Fifth Centuries B.C.E.," 323–76.

23. So Joseph Blenkinsopp, "The Bible, Archaeology and Politics; or The Empty Land Revisited," *JSOT* 27 (2002): 169–87, at 187: ". . . the Babylonian punitive expedition of 588–586 certainly caused significant loss of life, destruction of property, temporary interruption of economic activities and considerable ecological degradation, as had previous military incursions, but the destruction was neither indiscriminate nor total." See also Blenkinsopp's "The Babylonian Gap Revisited: There Was no Gap," *Biblical Archaeology Review* 28 (2002): 36–38, 59, and the dismissive reply by Ephraim Stern, "The Babylonian Gap Revisited: Yes There Was," *Biblical Archaeology Review* 28 (2002): 39, 55, and also Stern's "The Babylonian Gap: The Archaeological Reality," *JSOT* 28 (2004): 273–77, at 274: "The land was not 'emptied' but its great harbor cities in the north and south were totally destroyed, and the population, some of which was killed and some deported by the Babylonians, was sharply reduced. By the term 'empty'—as I maintain in all my writings—I refer to a land that was virtually depopulated." See also comments in Amihai Mazar, *Archaeology of the Land of the Bible, 10,000–586 B.C.E.* (New York: Doubleday, 1990), 458–60, 548–49; and earlier discussions of the "empty land" idea by Robert P. Carroll, "The Myth of the Empty Land," *Semeia* 59 (1992): 79–93, and Hans M. Barstad, *The Myth of the Empty Land* (Oslo: Scandinavian University Press, 1996).

24. Here I follow the review of data by Lester L. Grabbe, *A History of the Jews and Judaism in the Second Temple Period*, Vol. 1, *Yehud: A History of the Persian Province of Judah* (London: T & T Clark, 2004), esp. 197–207 on the economy, population, and archaeology of the period in question.

had always been, as when new "proto-Israelite" settlers made their rough home there some 600 to 700 years earlier in the late thirteenth through eleventh centuries BCE.

In this newly reduced area for agriculture and production there would be less support from nearby economic centers and simply fewer opportunities overall outside of small-scale subsistence farming. Year-to-year variations in rainfall made life unpredictable, putting increased pressure on agricultural timing; one side of a slope could receive all of the rain and the other none, increasing the urgency of choice of space.[25] The sites that do emerge after the Babylonian destruction were unwalled and very small, inhabited by only a few hundred people each; total population estimates for all of Yehud vary, but Oded Lipschits and others suggest around 30,000 total (compared to perhaps three times that number in preceding eras).[26] Though a mixed economy of animal herding and agriculture would be the norm in any location where both practices could be combined, those living on the desert fringes would rely more heavily on animal husbandry, and the discovery of (what are potentially) animal pens in Persian-period Benjamin territory attests to this fact.[27] The city of Jerusalem, once a symbolic and real capital of a proud nation, lost around ninety percent of its size and population. A small group of people remained or returned to and huddled in the City of David area, on around sixty dunams (less than 15 acres) of settled land. Some small farms cropped up near the city, leaving evidence of their

---

25. Grabbe, *History*, 198–99; see also Carol Meyers, "The Family in Early Israel," 1–47 in Leo G. Perdue, Joseph Blenkinsopp, John J. Collins, and Carol Meyers, eds., *Families in Ancient Israel* (The Family, Religion, and Culture; Louisville: Westminster John Knox, 1997), at 8–10.

26. Grabbe, *History*, 198–201, following Oded Lipschits, "Demographic Changes in Judah between the Seventh and the Fifth Centuries B.C.E.," 323–76 in Oded Lipschits and Joseph Blenkinsopp, eds., *Judah and Judeans in the Neo-Babylonian Period* (Winona Lake, IN: Eisenbrauns, 2003); idem, *The Fall and Rise of Jerusalem: Judah Under Babylonian Rule* (Winona Lake, IN: Eisenbrauns, 2005). Cf. Carter, *Emergence of Yehud*, 199–205.

27. Carter, *Emergence of Yehud*, 256.

agricultural function through modest installations of various kinds, including buildings and terraces.[28]

The loss of Jerusalem as a powerful economic and political center for the early post-exilic community can only have highlighted the failure of the influential "Zion theology" of the preceding centuries, especially as that theology was connected with ecological concerns. As J. J. M. Roberts puts it, the divine choice of Jerusalem as dwelling place "has implications for Zion's topography"; not only is it on a (metaphorically and cosmically) "high mountain," but it is also "watered by the river of paradise." The people must, of course, be fit to live in such a place (covenant), but their obedience under Yhwh's suzerainty would fire into motion a beneficent ecological process resulting in flowing water, growing plants, and successful people (as in Psalm 72).[29]

To account for this archaeological data Kenneth Hoglund proposed a "ruralization" hypothesis, arguing that Persia deliberately encouraged or mandated the settlement of certain rural regions in order to extract tax/tribute on the basis of the land.[30] Though many now agree that this ruralization hypothesis is overstated, the fact remains that Yehud was more rural than it had been. As Oded

---

28. Lipschits, "Demographic Changes," 331–32.

29. See J. J. M. Roberts, "Zion in the Theology of the Davidic-Solomonic Empire," 331–47 in idem, *The Bible and the Ancient Near East, Collected Essays of J. J. M. Roberts* (Winona Lake, IN: Eisenbrauns, 2002; orig. 1973), at 332, 338–40; also Ben C. Ollenburger, *Zion, City of the Great King: A Theological Symbol of the Jerusalem Cult* (JSOTSS 41; Sheffield: JSOT Press, 1987), esp. 155–58 on creation in the Zion tradition.

30. Kenneth G. Hoglund, *Achaemenid Imperial Administration in Syria* (SBLDS; Winona Lake, IN: Eisenbrauns, 1992); see also idem, "The Material Culture of the Persian Period and the Sociology of the Second Temple Period," 14–18 in Philip R. Davies and John M. Halligan, *Second Temple Studies III: Studies in Politics, Class and Material Culture* (JSOTSS 340; Sheffield: Sheffield Academic Press, 2002). Despite the lack of acceptance for the formal ruralization hypothesis, Hoglund's call ("Material Culture," 18) for studies that "bring a variety of social observations about rural agrarian society to the postexilic biblical materials in an effort to set them in an appropriate social context" is well placed, and his observation that "the overall portrait that emerges in the postexilic community is of a decentralized, ruralized population spread across the central Judean hill country" is broadly accepted.

Lipschits puts it, we see a "marked process of attenuation of urban life in Judah" during the Persian period.[31] Land that had been worked year after year lay abandoned; those who would resume the work faced an uphill battle, as the revitalization of neglected agricultural space can be nearly as difficult as bringing land under control from scratch.[32] Thus we do not need any formal notion of "ruralization" to see in the archaeological data and settlement pattern that, beginning in the sixth century, the population of the hill country would have been forced back to the land, and to the problems and promises the land holds, in new and challenging ways. Even if there were not massive waves of returnees,[33] the long lists of these who were to settle "each in his own town" in Ezra 2:1 and Nehemiah 7:6 offer a cryptic reminder of the importance of physical agricultural space for the returnees, and harks back to (or anticipates) Levitical laws regarding land and original ownership (Leviticus 25).[34]

The crises of economy, theology, and society that Rainer Albertz and Karel van der Toorn have suggested for the background of the book of Job were also, and perhaps as fundamentally, crises of ecology. How might the ecological context have influenced literary products from the sixth to fifth centuries BCE, and Job specifically? As the review and analysis in Chapters Three and Four of this book have, I hope, adequately suggested, the performance of the plant world and the behavior of animals is a central point of contention in the Prologue, the Dialogues, and the Divine Speech. The sheer focus on floral and faunal analogies suggests that nature's response to human activity stood as a massive concern for the Joban poet(s), and strongly

---

31. Lipschits, "Achaemenid Imperial Policy," 28.
32. Carol L. Meyers and Eric M. Meyers, *Haggai, Zechariah 1–8* (AB 25B; Garden City, NY: Doubleday, 1987), 41–42. Meyers and Meyers also explicitly compare this sixth-century situation to that of the initial early Iron Age settlers in the hill country.
33. So Lipschits, "Achaemenid Imperial Policy," 32.
34. Grabbe, *History*, 206.

hints at a period of ecological upheaval in which the relationship among humans, the deity, and the earth itself reeled in the balance. The theological question of whether the exilic generations had suffered under the weight of their own sins or of the sins of the pre-exilic generations finds repeated reference in the dialogical musings of Eliphaz and his lions and Bildad and his plants. Perhaps Eliphaz's speech in Job 15, riddled with ecological metaphors, comes closest to explicitly allegorizing the exilic situation vis-à-vis the land of the post-exilic return: the land was given to the ancestors, to them alone (15:19), and yet wickedness brings terror (15:20-22); people wander about in the wasteland looking for food and finding none (15:23); to be sure, they had arrogantly sinned against God (15:25-27) and as a result they will now live in desolated cites, among ruins (15:28); they cannot take root in the ground, their branches will not be green, and everything comes to nothing (15:30-35).

In the middle of Bildad's plant speech in Job 8, Bildad speaks of a "freshly watered plant," spreading out in a "garden," living in a "house" (*bêt*) of stones (8:16-17). But its "place" (*māqôm*) turned out to be precarious: God swallowed it up in "the pleasure of his way." Without wishing to push the language here too far we may wonder about double entendre: Job's blown-down "house" and lost "place" are surely one referent, and yet it would be hard to miss the association of terms like *bêt* (as in the *bêt yhwh*) and *māqôm* with the notion of a *sacred* place, a *temple*.[35] Whether the book of Job itself was

---

35. The Temple or divine dwelling in Israel is referred to as the *bêt yhwh* over 250 times in the Hebrew Bible. Though a very common word overall, *māqôm* also takes on a special sense as a "sacred place," such as the place of altars in the patriarchal narratives (e.g., Gen. 13:4; 22:4; 35:7, 13-15), the "place" where Yhwh will cause his name to dwell in the Deuteronomistic ideology (e.g., Deut. 12:5, 11-14), and then the formal Temple itself (e.g., Solomon's prayer in 1 Kgs. 8:29-35, with clear allusions to the exilic and post-exilic situation). In another post-exilic product, Esther, *māqôm* may very well be a coded reference to God or God's dwelling, as Mordecai assures Esther (4:14) that help may come from "another *māqôm*." *Māqôm* became a name for God in the rabbinic period, and the cryptic reference in Esth. 4:14 helps craft a theology of "a hidden force" that "arranges events in such a way that even against the most

composed anew during this period to address these concerns or took on its final shape in the midst of an era when Joban questions were most pertinent and painful, the focus for audiences in the sixth to fifth centuries would have been the same. Thus we must also ask how the book of Job could reflect back on that context and function as a guide in its own right, instructing an early-post-exilic audience in how they should view the products of their land and their communal fate in the face of the natural world they had been given.

Job's Ecological Competitors

As a way of briefly situating Job's nature discourse among other products from the same time period (and potentially, at least, for the same audience), let us consider a cluster of texts—Haggai, Zechariah 1–8, Isaiah 40–66, Genesis 1, and Deuteronomy—that prominently invoke ecological images to speak of the fate of people and land in the second half of the sixth century BCE.[36] At least the first three of these examples speak explicitly of a putative group of exilic returnees and their concerns for the rebuilding of the Temple around the year 515 BCE, though we should not rule out the possibility that those who had never left at all were also "audiences."[37]

---

daunting odds the Jews are protected and delivered" (Jon D. Levenson, *Esther* [OTL; London: SCM Press, 1997], 19–21; but on this point cf. Michael V. Fox, *Character and Ideology in the Book of Esther* [SBLMS 40; Atlanta: Scholars Press, 1991], 244).

36. As befits the rest of this study, I focus mainly on the floral and faunal images in these comparisons, though other points of contact exist; see, e.g., Urmas Nõmmik, *Die Freundesreden des ursprünglichen Hiobdialogs: Eine form- und traditionsgeschichtliche Studie* (B ZAW 410; Berlin: de Gruyter, 2010), 288–97.

37. As suggested through the discussion above on the archaeology of the sixth century BCE, there has been considerable disagreement over the past few decades regarding matters such as the number of returnees or the extent of the exile to begin with. We need not assert massive audiences for any of the texts in question, Job included; to use an analogy from Jeffrey Tigay, *You Shall Have No Other Gods: Israelite Religion in the Light of Hebrew Inscriptions* (Harvard Semitic Studies 31; Atlanta: Scholars Press, 1986), 39–40, problems loom large in a society based on the perceived immediacy of concern and the zeal of those involved in the debate, not abstract numbers of participants.

Haggai and Zechariah

Perhaps the most striking example of the intersection between societal behavior and ecological response comes in the short and often neglected book of Haggai. This prophet, working in the second year of Darius I (520 BCE), uses the response of the land as a rather crude gauge for divine activity.[38] In the opening oracle the prophet twice asks his hearers to "set your hearts upon your ways" (*śîmû lĕbabkem 'al darkêkem*; 1:5, 7) or more loosely, "think about how things are going." What do they see around them in the fields, in the skies, or upon the land? "You have sown a lot, but brought in a little" (1:6); and more specifically, because the people have rushed to build their own houses but not yet started on the Temple, for this exact reason ('*al kēn*)

> the heavens above you withhold moisture, and the earth withholds its produce; and I called forth a drought (*ḥōreb*) upon the earth, and upon the hills, and upon the grain, and upon the new wine, and upon the oil, and upon all that the earth brings forth, and upon human and upon beast, and upon all the labor of their hands. (Hag 1:10-11)

In the second half of the book Haggai returns to chide the people (2:15-19), using precipitation and plants as the primary argument. Again he asks them to carefully observe the natural world (2:15, *śîmû nā' lĕbabkem*): before Temple construction began, grain heaps and wine either mysteriously disappeared (2:16) or fell victim to "blight and mildew" (*baśśiddāpôn ûbayyērāqôn*) and "hail" (2:17), characterized as a direct divine assault on the land ("*I struck you* with blight and mildew and hail . . ."). As evidence of the interrelationship between

---

38. See Meyers and Meyers, *Haggai, Zechariah 1–8*, xxix–xcv on questions of historical situation and dating of Haggai; 24–34 on Hag. 1:5-11; and 58–66, 76–82 on Hag. 2:15-19. For other relevant commentary see David L. Petersen, *Haggai and Zechariah 1–8* (OTL; Philadelphia: Westminster, 1984), 42, 53–54, 85–96.

the peoples' deeds and their ecological world, Haggai asks his audience to observe their situation once again (2:18, *śîmû nā' lĕbabkem*), several months after the first oracle.

The repeated command to *observe* the situation on the ground, to *look*, is the first-order command of those who evoke the natural theology of the Joban Friends (e.g., Eliphaz in Job 4:8; 5:3, 24; compare Prov. 24:30-32; Eccl. 7:15). The Temple building process seems stalled out, or barely begun; Zerubbabel appears in 1:12 with other returnees (on the 24th day of the sixth month; 1:15), but weeks and then months later (2:1, 10) Haggai asks them to take note of how their produce has fared. The founding of the Temple—whether the laying of an actual cornerstone, as in ancient Near Eastern temple ritual, or a more abstract kind of beginning[39]—will, for Haggai, revivify the entire ecological process, just as in the classic expressions of Zion theology (e.g., Isa. 2:2-4, 12-14; 51:3; 61:3). All of this has a distinctly Deuteronomistic feel, not only in a general sense but also in linguistic detail—Deuteronomy 28:22 also specifically mentions "drought" (emending *ḥereb* to *ḥōreb*), "blight, and mildew" (*baśśiddāpôn ûbayyērāqôn*),[40] and the reference to new wine, oil, and earth, though not uniquely Deuteronomic, is certainly characteristic of the covenant expressions in Deuteronomy.[41]

But Haggai's confident proclamations, yoking deeds of rebuilding together with the surrounding agricultural land, come amid struggle and require constant updating. The book opens on the first day of

---

39. Meyers and Meyers, *Haggai, Zechariah 1–8*, 63–64, think the foundation in Hag. 2:18 (*yūssad*) is "symbolic," not literal through a specific foundation stone, though they acknowledge (64–65) a long tradition of Canaanite and broader Mesopotamian traditions that associate temple foundation events with blessing.

40. Petersen, *Haggai and Zechariah 1–8*, 53, 91–92. As Petersen notices, in this terminology Haggai also may be drawing on Amos 4:9.

41. Meyers and Meyers, *Haggai, Zechariah 1–8*, 33. They also (p. 25) compare the language in Hag. 1:6 to a curse formulation in the 9th-c. Aramaic Tell Fakhariyah inscription. Note also the statement on drought and human behavior related to the Temple in 1 Kgs. 8:35–37, in the midst of a straightforward exilic plea in Solomon's temple prayer.

the sixth month (1:1), after which point Zerubbabel and others return (1:12); work begins on the Temple on the twenty-fourth day of the sixth month, but by the twenty-first day of the seventh month (2:1) the prophet indicates that not much has been done. Haggai then asks the people (2:15) to consider what will happen "from this day on," which can only refer to the twenty-fourth day of the ninth month (2:10), a new beginning of sorts. Now they must look at their barns, their fig trees, pomegranates, and olive trees (2:19). Perhaps the reference to vine, fig, and pomegranate in 2:19 leads us to think of "abundance" (see Deut. 8:8), as opposed to "mere subsistence," thus indicating progress as time goes on.[42]

Does Haggai really mean all of this? In their commentary on Haggai, Carol and Eric Meyers assert that Haggai has been misunderstood because of the "brevity of his utterances"; he does not think the Temple will guarantee prosperity.[43] If this is true, though, why does he focus so much concern on the Temple-land relationship? Why keep repeating the terms of that relationship? If the situation is as Meyers and Meyers say, Haggai's brevity would be misleading indeed; in fact, he is working with a Deuteronomic and Zion-inspired view of self, society, and land: humans do not live in a discrete realm of abstract moral achievement where souls are edified but plants and animals languish in one's own yard. For Haggai the Temple sets down roots deep into the earth itself and, as we have already noticed in our long review of nature wisdom materials in the Hebrew Bible and a variety of expressions within Job itself, he stands in a long tradition of such thinking.[44] Whether or not Haggai was part of a "hierocratic" group as opposed to some

---

42. So Meyers and Meyers, *Haggai, Zechariah 1–8*, 64–65.

43. Ibid., 66. See the discussion on Isaiah 40–55 below for comments on whether audiences would have taken these images "literally."

44. *Pace* Petersen, *Haggai and Zechariah 1–8*, 54, who asserts that "rarely had the temple been so clearly linked to cosmic notions" as it is in Haggai.

other visionaries in his time, Paul Hanson is correct to assert that, in his nature theologizing, Haggai does not think of Yhwh's presence with the people outside of "this resurgent mythical equation" of Temple and land.[45] We may, of course, question the use of a term like "resurgent"—had this view of nature ever fallen away completely?

The status of the land had been controlled by covenant, but the people broke the covenant (so goes the Deuteronomistic History). What then happened to the covenant? For Haggai the ideals of old are still new. So, too, Zechariah, a contemporary of Haggai, invokes the same ideals;[46] he speaks of Yhwh's jealousy for Zion (8:2-3) along with ancient ideas of Zion as the mountain of divine residence and Jerusalem as the seat of divine presence (compare Isaiah 2:2-4). However, Zechariah claims that the new mode of interaction will not be like the past: formerly humans and animals went wageless and nature turned against itself (8:10), but now the "former days" (*yāmîm hāri'šōnîm*) are no longer the model (8:11). Now, Zechariah proclaims (8:12), there will be a "sowing of peace (*šālôm*). The vine will give its fruit, and the earth will give its produce, and the heavens will give their dew, and I will give the remnant of this people all of these things as an inheritance." This grand summation, which may be a redactional effort to connect Zechariah 1–8 with Haggai,[47] attempts to effect a disjunction with "the former days" that sits uneasily

---

45. Paul D. Hanson, *The Dawn of Apocalyptic: The Historical and Sociological Roots of Jewish Apocalyptic Eschatology*, 2d ed. (Philadelphia: Fortress Press, 1979), 248. Meyers and Meyers, *Haggai, Zechariah 1–8*, 66, oppose Hanson on this point.

46. Ezra 5:1 conflates these two prophets, though we need not see their messages as identical. Petersen sees the "sowing of peace" in Zech. 8:12 as a slow process, like the gradual growth of a seed, as opposed to Haggai, who wanted quicker results. For Petersen, then, Zechariah's situation is to be contrasted to Deut. 6:10; 8:7-10, etc., where the land is already fertile upon arrival—now the people must live in a land and see it through from barrenness to fertility. See Petersen, *Haggai and Zechariah 1–8*, 19, 307. Zechariah 1–8 makes up a unit separate from the rest of the book and addresses the situation around 520 BCE, while chs. 9–14 address a variety of concerns not specifically linked to chs. 1–8. But see also Zech. 10:1; 14:17-18 on ecological themes.

47. So Meyers and Meyers, *Haggai, Zechariah 1–8*, 32, 423.

alongside the direct appeal to what the Hebrew Bible presents as an archaic relationship between people and land, e.g., in Deuteronomy.

Isaiah 40-66

Also addressing a context of exile and return from exile, and probably the decades after the re-establishment of the Temple, the so-called "Second Isaiah" (Isaiah 40–55) not only exhibits a series of tantalizing connections to the book of Job but engages in a large amount of ecological discourse related to the late-sixth-century context.[48] As Joseph Blenkinsopp rightly points out in his commentary, "ecological transformation" is a very prominent theme in Isaiah 40–55.[49] The most striking expressions of this theme for Second Isaiah concern water in the wilderness (*midbār*) (41:18; 43:20; 44:3-4; 48:21; 49:10), the motif of a dry place blossoming to life as a sign of God's presence with the people (40:3; 41:18-19; 42:11; 43:19-20; 50:2; 51:3), and the leveling of high, rough, and twisted land to form an accessible

---

48. See William P. Brown, *The Ethos of Cosmos: The Genesis of Moral Imagination in the Bible* (Grand Rapids: Eerdmans, 1999), ch. 4, "'I Am About to Do a New Thing': Yawheh's Victory Garden in Second Isaiah," 229–69, for a robust floral reading of Isaiah 40–55. Two reliable commentaries on Isaiah 40–55 are Klaus Baltzer, *Deutero-Isaiah, A Commentary on Isaiah 40–55*, trans. Margaret Kohl, ed. Peter Machinist (Hermeneia; Minneapolis: Fortress Press, 2001), and Joseph Blenkinsopp, *Isaiah 40–55, A New Translation with Introduction and Commentary* (AB 19A; New York: Doubleday, 2002). For issues of date and context of Isaiah 40–55, which I assume here to be mid-to-late sixth century (and distinguished from Third Isaiah, chapters 56–66), see Blenkinsopp, *Isaiah 40–55*, 41–126, and Brian R. Doak, "Legalists, Visionaries, and New Names: Sectarianism and the Search for Apocalyptic Origins in Isaiah 56–66," BTB 40 (2010): 9–26, esp. 11–12. On the connections between Job and Isaiah 40–55 see Samuel Terrien, "Quelques remarques sur les affinities de Job avec la Deutéro-Esaïe," 295–310 in *Volume du Congres: Geneve, 1965* (VTSup 15; Leiden: Brill, 1965), especially the list of parallel passages at 301–8; Jean C. Bastiaens, "The Language of Suffering in Job 16–19 and in the Suffering Servant Passages," 421–32 in Jacques van Ruiten and Marc Vervenne, eds., *Studies in the Book of Isaiah: Festschrift Willem A. M. Beuken* (Leuven: Leuven University Press, 1997); Gunnel André, "Deuterojesaja och Jobsboken: En jämförande studie," *Svensk exegetisk årsbok* 54 (1989): 33–42; Henry Rowald, "Yahweh's Challenge to Rival: The Form and Function of the Yahweh-Speech in Job 38–39," CBQ 47 (1985): 199–211, esp. 207–9; Gerald J. Janzen, *Job* (Interpretation; Atlanta: John Knox, 1985), 238–41; Seow, *Job 1–21*, 42.

49. Blenkinsopp, *Isaiah 40–55*.

highway back to blessing (40:4; 42:16; 52:13). Consider, for example, the opening address in 40:3-5:

> (3) A voice cries out in the wilderness (*midbār*):
>   Prepare (*pannû*) the way of Yhwh!
>   Make straight (*yaššěrû*) in the desert (*'ărābāh*) a highway for our God!
> (4) Every valley shall be lifted up, and every mountain and hill made
>   low,
>   and the crooked places turned into flatland (*mîšôr*),
>   and the rough places (*rěkāsîm*) into a plain—
> (5) and the glory of Yhwh will be revealed,
>   and all flesh will see it together,
>   for the mouth of Yhwh has spoken.

Not only will rough and mountainous land go flat, but dry places also bloom to life (41:18-20):

> (18) I will open up rivers on the bare heights,
>   and in the midst of the valleys, fountains;
>   I will make the wilderness (*midbār*) a pool of water,
>   and the parched land into springs of water.
> (19) I will set the cedar tree in the wilderness (*midbār*),
>   the acacia, the myrtle, and the olive tree;
>   in the desert (*'ărābāh*) I will set the pine, plane, and boxtree
>   together,
> (20) so that they will see and know,
>   and direct their understanding together,
>   that the hand of Yhwh has done this,
>   the Holy One of Israel has created it.

Those who posit an exilic setting for the author and audience have to reckon with the fact that the ecological images in these chapters actually seem to refer to the situation in the land of Judah/Yehud; the various plant types in 41:19 are all native to the Levant and not to Mesopotamia (note the absence of the palm tree in the list).[50] The leveling of land can refer to the cosmic defeat of the "mountain"

(= Babylon) that stands in the way or rises up to challenge Zion's preeminence (compare with Isa. 2:2-4), yet simultaneously it is a *local, agricultural reference* for the arability of uncultivated or neglected farmland in the hill country that must be revivified.[51] Did Second Isaiah really believe that desert and rock would literally spring to life and gush miraculous water? Perhaps he did, but the core addressees here are not in Babylon; they are in the land, struggling in the new community.[52] Babylon is not the focus here; Babylon is transient and only the background of the struggle. At first the prophetic "voice" (Isa. 40:6a) expresses disorientation, but the response, a floral metaphor of empire, immediately follows (40:6b–8): "all flesh is like grass, and all their constancy (*ḥesed*) is like the flower of the field." Such things wither and fade, but the "word (*dābār*) of our God," by contrast, is constant.[53] The "grass" and "flower," then, are ciphers of empire; they are opposed to the *midbār*, which is Judah/Yehud itself.[54] Nature is thus a very malleable symbol for Second Isaiah, as it is for the Joban actors.

The references to water from the rock clearly link the ecological or geographical situation of the return from captivity to the wilderness period in Exodus–Numbers.[55] What is the nature narrative of the

50. Blenkinsopp, *Isaiah 40–55*, 203.

51. This is why Baltzer (*Deutero-Isaiah*, 54–55) is correct to say that the nature images are not exclusively "symbolic" or "literal." Roads can be straightened, and the desert is truly hostile; but the "mountain" is elsewhere also symbolic of political power (e.g., Jer. 51:24-26; Zech. 4:7). See also William Henry Propp, *Water in the Wilderness: A Biblical Motif and its Mythological Background* (Harvard Semitic Monographs; Atlanta: Scholars Press, 1987), 105–6, who also points to the "practical aspects of his message" for the fertility of the land.

52. See Blenkinsopp, *Isaiah 40–55*, 182, 203 on this point, as well as Michael Goulder, "Deutero-Isaiah of Jerusalem," *JSOT* 28.3 (2004): 351–62.

53. On this, see Baltzer, *Deutero-Isaiah*, 58–59.

54. Blenkinsopp, *Isaiah 40–55*, 183–84, 248; Baltzer, *Deutero-Isaiah*, 218–19. Notice also the streams running dry in 44:26-28, here also a symbol of Babylon and the defeated Sea (as in the *Chaoskampf*).

55. E.g., Exod. 17:1-7; Num. 20:11; Deut. 8:15, and many other reflections of this motif, discussed in Propp, *Water in the Wilderness*, and Enrique Farfan Navarro, *El desierto transformado: una imagen deuteroisaiana de regeneración* (Rome: Pontifical Biblical Institute, 1992).

Wilderness period? The land is harsh, even impossible, but God provides—which is an adequate way to describe Second Isaiah's own appeal. The temple-nature implications of the Zion mythology sprout up everywhere in these chapters (40:9; 41:27; 46:13; 49:14; 51:3, 11, 16; 52:1-2, 7-8); the fact that the "ruins," "wilderness," and "desert" that Second Isaiah speaks of are *within Judah* and a *part of Judah* and not a faraway desert is made clear in 51:3, where the prophet signals a return to the Garden of Eden:[56]

> For Yhwh has comforted Zion,
> he has comforted all of her ruins (*horbāh*),
> and he will make her wilderness (*midbār*) like Eden,
> and her desert (*ʿărābāh*) like the garden of Yhwh;
> joy and gladness will be found in her,
> thanksgiving and the sound of singing!

Just as for Haggai and Zechariah, the rebuilding the Temple has clear implications for revivified nature, as we would expect in the Zion-inspired theologies (especially in Isa. 44:26-28). The establishment of the Temple (via Cyrus; 45:1-7) results in the defeat of Chaos (Babylon) and the associated ecological result (45:8):

> Rain down from above, heavens,
> and let righteousness pour down!
> May the earth open up, and bear fruit of salvation—
> may righteousness sprout forth together with it.
> I, Yhwh, created this.

Given this pattern, it is not helpful to consider the Joban and Second Isaian view of rain in the same breath, as does Gerald Janzen, when he sees in both books evidence of a similar view of precipitation: "God's control of rain is not purely retributive but freely creative and redemptive in the divine wisdom" (here referring to Isa. 43:19-21

---

56. Propp, *Water in the Wilderness*, 106.

and Job 38:22-38).[57] Second Isaiah's ecological narrative is much friendlier than Job's and much more controlled in terms of human involvement. In Job 38:22-23 snow and hail are associated with trouble and divine warfare, and the rain on an empty land in Job 28:25-26 highlights not so much God's covenant predictability, garnered in a covenant scheme for human agricultural benefit, as God's mysterious *unpredictability* or glorious *wastefulness*—if provision and waste are only considered functions of human need. To anticipate some comments below on Job's ecological vision for those seeking to restore the land in the late sixth and early fifth centuries BCE, nature will remain hostile and harsh, outside of covenant control, whereas for Second Isaiah the pattern is all comfort. Ruins fill with settlers (Isa. 49:19) and people sprout up there like grass (44:3-4).

Job's opposition to Second Isaiah regarding ecological and cosmological issues can be charted in other areas as well. In a pioneering study Baruch Halpern has begun to investigate the extent to which the book of Job as a whole, and the Divine Speech in chapter 38 in particular, reflects a particular view of the astral bodies.[58] Halpern claims that the tripartite (i.e., traditional Canaanite) cosmology of heavens // earth/sea // underworld gave way to a very different conception by the seventh century BCE, one that saw the stars as "membranes" or portals through which divine light can shine (as opposed to stars as discrete entities or a divine retinue).[59]

---

57. Janzen, *Job*, 238. Janzen thinks that Job 38:31-32 "exemplifies" Isa. 40:26. At other points, however (pp. 240–41), he sees a Joban critique of views such as Genesis 1–2, Psalm 8, and, by implication, the "peaceable kingdom" scene in Isa. 11:6-9, 65:25, and perhaps 43:20.

58. Baruch Halpern, "Assyrian and pre-Socratic Astronomies and the Location of the Book of Job," 255–64 in Ulrich Hübner and Ernst A. Knauf, eds., *Kein Land für sich allein. Studien zum Kulturkontakt in Kanaan, Israel/Palästina und Ebirnâri für Manfred Weippert zum 65. Geburtstag* (OBO 186; Göttingen: Vandenhoeck & Ruprecht, 2002). Though I have not yet had access to this work, on this topic interested readers might also consult Jeffrey L. Cooley, *Poetic Astronomy in the Ancient Near East: The Reflexes of Celestial Science in Ancient Mesopotamian, Ugaritic, and Israelite Narrative* (History, Archaeology, and Culture of the Levant 5; Winona Lake, IN: Eisenbrauns, 2013), 6.7, "The Stars in Job."

59. Halpern, "Astronomies," 255–56.

If these shifting cosmological views can be charted historically, one might then be able to situate the Joban natural cosmology within this history—although, if we can find clear variation of views within a particular era (such as Second Isaiah versus Jeremiah on the extent of Yhwh's localization in or not in the heavenlies, which Halpern himself admits), it is not clear how one can confidently posit a typology for a single text based merely on that text's cosmological views.[60] Whatever the case, Halpern discusses Job's uniquely prominent focus on constellations within the Hebrew Bible, specifically in Job 9:9 and 38:31-32 (and possibly 38:36). For Job, in Halpern's analysis, "Yhwh had inscribed wisdom in the heavens, and particularly had written it in the stars. The stars of the vault are a text, in which YHWH has explained the way of the cosmos."[61]

This "rebuttal" of other voices, such as Second Isaiah (47:13), on the use of astral prediction techniques places Job in a period after Second Isaiah but before Greek cosmological thinkers such as Parmenides and Empedocles, hence Halpern's suggested date for the book near 500 BCE.[62] The possibility for Job's view of astronomy then makes most sense precisely in the matrix of empire, the late Babylonian and Persian empires to be exact, when an "elite intellectual culture" served to cultivate scientific thinking in the Mediterranean as a whole. Such knowledge was shared as never before and even relied on for imperial purposes.[63] Job's astrological musings may be an attempt to preserve theological tradition against "modernizing" tendencies in the seventh

---

60. All of this is not even to mention, of course, the problems that would be associated with locating distinct redactions or historical layers within a given text—for instance, competing cosmological views within a text could be the product of later editorial work not in step with the earlier vision, or they could simply be the result of (what to contemporary readers appear as) inconsistent thinking on the part of a single author.

61. Halpern, "Astronomies," 261–62.

62. Ibid., 262.

63. Halpern ("Astronomies," 262) suggests that the "Babylonians, who must have conveyed to Thales, perhaps with the intention of balancing Median and Lydian sovereignty, the news of the coming solar eclipse of 585, seem to have pursued the same strategy as Assyria before them."

to fifth centuries BCE that were cultivated among "peripheral elites" recruited by the empire. Second Isaiah says "look away from the stars" (Isa. 47:13; compare Jeremiah 10; Deuteronomy 4), whereas the Joban God says: look at them, and rejoice (see Job 38:31-33, *contra* Job himself in 3:9). Even the stars themselves are suggestively remythologized in the Joban Divine Speech, as the "morning stars" (*kôkbê bōqer*) shout for joy in parallel with other divine beings (*bĕnê 'ĕlōhîm*) at the creation event in Job 38:7.

All of this is not to say that Second Isaiah and Job do not share many features, some related to ecology. Many passages in Isaiah strike a similar tone to the Joban Divine Speech (Isa. 40:4-8, 21-26; 45:9-13; compare Job 38), as audiences are asked to consider God's overpowering position as creator.[64] Second Isaiah's explicit focus on theodicy (e.g., Isa 40:2; 50:1) suggests a world of concerns similar to Job's overall; indeed, the innocent crushed man who will save many in Isaiah 53 bears at least a superficial resemblance to Job's situation. At most, the similarities between Job and the Isaian suffering servant are even enough to lead some to conclude that Job *is* the Isaian suffering servant, based on some parallel passages (e.g., Isa. 53:9//Job 16:17) and other details (e.g., in Isaiah the speaking voice claims to have suffered double what was deserved [40:2], while in the Joban Epilogue [Job 42] Job's restoration involves double the amount of initial animal wealth).[65] Though Job does not develop an explicit concept of vicarious suffering, and Second Isaiah does (particularly Isa. 53:4-6, 10-12), one could no doubt extrapolate a "suffering servant" theology out of Job, given only the brute facts of the plot (an innocent man suffers and then receives back a great reward in the end).[66] If anything, however, the Joban Prologue would already seem to refute the Isaian successful-vicarious-suffering theme, as Job's

64. See Rowald, "Yahweh's Challenge," 207–9.
65. See references in Seow, *Job 1–21*, 42.

famous attempts to save his children through a kind of vicarious effort failed (Job 1:5).

Finally, we may point to the presence of desert animals in Isa. 43:16-21 (see also Isa 34:5-17) as a connection to Job. Not only does Job make use of a parade of strange steppeland creatures in the Divine Speech (38:39–39:30), but in the Dialogues Job refers to himself as a lonely desert animal, forced into exile outside of his land in a manner perhaps not unlike the wilderness-wandering imagery Second Isaiah imagines as part of his appeal (see Job 30:5-8). But Second Isaiah's brief reference to desert animals in 43:20, "the wild animals will honor me, jackals and ostriches . . ." quickly gives way to the prophet's openly anthropocentric intention: ". . . for I will provide water in the wilderness . . . to give drink to my people, my chosen ones." There is no sense here for Second Isaiah, as there is for Job, that the redeemed people would have to live like wild desert animals for very long. As the book of Isaiah comes to a close in chapters 56–66 nature images diminish greatly (but still see 58:11; 60:13; 65:17-25). The book ends on a utopian animal note in 65:17-25, picking up on the earlier theme in Isaiah 11:6-8 in which the prophet envisions a world devoid of animal violence. Wolf and lamb may lie down together, but only in a completely different world (Isa. 65:17).

Genesis 1

Without wishing to delve too deeply into problematic questions of dating for Genesis 1, we can hardly ignore the fact that at least the traditional source-critical scheme of the late nineteenth and early twentieth centuries ascribed the Bible's opening creation narrative to the Priestly source. This source ("P") is usually thought to have been composed in the post-exilic period, perhaps the sixth to fifth centuries

---

66. We will, of course, have to question the extent to which Job 42 actually represents a "reward" for suffering (see the Epilogue in this book for some comments).

BCE, though others have argued for an earlier date based on the fact that Ezekiel seems to quote or allude to elements of P already in the early sixth century (and thus the P corpus must have preexisted the sixth century).[67] If the early-date advocates are even partially correct, we might look to a historical context for at least the early reception and use of Genesis 1 (as in the references to the Priestly cosmos in Ezekiel 1) in the exilic and early post-exilic period. Even though I consider the date for Genesis 1 to be less secure than that for Haggai and Isaiah 40–55, some comments are still in order, especially given the prominent place of Genesis 1 in the Bible's overall conception of humans and ecology.

The emphasis on Sabbath as the climax of creation and the ordered, repetitive literary structure seemed to many to indicate affinity with an official, Temple-centric point of view (at least insofar as creation reaches its end with the Sabbath in Gen. 2:1-4). When noticing "structure" and "order" in Genesis 1 there should be no automatic implication that the ecological scene here is monotonous or uncreative,[68] and one might see broadly shared similarities between Genesis 1 and the Joban vision, such as the mastery of God over all things. In Genesis' famous seven-day scheme plants come on day three (1:11-13), sea creatures on day five (1:20-23), and then land animals and humans on the same day, day six (1:24-30); thus one

---

67. See the recent attempt to revive traditional elements of the documentary hypothesis by Joel S. Baden, *The Composition of the Pentateuch: Renewing the Documentary Hypothesis* (New Haven: Yale University Press, 2012), esp. 169–92, and the helpful overview of sources by Robert S. Kawashima, "Sources and Redaction," 47–70 in Ronald Hendel, ed., *Reading Genesis: Ten Methods* (Cambridge: Cambridge University Press, 2010). For commentary on Genesis 1 and a summary of the history of the source-critical debate through most of the twentieth century see Claus Westermann, *Genesis 1–11* trans. John J. Scullion (Continental Commentaries; Minneapolis: Fortress Press, 1994; first pub. 1974). For the earlier dating of P see, e.g., Avi Hurwitz, *A Linguistic Study of the Relationship Between the Priestly Source and the Book of Ezekiel* (Cahiers de la Revue biblique 20; Paris: Gabalda, 1982), and Israel Knohl, *The Sanctuary of Silence: The Priestly Torah and the Holiness School* (Minneapolis: Fortress Press, 1995).

68. See Brown, *Ethos of Cosmos*, 49 on the "creative 'madness'" of this account and 35–51 on literary themes in Genesis 1.

could advance an argument that Genesis 1 puts humans and other land animals on equal footing, over and against plants or sea creatures. As I discussed in more detail in Chapter Two, however, the author explicitly confirms the human place *over* land and sea animals:

> (1:26) God said, "let us make humans (*'ādām*) in our image, after our likeness—and may they rule over (*rādāh*) the fish of the sea, the birds of the heavens, the animals, and over all the earth, and over every creeping thing that creeps upon the earth." (27) So God created humankind (*hā'ādām*) in his image; in the image of God he created them, male and female he created them. (28) So God blessed them, and God said to them, "Be fruitful and multiply, and fill the earth, and subdue (*kābaš*) it, and rule over (*rādāh*) the fish of the sea and the birds of the heavens and all the living things that creep upon the earth."

The language of rulership here (*rādāh, kābaš*) could not be clearer.[69] Genesis 1:21 gives us a quick hint of the monster ("the great sea monsters," *hattannînim haggĕdōlîm*), but nothing more; as in Psalm 104, this is merely one part of creation to be conquered. Moreover, in Genesis 1 the repeated affirmation of the world's goodness (*ṭôb*) resides in a world without blood predation. Green plants are to serve as the only food for both humans and animals (with no comment on what sea creatures eat), and meat-eating is first introduced in the Noahide covenant of Genesis 9:1-7 (replete with P phraseology), after humans are put at some distance from the ground (3:17-19).

If Genesis 1 "demythologizes" the ecological world—humans are in charge of nature, sea monsters blithely swim about, the lights in the sky (sun and moon) are simply greater or lesser lights, the stars are an afterthought, and trees reproduce naturally from their own seeds—the

---

69. Compare Lev. 26:17; Num. 24:19; 32:22, 29; Josh. 18:1; 2 Sam. 8:11; 1 Kgs. 5:4 [English 4:24]; Isa. 14:2, 6; Jer. 34:11, 16; Ezek. 29:15; 34:4; Mic. 7:19; Zech. 9:15; Pss. 72:8; 110:2; 1 Chr. 22:18; 2 Chr. 28:10. On Genesis' language of human-to-animal relations, especially in comparison to Job, see Mary Ruth Windham, "An Examination of the Relationship between Humans and Animals in the Hebrew Bible," PhD dissertation (Harvard University, 2012).

book of Job reintroduces us to the post-Edenic world as the original, real world, at once broken in the way that Genesis may imagine it to be broken and also already filled with predation, myth, and wonder in a way that Genesis 1–3 does not imagine. Vultures lap up blood in Job 39:30, and children die or become alienated from parents as a matter of course (Job 39:4, 16).

What role might Genesis 1 have played during the early Second Temple period of the late sixth or early fifth centuries?[70] What did the author(s) of Genesis 1 want the vulnerable community to do or to believe about their ecology? The world of Genesis 1 is certainly "irenic," as William Brown puts it, though this does not have to mean that its conception of the world is without power; rather, people are called to be priests and engage in the task of making order out of the land, beating it into boundaries as God does in Genesis 1.[71] Any hint of conflict recedes into the background. In light of the Bible's other creation narratives that use conflict as the primary creative force (Psalm 74; Job 26) and other popular creation-conflict mythologies of the ancient Mediterranean world (*Enuma Elish*, the Baal Epic), this omission is deeply ideological and visionary in its own way. Instead of clashing gods and monsters, Genesis 1 gives us what Mark Smith refers to as "the priestly holiness of time and space" that cancels out conflict.[72] Is this cancellation a kind of denial? Perhaps the author of Job thought it was, but the choice here should not be thought of as between a stilted, fantasy world of the Priestly author

70. Mark S. Smith assumes that Genesis 1 was part of an emerging conversation on creation and the nature of God in the sixth century BCE; see his *The Priestly Vision of Genesis 1* (Minneapolis: Fortress Press, 1999), xi–xii; idem, *The Origins of Biblical Monotheism: Israel's Polytheistic Background and the Ugaritic Texts* (Oxford: Oxford University Press, 2001), 38–39, 89–90, 167–71, as well as William P. Brown, *The Seven Pillars of Creation: The Bible, Science, and the Ecology of Wonder* (Oxford: Oxford University Press, 2010), 48; idem, *Structure, Role, and Ideology in the Hebrew and Greek Texts of Genesis 1:1–2:3* (SBLDS 132; Atlanta: Society of Biblical Literature, 1993).

71. Brown, *Seven Pillars*, 48.

72. Smith, *Origins of Biblical Monotheism*, 170.

and the gritty, real world of Job (or the Yahwist in Genesis 2, for that matter), but rather between two different kinds of sensibilities or two ways of thinking about conflict. For the Joban God creation is a specific and ultimate theater of conflict; God's own dominance is no less in question in Job than it is in Genesis, but the Joban God reigns in the face of openly acknowledged problems—even as the creator of those problems. The paradoxical images of the creator-God in Job and Genesis continue to bristle with the same political and theological problems that plague the space between any of the "peaceful" creation narratives and any of the violent nature depictions (in Job or elsewhere in the Bible).

Deuteronomy

Having reviewed the nature imagery in Deuteronomy at length in Chapter Two, I return to it here simply to reiterate the fact that Deuteronomy is full of covenantal nature images, and the book may well have achieved its final form sometime during the same era as Job.[73] Themes of land possession reverberate throughout both books, more obviously in Deuteronomy (see the verb *yāraš* in Deuteronomy, with explicit connection to theodicy and covenant in Deut. 5:31, 33; 6:18; 8:1; 12:1; 30:5, 16; 32:47),[74] but also in Job (9:24; 15:19; 22:8).[75]

---

73. Notwithstanding the massive amount of secondary literature on the dating of Deuteronomy (see, e.g., Thomas Römer, *The So-Called Deuteronomistic History: A Sociological, Historical and Literary Introduction* [London: Bloomsbury T & T Clark, 2006]), we might for the moment be content to notice that several references in the book seem to presuppose the exile, such as the nature of the particular curses in Deut. 28:64-65 and 30:17-18. Such curses were part of stock ancient Near Eastern treaty formulae from early periods (and perhaps even very early layers of Deuteronomy), but they also echo what most would agree are historically *ex eventu* predictions of lost land and kingship spoken through the mouths of key characters in the Deuteronomistic History as a whole, such as Samuel (1 Sam. 12:20-25) and Solomon (1 Kgs. 8:46-51).

74. Note, however, the forceful and distinct theme in Deut. 9:4-6, which affirms that the people's covenant righteousness is not, in fact, the reason for their upcoming land possession; the reason, rather, is the unrighteousness of the current inhabitants. The exception here proves the rule, however: the covenant scheme regarding land possession is still very much in play, only in this case against the native inhabitants.

Whereas in Deuteronomy land possession is inextricably linked to covenant obligations, Job's land-possession musings are a matter of debate. Job and Eliphaz trade jabs on the topic of inhabiting the land, indicating that the question is very much in doubt. Recall Job's blustering accusation in 9:24, "The earth is given over (*'ereṣ nitĕnāh*) into the hands of the wicked; he covers up the eyes of its judges—if not, then who does it?" in competition with Eliphaz's Deuteronomy-like rejoinders (15:17-19): the righteous "wise men" (*ḥăkāmîm*) and "fathers/ancestors" (*'ābôt*) of the distant past received the land as their sole prerogative (*lāhem lĕbaddām nitĕnāh hā'āreṣ*), as opposed to Job's situation (in Eliphaz's opinion). Eliphaz returns to this argument again in 22:8, again arguing that Job is not worthy of land possession and the blessing it implies: "The land is for the strong man [lit., "man of arm"], and the favored [lit., "the one whose face is lifted up"] dwell in it."

The contrast between Job and Deuteronomy is at least obvious on the surface, so much so that David Wolfers ventured to say that "it is scarcely going too far to describe the Book of Job as an elaborate midrash on Deut 28 . . ."[76] As I have pointed out earlier, Bildad's use of the term *śwś* ("joy") in one of his plant analogies (Job 8:18-19) could be contrasted to Deuteronomy's use of *śwś* in situations of obedience to covenant (Deut. 28:63; 30:9; compare also Isa. 35:1, 66:14; Jer. 32:41).

If Deuteronomy was finalized in the sixth century BCE we would have to wonder with what spirit its ecological vision of blessing, curse, land possession, and fertility would have been received by the struggling post-exilic crowd who might attempt to rally around the new Temple and reinhabit the land. Presumably the Deuteronomic

75. On this see Moshe Weinfeld, *Deuteronomy and the Deuteronomic School* (Winona Lake, IN: Eisenbrauns, 1992), 307–16.
76. Wolfers, *Deep Things*, 53.

outlook was not entirely out of place. In their own ways authors such as Haggai and Second Isaiah could offer a program for plant and animal success in which fidelity (or, for Second Isaiah, at least forgiveness) drives the response of crops and waterways. Thus while Deuteronomy served its function as an explanation for past events it could also chart a way for the future—just as perhaps some version of the book did for king Josiah in the seventh century BCE (2 Kings 22–23).

The Book of Job as Natural Theology in Post-Exilic Yehud

Theologia naturalis

In classic theological nomenclature there are two major methods by which humans may collect data on the nature of the divine: "revelation" and "natural theology."[77] Essentially, revelation involves the direct divine beaming of information into the human soul, unfiltered by "nature" or reason or history or anything of the sort. "Reason" is not involved, and one does not (and cannot) confirm the message by thinking things through. Natural theology (*theologia naturalis* in the classic language of the church), on the other hand, is a basically self-directed and rationally motivated affair: through the use of reason humans perceive natural laws, mathematical principles, and other clues from the observation of nature by which to figure out God's ways—or the mere existence of God. Under this category God's ways can be "read" in the book of the observable world.[78] This

---

77. We are now fortunate to have a new volume that summarizes terminology, past research, trends, and future directions in *The Oxford Handbook of Natural Theology*, ed. Russell Re Manning (Oxford: Oxford University Press, 2013); of most interest to our topic within this volume see Russell Re Manning, "Introduction," 1–5; Stephen R. L. Clark, "The Classical Origins of Natural Theology," 9–22; Christopher Rowland, "Natural Theology and the Christian Bible," 23–37; Daniel H. Frank, "Jewish Perspectives on Natural Theology," 137–50; Christopher Southgate, "Natural Theology and Ecology," 459–74; Guy Bennett-Hunter, "Natural Theology and Literature," 551–65.

topic has a long history and a very complex philosophical pedigree that cannot be recounted in detail here. For Plato and Aristotle the development and expression of philosophy itself formed a base-level appeal to the struggle of observation, as expressed by Plato in the *Timaeus* dialogue and by Aristotle for his "prime mover" in the *Metaphysics*.[79] Philo of Alexandria adduced his own concept of natural theology, for he had said that the patriarchs, living before Torah, deduced the Torah from nature;[80] though it is difficult to know how nature teaches, for example, that one should not wear wool and linen together, perhaps one could figure it out by looking at sheep or any animals, who only wear one kind of fabric at a time. For thinkers like Thomas Aquinas both revelation and natural theology play their own roles, though in the tradition of Hume and Kant (in their own ways), the type of observation on which natural theology relies is tainted and thus cannot tell us much about God or religion.[81]

78. A definition like this, while fairly broad, is only one (simple) way to categorize this opposition; cf. James Barr, *Biblical Faith and Natural Theology*, The Gifford Lectures for 1991, Delivered at the University of Edinburgh (Oxford: Oxford University Press, 1993), 2–5. *The Oxford Handbook of Natural Theology* (Re Manning, "Introduction," 1) actually resists giving any single definition of the concept. As Barr points out (*Biblical Faith and Natural Theology*, 83), it is not always clear how or if a "theology of nature" is to be identified with or distinguished from "natural theology." In my view any musings on the moral status of humans or assertions about God's ways based on observation of the physical earth, the response of plants and animals, or even just the brute physical reality one sees is inevitably some kind of natural theology (as opposed to "revelation"). Thus I agree with Barr when he states that those who favor the "theology of nature" rubric over and against "natural theology" are actually engaged in "attempts to recognize the evidence that favours natural theology, but to evade the conclusion that natural theology is really there. For it seems to me that no theology of nature can really be purely 'revelational': any such theology must necessarily involve a combination of specifically Christian (or other religious) revelational insights with knowledge of the world gained through other approaches." On this see also Jan-Olav Henriksen, "How is Theology about Nature Natural Theology? Reflections on the Basis for a Christian Understanding of Nature," *Studia Theologica* 43 (1989): 197–209.

79. See Clark, "Classical Origins," esp. 14–17.

80. Discussion in Charles A. Anderson, *Philo of Alexandria's Views of the Physical World* (WUNT 2d ser. 309; Tübingen: Mohr Siebeck, 2011), 129–43.

81. See David Hume, *Dialogues Concerning Natural Religion: And Other Writings*, ed. Dorothy Coleman (Cambridge Texts in the History of Philosophy; Cambridge: Cambridge University Press, 2007) and Immanuel Kant, *Critique of Pure Reason*, trans. and ed. Paul Guyer and Allen

The natural theology debate, insofar as it reached educated Protestant Christian audiences, achieved a pinnacle of sorts in the mid-twentieth century with the famous and extended debate between Emil Brunner and Karl Barth.[82] For Barth, God's image in us has been obliterated by sin—so completely obliterated, in fact, that even the mildest attempts at human rationality are completely useless for knowledge of the divine (compare Bildad's remarks in Job 25:4-6). There is no such thing as "general" or "special" revelation for Barth, for revelation is unified only in Jesus Christ. Thus a motto such as Aquinas's *gratia non tollit naturam sed perficit* ("grace does not destroy nature, but perfects it") must be harshly rejected, as "nature" is simply imperfectible. Brunner agreed with Barth in thinking that humans have been marred in every way by sin, even to the point that we can no longer know what is good, but Brunner wished to preserve the idea, which he claimed can be found everywhere in Scripture, that God is revealed to the world through nature (e.g., plants, animals, stars, etc.) and human perception of that nature. Barth, on the other hand, according to Brunner, had run roughshod over the very teachings of Scripture in this regard, all in order to preserve the Bible's lone status as revelatory knowledge of Jesus—a "queer kind of loyalty," in Brunner's words.[83]

The very definition of the word "nature" and its putatively equivalent words in various languages is of course one issue of contention; compare, for example, the Protestant reformer John

W. Wood (Cambridge Edition of the Works of Immanuel Kant; Cambridge: Cambridge University Press, 1999) and *Prolegomena to Any Future Metaphysics That Will Be Able to Come Forward as Science; with Selections from the Critique of Pure Reason*, rev. ed., trans. Gary C. Hatfield (Cambridge Texts in the History of Philosophy; Cambridge: Cambridge University Press, 2004).

82. See Karl Barth and Emil Brunner, *Natural Theology, Comprising "Nature and Grace" by Professor D. Emil Brunner and the reply "No!" by Dr. Karl Barth*, with an Introduction by John Baillie; trans. Peter Fraenkel (Eugene, OR: Wipf & Stock, 2002; first published in German in 1934). For analysis see Moore, "Theological Critiques," 227–44.

83. Barth and Brunner (here Brunner), *Natural Theology*, 25.

Calvin's definition of nature as God's *original* creation versus "nature" as the sum of material objects—which would include trees, rocks, human bodies/minds, and so on.[84] On a basic level of language and philosophy Brunner seems to have understood much more clearly the fact that the *analogia entis* ("analogy of being," which could involve analogies based on nature) is not distinctive of Roman Catholic thought[85] but rather is "the basis of every theology, of Christian theology as much as of pagan." The question is not "*whether* the method of analogy may be used, but *how* this is to be done and what analogies are employed."[86] For Brunner, then, "the theologian's attitude to *theologia naturalis* decides the character of his ethics."[87]

Barth's rejoinder, aptly entitled "No!," refuses to admit the existence of any such topic to be debated at all: natural theology "does not exist as an entity capable of becoming a separate subject within which what I consider to be real theology—not even for the sake of being rejected. If one occupies oneself with real theology one can pass by so-called natural theology only as one would pass by an abyss into which it is inadvisable to step if one does not want to fall. . . . Really to reject natural theology means to refuse to admit it as a separate problem."[88] Barth apparently found the type of inquiry required of the natural theology debate impious: "Do we as 'believers' sit in the councils of God? . . . Can such a claim [i.e., any claim about natural theology] be anything other than the rebellious establishment of some very private *Weltanschauung* as a kind of papacy?"[89] Indeed, for Barth natural theology can only be of use for "the theology and

84. Barth and Brunner (here Brunner), *Natural Theology*, 36–37.
85. Barth is quick to point out that Catholic theologians had always viewed their concepts of natural theology as first mediated through "prevenient and preparatory grace," i.e., not arising from pure observation or reason; Barth and Brunner, *Natural Theology*, 96.
86. Barth and Brunner (here Brunner), *Natural Theology*, 55.
87. Ibid., 51.
88. Barth and Brunner (here Barth), *Natural Theology*, 75.
89. Ibid., 87.

the church of the antichrist,"[90] for it supplants the doctrine of *sola fidei*.

What might the book of Job have or not have to contribute to the development of natural theology as an ancient category of wisdom thought in Israel? The concept of natural theology has been much neglected as an intellectual development in ancient Israel, though arguably the ecological philosophy and self-making projects of Job have quite a bit to contribute to the discussion. To speak of wilting plant or dying animal analogies as a type of "natural theology" is a particularly folksy or pedestrian sort of approach to what can become a very lofty topic indeed, and yet readers of Job, and certainly of the Hebrew Bible as a whole, have found many points at which God's moral or divine qualities are revealed through observation of creation, plants, animals, and human bodies (see, e.g., Psalms 8, 19, 104, 147, 148;[91] and in the New Testament, Rom. 2:14-16, 1 Cor. 11:4-7). In his Gifford Lectures and subsequent book, *Biblical Faith and Natural Theology*, James Barr resurrected aspects of the natural theology debate specifically for thinking about the Bible in productive ways.[92] Through extended discussions of key texts for thinking about natural theology, such as Psalms 19, 104, and 119, Barr is able to show that the Bible engages with this type of thinking on a number of levels. However, he never discusses Job at all in a meaningful way, though he does make brief reference to wisdom

---

90. Ibid., 128.
91. Recall also the reference to Solomon's plant knowledge in 1 Kgs. 5:9-14 (English 4:29-34 (discussed in ch. 2 above), which implies that monarchic wisdom, the knowledge of God, and the knowledge of the plant world are bound together.
92. Barr, *Biblical Faith and Natural Theology*. The Gifford Lectures are devoted to the study of "natural theology" in a very broad sense, though many of the lectures and subsequent publications have focused on natural theology within its classical boundaries, even addressing issues of ecology and self-making (note, e.g., Paul Ricoeur's "Oneself as Another" [1985–1986], cited and discussed in ch. 1 of this book, as well as John S. Habgood, *The Concept of Nature*, delivered in 2000–2001, published under the same title [London: Darton, Longman & Todd, 2002]).

materials as a whole—which, he says, are most sympathetic to natural theology in that these books reveal truths that seem trans-cultural/historical, accessible to everyone.[93]

Nature and Revelation in Job

Most relevant for our purposes here is the intersection of this notion of natural theology, ecological analogies, and the evolving process of self-making in the book of Job. While one may assume that the thunder of the Joban Divine Speech and the clear and awkward inadequacy of the Dialogues put a hard stop to any attempt at natural theology, either within Job or within the Hebrew Bible as a whole—for who could say that anyone could have rationally known the reason for Job's predicament?—what we have found within Job suggests just the opposite: if anything, Job 38–41 can be read as a lengthy attempt to point humans directly toward the observable world. I will return to the Divine Speech presently, and there is no need to simply repeat the observations already made in the previous two chapters. However, I can now make some comments on the extent to which the book of Job offers an early Jewish meditation on the question of natural theology in terms of the agriculture and ecological challenge of the early post-exilic period and the

93. Barr, *Biblical Faith and Natural Theology*, 91–94; see also James Barr, *The Concept of Biblical Theology: An Old Testament Perspective* (London: SCM Press, 1999), 468–96, as well as John J. Collins, "The Biblical Precedent for Natural Theology," JAAR 45, Supplement B (1977): 35–67; perhaps Collins's best contribution in this article is to insist that wisdom literature is actually an important part of the biblical tradition, and from it one might understand important things about the history of Israel's theological thinking. Others have resisted these discussions; see, e.g., Odil Hannes Steck, *World and Environment* (Biblical Encounter Series; Nashville: Abingdon, 1980), 183. For Steck, Israel could not talk about Yhwh "in the context of the natural world" in terms of "self-evident deduction which would be bound to be drawn, with inner cogency, so to speak, from every reasonable consideration of experience of the world. The Old Testament's statements about Yahweh . . . are not deductions from natural experience . . . . These statements had actually to be made to Israel . . . they are in their own sense Yahweh's own revelations about what is indeed experienced. . . . They are proclamatory statements designed to guide Israel's experience with the world and give it bearings."

relationship of that challenge to the national history of sin, exile, and redemption. My argument here is that Job engages its audience on the terms of natural theology on multiple levels and, using farming analogies and animals of all kinds, alternatively challenges its audience to look at the rationally observable world and to draw conclusions from it. In this way Job warns its audience against the danger of reliance on traditional observational schemes bound to the covenant thinking of the past. To be sure, the observable world in Job contains horror as well as grace and beauty and thus cannot be pre-judged based on any preexisting theological scheme.

In the Prologue, Job's preeminence is proven by a kind of mathematics; his children had blossomed into a schematic number, seven sons and three daughters, known from myth and from elsewhere in the Bible (see, e.g., the numbers and ratios in 1 Kgs. 11:3; 1 Sam. 2:5; Ruth 4:15; and Baal's own children in the Baal Epic), as evidence of the claims the narrator makes about Job from the start. Moreover, the animal breeding in multiples of ten—e.g., the seven thousand sheep and the three thousand camels—suggests more than simply an ideal family, and invites readers to consider the unity between the moral claim of the Prologue about Job's righteousness and what we can simultaneously observe (through that same narrative) about his animals. In the world of the Prologue before the entry of the Adversary, in Job 1:1-5, why would one not continue to use principles of observation to judge Job's existence? The accusations of the Adversary, most often ridiculed as cynical in the extreme, turn out to be a rather painful observation on the distribution of wealth; we can "observe reality," but what is behind the curtain of reality?

The dilemma among competing claims of rational observation, nature, and other forms of knowledge comes into sharp relief in Job 4, where Eliphaz pits two recognized modes of knowledge, natural theology (based on nature analogy) against what many interpreters have categorized as a rather odd and stark appeal to a vision (revelation) accessible only to him. In 4:7-11 the challenge is to "remember" and to "see," "to observe" (*rā'îtî*; *zěkōr*)—and the combination of *covenant* (in the form of memory) and *observation* fuses what is to be the normative combination for Eliphaz between an understanding of the past (at this point we must dare to say *Israel's* past) and observation in the present. It is precisely at this point that Eliphaz speaks of sowing and reaping and, more ambiguously, about the lion family (4:8-9, 10-11).

After this appeal, however, we find a technique not tried anytime afterward in the Dialogues: appeal to a revelatory vision (4:12-21). The sudden nature of this claim is only bested by God's own appearance in the whirlwind; this is an attempt at an unveiling, an *apokalypsis* of sorts,[94] and readers are thrust into the position of wondering whether Eliphaz is telling the truth.[95] Eliphaz claims that a "word" (*dābār*) came to him secretly, at night, a truly dreadful thing causing his bones to shake and arm-hairs to bristle. A "spirit" (*rûaḥ*) glides past his face; he sees a ghostly "form" (*těmûnāh*) and then hears a voice (4:12-16). Presumably what follows in 4:17-20 is the content of that visionary speech, in which Eliphaz questions whether anyone can be righteous before God. "Even in his servants (*'ăbādîm*) he puts no trust, and even his messengers (*mal'ākîm*) he charges with error" (4:18). This is the basis for the claim that humans, especially, get crushed and buried, dying "without wisdom" (*lō' běḥokmāh*) (4:20). The speech could easily be read as a parody, for we may judge

---

94. One monograph has now attempted to speak of Job in "apocalyptic" terms, based partly on Eliphaz's vision in Job 4: Timothy J. Johnson, *Now My Eye Sees You: Unveiling an Apocalyptic Job* (Sheffield: Sheffield Phoenix Press, 2009).

95. See James E. Harding, "A Spirit of Deception in Job 4:15? Interpretive Indeterminacy and Eliphaz's Vision," *Biblical Interpretation* 13 (2005), 137–66.

Eliphaz on these same terms. He is the one who will be buried without wisdom, not Job, whom we know is, at some level, a trusted "servant" (*'ebed*) of God by God's own admission (1:8, and then 42:7-8). Perhaps it is unfair to play off Eliphaz's appeals to nature and vision in Job 4 as contradictory attempts. Perhaps he really means to emphasize that *everything* testifies to the truth of his view, but it is striking to see the appeal to spirit revelation placed alongside the observation of plants and animals in a short space.

No one character in Job voices the concerns of either a Barth or a Brunner in the natural theology debate, but we can find resonances of various views in the mouths of characters, suggesting that either these sorts of distinctions were completely foreign to them or (I think more correctly) that the genre of the Dialogue offers us a multiplicity of viewpoints that we are to consider as options, with no triumphant voice in the end.[96] We are thrust into the problems that an appeal to revelation (such as Eliphaz claims, or even such as readers get when reading the narrative of the divine council in 1:6-12 and 2:1-7) or observation of the visible world would always provide. Who is doing the interpreting? What do we know, or not know, about what we have perceived?[97] Job's own body comes up as a point of observational theology, from Job and Friends, as Job's skin blemishes (2:7-8; 11:15) and shriveled-up flesh (16:8) are accepted by all parties as "evidence" of the problem at hand.[98] Even so, as noted in Chapter Three, the Friends take a variety of positions. Eliphaz's exasperated question in 15:8, "have you listened in on the secret council (*sôd*) of Eloah?" seems like a *typos* of Barth's fiery rhetorical

---

96. As argued by Carol Newsom, *The Book of Job: A Contest of Moral Imaginations* (Oxford: Oxford University Press, 2003).

97. See Job 4:8; 5:3, 24; 9:24; 26:9; 28:7; compare Prov. 6:6; 7:7; 20:12; 24:30-32; 27:12; Eccl. 1:14; 3:16; 4:1; 7:15; Hag. 1:5, 7; 2:15-19.

98. On this see Amy Erickson, "'Without My Flesh I Will See God': Job's Rhetoric of the Body," *JBL* 132 (2013): 295–313, at 299, 302–4.

question against Brunner, "Do we as 'believers' sit in the councils of God?" Bildad supports this style of thinking in Job 8, arguing that everything is unpredictable; the manner in which he does so, however, reveals other convictions about what we can rationally know through nature, as all of his appeals come through commonsensical agricultural images. Even when he declares in Job 25 that all humans are maggots (hardly an endorsement of our capacity to know anything), he nevertheless affirms that God's ways can be known through nature, not totally unlike what the author of Psalm 8 believed—that is to say, we can compare ourselves to maggots and imagine, by analogy, that we are to maggots as God is to us.

As for God's own address in Job 38–41, the least we can say is that the deity invites Job and others to *look* at nature, to *look* at the structure and durability of the cosmos, and to *look* at the lives of animals as symbols of God's managerial power (39:29; 40:11). At most we may say that the deity *commands* the audience to observe all life-forms and the physical world in a rigorous manner, and to begin to draw conclusions alternative to those set out by Job and the Friends in dialogue. Readers critical of the divine voice in these chapters—critical, that is, of the deity's claim to absolute power—may still be forced to notice that, in the process of the heavenly harangue, God tips his hand to an astonishing degree, uncovering ecological dilemmas and revelations unconsidered by anyone else in the book. In the desert it is raining; the alienating and chaotic sea has a midwife; peripheral animals, armed with contradictory body parts and roaring with war lust, die or leave their young to die, even under divine design.

"Cults of the Little Community" After Empire

One additional avenue by which we might address the function of the book of Job in the face of the observable natural world, and even the Divine Speech in particular, is by considering Job's role as a foil to a certain kind of "natural religion" under terms set out by recent neuro-scientific and anthropological research. Indeed, the interplay between science and religion in the late twentieth and now the twenty-first century has been a major impetus for the revival of interest in the field of natural theology.[99] But how could contemporary science tell us anything about the book of Job? In a recent study the psychologist Justin Barrett devotes quite a bit of attention to the question of natural theology, dividing the concept into two categories: universal and confessional. Natural theology of the "universal" type relies on information that "all rational people *universally* would be inclined to accept," whereas "confessional" natural theology begins by assuming a particular confessional starting point (such as a certain kind of Christianity).[100] This confessional version does not start from the ground up, but rather seeks to "augment, disambiguate, and amplify" previous convictions by appeal to science or nature.[101] In Job's universe natural theology is certainly of the confessional kind, since God is a given, but more is assumed than just God's existence.

Drawing on his study of "content-specific cognitive systems," that is, those cognitive systems "responsible for [among other things] reasoning about the properties and movement of physical objects"

99. Re Manning, "Introduction," 3–4.
100. Justin L. Barrett, *Cognitive Science, Religion, and Theology: From Human Minds to Divine Minds* (Templeton Science and Religion Series; West Conshohocken, PA: Templeton Press, 2011), 147–48, 160.
101. Ibid., 160.

and "living things," Barrett suggests a tentative list of "assumptions" or "nonreflective beliefs" characteristic of "natural religion":[102]

> Elements of the natural world such as rocks, trees, mountains, and animals are purposefully and intentionally designed by someone(s);
> Things happen in the world that unseen agents cause. These agents are not human or animal;
> Humans have internal components (such as a mind, soul, and/or spirit) that are distinguishable from the body;
> Moral norms are unchangeable (even by gods);
> Immoral behavior leads to misfortune; moral behavior to fortune;
> Gods can and do interact with the natural world and people;
> Gods generally know things that humans do not;
> Gods . . . may be responsible for instances of fortune or misfortune; they can reward or punish human actions;
> Because of their superhuman power, when gods act, they act permanently.

Such views may be described as "cognitively optimal";[103] they work together and make sense as a system. As we have already seen, however, various actors in Job (particularly Job himself, and even God) pointedly resist some of these core assumptions of "natural religion"; they are heretics, out of step with its key components. They are, to adapt to the title of a recent book discussed by Barrett, *theologically incorrect*.[104] In Job the natural world is certainly designed by God, and unseen agents drive events, but it is not clear that anyone in Job believes that humans have a mind/soul/spirit apart

---

102. Ibid., 130–33. In what follows I have abridged Barrett's list of beliefs included under the category of "natural religion" on pp. 132–33.

103. See Harvey Whitehouse, *Modes of Religiosity: A Cognitive Theory of Religious Transmission* (Walnut Creek, CA: AltaMira Press, 2004), 29–47.

104. Barrett, *Cognitive Science*, 138; the book referenced is D. Jason Sloan, *Theological Incorrectness: Why Religious People Believe What They Shouldn't* (New York: Oxford University Press, 2004). Interestingly, Barrett (*Cognitive Science*, 136–38) describes a series of experiments he and others have conducted, showing that individuals will consistently mis-remember, distort, omit, or invent elements of a religious story so as to skew ambiguous elements in that story toward a "theologically correct" understanding (i.e., one in accordance with "natural religion").

from their bodies. Moral norms seem malleable and, most strikingly, behavior does not straightforwardly predict outcome in the book's central case study. Indeed, as Barrett points out, "natural religion" can become "specified, amplified, or even contradicted in particular cultural settings—what we often call theology—not unlike how we learn the particulars of our native language." Even so, intense effort is required for those who wish to affirm theology outside the bounds of this construct of "natural religion." "Cultural scaffolding" must appear to buttress and reinforce counterintuitive ideas.[105]

The anthropologist Harvey Whitehouse has recently discussed the varying ways a religious group can inculcate and reinforce "cognitively costly religion," that is, religion that runs hard against the grain of the types of beliefs Barrett described as "natural religion."[106] Whitehouse contends that many religions have within them two distinct (and even openly competing) "modes" of religious expression: the "doctrinal" and the "imagistic."[107] In the "doctrinal mode," often associated with "literati" and "social élites," religious knowledge is "codified as a body of doctrines," expressed through routine worship, accepted as "general knowledge," and meant to produce "anonymous communities."[108] Doctrinal mode communities are diffuse, and persuasion in this mode comes through the forms of universal, verbalized creeds, intellectual persuasion, and highlighting ideas linked by implicational logic.[109]

---

105. Barrett, *Cognitive Science*, 133, 143.
106. In addition to *Modes of Religiosity*, Whitehouse has discussed the "doctrinal" versus "imagistic" mode concepts in several works, including *Inside the Cult: Religious Innovation and Transmission in Papua New Guinea* (Oxford Studies in Social and Cultural Anthropology; Oxford: Oxford University Press, 1995); idem, *Arguments and Icons: Divergent Modes of Religiosity* (Oxford: Oxford University Press, 2000).
107. As Whitehouse himself points out, previous investigations have revealed partly overlapping categories: Weber's "routinized" and "charismatic" religions; Ruth Benedict's "Apollonian" and "Dionysian" modes; Jack Goody's split between "literate" and "nonliterate" religions, etc. See *Modes of Religiosity*, 63.
108. Whitehouse, *Arguments and Icons*, 1.

The "imagistic mode," on the other hand, represents "little traditions" or "cults of the little community." [110] Imagistic messages rely on terror, pain, and initiation; they evoke "multivocal iconic imagery" meant to produce "cognitive shocks."[111] In extreme (and ethnographically documented) cases, imagistic rituals can involve extended trance states, cannibalism, and ritual murder. Emotions run high; imagistic ritual produces intense arousal and expressions are infrequent (as opposed to the constant, measured nature of doctrinal mode expression). The summary effect of such a system is a body of what Whitehouse characterizes as "elaborate, if idiosyncratic, exegetical knowledge," and its attendant images "evoke abundant inferences, producing a sense of multivalence and multivocality of religious imagery, experienced as personal and unmediated inspiration."[112] The style of religion acquired through the imagistic approach is "cognitively costly religion," unintuitive, flouting the cognitively optimal views passed on through human biology and straightforward, everyday observation of the world.

This basic distinction between *doctrinal* and *imagistic* modes of religious communication will of course be familiar to readers of the book of Job, and there should be no obvious confusion regarding the modes of religiosity preferred by the book's actors. Nevertheless, Whitehouse's research breathes a new terminological life into the

---

109. The language here is drawn directly from Whitehouse's first major discussion of the doctrinal/imagistic split, in *Inside the Cult*, 197; see the more recent and comprehensive explication in his *Modes of Religiosity*, 63–82.

110. For the concepts of "little traditions" and "cults of the little community" Whitehouse refers to Robert Redfield, *The Little Community: Viewpoints for the Study of a Human Whole* (Chicago: University of Chicago Press, 1955), and Richard P. Werbner, ed., *Regional Cults* (London: Academic Press, 1977), respectively.

111. Whitehouse, *Inside the Cult*, 198; *Arguments and Icons*, 1.

112. Whitehouse, *Modes of Religiosity*, 70, 72. Whitehouse avers that this imagistic mode takes historical precedent over the doctrinal, based partly on "archaeological and historical evidence," though he seems not to consider the question of preservation bias—extreme, elaborate, or bizarre rituals would of course appear more prominently in material culture as well as in historical recollection, as opposed to frequent, routinized, verbal interactions. See ibid., 70, 77.

framing of the Joban drama. The book of Job is a textual icon of terror, a bold, imagistic attempt to freeze a moment in time where memory should remain fixated. It attempts to teach its audience through trauma, as an audience watches Job participate in an imagistic ritual initiated by God. Those looking for a take-home "message" or central meaning to this textual ritual, however, are mired in the doctrinal mode (no doubt preferred by biblical scholars with their penchant for textuality and thoughtful persuasion) and thus misunderstand the inevitable polyvalence of the imagistic mode. Still, even the imagistic ritual is meant to teach *something*, thus raising the question of what it is that the book of Job is supposed to teach through its shock narrative.

Something about the very nature of nature has changed for the Joban author, and this ecological drama shines forth everywhere with pathos and possibility in the book; the heavily unspoken Israel, lurking behind so many references in Job, functions not unlike the challenging absence of God and Israel in the book of Esther, another post-exilic product that struggles to work out the meaning of strange circumstance in a foreign land. We might add other pieces of short, speculative fiction in the Hebrew Bible, such as the books of Jonah and Ruth, to this same category, composed as they likely were in the post-exilic period. These books are more like "ecological congeners" as opposed to the "ecological competitors" described above. For Ruth, questions of land, famine, and agriculture all take center stage. The land is an active character in the book, as much as Naomi or Boaz or Ruth herself, and the inclusion of the Moabite woman into the community stands in stark contrast to the mid-fifth-century BCE program of Ezra and Nehemiah, who mention Moabites specifically as a group not to be admitted into at least the inner circle of Israelite inclusion (see Neh. 13:1-3).

In Jonah the author raises the question of empire and one's relation to it; despite the narrative setting of the book at the height of the Assyrian empire, the narrator gestures both forward and backward—backward to the brief reference to the jingoistic Jonah in 2 Kings 14:25, who encouraged the expansion of the Northern Kingdom under Jeroboam II in the eighth century BCE, and forward to the demise of the Assyrian empire in the late seventh century BCE, with a radically different approach from, say, the prophet Nahum. Jonah's world is strangely populated with nature images: fish, worms, and plants all curate and guide the angry prophet's experience with empire.[113] Weeds wrap around Jonah's head in the belly of the fish (Jon. 2:5), and the prophet struggles to find shade under plants after he delivers his message to the Ninevites (4:6-7). Animals repent (3:7-8), and the book ends on a question about animals in which God implies that the economic and social participation of the animals in that empire is to be a valuable part of Jonah's consideration. For the God of Jonah, humans are entwined in a seamless eco-anthropology, but Jonah doesn't think so; for that matter, one could say that Jonah even distinguishes between different species of humans (Assyrians versus his own people). The repentance of the Assyrian animals is not merely a comic attempt to show total Assyrian self-humiliation; it is a somber counterpoint to Jonah's own lack of concern with potentially lost animal life. This reflection on empire might lead one to read Jonah as a kind of midrash on 2 Kings 14, raising questions in retrospect about the meaning of empire, the ambitions of expansion, and the pain of acquiescence.[114]

---

113. On this see Raymond F. Person, Jr., "The Role of Nonhuman Characters in Jonah," 85–90 in Norman Habel and Peter Trudinger, eds., *Exploring Ecological Hermeneutics* (Atlanta: Society of Biblical Literature, 2008).

114. On problems with the midrash genre (and others) for Jonah see, e.g., Thomas M. Bolin, *Freedom Beyond Forgiveness: The Book of Jonah Re-Examined* (Copenhagen International Seminar; Sheffield: Sheffield Academic Press, 1997), 46–53.

Books like Jonah, Ruth, and Esther, all in their own ways, describe situations of the "little community" in the shadow of some much larger problem of empire, and I would like to suggest that Job, too, is a product of some aspect of the Judahite "little community" struggling in its land after exile.[115] In his own suffering body, unsure about how he relates to his land, animals, and plants, Job embodies Israel's story no less powerfully or meaningfully or prescriptively than do other embodied Israels in miniature, such as Abraham or Jacob or David.[116] What we might call the "mystery of Job's selfhood" in this sense is not, following the embodied hermeneutical direction of Paul Ricouer in *Oneself as Another*, a matter of abstract speculation but rather a practical matter indeed:[117] in Job the perception of the plant and the animal, and even the cosmos on the most spectacular

115. A correlation could be made here between the concept of the little community and Joel Weinberg's attempt to posit a "Citizen-Temple Community" (*Bürger-Tempel-Gemeinde*) of Jewish elites during the early post-exilic period. In Weinberg's view, these elites would have insulated themselves from others and functioned with relative political and economic autonomy. Many have rejected Weinberg's thesis, though it is nonetheless intriguing to consider how Job could be the project of a very small group of elites, charting their own idiosyncratic course. See Joel Weinberg, *The Citizen-Temple Community*, trans. Daniel L. Smith-Christopher (JSOTSup 151; Sheffield: JSOT Press, 1992).

116. The notion that Job represents Israel, and/or that the book of Job can be read as a cipher for Israel's story (or even that it was intentionally composed as such) is not a new one even in the secondary literature; see, e.g., Kathryn Schifferdecker, *Out of the Whirlwind: Creation Theology in the Book of Job* (HTS 61; Cambridge, MA: Harvard University Press, 2008), 19, who believes Job can represent the entire nation of Israel: Job is styled as a patriarch, and, like Abram, his fate represents the fate of the people; Peter Enns, *Ecclesiastes* (Two Horizons Old Testament Commentary; Grand Rapids: Eerdmans, 2011), 161–63, who interprets Job as a national tale; see also some comments in David Wolfers, *Deep Things*, 111–18; idem, "The Lord's Second Speech in the Book of Job," *VT* 40 (1990): 474–99, esp. 499 on Leviathan as a cipher for empire; and James Sanders, "The Book of Job and the Origins of Judaism," *BTB* 39 (2009): 60–70. Admittedly, in this early historical period (sixth to fifth centuries BCE) we will not be able to convincingly demonstrate the difference between the act of authors "intentionally" crafting Job as a response to their post-exilic dilemma and the act of taking up a traditional story as an interpretive move, using it as a parable for one's struggle at a later time, as national communities have felt free to do even into the modern period; see, e.g., Jonathan Lamb, *The Rhetoric of Suffering: Reading the Book of Job in the Eighteenth Century* (Oxford: Clarendon Press, 1995), 110–27.

117. Here I am following the language and analysis of Dan R. Stiver, *Theology After Ricoeur: New Directions in Hermeneutical Theology* (Louisville: Westminster John Knox, 2001), 176.

level, can become a matter of mundane human concern. One feels the whiplash of the ideology of the Divine Speech as it stretches from remote stars down to horses and ostriches, and then outward to Behemoth and Leviathan and back to Job again, who even eventually regains the safety of his domestic cattle (Job 42:12). The expanse of categories here invites us to consider what is distant, but also to forge links of meaning between what is distant (rain on deserts with no people) to what is near (rain on the highlands of Yehud), and between what is seen as a moral outrage in a world of regal self-understanding (the death of Job's children) and what is considered normal for life at the margins (the death of the ostrich children).

True, one could read the Joban Divine Speech as a reorientation away from the mundane, away from cattle and fields and food for people, and away from everything that would seem to matter for a struggling post-exilic community. One has only to imagine the deity bursting into the book of Haggai, for example, with a speech like the one in Job 38–41 to get a sense of how different Job and Haggai are on questions of God and nature's response to human activity. Yet Job does not give us a deity who is abstracted from Haggai's concerns with human effort; rather, Job gives us a God who is just as concerned, or arguably more concerned, but the scope of what could be included within the prospect of divine involvement is actually terrifying. For Job, God's involvement is not only to be seen in the "normal" (Proverbial, Deuteronomistic) cause-and-effect of nature or one's moral results in the world but also in an expanded range of twisted scenarios and paradoxes. Job's royal body of the Prologue is a vision of a fictive monarchic dreamworld of covenant fidelity (such "fidelity" is rarely actually achieved in the canonical storyline), but careful readers, doubtlessly already tainted with the knowledge of what becomes of that dreamworld in Israel's story, cannot remain innocent admirers of Job for very long. Job's references to his former kingly status—sometimes invoking the exact language of kings and kingship, sometimes alluding to long lists of royal stock-imagery for providing social justice (Job 3:13-14; 19:9; 29:7-17)—underscores the possibilities inherent in Job's suffering body. He is a mock-up of the Israelite "empire." When the Lord comes to dominate in that speech we may then read Leviathan and Behemoth as the new conquerors, more powerful and strange than any before; like the amoral Behemoth in Job 40, the Empire represents raw power and indifference to human concerns in the local community. God, however, is still the creator and thus the controller of this animal, and thus of empire.[118]

For this reason it is more appropriate to read Job not solely as a *Bildungroman* (an account of [individual] formation),[119] but also as a type of *Staatsroman* (a novel of state formation). As a formal German genre title the *Staatsroman* has its own complex history as a type of literature that can play out scenarios for the *ideal* state, engaging in utopian revelries and, to that same extent, in farcical depictions.[120] With this category in mind we could consider the reference in Job 42:10 as an irreverent or ironic twist on the Deuteronomistic theme of "returning" (*šûb*) from exile, emending šĕbît ("fortune") to šĕbût: "Then Yhwh restored (*šāb*) Job from his exile (*šĕbût*), when he had prayed (*pālal*) for his friends . . . ."[121] A complete turnaround like this seems as hard to comprehend in normal human terms as the initial

---

118. Here I take a cue from Wolfers, "The Lord's Second Speech," 499.

119. For this type of reading see Newsom, *Book of Job*, 16–17.

120. See, e.g., Martin Schwonke, *Vom Staatsroman zur Science Fiction: Eine Untersuchung über Geschichte und Funktion der naturwissenschaftlich-technischen Utopie* (Göttinger Abhandlungen zur Soziologie 2; Stuttgart: Ferdinand Enke Verlag, 1957); Helge Jordheim, *Der Staatsroman im Werk Wielands und Jean Pauls: Gattungsverhandlungen zwischen Poetologie und Politik* (Tübingen: Max Niemeyer, 2007).

121. See Enns, *Ecclesiastes*, 161–62. The *šûb* motif is a Deuteronomistic cliché; see Deut. 30:1-3 and the many passages cited by Enns in Ezekiel and Jeremiah specifically. In addition to Enns's own examples I would add Solomon's prayer in 1 Kings 8, replete with stock Deuteronomistic language of *šûb* ("turn/return"), *pālal* ("pray"), and forgiveness and restoration in general.

situation in the Prologue, but consider the message: Job does not have to pray *for himself* to achieve return from his exile, but rather for *others*, akin to the salvific power of the Isaian Suffering Servant. Once Job is able to forgive his own little community he moves forward, now in a renewed and doubled outburst of nature (42:14). In contrast to the Deuteronomic and Deuteronomistic narratives, in which all share in the community of guilt, for Job one repents not necessarily for oneself but for others among whom one must live in the land.

Conclusion

I have suggested that, on the historical level of the book's composition and earliest reception, Job should be read against the ecological backdrop of the exilic and early post-exilic period. In this context the intense focus on plant and animal analogies makes eminent sense and reflects concerns expressed in a range of other products in the Bible from this period, most notably Haggai, Zechariah, Second Isaiah, Genesis 1, and Deuteronomy. What archaeological evidence we have from this late sixth- and early fifth-century context suggests a nation devastated organizationally or politically and also a *devastated ecology* in which usable land had shrunk down to a minimum and the situation has reverted to something much like what Israel's earliest settlers faced throughout the thirteenth to eleventh centuries BCE in their attempt to control the rocky highlands. Anyone who spoke of miraculous or morally reciprocal renewal of land in such uncertain times can only have sounded like Job's Friends. Despite its putative focus on the individual, with Job standing radically apart from any community, we must notice the fact that the book of Job is still deeply communal; its struggle involves a community writ small, of the Friends and Job, the group of arguers there as a little government with their own failing king and their loyal but difficult subjects. This tiny kingdom-in-miniature represents and speaks to a small community in Yehud in this early post-exilic period.

Though speculative, the placement of Job within this context gives the book's outburst of nature imagery a real-world home after the exile and allows us to consider Job's radical theological direction against other "traditional" works as an expression of social and ecological crisis. To this end, on the basis of neuro-scientific categories of "natural religion" and the classical rubric of "natural theology," I have suggested that the book of Job functioned as a textual ritual of disorientation in order to inculcate in its audience a cognitively twisted message: rewards do not inevitably follow from one's deeds, and the God of the universe participates in the construction of the paradoxes and violence of the natural world. Such a view may lead to the eventual conclusion that God would redeem this world, or that only God *could* redeem this world (one thinks here of Heidegger's famous statement in the 1966 *Der Spiegel* interview, "only a god can save us"), but Job does not address this. Rather, following what David Clines identifies as a "principle of the world" for the Joban deity, "there is no problem with the world; there is nothing that Yahweh needs to set right"—that is, I would add, apart from the worldviews of the human characters in the book.[122] Although other late wisdom works, such as Qoheleth (perhaps much later, in the fourth century BCE) would reduce the world to a desert and the futility that comes when one's reward is totally unhitched from one's moral position, in the full force of its imagery Job comes around to take us back into nature, back into a world filled with teeming life and into the philosophical problems that nature creates and sustains.

---

122. David J. A. Clines, *Job 38–42* (WBC 18B; Nashville: Thomas Nelson, 2011), 1135.

Epilogue

The New Nature and the New Self

Through its multiple and sometimes shocking nature images Job provides an ecological transition for Israel that facilitates survival at the juncture between the older ideals of nature covenant and the new era of diaspora and the "little community" at home in Judah. The explosion of nature images in the Dialogues not only reflects the intense focus on the status of the land but also comes to function as a creative, metaphorical guide for several avenues of ecological thinking, none of which is ultimately regnant, and the intensity and indeterminacy of that debate demonstrates just how difficult it is to make simple pronouncements on "God and nature" in the Bible. Despite all the complexity we have introduced along the way, I hope these points emerge as clear and productive avenues through which we can begin to think more deeply about the theology of Job and the project of self-making in the context of the natural world in the Hebrew Bible's wisdom literature.

The book of Job, of course, does not end with the Dialogues, or even the Divine Speech, despite the massive importance I have accorded the invocation of floral and faunal analogies in these texts. The book ends with the Epilogue (ch. 42), in which Job famously repents (42:1-6). Now the theme of "seeing" takes on new meaning for Job (42:5): "My ears had heard of you, but now my eye sees you." God has been observed, as well as nature. Whether or not Job's ensuing "repentance" is more of a relenting, that is to say, an obvious acknowledgment of God's own power regardless of whose moral reasoning or nature analogizing prevailed in the debate, he does acquiesce, and the book ends with a return to prosperity for Job. In terms of the nature debates of the Dialogues, God's endorsement of Job in 42:7-8 tempts us to approve Job's views on nature (and everything else, for that matter) as the "correct" view:

> (6) Now after Yhwh had spoken these words to Job, Yhwh spoke to Eliphaz the Temanite: "My anger burns against you, and against your two friends, for you did not speak about me properly (*nĕkônāh*), like my servant Job. (7) Now, take seven bulls and seven rams for yourselves, and go to my servant Job, and offer them up as a burnt offering on your behalf. Then Job, my servant, will pray for you, for I will accept him (*'im pānâw 'eśā'*), so as not to deal with you (according to your) folly—for you did not speak about me properly (*nĕkônāh*), like my servant Job.

The precise nuance of the term translated here as "properly," *kwn* ("be established, firm, secure"), is not completely obvious in this statement. Does Yhwh mean "correctly" in terms of doctrinal content or the implication of his words? If so, then does Yhwh endorse *all* of Job's words, including Job's declarations about divine injustice and harrowing accusations of nature gone awry (recall chs. 9, 12, and 14), or just the "repentance" in 42:1-6? Or does Yhwh mean "properly" in terms of the character of Job's speech or the attitude with which it was taken up? Interpreters will continue to go back and forth on these issues, and they will not be resolved here. Moreover, the standard introductory phrase in 42:7, "Now after Yhwh had spoken these words to Job . . ." is a little awkward, since Yhwh was not actually the previous speaker (Job was), raising the suspicion, asserted in any faithful source-critical appraisal of the book, that Job's repentance sidled in here as a secondary accretion (see also 40:3-5).

Job's animal world not only returns to its pre-disaster state in 42:14 but doubles: fourteen thousand sheep, six thousand camels, a thousand yoke of oxen a thousand donkeys. Exactly seven sons and three daughters return—we know not how, they simply appear—but their numbers are no longer mystically equivalent in a 7:3 ratio of sons and daughters to the animals. Job's animal possessions now overflow beyond the bounds of the righteousness he supposedly had in the Prologue. The Adversary plays no further role. Job's wife is gone, too. The great drama of the Prologue, the debate with the Adversary, and the sheer length of the Dialogues and the Divine Speech only make the terse Epilogue seem all the stranger, and the Job we see here, briefly, says nothing after his repentance and he comes off as a flight of imagination and not a real character.

Perhaps Job is not easily reconciled to his new world, or perhaps the Epilogue has simply introduced something foreign and odd to the grand vision—and yet, readers have to contend with it. The Friends score one last point, at least, by way of the sheer plot of the book: Job persists in his righteousness, he does not curse God, and the crops of his moral success do eventually bloom. Nevertheless, it appears from my analysis of the Divine Speech in Chapter Four that God confirms Job's accusations of nature's violence and even raises the stakes to more frightening levels. Everyone is right and everyone is wrong. One senses some kind of avoidance or coverup in the Epilogue, and conclusions usually function this way—the solution comes too easily, or too quickly, or with not enough clarity.

This discussion of plants, animals, and the suffering of Job has shown us many things. The burst of nature imagery in Job is not without precedent in the Hebrew Bible or in the general ancient Near Eastern and Mediterranean world of the Iron Age. On the contrary; the floral and faunal world served as a primary site of wisdom meditation, and the Bible as a whole participates in this "nature wisdom" sub-genre to a great degree, evoking plants and animals in parables, proverbs, memories of sages, covenant forms, narrative, and poetry. In Job we found that plant and animal imagery was not confined to the "poetic" portions of the book (the Dialogues or the Divine Speech); instead, the Prologue framed the issue both explicitly and subtly in terms of an ongoing conversation between a Deuteronomic or Proverbial view of nature and other possibilities. Furthermore, the Friends did not offer a single, rigid point of view on nature but rather argued for a range of options, alternatively proposing that we reap what we sow, that nature is miraculous and incomprehensible, that nature is precarious and deadly, that humans are like plants, and that humans are not like plants. Job himself, despite his protests, finally returns to an appeal to the covenant vision of nature in which obedience yields abundance.

God's own speech demonstrates the grandiosity of the monotheistic vision with regard to nature (notwithstanding the Adversary or the court of divine beings in Job 1): there are no malevolent deities who deceive the ostrich or create the Behemoth. It is God, only God, through and through. Monotheism has ecological implications, for every rainstorm and every drought runs through God. As a whole the book of Job seems to argue that this is indeed the case, though not bound through previous traditional understandings of covenant. To be sure, the Deuteronomic and Proverbial understandings of nature as I have outlined them could only become terribly painful and nearly impossible for some to regard as meaningful after the demise of the nation in 586 BCE.

The point, though, is not that any notion of nature covenant thinking was "dead"; some tried to revive it (Haggai), or never thought it needed reviving. Others may live by it today. But for the community forged by the Joban ecological drama, the small community forged through initiation into God's secrets, there would always be a way forward in the land—through suffering imbued with meaning and through God's direct, hard presence. Despite the differences between Job and other traditions, there is an important point of similarity between the overarching ideologies of Deuteronomy and Proverbs on the one hand and Job on the other. It is often overlooked, but it is of great significance at least for the development of historical theology in the Hebrew Bible, if not for the history of ideas as it moves through the Bible from Torah to Nevi'im to Kethuvim, through the New Testament, into the history of the church, and into the entire development of the Western literary tradition: God is involved with nature, and God is involved with Israel's disasters.

Thus the Joban self-making project has important implications for thinking about the emergence of Judaism after the exile and the Bible's competing visions of the natural world. On many levels the book of Job repeatedly links self, land, plant, and animal with God's activity in the world. This affirmation, though basic, runs counter to the long-held assumption that Israel's God was involved with "history" and not "nature," and that on that basis Israel was to be differentiated from every other nation on earth. By involving God with nature in so many ways—even to the point of what many no doubt perceived and perceive as theological danger—the book of Job allows for an expanded range of possibilities for thinking about ecology, not constrained by the singular conclusions of the doctrinal mode of "natural religion." The journey into the Joban ancient anthropological debate takes us back into a past world where things were not clear or simple, despite illusions to the contrary. It is chronocentric arrogance to assume that the contemporary Western self is the definitive or final evolutionary self, or to automatically assume that current, regnant versions of the self that focus on "self-unity" are eternal, unproblematic, culturally necessary, or biologically helpful. In fact, the multiplicity of voices, both human and divine, seeking to characterize nature in Job could be read as evidence of a community in the throes of adaptation, ready to grow in many different soils and able to change as fast as their literal or symbolic ecologies demand. We know that in early post-exilic Persian Yehud the land itself provided an embodied, visceral challenge on these fronts. People had to symbolically reconstitute themselves, but the struggle to be *like* plants was also a struggle *with* plants.

Despite Job's loneliness in suffering, as perhaps the loneliest person in the entire Bible, he still lives in community. His community narrates his experience back to him when he cannot narrate it, and they provoke him back into his own competing narrations—that is, back to life. Job survives. The Friends survive. The God of Israel survives. The Joban self, for all its complications, is a survivor; the self takes root, and that root, for Israel, would ultimately be in the ancestral land of the Patriarchs among whom Job takes up mythical residence. At the risk of sentimentalizing, we might say that at the end of the book Job is "smaller but freer." Having been wrenched by God back into the natural cycles of plants and animals, Job is free *not* to be an "individual" in any modern sense of the word. Rather, he is free to observe an expanded natural universe, and an expanded moral universe, and is free, at least temporarily but maybe even permanently within the world of the book, from the fear of an unknown God. The stark visions of nature that Job receives, from Friends and from God, eventually remove him from the paranoid world of the Prologue in which he runs from sacrifice to sacrifice, a dismal monarch obsessed with sin, with nothing awaiting him but fear and loss; surely Job was revealing something profound in his opening lament when he exclaimed: "for I feared a fear, and it came to me; and that which I dreaded came to me" (3:25).

As the Divine Speech implies, however, fear may be an appropriate response when viewing some aspects of the world as it is. Despite the grandiosity of his great nature speech, by the end of the book the deity, too, is paradoxically smaller but freer, no longer under the burden of having to reward or punish for specific reasons, or at least without deviation. In the end he may reward the righteous, but all in due time. Those who suffer unjustly have to put up with the pain during that weird interim. Job himself is invited to embrace his status not at the center of the world but rather as a human freak, now in beautiful—even if terrifying—concert with all of creation, from the ordered to the monstrous. Now he can restart his family; now he can finally live. Likewise, as I have argued, the book of Job began as a generative, living model for a new Israel in a new era. If Job offers its audiences anything today it does so by pointing us back to Israel's tragedies. Job may not be able to articulate any clear program for contemporary theological thinking about saving or destroying the environment as political action; if anything, though, as the Joban Divine Speech seems to suggest, the environment may come to save or destroy us.

Index